Limited Edition

Limited Edition

Voices of Women, Voices of Feminism

Geraldine Finn, editor

Fernwood Publishing
Halifax

To my mother, and in memory of my father

Editing: Jane Butler
Copy editing: Brenda Conroy
Cover design: Shelagh Corbett
Design and production: Debbie Mathers
Printed and bound in Canada

A publication of:
Fernwood Publishing
Box 9409, Station A
Halifax, Nova Sotia
B3K 5S3

Canadian Cataloguing in Publication Data

Main entry under title:
Limited Edition
  Includes biliographical references
  ISBN 1-895686-13-X

1. Feminism.   2. Women.   I. Finn, Geraldine.

HQ1111.L56 1993   305.42   C93-098537-0

Contents

Acknowledgements

I would like to thank the following individuals whose intellectual and practical support at various times and on different occasions helped me to see this project through to its conclusion: Caroline Andrews, Peter Bruck, Anne Bullock, Fred Caloren, Naomi Goldenberg, Kate Hughes, Donna Jowett, Angela Miles, Clare Pain, John Shepherd, Caryll Steffens, and Derek Taylor.

I extend special thanks to the contributors for the originality of their work and the patience and tenacity they have shown through the rather lengthy process of the production of this book; to my editor at Fernwood Publishing, Jane Butler, who has done such a wonderful job with the original manuscript; and to my publisher, Errol Sharpe, whose enthusiasm and commitment to this project made the completion of Limited Edition possible.

Notes on Contributors

MICHELE BOURGON is a professor of Social Work at the University of Québec in Montréal. She has been involved in the field of feminist practice as a teacher, a counsellor, and a researcher for many years. She is currently carrying out research and intervening in the area of AIDS and its impact on caregivers.

JUDY BRUNDIGE is Ojibwa and considers herself a traditional Native woman. She grew up in Winnipeg and was living and working in Thunder Bay when we last spoke (1990). She has been actively involved in treaty negotiations for the north western Ontario region, in the Ontario Native Women's Association, and especially in work with Native youth.

SUSAN COLE is the author of *Pornography and the Sex Crisis* (Amanita-Second Story) and is currently senior editor of NOW magazine in Toronto.

JOANNA DEAN re-entered the paid labour force when her youngest child was two years old. She is now a doctoral student at Carleton University preparing a dissertation on spirituality, women, and the church in Canada at the turn of the century. The tensions described in her paper have now been eased, simply by the fact that children grow up; and a new group of mothers continues to work within MAW for recognition of their work.

MARYMAY DOWNING teaches Women's Studies and currently resides in Ottawa.

MARY EATON is a lesbian, a feminist, a law teacher, and a dog lover, presently struggling with a bad case of postmodern blahs. For the past few years her work has focused on developing a lesbian vision of anti-discrimination law, a project inspired by the events described in her contribution to this book.

JOY FEDORICK is a writer and activist. She was born Cree-Métis in a small interlake community in Manitoba. She has a long history of activism in the Native women's movement and in the development of literature programs for Native communities. She is founder and director of *Earthtones North,* a community-based aboriginal writing and publishing project in North Bay, Ontario.

GERALDINE FINN is associate professor of Cultural Studies at Carleton University. She was trained as a philosopher and has published widely on issues arising from the intersection of feminism, philosophy, and cultural studies. She is co-editor with Angela Miles of *Feminism in Canada: From Pressure to Politics* (Montreal: Black Rose Books, 1982, 1989).

NAOMI GOLDENBERG is professor of Religious Studies and former director of Women's Studies at the University of Ottawa. She works in the area of psychoanalysis, feminism, and religion and is the author of *Changing of the Gods: Feminism and the End of Traditional Religions* (Boston: Beacon Press, 1979) and *Returning Words to Flesh: Feminism, Psychoanalysis and the Resurrection of the Body* (Boston: Beacon Press, 1990).

NANCY GUBERMAN is a professor in the Social Work Department at the University of Québec at Montréal where she teaches courses in Women's Studies and community organization. Her research interests include family caregiving to adult relatives; sex, gender and mental health; and feminist practice. She is active in the Québec women's movement.

PEGGY KELLY is studying English Literature and Women's Studies at Carleton University. Previously she studied film production and worked in the television industry for eight years. She served on the Ontario Film Review Board for two years. In 1991 she received literary awards from the Jane Austen Society of North America and from *Atlantis: A Women's Studies Journal*.

ANNA LATTANZI lives in Ottawa. She is completing her B.A. part-time at Carleton University and is employed in non-traditional work.

HELEN LENSKYJ has written two books on women and sport: *Out of Bounds: Women, Sport and Sexuality* (Toronto: Women's Press, 1986), and *Women, Sport and Physical Activity: Research and Bibliography* (Ottawa: Fitness and Amateur Sport, 1988 and 1991). She is an Associate Professor in Feminist Studies at the Ontario Institute for Studies in Education, Toronto.

MARILYN MACDONALD has a background in biology, environmentalism, and education. She is currently Chair of Women's Studies at Simon Fraser University in British Columbia. She has given up ice hockey because of slower reflexes.

MARTHA MACDONALD is a professor in the Department of Economics at Saint Mary's University in Halifax and Vice-President of the International Association for Feminist Economics.

SUZANNE MACKENZIE is a feminist geographer with an intense interest in the creation and change of environments, her own and other people's. She has published books and articles on women's role in changing cities and is currently looking at people's responses to de-industrialization in resource-based towns. She teaches Geography at Carleton University.

HEATHER MENZIES is an Ottawa-based writer, an activist in the peace and women's movements, and adjunct professor of Women's Studies and Canadian Studies at Carleton University. Her books include: *Fast Forward and Out of Control* (1989), *Women and the Chip* (1981), and *The Railroad's Not Enough: Canada Now* (1978).

PATRICIA MONTURE is a citizen of the Mohawk nation, Grand River Territory. She is mother to Justin, Blake and Kathleen, and is married to a man from the Thunderchild First Nation (Cree) in Saskatchewan. She is currently teaching property law, constitutional law, criminology, and Aboriginal rights in the Faculty of Common Law at the University of Ottawa. Patricia is a committed activist and author in matters of criminal justice, Aboriginal rights, social justice, children's rights, and women's issues. All of her work emphasizes the reality that her heart rests with First Nations people.

ROSEMARY MURPHY is a nurse educator and co-ordinator of the Nursing Program at Heritage College in Hull, Québec. Prior to her career in nursing education, Rosemary worked as a general duty nurse in Kitchener, a clinical instructor with CUSO in West Africa, and as a public health nurse for the Ottawa-Carleton Regional Health Unit. She is a member of Women's Health Interaction, a feminist advocacy group, and is active in a number of different women's health organizations.

MARILYN PORTER was born in Wales, went to university in Ireland, taught school in Bristol and Botswana, and university in Bristol, Manchester and St. John's, Newfoundland. She teaches in the Department of Sociology at Memorial University. She has a daughter who is now an active feminist, which takes a remarkable burden off her shoulders, and a son who at least knows what it is about.

PAMELA SACHS teaches English and Women's Studies at Dawson College in Montréal and is the co-ordinator of Access, the college's daytime adult education program.

PAT SMART is a Professor of French at Carleton University and a Fellow of the Royal Society of Canada. Her book *Writing in the Father's House: The Emergence of the Feminine in the Québec Literary Tradition* (Toronto: University of Toronto Press, 1991) won the Governor General's Award for its original French version published in 1989.

SUSAN SORRELL lives in Ottawa where she works as a counsellor in a women's pre-employment counselling agency. Her leisure time is spent socializing and playing sports in the lesbian community.

CARYLL STEFFENS is a feminist interested in psychoanalytic theory. She teaches in the Department of Sociology and Anthropology at Carleton University.

JILL VICKERS is a Professor of Political Science and Canadian Studies at Carleton University. She is the author of *But Can You Type?: Women and Canadian Universities* and *Taking Sex Into Account: The Policy Consequences of Sexist Research* in addition to many works on women and politics in Canada. She is past president of CRIAW (the Canadian Research Institute for the Advancement of Women) and CAUT (the Canadian Association of University Teachers). She was Parliamentarian of NAC (the National Action Committee on the Status of Women) for five years and has just finished a new book about NAC called *Politics as if Women Mattered.*

Introduction

This collection of essays is intended as an introductory reader to feminism and Women's Studies. In it, feminist activists, teachers, and students of Women's Studies speak about their own experiences of feminism and the difference feminism has made and continues to make to their public and private lives.

Feminism

The feminism espoused by this collection designates not so much a set of shared beliefs about the world as a common standpoint towards it. The standpoint is that of women.[1] To take this standpoint is to look at the world from the perspective of those who have been systematically excluded from key aspects of organization, regulation, and interpretation simply because they are women. It is to adopt the perspective of those whose knowledge and experience have been first constrained and devalued, and then disqualified, from the record of human history merely because they do not, because they cannot, conform to the knowledge and experience of men. To begin from such a standpoint does not imply a common point of view, experience, consciousness, psychology, or "nature" among women, but rather a common situation of exclusion and subordination.[2] What women have in common is a specific position in a hierarchy of knowledge and power: our status as subordinates in a social world ordered and divided by sex.[3]

Understanding the scope, the structures, and the mechanisms of this ordering and dividing by sex, to most effectively fight against it, is the specific task of feminism and Women's Studies. Traditional knowledges, which have served to reproduce as well as describe a world already divided by sex, have been and continue to be developed by and from the standpoint of men: that is, by and from the standpoint of people in positions of relative privilege and power in society. The knowledge so produced, not surprisingly, both reflects and vindicates the privilege and power of the authorized knowers as well as the continuing subordination, silence, and relative powerlessness of those who are not so privileged: this includes, of course, not only women but male members of other subordinated groups such as Blacks and citizens of First Nations in North America. Think of the status of women in the theories and practices of mainstream/malestream religions, medicine, economics, politics, or popular music: all of them are dominated by men (by white middle-class men in our society) with women participating only on men's terms, i.e., terms determined by, and in the interests of, men. Marymay Downing, Rosemary Murphy, Martha MacDonald, Jill Vickers, and Susan Cole demonstrate this in their contributions.

Taking the standpoint of women, then, means taking the standpoint of those situated on the subordinated pole of gender hierarchy whenever and wherever it appears: in the bedroom as well as in the boardroom; in the kitchen as well as in the church. Notice that you do not have to be a woman to take this standpoint, nor does being a woman spontaneously deliver it to you. Taking the standpoint of women in the given sense requires a sustained and constantly renewed effort of intellectual and political self-discipline: a habit of thought and practice which comes easier to some than others according to the particularities of their personal circumstances, history, and everyday life. It is a standpoint that could come easier to some men than some women in some circumstances.[4] For women, taking the standpoint of women means first of all taking ourselves and other women and what we know and feel *as women* seriously. It means listening to all aspects of our experience, especially those that seem to differentiate us from men and from what is taken for "common sense" in our society. It means trusting the authority of what we hear and drawing upon it as a source of counter-knowledge, creativity, community, and power.[5]

Although, as women, we share a common position in the social and political hierarchy organized by the sex-gender system[6] and can therefore expect to have at least some experiences in common, we do not even as women have *equal* shares or stakes in, or experiences of, the system itself. Our political status as women and our experience as subordinates in the hierarchy organized by sex is always mediated by our status in other political hierarchies based on other differences: on race, class, colour, creed, religion, age, occupation, education, sexual orientation, physical and mental ability, etc. All of these (together with the particularities of our birth and nurture, which is the subject of Caryll Steffens's essay on psychoanalysis, chapter 13) intersect to determine the quality of our individual lives as women and likewise our experience and understanding of patriarchy[7]: its structures and mechanisms, its limits and scope, its causes and effects. As a consequence, no woman starting from her own experience can presume to speak for all women, though all women can usually speak for more than just themselves. Likewise, no woman (or group of women) starting from her own experience can claim privileged access to or a monopoly on "The Truth" of women's condition, though all women do have privileged access to some important truths.

Within feminism, therefore, there can be no privileged knowers and no privileged voices. Obviously there are privileged women who are feminists, and in fact, privileged women have dominated the development and definition of feminism up until now. These are women whose public voice has been both more easily acquired and more readily attended to because of their privileged status in the other political hierarchies listed above, i.e., because they are white, urban, educated, able-bodied, middle-class, heterosexual, or professional women, for example. But this privilege *within* patriarchy does not automatically translate into privileged access to feminist knowledge *about* patriarchy, i.e., knowledge developed *from the standpoint of women* as specified above: knowledge from the standpoint of those who are excluded from and subordinated to the major institutions of political and social power in our culture. On the contrary, the experience and counter-knowledge feminists seek, in fighting *against* patriarchy and in the struggle to develop alternatives to it, are more likely to come from those with the *least* investment in its various rewards and privileges: those whose experience of exclusion, subordination, and silence has been most systematic and relentless and at the same time most invisible, even to feminists. *For privilege tends to blind the privileged to the mechanisms and effects of its own operations.* This is one of the ways it maintains and reproduces itself: by rendering itself invisible to those with access to power and the instruments of social change. Those on the nether side of power, those who are systematically disabled by its various operations, know only too well how privilege works and how it is reproduced in the ideologies and practices of would-be dissidents and reformers: like feminists.

Both the content and organization of this collection try to reflect this understanding of the politics of feminism as well as the complexity and challenge of being a feminist and doing Women's Studies from the standpoint of women as clarified above. The essays have been arranged so that the first and the last words go to women who speak from the margins of social privilege and power rather than from its centre: to women who speak as mothers, as lesbians, as First Nations women. They speak, that is, from experiences and locations which have been consistently silenced, invalidated, and/or pathologized in our culture: experiences which have been spoken *for* and *of* by others, if they have been spoken at all. This has been as true of feminist culture as it has of patriarchal culture, and of Women's Studies courses as much as of traditional classrooms (see Part Four for more on this).

The first essay speaks from, and to, the experience of mothers looking after their children at home. This is an experience not uncommon to women, but their voice nevertheless is seldom heard in the public sphere and rarely attended to as a source of authoritative knowing. Speaking as a feminist who is also a mother at home, Joanna Dean describes her days and explains why mothers at home do not always feel supported by feminism or recognize themselves as one of the women in whose name the public voice of feminism is heard to speak. There is a certain irony in this, given that according to accepted feminist wisdom, motherhood defines the very condition of women in patriarchal society, constituting both our specific difference from men as well as the occasion of our specific oppression by and subordination to them.[8] This theme of motherhood is picked up in subsequent essays: as an unacknowledged aspect of women's traditional work,[9] as a controlling image in religion, literature, and popular culture,[10] and as an enabling social and political strength for women of North America's First Nations.[11]

The lesbian women and First Nations women whose stories constitute the closing section of this book make similar points: the lesbian women against the exclusionary and oppressive heterosexism of the voice of mainstream feminism, the First Nations women against its continuing assumption of the prejudices and power of European imperialism. Although both Judy Brundige and Joy Fedorick are or have been actively involved in the organization and movement of Native women and clearly adopt "the standpoint of women" in their work (which I have identified as the hallmark of feminism), neither of them will call herself a feminist, so ignored and betrayed has she been as a First Nations woman by the non-Native white women's movement which has paraded the label. I have placed their particular voices last in the collection in the hopes that they will continue to ring in our ears when we close this book and change the way we see, hear, and do feminism and Women's Studies in the future.

As these essays show, feminism does not speak with one voice. It does not describe an established body of knowledge, a shared set of beliefs, or even a single strategy for social change, but rather a *movement* and a commitment of and to women, and to women's liberation from the historic rule of men. Feminism cannot, and should not, therefore, be defined once and for all. What feminism is at any one time is always a function of the concrete and ideological realities particular women find themselves up against; realities which are constantly changing and which shift in response to our own feminist interventions in them. Feminism is in a permanent state of flux and re-vision, that is, it responds to the shifting circumstances of women's lives and developments in our own individual and collective understanding of them. Feminism designates an *unfinished* task of social transformation whose end remains contested and undecided (undecidable), and not a fully realized, agreed upon, or even determinable ideology, politics, or practice. All the essays in this collection recognize this truth of feminism as an *unfinished* project of social change. Some speak directly of or to the necessarily provisional and partial nature of feminist work, describing the experiences and understandings of their authors at the time the article was written, experiences and understandings which have continued to develop and change since then. These have been identified in the text with an editor's footnote.

Women's Studies

Women's Studies did not always and still does not always adopt the standpoint of women as I have described it above. Women's Studies began as studies *of* women rather than studies from the standpoint of women. In the late sixties and early seventies, at the height of the second wave of the Women's Liberation Movement, women teachers in colleges and universities started to develop courses which focused on women, which took women into account and presented knowledge about the world *"as if women mattered"* both as knowers (students, teachers, researchers, and writers) and as social actors (fifty-one per cent of the population who also work, think, create, respond to, and reproduce the world). The immediate objective of these courses was to get women on the intellectual agenda and into the curriculum: to make women visible in academia and to make academia more hospitable to women as well as more responsive to its own limitations as a system of knowledge production which takes Man/men for granted as both the norm and measure of humanity as a whole and thereby proceeds as if women do not and did not matter.[12] "Women and..." courses (Women and Psychology, Women and History, Women and Literature, Women and Health, etc.) blossomed in the universities in the mid- and late seventies, attempting to set the record straight; until then women had simply been left out as actors or agents (as in history, political science, or economics), or included only as exceptions (the "great woman" syndrome) or more commonly as deviants, delinquents, or dependents (as in psychology, sociology, or philosophy). Getting women onto the curriculum took a number of different forms then: looking at the ways women have been represented in traditional male-stream studies; seeking out and examining research and writing by women, sometimes in search of its specific difference from work done by men in the same disciplinary area; applying and adjusting the theories and methods of a particular discipline to women; developing new theories and methods within disciplines for studies *of* women *by* women *for* women...and so forth.

It quickly became clear, however, that the objectives of "Women and..." courses—to get women into the curriculum and onto the academic record *on equal terms with men*—could not be achieved within the terms and relevancies of the academic disciplines as traditionally practised: that the boundaries, definitions, and methods of the disciplines themselves actually accomplish our exclusion and our continuing silence by constructing women's experience as marginal and women's knowledge as either exceptional or deviant and thus devoid of any general human, social, or scientific interest or relevance. Jill Vickers and Martha MacDonald in this collection show how this has worked in political science and economics respectively: how the definitions of political and economic behaviour, of power and work which govern the methods and practices of political science and economics render women's political and economic behaviour and women's relationship to power and work invisible to the social scientist who would study them on its terms. As a consequence, women have been perceived, and continue to be perceived, in male-stream thinking as politically inactive, as passive or conservative, and the unpaid work women perform in the home and in the "community" is deemed to have no economic value and is thus excluded from calculations of the GNP. Both Vickers and MacDonald offer alternative terms and relevancies, rooted in women's experience of power and work, for a political science and an economics which would not leave out of the account the experience and knowledge of over half the population. Similar processes of exclusion (of male bias) occur across the academic spectrum. Traditional methods of determining what counts as "art" and "literature," for example, and of evaluating creative and imaginative achievement in these fields have rendered women's literary and artistic accomplishments invisible and/or irrelevant: if visible, they are always portrayed as secondary, derivative, and subordinate to the "real" art and literature, the "great" art and literature, which is always accomplished by men—or by the "exceptional" woman.

Making women's experience and knowledge visible in academia came to entail, therefore, a transformation of the terms and relevancies of the disciplines themselves, together with a relaxation of their traditional boundaries, definitions, and methods. Political and economic considerations are introduced into psychology courses "on women" to challenge traditional conceptions of maturity, autonomy, mental health, and madness and to explain women's apparently "deviant" or "delinquent" relationship to the norms of traditional psychological discourse. Likewise, observations and analyses from psychoanalysis or sociology find their way into courses "on women" in philosophy or literature to clarify men and women's different relationship to language in general and to "reason," "creativity," and "culture," in particular, all of which have come to be seen as *political* categories of exclusion rather than neutral concepts of "reason:" as categories which set up systematic discourses which in turn actually organize both consciousness and reality so that men and women occupy different sites and different, and unequal, social and political statuses. "Women and..." courses thus became increasingly inter-disciplinary with considerable overlap occurring between courses "on women" offered by the different disciplines. *Women's Studies* as a distinct, unified, and interdisciplinary program, with a special focus on and commitment to women, emerged from these developments within the individual disciplines.

In her essay on "Feminism, Literature and Women's Studies" (chapter 11) Pamela Sachs identifies four stages in the development of a Women's Studies approach to the teaching and practice of Literature which could, in fact, be equally applied to the development of Women's Studies courses in other disciplines, like political science, social work, sociology, nursing or religion. These are the stages of *critique, recovery, reassessment,* and *gynocriticism.* Although they seem to have emerged chronologically, one following from the other, there is considerable overlap in these approaches, and Women's Studies scholars tend to wander somewhat freely between them. (Pat Smart's discussion of women and Québec literature in chapter 12 is a good example of this.) The first stage of *critique* focuses on the images of women in a particular discipline and on the fact that women have traditionally appeared only and always in relation to men: as men's mothers, wives, sisters, lovers; and only and always from men's point of view: as good or bad mothers, wives, sisters, lovers *to men*. Sachs describes the effect of this on women readers of English literature which, as she puts it, has obliged women to identify against themselves: to read about women as if we were not ourselves women, i.e., to read as men. She uses the example of D.H. Lawrence's novel *Sons and Lovers* to show how if you, the reader, are to take the side of "life" in this story, you have to side with the son against the (smothering) mother. A similar dilemma is posed for women in the Judaeo-Christian religious tradition which Marymay Downing discusses in chapter 3. Fathers and sons are the important figures in this tradition, the givers and takers of life, the savers of souls, the sowers of seeds, and the creators and redeemers of the universe itself. Women get the bit parts—as mothers, sisters, wives and lovers of men—in what is essentially a male melodrama, a very masculine myth of social, political, and moral origins. Downing discusses the difficulties this poses to women who want to take both their religions and themselves seriously, and describes her own journey away from the patriarchal religion of Christianity to the goddess religions of the ancient Greeks and pre-colonial Amerindians.

The second stage in the development of a Women's Studies approach identified by Sachs is that of *"recovery,"* which refers to the activity of discovering and re-evaluating works by women otherwise neglected or marginalized in male-stream studies and to the organization of courses around them: courses on women poets, or novelists, or artists, or musicians, or inventors, or scientists, or, in my own case, women philosophers, or in the case of Marymay Downing, woman-centred religions.

The third approach described by Sachs, she calls the stage of *reassessment*. This involves a return to work previously critiqued and possibly dismissed as hopelessly male-biased at the "images of women" stage, and a re-engagement with it from "the standpoint of women" as outlined above: a reading between the lines, so to speak, which spotlights "the woman's part" from the woman's point of view, to identify and re-interpret what she does and what she reveals *subversively* about the condition of women in patriarchal society, which we can continue to draw upon in our own struggle for a voice and for change. *Gynocriticism,* the fourth and most recent (and still emerging) stage in the development of a Women's Studies approach continues this movement towards "woman-centred" scholarship. It involves, among other things, looking at women's writing (or art or music or religious practices, etc.) as a tradition of its own: "thinking through our mothers" as Adrienne Rich once expressed it. It is a development which has led to complex, difficult, and often divisive debates within feminism around feminism's key organizing terms of sexual difference; terms like woman, sex, gender, mother, lesbian, female, feminine, experience—even writing itself—have become enormously problematic while no less indispensable to feminist praxis. The dust is a long way from settling on these issues within feminism and each contributor to this volume has had to work out her own (provisional) negotiation of this difficult but now absolutely central terrain—the language of sexual difference itself—in her own way.[13]

The Collection

The collection is divided into four sections, each of which focuses on a different aspect of *feminism as a politics,* as both a standpoint and a movement for social change which investigates and at the same time intervenes in contemporary social reality. Part One focuses on the Politics of the Personal, Part Two on the Politics of Science, Part Three on the Politics of Knowledge, and Part Four on the Politics of Feminism itself. Each of the four sections is preceded by an introduction to its focus and problematic, and to the scope and limits of its constituent chapters. Each chapter presents aspects of feminism as they have been encountered, experienced, and understood by the particular writer in her own field of work or interest. A selective bibliography is attached to each essay to direct the reader to additional reading material if she wishes to extend her studies in this area.[14]

The collection has not aimed for consensus but for specificity and complexity. It has, however, aimed for a certain coherence which depends on the essays being read in their order of appearance. Cumulatively and collectively the chapters develop an argument, a set of questions, and a perspective which culminates in the voices, knowledges, experiences, and challenges of the final section. Nevertheless, the collection lays no claim to being conclusive or complete, representative of feminism in general or Women's Studies in particular. It has aimed rather to demonstrate the specificity and scope, the energy, creativity, richness, complexity and promise of Women's Studies. Some women will recognize themselves and their experiences in these stories and, inevitably, some women will not. As indicated by its title, this collection, as any collection, offers only a "limited edition" of contemporary feminist thought and practice and a "limited edition" of the reality and aspirations of Women's Studies. This is an edition limited by the particular social and political location of its producers.[15] As a result, many voices are missing: the voices of women from the Third World and the voices of Canada's immigrant women, women of colour, and women from rural and regional communities. The absence of these voices should not be overlooked nor their relevance discounted. As indicated earlier, feminism and Women's Studies have been dominated and defined by privileged women, women whose public voice has been more easily acquired and more readily attended to because of their privileged status in hierarchies of power. These hierarchies collaborate with patriarchy in the determination of our individual destinies and desires: privilege is accorded women who are white, urban, able-bodied, educated, middle-class, heterosexual, and professional. This edition is no exception. It, too, speaks for the most part with this voice of privilege, i.e., with the voice of women privileged in our society by virtue of their positions in political hierarchies based on race, class, sexuality, education, location, etc. And while none of these women believes (or maintains) that her experience is representative of women as such, or that her understanding of feminism is definitive or final, or that she has nothing to learn from women who do not share her privilege, the collection nevertheless continues the tradition of advancing the visions and voices of privileged women within feminism and Women's Studies and marginalizing the experiences and knowledges of women who lack a public voice and who are already on the margins of power in our culture. (See Part Four for more on this). This is a serious limitation of this collection. On the other hand, it should not prevent us from hearing the voices that are present in the text and testing them against our own experience and knowledge of what it means to be a woman in patriarchal society and what exactly is at stake in the collective struggle against it.

The collection does not offer a definitive statement of what feminism is or should be, but is rather a sampling of what is being done and said in its name in a number of different contexts so the reader can decide for herself what feminism means and means to her. To this end, *Limited Edition* is offered as an excerpt from a conversation among women which is going on all around us and all over the world, and as an invitation to the reader to join in: to contest, confirm, or refine its terms and relevancies, observations, and conclusions, and above all to continue its investigations, inquiries, and critiques upon which some of us believe not only the future of women depends but also the very survival of our world. I hope you will accept this invitation and add your voice and experience to this conversation, this revolution, among women.

Notes

1. Of course, as all feminisms, the feminism espoused by this collection is premised on the belief that: (i) we live in a male-dominated society, (ii) this is a bad thing: both unjust and unncesssary, and (iii) it can and must be changed. The particularities of the substance, content and extent of male-dominance; of its origins, mechanisms, causes and effects; and of precisely what can and should be done about it, remain open questions within feminism, however. These are questions which the essays in this collection address and explore, each in their own way and from their own perspective, but all, I believe, are from the "standpoint of women" as described below.

2. For more on the "standpoint of women" from a similar perspective see Dorothy Smith, *The Everyday World as Problematic,* University of Toronto Press, 1987, esp. 77-88. My own understanding of this standpoint owes much to Smith's analysis but does not coincide precisely with it.

3. By "sex" I mean sexual difference, not sexual desire, orientation, pleasure, or experience. By "gender" I mean the masculine/feminine difference as a hierarchy. Gender is built on sexual difference but does not coincide with it. Hence the reality of feminine men and masculine women. Sexual differences between men and women (or more precisely, males and females) occur in "nature:" like the weather, they are accidents of being. Gender differences, the social differentiation and hierarchy of

masculine/feminine, man/woman, is entirely cultural: like umbrellas and igloos. Gender refers to the social organization and evaluation of sexual difference. It is inseparable from its particular social and historical context. This relationship between sex and gender has been the subject of much research and debate in feminist scholarship. I particularly recommend: Simone de Beavoir, *The Second Sex,* Bantam Books, 1970, and Gayle Rubin, "The Traffic in Women: Notes on the Political Economy of Sex", in Rayna Reiter (ed.) *Toward an Anthropology of Women,* Monthly Review Press, 1975. For my own account of the relationship between sex, gender and sexual pleasure, desire, orientation and experience (sexuality), see Geraldine Finn, "Patriarchy and Pleasure: The Pornographic Eye/I," *The Canadian Journal of Political and Social Theory,* IX, nos 1-2, 1985.

4. It may come easier to men in subordinate positions in the hierarchies of race, religion, language, and sexual orientation, for example, than it does to women in privileged positions in the same hierarchies. I, for example, have learned much about the structures and mechanisms of my own oppression *as a woman* from the writings and experiences of working-class men and men from formerly colonized countries. (See especially, Franz Fanon, *The Wretched of the Earth,* Macgibbon and Kee, London, 1965; Albert Memmi, *The Colonizer and the Oppressed,* Seabury Press, New York, 1970). Obviously men cannot speak as or on behalf of the *experiences,* knowledges and values of women because they are not women. They cannot know or have women's experiences. But they can, to varying degrees, take "the standpoint of women" as it is specified here. This is obviously a moot point which needs to be debated and decided *in context* and which cannot be decided once and for all. If feminism is a politics, as this collection argues, then its theories, methods, and working definitions must always be open to revision and change in response to the emergence of new knowledges and conditions and the strategic needs of particular persons, places, and times. At *this* time and in *this* context I am espousing a feminism which requires its advocates to assume "the standpoint of women" as specified. It is quite possible that at a future date I might espouse a feminism which is more exclusive or inclusive in its specifications, depending on the context and the particular political challenges it poses.

5. See Michael Focault, *Power/Knowledge.* Selected Interviews and Other Writings 1972-1977, edited by Colin Gordon, Pantheon Books, New York, 1980, for an explication of these terms and the relationship between knowledge, power, subjectivity, truth, and resistance they imply and designate.

6. Gayle Rubin uses this term to designate the system of male-dominance (gender) which is organized by and upon sexual differences (sex). See note 3 above.

7. Patriarchy literally means "rule by the fathers." The term is often used loosely by feminists as the equivalent of "male dominance." I believe that male dominance and rule by the fathers (patriarchy) are historically linked and will stand and fall together: that the one, knowledge of and desire for paternity rights and privileges (patriarchy) was/is the precondition and social determinant of the other, the subordination and oppression of women by men (male dominance). See Mary O'Brien, *The Politics of Reproduction,* Routledge and Kegan Paul, 1981, and Evelyn Reed, *Woman's Evolution* from matriarchal clan to patriarchal family, Pathfinder Press, New York, 1975, for two different, though compatible, accounts of the origins and mechanisms of this historical link.

8. See, for example, Mary O'Brien op.cit., note 7.

9. Chapters 2, 7 and 8.
10. Chapters 3, 12 and 17.
11. Chapter 22.
12. There have been many feminist publications which explore the specificities and consequences of this reality. My own personal favourites are Virginia Woolf, *Three Guineas,* Penguin Books, 1977, and Dale Spender, *Invisible Women:The Schooling Scandal,* Writers and Readers, London 1982. See also, Angela Miles and Geraldine Finn (eds.) *Feminism: From Pressure to Politics,* Black Rose Books, Montréal 1989; Angela McRobbie and Trisha McCabe (eds.) *Feminism for Girls: An Adventure Story,* Routledge and Kegan Paul, 1981; Dale Spender (ed.) *Men's Studies Modified: The Impact of Feminism on the Academic Disciplines,* Pergamon Press 1981.
13. My description of the "standpoint of women" earlier in this Introduction both illustrates and engages with some of these difficulties and debates around the very language of feminism itself. The essays in Part Four on "The Politics of Feminism: Am I That Woman?" address these questions directly.
14. I use the feminine pronoun and possessive but, of course, they include men in their address.
15. I, for example, have lived and worked in Hull, Québec for the last fifteen years. I am white, anglophone, and originally from a working-class family. I came to Canada from England in 1970 to do graduate work in philosophy. It was my experience of the lack of any similar resource for my own teaching needs that motivated me to initiate this collection of introductory essays to feminism and Women's Studies. I also wanted a book my mother would be able to understand and read. (I'm not yet sure I have it). I circulated a description of the collection I had in mind and a call for papers where I could and wherever I happened to be over a period of two to three years. I had a vision of the range of voices I wanted to include in the text and this general call for papers was supplemented by specific solicitations of specific voices which had not responded to or been reached by (more likely) the original general notice. This collection is limited, therefore, by both my own experience, understanding, and vision of feminism, and the particular circumstances and context within which I live and work, as well as by the necessary selectivity and partiality of any piece of writing.

PART ONE

The Politics of the Personal:
Image and Reality

Introduction

One of the distinguishing marks of feminism as a politics is its insistence on making the connection between the personal and the political: connecting what has traditionally been regarded as women's "personal" pain and the political context within which it is organized; between the quality of what has been called women's "private" life in the family, and the institutions and ideologies of the public world which determine it.

While all the essays in this collection make these links between the "personal" and the "political," the "private" and the "public," those in the first and last sections speak of and from them most directly. Joanna Dean in chapter 1 describes her own experience of full-time *mothering* in a traditional nuclear family and shows how it is organized and structured not by and for her or her children's interests and needs but by and for the economic and political priorities of the "public" sphere. These are priorities which entail the exclusion of mothers and children from "public" space, their isolation in what can only therefore be *men's* "private" sphere, and the corresponding concealment from "public" consciousness of the work mothers do in the home, work which is indispensable to, yet excluded from, all calculations of the nation's economy.* (We have to ask just how "public" public is, therefore, when mothers and children are not welcome there, and likewise how "private" is private when it is your place of work?)

More importantly, perhaps, Joanna charges feminism with the same political tendencies to privileging the "public" over the "private" sphere, and thereby excluding the interests and concerns of full-time mothers (and housewives) from the feminist agenda, in favour of demands for universal day care, affirmative action, and equal pay for work of equal value. She raises some difficult, divisive and sensitive, but nevertheless absolutely central, questions for and to feminism in her essay, about who should look after the children, for example, and who should foot the bill—questions echoed throughout the book in one context or another but never finally resolved.

---

* See Martha MacDonald in this collection.

12

Rosemary Murphy continues to explore the theme of women's mothering in chapter 2 in the context of her experience as a mother and wife, and *nurse* and *teacher*, and in relation to the emergence and development of her own feminist consciousness. Through a combination of anecdotes and analyses she makes the connections between her childhood experience as one of three daughters in a large, rural, Catholic, and patriarchal family of eight; her early aspirations to and continuing pride in being a good wife and mother and a good nurse; and what she has now come to see as her internalization of patriarchal prescriptions for femininity for being a "good woman"—which allowed her, as she puts it, to become her "own oppressor." Rosemary makes the links between her own story (the "personal") and the history, practice, and ideology of *nursing* (the "political"), a profession which continues to both attract and oppress women by exploiting women's commitment to "care": to bringing the skills and values of the "good mother" out of the "private" and into the "public" sphere. Rosemary thus politicizes "caring" by recognizing it as both a value or resource and *a liability* for women: as an occasion for our exploitation as well as for the expression of our particular talents and strengths. She too, thereby, places another difficult issue on the feminist agenda.

In chapter 3 Marymay Downing shifts the focus of discussion from the concrete reality of the experiences of mothering to its ideological representation in *religious imagery*. The essay opens with a description of the challenging and controversial video image of the rock singer Madonna dressed in sexy black underwear singing "Like a Virgin." An image which brings together two dominant images of womanhood in Christianity which are usually kept strictly apart: the images of Mary and Eve; the Virgin and the whore; the asexual, innocent Mother of God and the sinful, sexual, godless seductress. Marymay reviews the history of the representation and participation of women in the Christian Church, her own personal efforts to find a place of dignity and respect within it, and the two traditions of feminist intervention in religion(s) which have emerged over the last twenty years: the critique and reform of traditional religion(s) on the one hand and the renaissance of female polytheism on the other. She explains why and how she came to choose the second route—the goddesses of ancient Greece and the Amerindians over the monotheistic God of traditional Christianity. The latter's continuing idealization of the Madonna, which equates motherhood with silence and submission, is not the least of those reasons supporting, as it does, not only the institutionalized oppression of and violence towards "knowing" and self-determined (especially sexual) women but also the everyday silencing, subordination, and exploitation of the mother-work described by Rosemary and Joanna in previous chapters. Marymay thus makes the connections between the representation of women, in this case in the sphere of religion, and the contradictions and conflicts of the experienced realities of women's so-called "private" lives and their lives as mothers in particular.

Susan Cole makes similar connections in chapter 4, between the popular and persistent representation of women as sex-for-men in the so-called "public" sphere (as pornography, that is) and the real problems women face in that sphere when they presume to occupy it on the same terms as men and as men's equals. In her case, it was as a member of a late seventies feminist *rock band* called Mama Quilla II. Susan picks up the Madonna theme of the previous essay to show how it organizes women's exclusion from, and oppression and exploitation in, the "public" sphere where we appear always and only as sex-for-men. The "good" woman, the Virgin Mother, stays at home where she belongs; only the "bad" woman, the whore, circulates in "public" and walks the streets. Susan points out that the only industry in which women make more money than men is, predictably enough, the sex industry: prostitution and "modelling."

Like the other contributors to this section, Susan uses a combination of personal anecdote and feminist analysis to show how and why women do not succeed in the music industry as men do and to demonstrate thereby popular culture's powerful role in the production and reproduction of gender as a politics: the masculine-feminine difference as a hierarchy of male/Man over female/ Woman. She concludes her essay by describing some of the ways this pornographic culture can be and is being resisted: by teaching "media literacy" in schools as she does, for example, (teaching students to read cultural imagery in order to see how it shapes our consciousness, aspirations and desires) and by the innovations and challenges of women in the music industry itself, women like k.d. lang, Madonna, Pat Benetar, Annie Lennox, Cyndi Lauper, Tina Turner, and others.

Susan's analysis of the structures and processes of male dominance in the "public" space of the popular music industry is echoed in chapter 5 by Peggy Kelly's account of her experience as a technician in a Canadian *television station*.

Susan describes how women are neither expected nor encouraged to either make or play musical instruments or make or manage the various technologies of sound production in the popular music industry. These powerful determinants of musical success (its technology) are securely maintained and jealously guarded in and by the hands of men. The only musical "instrument" women are actively encouraged to use is the one that confirms our "object" status in this hierarchy and our status as "nature" and as sex-for-men: that is, our body and our voice performing the rhythms, gestures, and words scripted *for us by men*. Male monopoly of the various musical technologies thus assures the continuing sexualization, objectification, and marginalisation of women in, and/or exclusion from, the popular music industry.

In chapter 5, Peggy Kelly shows how the same male monopoly of technology achieves the same effects in the Canadian broadcasting industries: male domination of cultural representation (of who and what is represented in the media and how) and the corresponding objectification, sexualization, and marginalization of women in the "public" sphere. Peggy brings together her experience of viewing pornography as a member of the Ontario Film Review Board, her experience working in a Canadian television production studio, and her understanding of feminism as political critique to show how pornography, technology, and the scientific demand for "objectivity" are linked in our culture to the constitution of the masculine-feminine difference as a hierarchical separation of Man over Woman, subject over object, mind over body, and culture over nature. And she wonders whether we should encourage women to go into "technology" at all, given its constitutive hostility towards women and its corresponding insistence on the "objectivity" and "neutrality" of its ways. These themes and related issues associated with men's domination and control of the powerful "public" arenas of science and technology are explored in greater detail in the next section.

Chapter 1

Mothers are Women

Joanna Dean

Housework is the bond that virtually all women share. Whether we get down on our knees and scrub the floor ourselves, or oversee someone else's scrubbing, women have always had the responsibility for maintaining the household and raising the children. This common experience has been at the root of our oppression. Tied down by household and children, women have not been able to compete on an equal basis with men in the working world. Housework is dull, tedious stuff, most of it, but until we take it seriously, and change the power relations that structure this work, women will continue to be burdened by our household responsibilities.

Domestic labour has preoccupied me for the last few years, both materially and ideologically. Whenever I have been able to catch my breath between babies, laundry, and cooking, I have struggled with the contradictions between my feminist politics and my day-to-day life as a mother and housewife. The issues are both personal and political, so I shall attempt to describe my own situation as well as provide an introduction to the current analysis and debate on the issue.

First, a few definitions. Housework is difficult to clearly define because it is a catch-all term that includes all unpaid work done in the home. It incorporates cleaning, cooking, laundry, budgeting, shopping, and possibly gardening, decorating, sewing and such traditionally male jobs as home repairs, car maintenance and lawn care. It has become popular to separate housework and childcare conceptually, perhaps out of recognition that it is no more "natural" for a mother to cook with a child under foot than it is for a cabby to drive with his or her child in the car or a plumber to work while watching a toddler. For this reason I will distinguish here between motherwork and housework, although society is structured in such a way that for most of us doing the work the distinction is an artificial one.

Motherwork and housework are very tangled today, and many of us who have chosen to do full-time motherwork find ourselves doing a great deal of housework. Spooning the pablum into the baby is clearly childcare, but cooking it and cleaning it off the floor is probably housework. Not only do children create housework, but housework is one of the few things that can be done, albeit with difficulty, with children around. The marxist term "domestic labour" is one that I turn to frequently because it recognizes existing linkages between housework and motherwork and acknowledges the labour involved in both (Fox, 1980).

Another difficulty is that everyone, even the most privileged man, does some housework, if only to throw his socks in the laundry hamper. How do we distinguish between the housewife and the woman who works for a wage and does an equal amount of domestic labour? Without intending to deny the household labour of the woman in the paid workforce, I will use the term housewife as it is commonly used, to refer to the full-time housewife, someone who has no paid job and identifies herself as a housewife or "homemaker." Those women who work part-time, but whose primary allegiance is to the homefront, might also be included in the definition. The distinction is important because, although all women have common problems with the burdens of housework, there are issues involved in housework done by a dependent wife that do not affect those who do it in addition to paid work. Full-time housewives and full-time mothers are financially dependent, often isolated, and have little status in a world where people are defined by their work.

To give a little personal history, (the personal is so clearly political in this area) I am, temporarily, a full-time mother and housewife. It was not something I planned; in fact, as a young feminist I had assumed that housewives and full-time housework were relics of the past. While at university it had taken only the minimum of power struggles with a reasonably liberated partner to establish an egalitarian household. Neither of us had to make any real sacrifices to keep the household functioning, admittedly, on a fairly minimal level. Then our first child arrived and my idealism came crashing down around my ears. I had planned to return to work and put the baby in daycare, but I found, somewhat to my surprise, that I could not leave my infinitely precious child in anyone else's care. My husband was caught up in the demands of a professional career, not willing to give it up to share parenting, and unable to understand my doubts about substitute care. I found myself at home all day with the baby, taking on most of the household tasks because I was there and because I was making no direct financial contribution to the household.

For someone who had been used to a very active lifestyle, the change was traumatic. I missed the excitement and mental stimulation of my work as well as the casual social contact that most working people take for granted. The baby slept very little and I was often stupid and disoriented for lack of sleep. I was isolated in a small basement apartment in a new city, and was desperately lonely. The biggest problem, however, was the loss of the respect I had received as a working person.

As my daughter grew older, I tried part-time work, and then full-time work. In the paid workforce all day, I found myself torn between two worlds and making compromises in both. The stress of getting my child to daycare, myself to a demanding job, and then sharing housework and childcare with my husband at night negated the very real satisfactions of my career. I also desperately missed my daughter. With the birth of a second and then a third child in the next few years, I gave up paid work altogether. I found friends who had made the same choices and joined an Ottawa-based support group for at-home mothers, Mothers Are Women.* Discovering that I was not alone, I stopped blaming myself for my situation and started looking at the structures in our society that had precipitated it.

My experiences are personal, yet they reflect a common reality. Many women today find themselves at home with small children, unable to manage the double burden of housework and childcare on top of a career or unwilling to leave childcare up to someone else. In 1987, 42.7 percent of Canadian mothers of children under three were not in the labour force at all. Another one-third were working in the labour force part-time, from one to thirty hours a week, and working at home the rest of the time. Overall, roughly 60 percent of mothers of children under three are stepping out of the labour force to some extent to care for their children (Statistics Canada).

The effects of staying at home to care for children, whether full- or part-time, are enormous and often under-estimated. The woman who drops out of the labour force for five years to raise a family loses not only the income from those years, but also her seniority, her pension, and most important, her place in the work force. The years she misses are crucial ones for job advancement, and most women never catch up. Taken over a lifetime, the cost of this setback can run into hundreds of thousands of dollars. Personal costs are even more difficult to calculate. Women who are isolated in the home all day and financially and emotionally dependent on one man lose self-esteem and the confidence they had while in the work force.

Those who stay in the labour force and shoulder the double burden are also handicapped by housework and motherwork; the effects are less obvious but significant. Husbands only slightly increase their participation in the household when their wives enter the labour force, and women continue to do most of the work (Michelson, 1985, Lewis, 1986, and Meissner, 1975). The woman who misses a day because of a sick child, who cannot work overtime because of school hours, who is exhausted at work because of the stress, is clearly not going to advance as quickly as the woman with fewer household responsibilities or the man with a full-time housewife assisting him. When we consider why so few women reach the top of their fields—whether that means chief surgeon or head cook— we must consider not only sexism in promotion and hiring, but also the millstone of household responsibility that hangs on women's necks (see Eichler, 1982).

Because most of us were raised in households with housewives in attendance, we often take their work for granted and it is not until we have a child and

---

*MAW, P.O. Box 4104, Station E, Ottawa, Ontario, K1S 5B1.

try to run our own house that we appreciate how much work is entailed. One mother tied a tape recorder around her waist while caring for a small child in an attempt to record exactly where her day went. I read her account of lost mittens, forgotten errands, and general mayhem during my first pregnancy and wrote her off as a disorganized fool, but a year later I was shocked to see how closely my days matched hers.

Every new mother swears that she will do things efficiently, and inevitably she finds herself overwhelmed by chaos. No one is ever really prepared for the unending nature of full-time childcare, the unpredictability of children's needs, or the way they soak up endless amounts of love and attention. Apart from needing care, they also generate a surprising amount of housework. The kitchen floor that once got a cursory mop every week now needs to be washed daily as mud is tracked in and juice spilt. The laundry pile soars with wet sheets, dirty T-shirts and diapers; dishes pile up. It is estimated that the first child generates more than 9,000 hours of extra housework between birth and leaving school. A second child generates an additional 3,500 hours or more.

A Day in the Life of...

To give some idea of the day of a mother/housewife, I will describe a typical day when my children were five years, three years and nine months old. The day begins when the first child awakes anywhere from 5:30 to 7:30 a.m. The first two hours of the morning are a hectic scramble to dress three small, moving bodies with matching clean clothes, to wash faces, brush teeth, cook, serve and clean up breakfast, pack lunches, organize school bags, and finally put on snowsuits and escort children to school. Sometimes I throw a load of laundry on, or make the beds at this time, but more often I don't even finish tidying up breakfast and must come home to sweep the floor or wash the dishes. Generally there is at least one morning crisis, a temper tantrum, a lost mitten, or a fall out of the high-chair.

I am lucky to be able to afford nursery school, so from 9 till 11:30 a.m. I have only my youngest with me, and at nine months he usually sleeps for an hour in the morning. A more meticulous housewife would probably devote the hour to getting the Cheerios out from behind the refrigerator, but I have been working on my Masters degree and use every spare moment to read or write. Napping babies are notoriously unreliable, and mine can be counted on to miss his nap if a deadline looms, or wake up just as things are going well. When the baby is awake, I run errands or do some housework. This can be fun or incredibly frustrating; he will turn the machine off and on while I try to vacuum, or play peek-a-boo in the laundry hamper I am filling. Everything takes twice as long as it would alone. Sometimes a friend will drop by and have a cup of coffee while we watch the children, and sometimes I will babysit a friend's child in return for a few hours off later in the week.

At 11:30 I pick up the older children and feed them lunch. I do a lot of childcare at this time, listening to stories about the morning, admiring art-work. After lunch is cleaned up, at about 1 p.m., we have a cuddle and a story upstairs and the children are supposed to play quietly or sleep for an hour while I nurse the baby, read, or catch up on sleep after a broken night. The afternoons vary a great deal: the children often have a friend over, we will walk to the park, go grocery shopping, do some arts and crafts, or bake cookies. Going anywhere requires great preparation, especially in the winter, i.e., packing a diaper bag, finding mitts, boots, scarves, etc., herding the children into the car, and then undressing on arrival. I spend one afternoon a week at university attending classes.

From 5 until 8 p.m. there is a repeat of the morning's busy pace, this time with preparation of the children's dinner for 5:30, and our dinner for 6:30... My husband bathes the children while I clean the kitchen, then we both read stories and put them to bed. Sometimes they are all asleep by 8:30 and I can have some time to myself, but more often the baby is up until 9 or 10.

The routine is much the same from Monday to Friday, altered only by my classes and incidental outings like a trip to the doctor. I spend one day doing laundry off-and-on all day, and another day getting groceries. Other errands fit in here and there—buying shoes with all three in attendance will fill an afternoon. On the weekends the routine is somewhat more relaxed, with two of us to share the load, but the work of three meals a day, dressing, minding, and tidying up after the children continues.

An outline of the day, however, gives little sense of its texture. A walk to the park can be idyllic, but it differs fundamentally from a walk alone. There are questions to answer, shoelaces to tie, scraped knees to bandage, and at least one child who refuses either to go to the park or come home once she is there. Cooking a simple dinner with three tired children is an exercise in agility, diplomacy, and organization. There is almost always someone wanting to talk to me, sit on my knee, or nurse.

The days are long, often monotonous, relieved by moments of hilarity, tenderness, and anger. Isolation is a problem for most at-home mothers. Most of us search out and treasure friends and neighbours we can drop in on, but dropping in involves bringing along a crew of children and talking above the mayhem. A sick child can mean that I am literally locked in for days on end, unable to take the contagious child out or invite many friends or sitters in. Even when the children are well there are limits on one's activity. As Germaine Greer (Greer, 1984) demonstrated, our society romanticizes children but does not really accommodate them, and the woman with children finds there are very few places where she is welcome. Shopping is the stereotypical mother's activity, but small children pull things off shelves, make noise and disrupt the order of adult-oriented stores. Normally an hour in a shopping mall is the limit of my children's good behaviour and my patience. On bad days it is easier not to try to go anywhere at all.

On the other hand, there are real pleasures in full-time child-raising. Most mothers speak about their joy in watching a child progress and grow under their guidance and their sense of making a real contribution. In comparison to mothers in the labour force, the at-home mother has the luxury of time with her children, time to fritter away at the park or over a picture-book, time to dandle a baby on her knee or teach a four-year-old to ride a bike. (On the other hand she rarely has time to herself; I have often envied the mothers walking alone to work). And within the constraints of the children's needs there is some flexibility to structure your own life. (For a more comprehensive account of the realities of mothering see McConville, 1987.)

Public and Private Spheres—Then and Now...

Although the stay-at-home mother is considered the traditional woman today, her isolated and child-centred role is very different from that played in the past. In pre-industrial societies, women were responsible for most childcare and house-work, but they often shared this work with other members of the extended family and engaged in other forms of productive labour. Work was not separated from the home: family members contributed in different ways to feeding and clothing each other and to producing commodities for sale or barter. In much of the Third World this pattern continues, but in the "developed" world it changed drastically with the Industrial Revolution. Members of the household became absorbed into the "outside world": the teenagers found employment or went to school, the husband and unmarried sisters and daughters went to work, and the extended family was lost as the nuclear family moved to the city. Many of the household tasks were also moved into the public sphere: shoes and clothes were made in factories; food was produced on large farms, processed commercially and sold in stores; energy and water were produced outside; medical care was provided in hospitals; training in public schools. Left at home, in the private sphere, were the small children and the mother who minded them. She was given, by default, those tasks that wouldn't fit into the industrial world: the raising of small children, the emotional support of family members and the daily household maintenance (Strasser, 1982 and Cowan, 1983).

Two worlds developed, the public sphere of business and industry and the private sphere of the home, and although much lip service was paid to the values of the home, the values of the public sphere came to dominate. Work was defined as concrete, separable tasks valued for the income it produced, and sharp distinctions were drawn between work and leisure. The private sphere was no longer considered part of the real world; it was seen as a haven from the rough and tumble public sphere.

Several different attempts were made in the nineteenth century to change the structures defining housework and to bring the household into the modern industrial world. Home economists tried to bring the rationality and efficiency of the modern factory into the home. They tried to make homemaking a profession and so raise the status of the housewife (Strasser, 1982, and Ehrenreich and English, 1979). Other less widely-known campaigners tried to do the opposite: to take the housework out of the home and put it into the public sphere. They advocated public laundries, cafeterias, apartment hotels, and daycares (Hayden, 1980). Neither of these attempts, however, had much impact on the role of the housewife. The rationalization of duties that made the factory so efficient didn't work in the single home where a woman was juggling a multitude of different tasks. The professionalization of housework overlooked the fact that the housewife was, in most cases, both manager and worker. The idealistic attempts to move housework into the public sphere also failed for a variety of reasons, including the resistance of husbands and the allegiance of men and women alike to the nuclear, private household.

Where the public sphere did have a great deal of impact on the private was in the introduction of the technology of the factory into the home. In the last 150 years, electricity and plumbing, and more recently dishwashers and microwaves, have fundamentally lightened women's load without, however, changing her role or responsibility. As Ruth Cowan (1983) observes, women continued to remain at home full-time and used the extra time provided by the new "labour-saving" devices to elevate their standards of housekeeping and childcare. Laundry was done every day instead of once a week, more elaborate meals were prepared, and children received unprecedented amounts of attention. Technology has also had the effect of further isolating women. Inner-city neighbourhoods and primitive household technology provided many opportunities for contact and mutual help, but with the introduction of new machines women never had to leave their homes. They no longer gathered at the laundry, thanks to the washing machine, or at the grocery, thanks to the refrigerator. The car meant they lived farther apart in the suburbs. Except for the baby boom after World War II, family size steadily decreased. Women's work was lighter, but their lives became emptier and lonelier. The romanticized image of the homemaker in the fifties masked an increasingly empty life for many women.

What is Work?

The historical genesis of domestic labour has resulted in a number of contradictions that are worth exploring. The first is the definition of work as paid employment in the public sphere. Housework and motherwork are seldom considered work. A woman will often say, "No I don't work, I am just a housewife." New mothers will talk about "going back to work." The blindness to the truth of domestic labour is evident not only in romantic idealizations of housewives and mothers but also in serious, purportedly objective disciplines such as politics and economics.* Economists routinely ignore housework and childcare when calculating Gross National Product, and sociologists looking at the workplace forget to consider the home. Feminist marxists have pointed out that marxist class analysis often ignored half the population. This is not only because work has been defined in a certain way, but also because housework, done in the private sphere, is invisible. At the end of the day, the meals are eaten, the clothes dirtied, and the house untidy. There is no pay-cheque to show for it and no satisfied boss to comment on it. The work of childcare is doubly invisible. It is mystified as a labour of love and considered the natural function of every woman. Meg Luxton distinguishes between the work of childcare and the social relations between mother and child and says the two aspects are confused in our society. Women are torn between their very real love for their children and their frustration at the repetitive and endless work involved in caring for them (Luxton, 1980). Mothers who find satisfaction and joy in their relationship with their children may deny that the care is work: they say that they cook and clean for the family out of love. Indeed, the work and the relationship are inextricably linked. A mother changing a diaper is clearly doing work, but the tickle she gives the baby and the smile she gets in response are part of a loving relationship. Even in a daycare setting, where we recognize the work, we often expect the caregivers to love our children.

Adrienne Rich sorts out the contradictions involved in motherwork in another way (Rich, 1976). She distinguishes between the experience of mothering, the rewarding and creative relationship each mother has with her child, and the institution of mothering, the isolated and difficult circumstances in which we experience this relationship. She blames patriarchal society for structuring mothering in this way. While Rich celebrates motherhood, she challenges our acceptance of motherwork as unpaid, isolated, endless labour.

In the seventies and eighties, a number of feminists tried to bring domestic labour into the open and give it the analysis and recognition it needed. Adrienne Rich, as we have seen, analyzed motherhood, Ann Oakley in Britain looked at housework through a sociologist's eyes (Oakley, 1974, 1976), and in Canada, Meg Luxton wrote a perceptive and understanding account of housewives in a northern community (Luxton, 1980). Other marxist-feminists tried to work domestic labour into a marxist analysis of capital (Fox, 1980 and Malos, 1980). Penney Kome wrote a more accessible, popular book on housework based on a national survey of housewives (Kome, 1982).

Housework and the Economy

What has become clear in this ongoing feminist discussion is that the private sphere is not simply a hold-over from the past; it plays a crucial role in supporting the modern public sphere. The survival of the housewife is no accident, society

---

* See Martha MacDonald, Jill Vickers, and Marilyn Porter in this collection.

has depended on her unpaid and unrecognized labour. As marxist feminists such as Luxton (Luxton, 1980) and Wally Seccombe (see Fox, 1980) make clear, the housewife's key economic role in modern industrial capitalism is the production and reproduction of the labour force. Housewives produce a clean, well-fed and rested labour force ready for work each day, and they reproduce and socialize the next generation's labour force. Although she does not appear on the payroll or the pension list, the housewife's work is integral to the factory's operation.

Housewives also serve as a reserve army of labour. This term usually refers to the fact that housewives can be recruited into the labour force at times when the need for labour is high, such as in wartime, and then be absorbed back into the household at times of unemployment. However, the housewife not only accommodates changing labour force requirements, she also buffers fluctuating family needs. The housewife puts in very long hours of domestic labour when the children are small or a family member is sick, and far fewer when the nest is empty. She cushions the rigid demands of the workplace on the husband by taking on more responsibility if he has to work late or travel. In fact, the public sphere has taken on its rational, organized character in large part because there is a private sphere that absorbs life's irregularities.

The private sphere has also been left, by default, with the less profitable tasks. Emily Blumenfeld and Susan Mann Troffimenkoff (Fox, 1980) have pointed out that capitalists have left housework to housewives because much of it is not suited to maximizing profit. The sporadic, unrelated tasks that make up so much of domestic labour would be difficult to profitably organize. The affective ties surrounding childcare make it difficult to "rationalize": few of us want the efficiency of the factory in our families.

Clearly the public and private are not separate spheres but are inextricably linked with changes in one having dramatic implications for the other. Although we romanticize the home as a haven from the modern world (Lash, 1977), it is part of modern capitalism and has been defined by the developments in the public world.

Central to much feminist analysis is housework's effectiveness in maintaining male dominance. By organizing housework and childcare as unpaid female tasks, society simultaneously frees men for paid labour and forces women into dependency on men. The work that a woman does in raising a family is only recognized in our society if she finds a place within a patriarchal family. A housewife and mother is entitled to support from a husband on an almost feudal basis. The amount of support bears no relation to the amount of work she does, the standard of housekeeping, or the number of children she bears. Beyond a minimal level required by law, it is dependent upon the husband's "generosity" and is contingent upon the housewife pleasing him.

There is only one other way our society recognizes domestic labour. At times, the state will play the role of the father: a single woman can get government support for raising children. The support is given grudgingly, however, and at such a minimal level that it encourages a woman to return to dependence on a husband. Often women will put up with physical and mental abuse rather than lose the husband's support for themselves and their children.

What Is To Be Done?

Although feminists have been clear in their denunciation of the housewife's economic dependence on her husband, there has been some controversy about how to improve the situation. Should we recognize a housewife's labour by fighting for pay? Margrit Eichler has proposed that a housewife who is caring for a dependent, whether a child or disabled adult, should be paid by the state for this socially valuable work. Women caring for an able-bodied husband, however, are not doing a social service and should not be paid by the state but by the man receiving the service (Eichler, 1982). A campaign for *Wages for Housework* has lobbied for wages for domestic labour to be paid by the state or by the individual, usually the husband, who benefits. The campaign has gained some publicity for housewives but little in the way of real reforms, in part because of opposition from within the feminist ranks. In the late 1970s, Canada's National Action Committee on the Status of Women voted down proposals for Wages for Housework.[1] Some feminists argued, for example, that wages would only serve to perpetuate a social structure that has subjugated women. These feminists would prefer to bury the role of housewife and encourage women to enter the public sphere. The vision of society as presented by these feminists can be seen in such popular works as Betty Friedan's (Friedan, 1964 and 1981) and in media portrayal of the new superwoman, briefcase on one arm and baby in the other.

This vision has not been articulated so clearly in Canada, but it is implicit in the social policy positions of many groups. There is widespread support for campaigns for universally accessible government-funded daycare and general opposition to campaigns for wages for housewives. When Mothers Are Women proposed government support for at-home childcare at the National Action Committee on the Status of Women, the largest women's lobby group in Canada, we received support and understanding from some women and outright hostility from a few others, but generally the response was a patient explanation that we had profoundly misunderstood the aims of feminism.

The vision of most of the feminists with whom we spoke was an equality in which both men and women work at full-time jobs and neither is dependent on or supporting the other. The work traditionally done by the housewife would be transferred into the public sphere: domestic labour could be taken on by the state with old-age homes and hospitals, by the community with daycares, or by private enterprise with fast-food chains. The more privileged feminists turn to servants and argue that if we pay someone a fair wage to clean our house or care for our children, it becomes a job like any other. The small amount of work left should be shared by both men and women so that neither would have to do it full-time and neither would be defined or oppressed by it. Implicit in this vision is the assumption that many housewives are engaged in compulsive cleaning and trivial chores: if we stop polishing lightbulbs and decorating cakes and simply lower our standards, there would be a lot less housework to do.

The past twenty years have seen radical changes as many women have re-entered the labour force and put ideas such as these into practice. For some, in particular professional women, they have worked admirably: technology has lightened housework significantly so that it is easier to juggle the paid work and domestic labour. The growth in fast-food chains, laundry services, and maid services has demonstrated the popularity of turning much of the work over to the public sphere.

Fundamental problems persist, however, even when the work is in the public sphere. The status and pay for domestic labour continues to be low and the workers are predominantly women. Working in the public sphere has the advantage of being comparable to other forms of work, so that we can point out the incongruities of the low pay of a daycare worker compared to a zookeeper, and workers can unite to fight for better pay. Although we still have a long way to go in getting husbands to share the load of the housework remaining in the home, attitudes are slowly changing. For many women, housework is an annoyance rather than the central responsibility it once was.

Who Will Look After the Children?

Where the proposed solutions have clearly failed, however, is in meeting the needs of mothers of young children and other women with dependents such as the aged, disabled, and the chronically ill. Childcare and the attendant cooking and cleaning are onerous tasks that have not been much lightened by technology. They are not easily transferred to the public sphere. The burden of getting small children off to daycare every morning, working at a job all day and then putting hours into housework at night is exhausting, and many women are questioning the "Superwoman" image they have been trying to live up to. The full-time housewife served as a cushion between the rigid demands of the workplace and the irregular and unpredictable demands of a family, but the mother in the paid work-force has no such cushion and struggles with a workplace that does not readily accommodate family needs. Feminists in Canada are pushing to change the workplace to allow for family responsibilities by providing greater flexibility and such things as workplace daycare. These changes are crucial, but the short phase of child-rearing will continue to be a stressful and difficult one for most parents.

Potentially more problematic, however, is that not all women share the vision of these "liberal" feminists. The two-career marriage is a dream more attractive to the young, upwardly mobile professional couple than it is to the older woman who has few job skills after a lifetime of homemaking or the working-class mother whose marginal place in the work force provides little satisfaction and less security. For these women, the working world may provide a more precarious and difficult existence than dependence on a husband.

Another group questioning the cost of independence is mothers of young children, like myself, who want to raise their own infants and preschoolers. For us, an equality gained at the expense of a full-time relationship with our small children is not worth the price. Some women are totally opposed to non-parental childcare and feel adamantly that paid professionals, no matter how qualified, cannot provide the constancy, the familiarity, and the intimacy that is offered by someone who had known the child since birth and loves her deeply. Only as the infant grows older can we relinquish her to increasing amounts of alternative care. Others, like myself, are more willing to accept the adequacy of good quality alternative care but find that they really *want* to do it themselves. When my eighteen-month-old daughter was in daycare full-time, I quite simply missed her. I knew she was well cared for but *I* wanted to be the one doing the caring. Many women have told me that they have similar, gut-level reactions. So often mothers who are at home say "I wanted to be the one—the one who heard her first words, the one who taught him to swim, the one who dried the tears."

It can be extremely difficult to explain this reasoning to people who do not have children. It sounds sentimental and self-indulgent. Not everyone shares it to the same extent. People seem to be able to let go of their children at different ages and stages, depending in part on what is pulling them away. I have found that at six months I am happy to leave a child for a few hours a day, and at two years I can, with some doubts, leave the child for a full day, several days a week. Some of my friends want to be there until their children are in school all day. Others seem unconcerned about leaving a baby in care shortly after birth. It depends, of course, upon outside factors like their confidence in the childcare and the need to work, their income level or the satisfaction they derive from their work.

It is easy to hurt or offend women who feel differently about this. Most women are at least a little bit ambivalent about leaving their child with another caregiver and are vulnerable to criticism. Likewise, women who do their own childcare are sensitive to patronizing remarks about their mothering. I have been hurt by women who assumed I was unambitious, stupid, or "naturally" domestic when they saw I was at home. I suspect I have hurt others when I defended my staying at home by implying that I was a better mother. The liberal feminist vision I have referred to has made very little allowance for these feelings. Women are told that the regret they feel on leaving their children in care is socially conditioned guilt; something they should be strong enough to overcome. In my work for Mothers Are Women I found myself trying to explain to a variety of activists why I was at home. Most assumed that *they* knew that full-time daycare was in my best interest and that *I* was merely misguided to believe otherwise. I was told I was privileged, shortsighted, or that my children might be better off in professional care. I was told that my form of childcare was too expensive; that in the interests of economy I should put my children in group care. But, in fact, apart from concern for their relationship with their infants, many at-home mothers find the logistics of combining family and career overwhelming. With one child it is difficult, but with two or three children the stress of getting them all dressed and off to (often different) daycares each morning is exhausting. Finding "quality time" with each in the evening would be impossible on top of even minimal housework. The chances of having to stay at home with a sick child are fairly high, and even with leave for family responsibilities it is hard to maintain a position of any responsibility in the working world. (Recent proposals for overcoming this problem: a (strange) caregiver to be brought in to the home at a day's notice to care for sick children of working parents would seem to meet the needs of the employers rather than the children.) The cost of substitute care also enters into the decision to stay at home. Even with the low salaries now paid to daycare workers, the cost for me to send my three children to daycare would be more than most people earn.

Excluded From the Women's Movement?

Those women who opt to stay at home full-time for a few years often feel excluded by the mainstream women's movement. As more women enter the labour force, the at-home mother has become more isolated, more clearly dependent, and lower in status. Without the network of neighbourhood support provided in the past by the numbers of full-time housewives, she must constantly question her choice to stay at home and is probably far more aware of the sacrifices she is making. Very often the reforms proposed by feminists to ease the entry of women into the labour force are seen as threats by full-time housewives. For example, the feminist campaign for publicly-funded daycare provides very little for the mother who is at home all day, and in fact penalizes her by funding the childcare of parents in the paid workforce. Extended parental leave also usually excludes the woman who is at home before the baby is born. Older women have also felt alienated by a feminism that implicitly devalues the work that many of them have devoted their lives to. They argue, with some logic, that these feminists have accepted male myths about the value of the public sphere and the parasitic role of the housewife. Knowing themselves the value and the difficulties of the work they did, they are often hurt by this apparent lack of respect.

Although statistically housewives are an increasingly small minority, there will continue to be a number of women (and men) choosing this role. For some it is because of temperament and/or privilege: their partners *can* afford to support them and they enjoy the life. For others it is because their partner's jobs make such demands on the family—in terms of long hours, travelling, or moving—that it is difficult for them to do paid work. These women get little in the way of sympathy or support from the women's movement. In fact, they frequently feel blamed by feminists for their situation. And, indeed, there often *is* an implicit criticism of the overburdened wife for *letting* her husband take advantage of her. It is revealing that the women's movement has left the battles for sharing housework and childcare to the individual woman to fight, while feminists would never expect a woman to fight for pay equity on her own.

The disaffection from feminism of these housewives is now being used by groups in Canada and the United States to support an anti-feminist campaign. REAL Women in Canada and the Eagle Forum in the United States have claimed full-time homemakers as their constituency and tried to mobilize the alienation of older housewives as well as younger women. With shortsighted logic they argue that a dependent relationship with a husband is preferable to equality in a world that is biased against women and does not allow for the family responsibilities that most women shoulder. They prefer the enemy they know to the one they don't and choose the flawed haven of the home over the unpredictable freedom offered by feminists. They turn a blind eye to many of the flaws in the traditional family, and in fact often blame feminism for pointing out these flaws, for divorce, for example. But they offer little in the way of reforms to make the home a better place for women (Dubinsky, 1985, and Eichler, 1985).

Although the program offered by such groups is a backwards-looking, anti-feminist one, and their pro-homemaker stance masks a conservative, anti-choice, anti-homosexual agenda, some of their criticisms are important (Dubinsky, 1987). They point out that the mainstream feminists' emphasis on bringing women into the public sphere has removed many of the traditional supports for women before new ones are put in place. For example, in the past a married woman could expect to be supported in return for her housekeeping and childcare work; today she is expected to support herself as well as shoulder an inordinate share of these responsibilities. Women are increasingly expected to be independent shortly after divorce and they receive little compensation for the losses in earning power they have suffered because of their domestic work. In other words, feminists advocate independence for women in a world which is still organized on the assumption of their dependence: they expect women to assume an equality which has not yet been achieved.

The facile misrepresentation of feminism by groups like REAL Women and Eagle Forum, however, makes it clear that many women do not really understand the range and complexity of feminist analysis. The liberal or mainstream feminist vision is the only one most women are familiar with, and their picture of it often comes from distorted media accounts that romanticize the career woman. The perceptive and understanding views of a Margrit Eichler, Meg Luxton, or Penney Kome are not generally known, and the successful campaigns of feminist organizations for improvements in such things as divorce settlements and child support are seldom attributed to the women's movement.

Feminism must continue to meet these problems head-on by publicly discussing issues raised by anti-feminist groups like REAL Women. We must question the mainstream feminist analysis—a process that is taking place in the United States in debates between feminists like Jean Bethke Elshtain and Zillah Eisenstein (Elshtain, 1981, and Eisenstein, 1984). Elshtain calls for a revaluing of the private sphere, a proposal that Eisenstein condemns as a retreat from the difficult struggle for full equality. Ideological differences like these, however, must not prevent us from continuing to work for recognition and pay for the domestic labour women do. This is being done already where the support structures are part of the public sphere. The demand for universal, government-funded daycare, the pressure in the workplace to provide extended maternity and paternity leaves and part-time work with pro-rated benefits, and the attempts to ensure child support payments after divorce are all important feminist platforms.

Feminism needs to look further, however, at the private sphere to ensure recognition for the work women do there. If a woman chooses to raise her own children she should not be doubly penalized by a subsidized daycare structure that excludes her form of childcare. Rather, her childcare should be incorporated into a daycare system so that she receives some financial compensation for the work she is doing. At the time I was doing this research, Hungary provided a three year parental leave with partial benefits (for the woman) as well as subsidized infant daycares. While professional women who would lose seniority preferred not to take the leave, many others welcomed the opportunity. We should also start to question the forty-hour week. We have jumped abruptly from one forty-hour week supporting a family to expecting two work weeks—a total of eighty hours—from the family. Given the domestic responsibilities now carried by many people in the workforce, we should be considering a thirty-hour week for people with children. Many women already see part-time work and job-sharing as ideal ways to balance the demands of family and career, and we need to continue working to improve the job status and security of part-time workers while making sure that the child-care they also do part-time is recognized as well.[2]

Programs like parental leave and job-sharing are overwhelmingly used by women and there is a real danger that these will only perpetuate women's inequality. Women also predominate in the childcare and housework done in daycare centres and cleaning agencies. It is clear that until men are socialized to take a nurturing role and until the pay and status of this type of work is improved, few men will choose to take on the tasks, whether in the private or public sphere. Some European countries are considering an incentive for fathers to take parental leave: if he does not take his share of the leave, the family will lose it. Following the same reasoning, we might also require daycares to hire men. Because women have been exploited in the private sphere for so long, we have looked perhaps blindly to the public sphere for our equality. If we could envision a private sphere with equal participation by men, we might not be so defensive about parental childcare.

My own vision of the future is one where women will not have to make the impossible choice between full-time work and full-time mothering, where the mother or the father—probably both at different times—could stay at home with a baby for a year or more. And then, on return to the workforce, the parents might be able to work shorter days without losing benefits. If a child is sick the parents could remain at home to nurse her themselves. These changes will be hard to win because they will affect the employer far more than current proposals for daycare and pay equity.

Women who stay at home after their children are in school are still ignored in this vision, and we must ensure that they see their interests protected by the feminist movement. We should consider mechanisms to ensure that these women have access to the family income so that the men who are benefitting by their labour are actually paying them for it. We must continue to work for a homemaker's pension for these women and ensure that divorce settlements recognize the value of work done in the home.

Modern feminism, in its early days in the sixties, prided itself on listening to each woman's experience and respecting her decisions. We must return to this tradition, and work from the reality that most housewives experience, taking into account their values when advocating social policy reforms. The homemaker's life is not one that others might choose, but if feminism is not to become a rigid dogma, dictating but one correct option, it must allow women this choice.

Afterword

This paper comes out of a political struggle to bring the voices of women at home into the Canadian women's movement. Until I had children I had assumed the movement was my movement. As a young mother I was disturbed to find myself on the outside, my passionate commitment to my children viewed as misguided and backward.

I used a Women's Studies course with a supportive professor as an opportunity to explore feminist theory. I met other women in the same situation, and we began to raise our concerns within forums like the National Action Committee. We tried to develop alternatives to NAC's childcare policies that would allow parents more time with their small children. Some of these I mention in the article: extended parental leave, increased time off for family responsibility, the inclusion of parental childcare in provisions for paid childcare.

We were met with some hostility—many feminists, quite understandably, assumed we were a new variant on REAL Women—and with a great deal of condescension. We joined NAC committees, spoke at a daycare conference, attended meetings. There were important pockets of support, but overall it was an alienating experience.

Most of us have moved on to other things, but some of the women in Mothers Are Women continue to propose policy changes. Attitudes have shifted. There seems to be increased recognition that simply inserting women into a work world designed for men who enjoy the support of housewives has not worked. We hear less about the superwoman and more about the unequal load carried by women with young children. Among feminists there is now increased awareness that there are multiple feminisms. The authority of what I dubbed "mainstream feminism" has been challenged by others far more disenfranchised than myself, especially women of colour.

Mothering continues to be a difficult issue. We mothers have a great deal invested emotionally in the way we look after our children. I fear that my outspoken defence of parental care will anger and possibly hurt women who have trusted their children to alternate caregivers. No matter how carefully I chose my words, explaining my own decision to stay home implicitly raised doubts about other forms of childcare. Yet it seemed important to be clear about my decision— so many women have assumed that I stayed home out of innate domesticity or a lack of initiative.

Childcare is also a highly sensitive issue politically. I think that many women cannot imagine the liberation of women without daycare. So much rested upon daycare that it is very threatening to question it. Perhaps as we imagine alternate methods of accommodating the needs of children, without unfairly burdening their mothers, then we might be able to discuss daycare critically.

For I continue to think there are serious problems with daycare—specifically with the full-day group care of infants and toddlers. It seems to meet the needs of the work world better than the needs of the child or parent. It involves the state in one of our most intimate relationships and imposes the authority of the professional caregiver over the untrained mother. It has been highly gendered and class based: organized by middle-class women, staffed by poorly-paid women, promoted as a solution for the problems of the poor.

Beyond these concerns lies a very personal gut reaction. Group care was quite simply not able to provide the emotional context that I wanted for my children. Mothering, for me, was an emotionally intense, physically close, and highly personal relationship. Like many parents, I felt an emotional wrench on leaving my child in group care and only felt comfortable leaving my children when I was able to duplicate the mothering relationship.

After the article was written, my youngest child—then two—was cared for by a nanny for two years. She stepped into my shoes, he fell deeply in love with her, and I felt no guilt about his care. (Instead I felt guilty about the caregiver— a bright Third World doctor who was forced to give childcare to get into Canada. It was so clear that my freedom was bought at the expense of hers.) It is possible that group care could duplicate this one-to-one relationship, but the otherwise excellent daycare I experienced did not.

Given my focus on mothering, I am surprised at the extent to which I identify myself as a housewife in the article. Rather than describe myself as a graduate student struggling with three small children, I perversely identified myself with all that had been rejected by feminism, as a housewife. This was partly out of my own loss of confidence at the time, but it was also out of a recognition that most of my energy and intelligence was going into raising those children, and to call myself a student would be to deny my own work and to buy into a world view that denied the existence of children and the effort required to raise them.

Anyone familiar with the chaotic and untidy character of my house would probably agree that I would have been wiser to call myself a mother. As soon as my mothering responsibilities eased—shortly after writing the article—I re-entered the labour force. My public identity is now that of a doctoral student, and my mothering responsibilities are carried in private. I have been advised not to mention them too much on campus, advice I have largely ignored, but I know that being seen with a child subtly undermines my status as a potential academic. The private world collides with the public, and I forget children's appointments when I become absorbed in my thesis and miss academic deadlines when worried about a sick child. I worry that the distraction of my children will prevent me from the kind of single-minded commitment required for a thesis; that being a mother does make me less of a student.

But in these worries I am now part of the mainstream and able to share my concerns with other parents and see them addressed by the women's movement. Recently, at a dinner celebrating some anniversary in the women's movement, a woman I had worked with came up and asked what I was up to. I told her and she smiled. "We knew you would return to work," she said. Her welcome was kind, but revealing. I was back on track, on the inside, in the paid work world, and now sharing the concerns of the women's movement. We were now clearly on the same side.

Notes

1. A vote taken in the late 1980s indicated that N.A.C. had reversed its earlier position on Wages for Housework.
2. For a more exhaustive discussion of part-time work, see Duffy, Mandell and Pupo, 1989, and Duffy and Pupo, 1992.

References

Cowan, Ruth Schwartz, 1983. *More Work for Mother: The Ironies of Household Technology from the Open Hearth to the Microwave.* New York: Basic Books Inc.

Dubinsky, Karen, 1985. *Lament for a "Patriarchy Lost?" Anti-feminism, Anti-abortion, and R.E.A.L. Women in Canada.* Ottawa: The Canadian Research Institute for the Advancement of Women.

——, 1987. "R.E.A.L. Women–Really Dangerous." *Canadian Dimension* 21(6): 4.

Duffy, Ann, and Norene Pupo, 1992. *The Part Time Paradox: Connecting Gender, Work and Family*. Toronto: McClelland & Stewart.

Duffy, Ann, Nancy Mandell, and Norene Pupo, 1989. *Few Choices: Women, Work and Family*. Toronto: Garamond.

Ehrenreich, Barbara, and Dierdre English, 1979. *For Her Own Good: 150 Years of the Experts Advice to Women*. Garden City, N.Y.: Anchor Books.

Eichler, Margrit, 1985. *The Pro-Family Movement: Are They For or Against Families?* Ottawa: The Canadian Research Institute for the Advancement of Women.

——, 1985. "The Connection between Paid and Unpaid Labour and Its Implication for Creating Equality for Women in Employment," *Research Studies of the Commission on Equality for Employment*. Judge Rosalie Silberman Abella (April).

Eisenstein, Zillah, 1984. *Feminism and Sexual Equality, Crisis in Liberal Amercia*. New York: Monthly Review Press.

Elshtain, Jean Bethke, 1981. *Public Man, Private Woman, Women in Social and Political Thought*. Princeton: Princeton University Press.

Finch, Janet, 1983. *Married to the Job: Wives' Incorporation in Men's Work*. London: George Allen and Unwin.

Fox, Bonnie (ed.), 1980. *Hidden in the Household*. Toronto: Canadian Women's Educational Press.

Friedan, Betty, 1964. *The Feminine Mystique*. New York: Dell Publishing.

——, 1981. *The Second Stage*. New York: Summit Books.

Greer, Germaine, 1984. *Sex and Destiny: The Politics of Human Fertility*. New York: Harper and Row.

Hayden, Delores, 1980. *The Grand Domestic Revolution*. Cambridge: MIT Press.

Kome, Penney, 1977. *About Face: Towards a Positive Image of Housewives*. Ontario Status of Women Council.

——, 1982. *Somebody Has To Do It: Whose Work is Housework?* Toronto: McClelland and Stewart.

Lash, Christopher, 1979. *Haven in a Heartless World: The Family Besieged*. New York: Basic Books.

Lewis, Robert A., and Robert E. Salt, 1986. *Men in Families*. Beverley Hills, C.A.: Sage.

Luxton, Meg, 1980. *More Than A Labour of Love: Three Generations of Women's Work in the Home*. Toronto: Women's Educational Press.

Luxton, Meg, and Harriet Rosenberg, 1986. *Through the Kitchen Window: The Politics of Home and Family*. Toronto: Garamond Press, 1986.

Malos, Ellen (ed.), 1980. *The Politics of Housework*. London, England: Alison and Busby Ltd.

Mackie, Marlene, 1983. *Exploring Gender Relations: A Canadian Perspective*. Toronto: Butterworths.

McConville, Brigid, 1987. *Mad To Be A Mother: Is There Life after Birth for Women Today?* London: Century.

Meissner, Martin, 1975. "No Exit for Wives: Sexual Division of Labour and the Cumulation of Household Demands," *Canadian Review of Sociology and Anthropology* 2(4), Part I.

Michelson, William, 1985. *From Sun to Sun – Daily Obligations and Community Structure in the Lives of Employed Women and Their Families*. Totawa, N.J.: Rowman and Allenheald. (Michelson is a professor at University of Toronto and gives Canadian findings).

New Internationalist. March 1988, No. 181. Issue on "Life Sentence, The Politics of

Housework."

Oakley, Ann, 1974. *The Sociology of Housework*. New York: Random House.

——, 1976. *Women's Work: The Housewife, Past and Present*. New York: Random House.

Pogrebin, Letty, 1983. *Family Politics, Love and Power on an Intimate Frontier*. New York: McGraw-Hill Book Co.

Rich, Adrienne, 1976. *Of Woman Born: Motherhood as Experience and Institution*. New York: Bantam Books.

Snitow, Ann, 1992. "Feminism and Motherhood: An American Reading," *Feminist Review* 40 (Spring).

Strasser, Susan, 1982. *Never Done: A History of American Housework*. New York: Pantheon Books.

Chapter 2

Nurse as/and Mother
Rosemary Murphy

I am a nurse currently teaching psychiatric nursing. I am also a wife, a mother, and a feminist. Over the years I have learned the extent and depth of patriarchal sexism which pervasively and systematically discriminates against women. I have learned how sexism specifically allows nurses to be controlled and dominated. I didn't always understand the degree of subservience demanded of nurses nor the reasons for the discrimination that nurses suffered. We must know our history, our past, and understand our present, daily lives because it is only through sharing our knowledge that we can jointly value our experience and fight against the injustices, oppression, and violence experienced by women, and nurses in particular.

This paper is divided into four parts. In the introduction I briefly outline my present understanding and analyses of nursing. In the second part I describe my life as a woman and nurse and how I gained insight into the meaning of my experiences in these roles. The third part of the paper describes the daily life of the nurse, the exploitive working conditions and how the social relations with doctors* and administrators are oppressive. In the last section I describe the changes occurring in nursing with the growing politicization of nurses and the influence of the women's health movement on our health care system.

Introduction

I See and Am Silent

Nurses are treated as second-class citizens by the male-dominated medical establishment and hospital administrators who control the entire health care system. Nurses, who make up the majority of workers in this health care system, have no "real" decisional input and, furthermore, have exploitative working conditions and oppressive social relations with physicians who, in essence, control their daily work. The nurse's work is equated with that of the good mother

---

* When referring to doctors, I use the male pronoun for several reasons: 1. the majority of doctors are male; 2. while women are entering the field in large numbers, control of the profession remains in the hands of men; and 3. teaching methods in medical school are, for the most part, from a male point of view. I refer to nurses as female because the majority of them are women and this paper is written from the perspective of a female nurse.

and wife. Both clean, feed, bathe, care for, listen, take orders, and smile. Both nursing and mothering roles are presumed to be "natural" to women and because of this they are taken for granted and even devalued. Nurses are socialized to believe that a professional nurse does not rebel. An examination of our history demonstrates the roots of nursing as the work of an "angel," as a "Christian" duty to care for the sick. Rebelling is still considered unfeminine and unprofessional. Women are expected to do what they are told and fulfil their "natural" function of caring for others. And so it is no surprise that so few nurses (like so few mothers and wives) even recognize that they are oppressed and exploited. We were taught to suffer in silence. Most nurses (again, like mothers) blame themselves when they feel abused or resentful, believing that they just aren't "good" nurses.

In this paper I am examining my own experience as a nurse and how I gradually came to embrace the feminist analysis of nursing. Through my personal experience in nursing, which I believe is typical, and through the study of feminist scholars, I realized the necessity for breaking the silence about the real lives of nurses. Although nursing has a long history of oppression and subservience, this isn't taught to nursing students (see Kalisch and Kalisch, 1992; Melosh, 1982; Coburn, 1981; Ehrenreich & English, 1973).

Furthermore, nursing abounds with myths, stereotypes, and untruths (see Muff, 1982, for an extensive academic examination of this topic). All of this contributes to the conspiracy of silence that keeps us in our place. It is no accident that the inspirational motto of Canada's first nurses' training school is "I See and Am Silent." More and more nurses are refusing to remain silent. To become empowered, to identify the real causes of exploitation and to make real changes requires an understanding of the various forms of patriarchal discrimination. It is only through understanding that we can stop complying with our exploitation. It is only in the last few years that nurses have begun to reclaim their autonomy and power and to speak out on health care issues, as well as to demand fair working conditions. If nursing is permitted to develop, the health care system will be improved. There will be greater emphasis on the whole person and on the prevention of disease. The nursing role would be to help people take greater control over their own health and bodies. Working relationships with doctors will be equal, each having a domain of knowledge and responsibility, and will be truly interdependent. Relationships with clients (patients) will also be egalitarian.

My Personal is Political

"The personal is political," a popular slogan of the feminist movement, posits that personal, intimate experiences are not isolated or individual to one woman nor the result of their "nature." One woman's experience is often very much like another woman's experience. One distinctive shared experience is that women are relatively powerless in a man's world. Feminists value women's personal experiences and analyze the connections common to them in an effort to empower women to effect change. This personal kind of knowledge and insight is valued and used to critique traditional (male) explanations for why women are exploited, abused, lack power, or remain in independent roles both within the private sphere of the home and within the public sphere. This definition of "political" is quite different than the traditional one which denies the validity of personal, private experiences and remains abstract, theoretical, and so-called "scientific." For these reasons I begin my analysis of nursing from an examination of my own life, making connections between my private life as a nurse and woman and that of other nurses and other women.

My early life experiences, I think, are quite representative of nurses from my generation and illustrate how my life as a girl, and a young woman, prepared me to uncritically accept, and then reproduce, the oppressive forces in the nursing profession that I am now trying to change.

I grew up on a farm in a large family of eight. I had four brothers and three sisters, close in age, with only ten years from the oldest to the youngest. My mother was trained as a nurse. She had an enormous influence on me and on my sisters. She encouraged us to stay in school—to be educated—to be nurses. Three of us became nurses and one is a teacher. We were told that a career would mean we would never have to be financially dependent on a man. This has had a profound effect on me. These ideas were the seeds of my feminism. At the same time, the values of working hard, caring for and serving others contributed to my vulnerability for oppression. I was being socialized to take on the role of a woman in this society. These values were internalized and prepared me well for the profession of nursing. Nursing is nurturing and hard work.

At mealtimes in our home, my father and brothers were served first, receiving the most and best food. Women set the table and cleaned up afterwards. The men made demands and we met them, at least until my sisters and I were teenagers. We cleaned the house and they, disrespecting our work, walked over scrubbed floors with muddy boots. We cleaned up, picked up, laundered and ironed. I even remember carrying my brother's lunch-pail to school for him. Our home wasn't that unusual. We learned to serve. We saw: we knew that men had a more privileged position in society. They *certainly* did in our home.

During high school I worked in a "home for the aged," as a nurse's aide. My reputation as a willing, hard worker earned me praise but little money; and it also earned me more of other people's work. I thrived on the praise I received. I worked harder. I never complained. I can see now that I was used. I would often work the weekend for the permanent aide. She would collect her regular pay of $8 and give me the part-time rate of $5 for an eight-hour shift. I would come home from work exhausted. To protest never crossed my mind. In fact, I had a "beautiful smile" and was pleasantly compliant with all the demands made of me. Our smiles, mine and my sisters, were often praised and commented upon: "Oh what a beautiful smile!" "You're so kind and cheerful!" Even, "You have beautiful teeth!" Sometimes I smiled so much my face ached. Imagine! I think this experience is familiar to many women. And it is crucial we understand the meaning of this kind of praise and what smiling represents. Smiling as a greeting is a caring gesture we all like to share. Smiling as a conditioned response to submission, compliance to others, objectification of oneself, or denial of one's needs, is injurious to oneself as a complete human being. I didn't realize all this when I was sixteen. I didn't know the depth and extent of the oppression of women, and nurses in particular, until many years later.

Although I always asserted myself to some extent, the responses I received ranged from considering my ideas "high-faluting," to dismissing them as cute or funny. In primary school I was often punished for being impolite and for talking back to teachers. By high school I had learned to keep my ideas to myself and to carefully memorize the teacher's words. This paid off. I began to receive good marks.

I entered a Catholic nursing school in a medium-sized city, determined to be the best, most caring nurse I could be. I took seriously all the hours of lectures and adopted whole-heartedly the Christian and nursing philosophy of giving obedient, loving care. I remember learning that TLC meant "Tender Loving Care," which I intended to provide. I was always pleasant and willing to work hard. My own aching feet and back never interfered with the needs and demands of my patients, head nurses, teachers, directors, doctors, and house-mother. It is no surprise that I was a successful student. I was rewarded for my hard work by winning the Proficiency Award for First Year Nursing.

I was even self-righteous and judgmental of peers who weren't as dedicated, efficient, and hard working. I had internalized these values. I had become my own oppressor. These behaviours weren't defined as exploitation: this was called being a professional, dedicated, caring nurse.

After graduation I got married immediately. Most of my classmates, in fact, were engaged to be married within a year from graduation. I had never lived independently. I went from my father's home to a nurses' residence and then to my husband's home. For the next year I worked on a demanding male surgical ward while my spouse finished university.

Challenging the Medical Model
We spent the next two years living and working in Nigeria with CUSO: teaching, nursing and seeing the world. This experience was non-traditional and influenced me greatly. I learned about nursing, culture, power, and about women's work. The year was 1968. We saw a nation torn by tribal war; a nation struggling to find an identity following its independence from Britain. The British influence was still very present. The hospital was run by a British matron. The school of nursing had a British director and the nursing structure was based on the British military hospital system. Authoritarian, hierarchical order was imposed. The hospital-

based health care was from a medical model focusing on diseases, cures, surgery, and drugs. The medical model views illness and disease as an invasion of the body by germs. The doctor focuses on the diseased body part, makes a diagnosis, and then prescribes a cure. The cure consists of drugs, or of cutting out the offending disease, or of replacing the diseased body part. This type of health care is criticized by the women's health movement because it focuses on individual patients or their body parts instead of a holistic and community view; disease and treatment rather than health and prevention; high technology and hospitals rather than small community-controlled centres; and "experts"—highly-trained physicians who control almost all decisions about health care and policies—rather than sharing responsibilities with the consumer as well as with nurses, midwives, health educators, physiotherapists, to name just a few other important participants in the health care process. The medical model does have its place in the diagnosis and treatment of diseases, but it should not have authority over social problems and should be considered in its place, along with other models of health care, instead of dominating and controlling all other participants.

The medical model was totally inappropriate to the real needs of the country I was in. Nurses were trained to function within this model and the hospital-based system of health care. At the time, as at present, millions of people required basic health education, primary prevention, immunization, a basic balanced diet, clean water, safe child-birthing and family planning assistance. Individuals and communities must take control of their health and health care needs. This is a nursing approach and is valued by the women's health movement. It is called primary health care and is promoted by the World Health Organization.

Instead, we took care of a few while the majority suffered. We put on Band-aids rather than educating and organizing communities to meet their own basic health needs. The medical model is valued by traditional doctors and the patriarchy. The experience helped me to demystify modern medicine, to critique its value, and to see its limitations.

I was also learning about women's work, specifically housework. We, like most ex-patriots, had a cook/housekeeper. He did all the cooking, cleaning, laundry, and shopping. I had never experienced such service. I was the recipient of the care I had always provided. It was great! Never again would housework be my responsibility alone. But the egalitarian distribution of housework between myself and my husband took many years to achieve.

I returned to Canada and to university, to obtain a degree in nursing. I had always wanted to go to university but thought I wasn't capable of passing the courses. No one had encouraged me. Now I saw university education as a way to advance my nursing career, to explore my intellectual interests, and mostly to escape the exploitive working conditions of hospital nursing.

I was at first intimidated by the idea of studying in a university. But soon another male stronghold was demystified for me. University courses were interesting, fun, and relatively easy. It was rewarding to discuss ideas and learn aboutithe world. It was empowering.

Public Health Nursing

After graduation, I got a job as a public health nurse in a poor rural district. My job involved teaching individuals and families about disease prevention and identification of early health problems through such programs as immunization and well-baby clinics, school health programs, pre-natal classes and follow-up home visits to new mothers and their babies, visiting the homes of old people and people who have had psychiatric problems. Public health nursing meant I was working with families in the community, helping them take control over their lives by providing them with knowledge about their bodies, health, and perhaps most important, their rights in the health care system, for example, teaching pregnant women about their right to choose alternative forms of labour and delivery, their right to full explanations and choices in health care.

For the first time I was functioning independently from authoritarian, medically-controlled structures. I was freed from the medical model. The focus was on the client. It was holistic, concerned with the person's emotional, social, and physical needs rather than with any specific disease. My role changed from the restricted, subservient role of the hospital nurse carrying out doctors' orders and helping with the cure of specific diseases to the expanded, independent role of an educator in the prevention of disease and the promotion of health. Sometimes I was even involved in community activism: for example, helping a community organize a day care centre, or ensuring a safe water supply in rural areas, or assisting families with special needs children to get specialized services. I worked in collaboration with clients, helping them meet their own needs rather than telling or instructing them as an "expert." The relationship was more balanced. I was invited into their homes, and many times they taught me about health problems and their ways of coping with them, and I learned from them.

My clients were primarily women whom I met in their homes. Some of the problems I was helping with involved caring for newborn babies, caring for children after hospitalization, caring for mentally and physically handicapped children, helping with school health problems, helping women with depression and other kinds of psychiatric problems, helping old people with their health,problems and with remaining independent in their homes as long as they wanted.

These women taught me a great deal about the lives of ordinary women, about their strength and about their pain. They told me their problems, discussed their depression and their difficulty coping with small children and adolescents. They talked about their fears of beating their children out of frustration, isolation, loneliness, and overwork. Many women felt that their mothering and housework was devalued and taken for granted by their families. They often said they felt like servants to their children and husbands and at the same time felt guilty for having such negative, angry thoughts. Some women really felt trapped. They disliked being at home but lacked either the education or the confidence to go out into the work world. They felt they had no choice but to "make do." Being a housewife was viewed as better than being a waitress for someone else and *also* a housewife and mother. Women felt exhausted and frustrated. They talked about their husband's affairs, their feelings of powerlessness and helplessness, fears of being abandoned by their husbands, of poverty, and of being inadequate mothers and workers. These women's personal lives are testimony to the abuses women everywhere experience, abuses that should no longer be tolerated. They taught me to appreciate and admire the strength of women. I was determined, at least, to avoid falling into the traps I saw these women in.

At this time something happened in my life that would shake up my view of the world. I had a baby, a boy. I had romanticized and idealized motherhood and family life. Despite my work experiences, I was unprepared for the reality. Parenthood shook the foundations of my relationship with my partner. To this day, I'm not altogether sure I understand what happened. I demanded that we share equally in the parenting and housework tasks. It was a struggle. I was working full-time outside the home, earning more money than my partner. But he still considered childcare and housework to be primarily my job. I really began to see how women in traditional roles become subservient by always caring for others. When I was taking care of my baby, I anticipated his every need and juggled my priorities to meet his needs as well as those of my husband. It wasn't long before I realized that my chronic frustration and anger were the result of the overwork, the injustice of the workload distribution, and the fact that I had entirely pushed my needs aside. I wasn't articulate about what was happening to me at the time, but I complained. Everyone thought I was at the very least being picky, and some felt I was hen-pecking, demanding, and even lazy. Just about everybody had some comment, and none were unconditionally supportive. My partner and I struggled, talked, and worked through every issue as it arose. It was my job (and still is) to raise the problems and bring them into the open for resolution. My career helped keep me sane. My job gave me a separate identity as one who is a capable, knowledgeable person. It provided intellectual stimulation, confidence, self-esteem, and financial independence.

Psychiatric Nurse

I again returned to school for a Masters degree in Education and got the job I still hold, teaching psychiatric nursing in a community college. Psychiatric nursing, as I teach it, is similar to public health nursing in that the nurse educates and emotionally supports clients to gain the insight, knowledge, and ability necessary to regain control over their lives and to make choices about how to proceed with their lives. In the psychiatric hospital setting, the clients are often emotionally distraught and confused. They are especially vulnerable and need to know they will be protected and cared for.

Here, too, my views evolved as I studied and witnessed the sexism in psychiatry. Sexism in psychiatry is a book in itself, but very briefly, all the psychological theories of personality development as well as the explanations for mental illness and treatments are biased, inadequate, and often violent to women (Ashley, 1980; Chesler, 1972; Smith and David, 1975). Women are labelled mentally ill more often than men and called sick when they rebel. Examples are the "Angry Woman Syndrome" (Rickles, 1971) and the "Hysterical" personality diagnosis. Moreover, the treatments and drugs which women receive are more violent. In Canada, women are prescribed two-thirds of all tranquillizers. Especially vulnerable are women of child-bearing age and housewives (Cooperstock, 1982). In one Saskatchewan study, women received anti-depressant drugs eight times as often as men in the same age group (Harding, 1981). Women receive twice as many electric shock treatments as men, even though it is known that shock treatments are ineffective for treating depression and can cause brain damage (Weitz, 1985; Burstow, 1985). Another aspect of sexism is that psychiatry generally ignores the roots of women's problems, many of which are found in society. More and more women are bringing incest into the open. Many times reports of this kind are recorded in the physician's history but rarely does the woman receive any help in dealing with sexual violence. She is given treatment as though such violence were *her* problem and she is expected to see such events as "past history" and to get on with her life as if these events meant nothing. So women come to believe they are "sick" and are thus further violated and isolated by their "helpers." They are left alone with their anger, fear, and shame (Chesler, 1972; Smith and David, 1975). A great number of women's mental health problems are rooted in the social conditions of their lives, and solutions rest in changing these social inequalities, often through women working together. Over the years, I have added to my psychiatric nursing course specific women's issues such as examination of sexism in mental health care, eating disorders, addictions, battering, rape and incest, all from a feminist perspective.

An Historical Perspective

I love teaching; I enjoy students and being able to provide a feminist perspective to my course, not only in content but also in process. By this I mean that I try to strengthen the individual student through building on her strengths; I ask students to analyze their own lives before prescribing for others; I encourage students to see the commonality of experience in women and to endorse the need for collective, collaborative action to make changes, both in the student's life and in the clients' lives; I encourage self-assertion and self-esteem. Above all, I believe it is essential for a student to experience her own strength and value; this in itself will be an empowering experience to transfer to her personal and work life.

To reinforce my feminist perspective and to thoroughly ground my experience in theory, I returned again to university, this time to a Women's Studies program. I was shocked by the literature from all disciplines, again and again documenting the depth and breadth of sexism in patriarchal society. The Women's Studies program helped me gain a theoretical and political understanding of what had happened to me. These studies helped me see the connections between what was happening to me as a woman and nurse, among all women and all nurses.

I discovered the history of women as healers. It was exhilarating to learn about the wisdom of our foresisters, yet sad to read about the hatred focused on women healers. This "history" was not taught to me nor to other nursing students. I am just now introducing it into my courses. It is essential to know our past to understand our present and to gain autonomy. I learned that in the middle ages, women were healers with a great deal of knowledge about herbs, treatments, and midwifery. They were scientific, astute observers and diagnosticians as well as practitioners able to give holistic care to sick people. The Middle Ages also marked the beginning of a campaign by the male ruling class of doctors and priests to take over women's role in healing (Ehrenreich and English, 1973). Nine million people were exterminated in the infamous witch hunts. Most were poor women, healers and midwives. They were believed to be possessed by the devil because they were able to heal, while doctors who used superstitious and dangerous treatments such as blood-letting and leeches were viewed as authorities. The witch hunts have had a lasting effect on our attitudes toward women and nurses. Medicine was established as a profession requiring university training. This eliminated not only the poor, but women as well, because women were legally barred from going to university. The last domain to be taken over by physicians was midwifery. This was achieved by refusing training to midwives and restricting the use of obstetrical forceps to surgeons only. Finally, the university-trained middle-class male physicians lobbied legislators to pass licensing laws forbidding the practice of lay healers. Although doctors finally gained monopoly over the practice of medicine by the turn of the twentieth century, the popular health movement, of which women were the backbone, fought a long and difficult struggle against the monopoly that medicine still enjoys. They fought for women's legal rights, public health principles, birth control, and the right to have their own schools. Doctors did not allow medicine to be shared. Their schools were closed.

At the same time that lay healers were losing the battle with doctors, Florence Nightingale was reforming nursing, making it an acceptable place for women in health care. Nursing was made into a subservient "profession" for respectable middle-class women, emphasizing character and minimizing skill (Ehrenreich and English, 1973; Leininger, 1970; Melosh, 1982). The physicians used hospitals to practice medicine and needed nurses to carry out their orders and treatments in caring for the patient. In so doing, doctors split healing into two distinct parts: curing and caring. Curing, the prescription of drugs, treatments, and surgery, was the domain they claimed for themselves and attributed all recovery to their intervention. The caring role was left to the nurse and was considered a "natural" skill of women, not requiring intelligence or study nor deserving of financial reward.

Since nursing was mostly heavy-duty housework, it didn't attract the middle- and upper-class woman, as Florence Nightingale had hoped. It therefore became necessary to *teach* nursing students upper-class values and graces. A great deal of this kind of teaching persisted into the mid-1960s when I was a student. We were told how often to bathe; to wear girdles, hats and gloves; to show respect to those with more status than ourselves by standing at attention, not speaking until spoken to; we were even to address each other by our surnames. Our leisure time was regulated and restricted by curfews, and our beds were checked to be sure that curfews weren't broken. Finally, no student nurse was allowed to be pregnant. Married women were not accepted into training programs. Only twenty-five years ago, pregnancy meant shame and immediate dismissal.

The early schools of nursing instilled strict authoritarian values stressing the need for complete subservience to the doctor. The nurse was to be the obedient handmaiden to the doctor (Melosh, 1982; Coburn, 1981; Leininger, 1970).

The two institutions that had a profound effect on nursing were the military and the religious orders. Both valued and instilled the ethics of authoritarian hierarchical structure, obedience, and service. Hospitals were hierarchical and authoritarian, run by male administrators and male doctors. Until World War II they were staffed completely by student nurses. Hospitals recognized the value of this pool of cheap labour. Large and small hospitals opened training schools just for the labour the students provided, often offering them only minimal education in exchange. The students received no pay, only room and board. Their conditions of work were deplorable. Only after World War II did hospitals employ graduate nurses, and then it was for low pay and poor working conditions. The justification for such low wages was that nursing was a labour of love and inherent in femininity, as were housework and mothering. Coburn (1981, 193) explains that marriage was looked upon as a lifesaver, "rescuing" nurses from exploitation, overwork, and the threat of long periods of unemployment and poverty-stricken old- or even middle-age. Women's employment was seen as supplementary to the primary duties of that woman to her family. This attitude still prevails. Nurses' work was considered a public service and similar to unpaid work in the home. Because nursing and mothering were seen as labours of love, nurses were denied decent wages and working conditions, and law-makers actually blocked legislation recognizing the skilled nature of their work. Coburn (1981, 198) maintains that governments justified exploitation of nurses by arguing that nurses' duties were "not only an extension of the work they would do in the home for free, but also a training ground for married life."

Exploitation of nurses was also entrenched through a set of professional attitudes that still rule nursing. Nurses were taught blind obedience to authority, subordination to physicians, and professional loyalty to institutions. These attitudes prevented nurses from uniting with each other, let alone with other pink-collar labourers in the hospitals such as the cleaning women. It was considered unprofessional, disloyal, and even unholy to complain, let alone to demand. Certainly "striking" was considered a dirty word by nurses. But nurses are now becoming politically active and we are re-defining what it means to be professional and in what directions nursing can develop. I will discuss some of these activities in the last section.

The Life of a Nurse: Exploitation and Oppression

So much glorification and stereotyping surrounds the practice of nursing that their daily exploitation is almost completely hidden and denied, even by nurses themselves. Nurses reinforce this oppression by internalizing the myths and the expectations of the dominant culture. We must sort out the reality and understand how these myths serve to keep us as subservient "angels of mercy" engaged in "labours of love," rather than autonomous, powerful, caring health professionals. We must redefine our needs, our rights and our work as women and as nurses. To do this requires an understanding of apparently insignificant details which belie the systematic and powerful ways that nurses are dominated and controlled by others.

Overworked and Undervalued: Exploitation

Nursing is an enormous amount of hard work carried out under the authority of others. Furthermore, a great deal of nurses' work is obscured, hidden from the public, or not called work at all. This is similar to housework and the work of mothers. Nurses' conditions of work are exploitative.

Nurses carry out intensive and extreme physical and emotional labour. They are responsible for critically ill patients, which requires knowledge of complex medical and technological developments. Nurses are on the front line twenty-four hours a day, unlike doctors who only come in briefly to "visit" the patient and write orders to be carried out by nurses. The nurse keeps the machines operating and the patients comfortable and alive. The nurse does so much work that to detail it would be time-consuming and frustrating for the reader, so instead I'll present a snapshot view of a nurse's day. On a typical day a nurse bathes, feeds, toilets, and exercises about five patients; she makes their beds; she lifts hundreds of pounds of flesh, positioning and turning immobilized patients; she educates, comforts and supports patients and their families; she administers about two hundred medications; she administers treatments, dressings and intravenous feedings; records and reports the patients' conditions to co-workers, supervisors, and doctors; answers telephones, doctors' requests and orders; makes countless decisions, some of which are life-saving; and plans and co-ordinates her patients' care with other health care workers, such as social workers and physiotherapists. The nurse rarely has time to sit down during the day. In fact, one nurse who wore a pedometer recorded walking ten miles during one tour of duty! The conditions make a nurse's work even more difficult and burdensome.

One of the most frustrating aspects of a nurse's work is the constant interruption nurses endure. They, like secretaries and mothers, must rearrange their priorities to meet other people's needs. It is difficult to complete even one task without interruption. Patient call-bells and telephones ring constantly. Patients, families, visitors, and doctors all demand immediate attention, each believing their request deserves the nurse's immediate attention.

She does all this without taking credit for her accomplishments and certainly without errors. Mistakes are not well tolerated. They are recorded, reported, analyzed, and kept in the nurse's and patient's files. The nurse is not only responsible for her own work but also must ensure that doctors don't prescribe incorrect treatments. In short, nurses are expected to carry an impossible workload, leaving them with a chronic sense of fatigue, anxiety, inadequacy, and failure. To make matters even worse, the problem of overwork is denied and hidden, or the individual nurse is made to feel responsible. *She* is accused of being the cause of her overwork. Not only does the hospital administration hold her responsible, but so do her peers, who have internalized these impossible standards.

Work that is poorly done or left undone by one nurse is picked up by the next, further overburdening her. And if an emergency or crisis arises, the nurse is expected to sacrifice her coffee break, and sometimes her lunch, and to work mandatory overtime when necessary. If it is an especially hectic, short-staffed day, the nurse is expected to use her time ever-so-efficiently, without additional compensation and without complaint. In one hospital the nurses were told not to tell the patients when they were short-staffed because administration did not want patients complaining about the hospital. This means that the nurse must quietly accept the blame for the inadequate care a patient is receiving instead of placing the responsibility for staffing on the administration where it rightfully belongs.

If a nurse is consistently unable to complete her work and is behind schedule, she is considered disorganized, inefficient, unable to establish priorities; if the problem is long-standing, she is judged a poor nurse. She may be ostracized, criticized, or fired.

Understaffed, it is impossible to do what you know you should. The hospital nurse often has to feel satisfied with maintaining minimum standards of care— of preventing major problems. She rarely has the leisure of enjoying her work and feeling gratified for doing it well!

Nurses are required to rotate shifts, weekends, holidays and to work mandatory overtime. A subtle, unwritten rule prevents many nurses from requesting overtime pay. All requests are recorded and analyzed. They are afraid of being judged "uncaring" or "inefficient." Many feel they should be able to be more productive and give the patient more, even if it's at their own expense. Rarely do you find nurses asking for extra staff, let alone demanding it, and seldom, if ever, do you find nurses refusing to take on heavier and heavier workloads. Sometimes I would be so exhausted, my feet and back aching, that I felt I could not walk down the hall to answer one more bell.

Although some nurses have negotiated "professional responsibility" clauses which allow them to grieve if they believe their work is being handicapped by an overload of patients, nurses rarely invoke this clause. Not only do nurses feel they should be able to cope, they are also afraid to take any sort of official action against their employer.

Another astonishing example of overworking the nursing staff illustrates the extent to which nurses carry the burden of budgetary restraint. This hospital had adopted a scoring system that determined staffing according to patients' needs for nursing care. It was found that the unit was understaffed and more nurses were hired. After several months, however, the administration abandoned the system because it cost too much to hire the number of nurses actually required. The nurses had no input or choice about this arbitrary decision to increase their workload, even when objective evidence validated their need for more staff.

Adding to the workload is the nurses' practice of covering each other during coffee breaks, lunch, and even for meetings. Relief nurses are not hired while regular nurses attend meetings. While she is off the unit, the nurse continues to be responsible for her patients and feels the pressure to return quickly to the unit. Nurses are even subtly pressured to attend staff meetings on their days off.

These are some of ways in which nurses' conditions of work are exploitative. In the next section I will analyze how nurses' social relations with doctors are oppressive.

Relations with Doctors: Oppression
Physicians dominate not only their patients and the public but also nurses. Curtin (1982, 144) explains that while nurses, the largest group of health care professionals, are employees of a health care agency, their supposed "co-workers," that is, physicians, are "guest practitioners" with enormous power over most aspects of the organization.

Examples of doctors controlling nurses' work are found in doctors writing orders for such nursing decisions as diets, exercise, dressing changes, and when a patient can be discharged. Doctors continue to insist on writing orders specifying not only what care a patient should receive but also when it should be given. If a nurse doesn't follow an order exactly, she must file an incident report.

Nurses have no real input into how the institution is organized or run. Doctors are the gatekeepers for patient entry to hospitals. They also dominate and control the committee and the decision-making hospital policy process within departments and at the government level. And doctors want to keep their superior positions. A U.S. survey found that 78 percent of MDs believe nurses already have enough say in patient care, and close to another 10 percent believe they have too much authority already! (Lee, 1979, 27).

Doctors and others also dominate nurses through their social relations, as illustrated by the use of time, space, and language. Social scientists have analyzed their use in terms of social power. High status, dominant groups of people have more rights to control their time, which is seen as more valuable, than do subordinate groups; they have larger, more comfortable and private spaces, and their use of language reflects and reinforces their privilege, status, and social order (Tellis-Nayak, 1984). In a patriarchal society men belong to the dominant group while women are in the subordinate group.

Nurses, as a subordinate group, have little control over their use of time: it is not valued by others, especially by doctors, who are free to interrupt nurses' work, and to keep *them* waiting. Nurses, like mothers, are to be available to everyone, on demand. Furthermore, their time is closely regulated and supervised, like that of unskilled labourers. Sanctions govern late arrivals and early departures. Coffee breaks and lunch times are closely regulated and specified. One intensive care unit nurse told me that coffee breaks were seen almost as a privilege, to be taken if nothing else required the nurses' attention and this rarely was the case. She felt that the scheduling of coffee and lunch was so rigid that it was like being in the army or on an assembly line. Also rigidly scheduled are nursing procedures and treatments; being late in administering a treatment may be cause for reprimand.

Nurses' holidays and sick days are closely regulated. Only a limited number of days can be taken during the summer and none over the Christmas season. Sick days require a physician's certificate and no salary is given for the first sick day if a nurse has already had three sick days in one year! There is considerable pressure not to take a sick day on a weekend or holiday. A nurse will often work when she is sick because she recognizes the heavy burden placed on her peers if a relief nurse can't be "found." She also expects the same of her co-workers.

Another demand placed upon the nurse is to upgrade her education, on her own time and at her own expense. There are no paid "professional development" days for nurses. I've known nursing staffs to raise money for conferences (and even for hospital equipment) through bake sales and raffles. And all nurses are expected to have at least a B.Sc. in Nursing by the year 2000, but the responsibility for getting time off for study is left entirely to the individual nurse. This can mean great hardship, for the nurse must work extra nights and weekends, or work part-time. She loses her salary, seniority, benefits, and job security. What does she get in return for these hardships? Nothing, if she returns to the bedside. Nurses are not paid for their degrees. In fact, as of the late eighties, some Ontario public health nurses with degrees were being paid up to 40 percent less than hospital non-degree nurses. Some hospitals don't even pay for a nurse's past experience! In Ontario, when a nurse leaves one hospital to work in another, she must begin at the bottom of the salary scale no matter how much experience she has. This illustrates clearly the low value put on nurses' time and labour.

Another frustrating, demanding, and difficult aspect of a nurse's work day is having to be available to the doctor and other senior staff. This means constant interruptions. The Tellis-Nayak study (1984, 1066) found the doctor delegating time-wasting tasks to the nurse, making her wait around for him because his time is considered more valuable. It is a common experience for the nurse to be interrupted by the doctor, whatever she is doing. It doesn't matter if she is talking on the telephone, preparing medications, charting, reading a report, talking to or even bathing a patient. The nurse complies with the physician request, adjusting her priorities to meet his needs. I've never heard a nurse ask a doctor to wait until she has finished the task she is engaged in. A nurse carefully evaluates whether to call and disturb the physician during a crisis, especially if it is at night. She must have absolute justification for disturbing the doctor, always weighing the needs of the patient against those of the physician. If she calls him for what he deems a minor concern, she risks being ridiculed, yelled at, or even reported.

A final example of the disrespect for nurses' time and the over-valuing of doctors' time is the ritual around patients' charts. Whenever a doctor wants a chart, no matter who is using it, it must be given up immediately. The nurse is even expected to fetch and retrieve charts for the doctor (Tellis-Nayak, 1984, 1067). These "handmaiden" behaviours support the superior ranking of the physician's time.

Nurses, in common with other women in subordinate positions, do not have control over their spaces in terms of amount, type and rights to privacy. Nurses generally don't have separate offices or lounges. Doctors, patients, and families saunter into the nurses' station, charting rooms, and treatment rooms without asking permission and without respect for what the nurse is doing. By contrast, the doctor's territory is usually guarded by a nurse or secretary.

Invasion of the nurses' station is so pervasive and routine that most nurses don't even consider it an interruption or a violation of their privacy. In fact, many believe these interruptions are normal and necessary for the functioning of the unit. Occasionally, when the noise level is high with talking, joking, and general confusion, a nurse may quietly suggest that it is difficult for them to concentrate, but she will not ask doctors to be quiet.

I observed one blatant example of territorial ownership by a ward psychiatrist which would be almost humorous if not for the destructive power imbalance it represents. This doctor insisted on always having the same chair in the nurses' charting room to complete records. Whenever he arrived, everyone literally jumped off the "doctor's chair." No words were spoken; not even eye contact was made. Everyone automatically changed places at the sound of his footsteps. Social superiors have the privilege of entering the personal space of social inferiors. The Tellis-Nayak (1984, 1066) study observed that physicians regularly moved into the personal zones of nurses, yet nurses rarely violated a physician's space bubble.

In the hospital setting, the way people relate not only abuses nurses but also reflects and reinforces their subordinate position. This is illustrated through the manner in which people are addressed; how mistakes are pointed out; through patterns of interruptions; and in sexist jokes, harassment, and finally, even sexual assault. Social superiors are addressed by their title and/or last name; for example, Doctor Smith, Mr. Rogers, Sister Mary. The nurse is called by her first name and as a group are referred to as "girls," while doctors are rarely referred to by their first names, especially in the presence of a patient, and as a group are never called the "boys." Subordinates don't point out the mistakes of their superiors. When a doctor errs or requires a nurse's advice, she takes great care to gently correct or indirectly provide clues by making suggestions, underplaying her superior knowledge and ability. In contrast, it isn't uncommon for doctors to confront a nurse directly about any slip-ups, publicly reprimanding and even humiliating her even when the nurse isn't responsible for the mistake (Tellis-Nayak, 1984, 1067). It isn't uncommon that her intelligence is questioned. I heard one psychiatrist say that student nurses always ask stupid questions, even when speaking to each other.

Study after study have clearly documented men's right to express power through controlling conversations. This is done by dominating, monopolizing, contradicting, and interrupting others (Zimmerman and West, in Thorne, 1983). Doctors do it "naturally." They dominate meetings and interdisciplinary conferences. Nurses learn not to speak out of turn or contradict doctors' information, and many times they don't speak unless spoken to. By contrast, when the nurse is giving her report, the doctor may not pay attention or may respond by flipping through papers or continuing to write while he advises, gives orders, and points out mistakes.

Sexist jokes and humour are now recognized as forms of domination and harassment. Nurses are so frequently the butt of sexist jokes that some have become so desensitized that they will repeat the same jokes that violate them, further reinforcing their own powerlessness and degradation. Even when nurses protest, their objections and their rights are not considered valid. One appalling example illustrates the extent of this problem: on one orthopaedic unit, young men who had their bodies, legs, or arms in casts and were hospitalized for lengthy periods of time were making sexual gestures, jokes, and advances towards the nurses on their unit. The nurses were angered about this behaviour and they requested in-service education on how to adequately deal with these men. The male "expert" psychologist told the nurses that the men were behaving normally, that they had to expend their pent-up sexual energy in these ways and this was healthy for them. The nurses were told they were being prudish, had sexual hangups, were being overly religious and were imposing *their* value systems on patients and this had to stop. This is clearly sexual harassment and a violation of the nurses, first by patients and then by the psychologist who made them feel guilty, inadequate, and to blame for the problem. Their legitimate anger was denied and turned against them.

Nurses risk and endure much more than sexual and verbal harassment. They also risk physical and sometimes sexual assault. A recent article in the *Canadian Nurse* (Cust, 1986) poignantly describes a situation where two nurses laid assault charges against a forensic patient (under assessment for alleged criminal activity) who did not have a psychiatric disorder. This patient attacked and severely injured the two nurses by beating them with his arm, which was in a cast. The charged person was found "not guilty" although there was no dispute about the events of the assault or the extent of the injuries. The defence argued that nurses choose to work in psychiatric hospitals, knowing that assault by patients is a fairly common occurrence. "Thus, consent to work there amounted to consent to be assaulted" (Cust, 1986, 20).

When a patient assaults someone, the entire incident is reviewed, documented, and everyone's actions are evaluated. Sometimes this investigation makes the nurse feel responsible for the injury inflicted upon her by the patient. She is questioned about why she couldn't predict the behaviour, intervene earlier, and somehow prevent it. It may even be implied that injury results from her poor management of disturbed behaviour. And assault can also include attempted rape. A friend of mine told me about a psychotic patient who attempted to rape her. Her fellow nurses were supportive, but she actually heard doctors laughing about and belittling the incident, implying that my friend had exaggerated. This patient later raped a helpless co-patient. The hospital officials then become very concerned about the legal implications and their solution was to discharge this violent patient to the streets.

This "day-in-the-life" of a nurse describes how her conditions of work are exploitative and how her social relations with others, specifically with physicians, are oppressive and demanding. In the following and concluding section, I present a feminist analysis of why nurses have been oppressed and how, with the women's health movement and the politicization of nurses, nursing is becoming liberated.

The Politicization of Nurses
Nursing as Nurturing and Self-Sacrifice
The traditional values of nursing which make nurses "admired": respect for paternalism, self-sacrifice, and self-dedication, are also those qualities which make them so vulnerable to being exploited and kept in powerless and dependent second-class positions.

To be a nurse has meant to live out the socialization of a woman. Psychoanalyst Jean Baker-Miller describes women's development in terms of her relationship to others (Miller, 1976).* She is taught to value and care for others—husbands, children, friends, patients—to such an extent that her very identity is constituted as one-who-cares-for-others, one-in-relationship-to someone else. Her identity and needs become so enmeshed with those she cares for that she never really knows who she is, what she wants or how to act on behalf of herself.** The notion of woman as nurturer, care-taker, as co-operative being with strong affiliative needs is reinforced and demanded by the patriarchal culture in which she occupies a subordinate, second-class position. Miller believes that women must know well the powerful dominant group, men. We listen carefully and become sensitive to their wishes and needs because our very survival is dependent upon that knowledge.

Carol Gilligan** describes women's moral development, which also helps us to understand our nursing values. Women's moral development centres on highly valued responsibility and care for others, including co-operative behaviour and affiliation.

In this context the nurse, who is already predisposed to caring because of her socialization as a woman, becomes a professionally-trained nurturer. Self-sacrifice is admired and encouraged. Nursing by definition is caring, serving others, meeting the needs of patients. The sick are made comfortable. Those in emotional pain are given empathetic, loving care. A nurse, because she is so tuned in to the needs of others, often knows someone is distressed even before the patient has admitted s/he has a problem. This is especially true when identifying psychological needs. The nurse's ability to meet the needs of others isn't restricted to her patients but includes families, administrators, head nurses, other health care workers, and, of course, doctors. She tries to meet everyone's needs but must deny her own. This is justified on the basis of professional responsibility. After a while she may not be able even to identify her own inner needs. She may say she needs to do what makes other people happy. She may become totally out of touch with her own inner strengths, thoughts, emotions, and desires because she is praised and valued for her ability to anticipate and care for others; for how responsible she is (for others), for putting everyone else first, for self-sacrifice, for being a professional nurse. There is little recognition of or reinforcement for focusing on herself, and there is virtually no time left even to reflect, let alone identify, clarify, and articulate her own needs and ideas. There is a price to pay for this self-denial. Unconsciously, and sometimes consciously, she begins to feel exploited. She may expect her loved ones, or her peers and friends, to see and recognize her needs and feelings just as she recognizes theirs. She may feel resentful, alienated, and depressed when she is treated as unworthy of others' care. She may feel like a

---

* See also Caryll Steffens in this collection.
** Susan Sorrell talks about this in her contribution to this collection.

failure because no matter how much she gives or nurtures, she is taken for granted, like a mother. She feels unhappy, unrecognized, and devalued and she doesn't know what else she can do. She rarely recognizes the underlying structural causes for these feelings. She hasn't analyzed that this is the experience of all nurses, and of all women to some extent. And it is only recently, with the women's movement, that she has realized that collective *action* is necessary to change these relationships.

Rarely, if ever, does she get in touch with her anger. Anger is not an acceptable emotion for any woman, let alone for a nurse. To be angry means you are temporarily alone; you are not in relationship to the person you are angry with. It means being willing to risk that others will reject, abandon, dislike, even hate you. To many this would represent psychological death. It threatens the established pattern and can mean change. But anger provides energy for change. Women and nurses have to redefine anger and use it for our own development. We have to stop idealizing self-sacrifice, and at the same time we must redefine and reclaim our justified anger.

Feminist have argued that anger and conflict are necessary for liberation and self-enhancement, for releasing our creative abilities, for serving our self, and for full development (Miller, 1976). Anger is a rational response to the injustice, exploitation, and denigration surrounding the dedicated nurturance and self-sacrifice of nursing. Self-sacrifice is exactly that: sacrifice or denial of the self, of one's identity, needs, desires in order to serve others. Nurses must redefine nurturance and care because nursing cannot continue its care of others through exploitation of its workers. Caring must begin with caring for ourselves. Caring can be collaborative with parity between the recipients. Nurses must begin to care for themselves and for each other, and they must nurture their own abilities, validate their own experience, desires, needs and ideas. Nurses have been notoriously negligent at supporting each other. We need to build solidarity. We need to develop an identity that defines caring and responsibility for others to also include ourselves. This means we will have to care less for others and allow some suffering and pain where we would otherwise work hard to prevent it. This is a difficult task for women and a contradiction for a nurse. I find this conflict very difficult to resolve, but at least now I am aware of the choice I am making when I sacrifice myself for another. Caring for ourselves means we must not accept overwork, or if we do, we must demand appropriate pay when we work overtime. We must lobby for better conditions of work, more time off, and better pay. We must document and confront sexism and sexual harassment in our daily work and in advertising, supporting each other in these confrontations.

If we care for ourselves and we demand equality, it will end the relegation of nurses to the "handmaiden" role. Nurses will have adequate nursing budgets controlled by nurses. We will define the practice of nursing as an autonomous complementary profession with *full*, not auxiliary, representation on health advisory committees, hospital boards, and government policy-making committees. This is what caring means. The nurse will become political.

The Political Nurse

Nurses, like other women in our society, have not been involved in the mainstream political process. They have been socialized, indeed taught, not to get involved in public confrontation, for example. They have been taught to rely upon and trust their men or superiors to "look after them." A woman's first responsibility was, and still is, to her family, then to career, and then possibly to politics (Kalisch and Kalisch, 1982, 379). Today many nurses want their careers in nursing to come first. They are beginning to demand better conditions of work and the right to participate in health care policy and decision-making.

Traditionally nurses have resisted forming unions because we were taught that *striking is unprofessional* and *unionism is for blue collar workers,* which we certainly are not. It was ingrained in us that our patients must always come first. This is a common belief among the public as well. I remember being told that any nurse who would strike must be a cold, unfeeling, money-seeking, selfish person, unworthy of her profession. I was asked how I could leave a sick child who needed me. This is, in fact, a difficult dilemma, but it can be resolved by sharing the problem with institutions and policy-makers.

Many places now have collective bargaining. Where striking is allowed, nurses are considered essential workers and a level of service for the critically ill must, therefore, be maintained. Strikes in these cases only disrupt service for less serious problems and for "elective" surgery, and they certainly don't threaten patients' lives. Striking is seen as a last resort for protesting impossible working conditions imposed by hospital administrators and governments who must, therefore, share responsibility for the strike. But many nurses abhor the idea of a strike. They find it difficult to speak up for their rights, let alone openly defy administrators and physicians. What is essential, however, is that we rephrase the problems: we must disclose and articulate contradictions in the nursing situation and redefine professionalism and professional responsibilities. And this is happening. Nurses now *are* saying they aren't responsible for poor nursing care when they are understaffed and overworked. Health ministries and administrators are responsible. Nurses aren't neglecting their patients when they strike; rather, they are fighting for a better health care system, one that doesn't exploit and abuse its workers but encourages professional development by providing financial rewards and supportive working conditions. However, there are other, possibly more effective, ways of politicizing nursing besides the methods and strategies of traditional labour unions.

Kalisch and Kalisch describe the need for and the process of political mobilization of nurses. Nurses must first develop a group consciousness which requires individual members perceiving themselves as having common problems, "a shared sense of deprivation and discrimination" (Kalisch and Kalisch, 1982, 444). Through development of group consciousness, individual nurses will identify with and develop allegiance with other nurses, recognizing the necessity of working collectively to make improvements. For these things to happen, nurses must recognize their current powerless state and envision a new identity for the future (Kalisch and Kalisch, 1982, 445). As they develop solidarity, they will analyze and communicate their common problems, ideas and solutions. Individual nurses will no longer blame themselves for inadequacies in health care but will realize they have been discriminated against as workers; that their concerns have not been taken into account in developing health care policies; and they haven't been considered when decisions for the distribution of resources are made.

Time together and communication are essential for nurses to develop a group consciousness, solidarity, and to articulate their common problems and propose solutions. Often nurses have no time left for themselves. They are isolated from each other although they may have worked together for years in the service of others in the same institution. Socializing with colleagues after hours is rare.

Getting to a professional or union meeting requires an extraordinary effort, as these meetings come after work, children, husbands, and toilet-cleaning. Attending a meeting is not supported and may even be devalued by husbands. I was told by an insider that members of the board of the largest Canadian nurses' union are often teased by their husbands who accuse them of being interested in attending board meetings only so they can shop in the big city. Women's work and issues aren't considered important or serious. Historically, nurses haven't had the time or the energy to attend meetings. Yet only through communication can a powerful group develop, believing in their ability to demand and make changes; seeing their problems as the result of discrimination and not a reflection of personal failure. "If nurses feel weak and dependent, they will act as if they are weak, and in actuality will become weaker and more dependent..." (Kalisch and Kalisch, 1982, 446).

The emphasis that schools of nursing put on conformity and acceptance of established sexist psychological theories and the medical model health care system doesn't lead to healthy questioning of the system, of our conditions of work or our salaries. Nurses are just beginning to realize that it is a false dichotomy to separate professional concern for nursing practice from the concern for salary, benefits, and workload. Staffing patterns jeopardize patient safety. Nurses want professional autonomy not rhetoric. They want to determine and develop nursing practice and control their working conditions. Nurses want a satisfying career financially, intellectually, and emotionally. Nurses no longer accept nursing education as the finishing school for marriage and motherhood, nor the job as providing a few extras for the home. Nurses are viewing professionalism in a new way, one that empowers the nurse. Nursing is becoming autonomous.

Professional nursing also means developing health care policies from a different perspective: we need an alternative to the medical-disease perspective which is cure-oriented, hospital-dependent, expensive and male-controlled. Illich (Illich, 1976) analyzes how the modern medical system is a major threat to health, causing disease, disability and death. He calls this phenomena "iatrogenesis." Illich outlines how complications from medical intervention, technology, surgery, and drug therapy in a large percentage of cases make the patient sicker than if s/he had never sought medical assistance. Like the women's health movement, Illich argues that medical control over illness must be limited and lay persons must have control over medical decisions.

The nursing profession is increasingly focusing on the health needs of well persons and on the prevention of illness. Along with advocates in the women's health movement, nurses are providing a critique of modern medicine and suggesting alternative forms of health care service. This is especially important for women, as women's health critics (Corea, 1977; Dreifus, 1978; Scully, 1980; and Seaman, 1977) have documented how destructive medicine can be, especially for women. These authors show how doctors have made women suffer unnecessary and damaging hysterectomies, mastectomies, caesarian sections, forceps deliveries, medicated birthing. Doctors have prescribed experimental and cancer-producing drugs such as DES and Depo-Provera (which women in the "Third" World still receive although they are now banned in North America because of their known danger.) Doctors have inserted hemorrhage-producing devices in women's uteri for contraception, as in case of the Dalkon Sheild IUD. Doctors have over-medicated and tranquillized distraught, overworked, depressed, and menopausal women. Doctors still give women electric shock treatment twice as often as men although it can cause brain damage and isn't proven to be an effective treatment for depression. And doctors and law-makers still fight to control who can have an abortion.

The women's health movement, mobilized to confront the worst of these practices, can provide an alternative form of care, especially around reproductive functions (Ruzek, 1978). The women's health movement advocates for women to have medical knowledge about their bodies so they can have control and make responsible decisions based on accurate knowledge. They are advocating the training of nurses and midwives to perform routine well-woman care which will free doctors to treat sick women. Well-woman health care includes self-help groups, prescribing birth control methods and fitting contraceptive devices, midwifery, gynecological examinations and even abortion. They argue that women's life events have unnecessarily been made into medical diseases. Women want to regain control of their reproductive functions and seize the technology to control fertility. This is particularly necessary now that medical advances have made the "test-tube" baby a reality. At present it is men who control this knowledge and technology (Finkelstein and Clough, 1983).

Nursing is at a turning point. In co-operation with the women's health movement, we are creating a vision of health care that promotes the health of all people; that empowers people through sharing knowledge and putting control for health care decisions in the hands of clients. Nursing organizations are developing alternative perspectives on social problems that affect people's health by presenting papers to policy-makers on such topics as wife abuse, the elderly, extra-billing, and controlling health care costs. Nurses are criticizing medically-controlled hospital-based care as both expensive and ineffective. They are focusing on primary health care and the prevention of disease. The foremost causes of death in Canada are largely self-induced and preventable: heart disease, cancer, strokes, liver cirrhosis, and accidents *(Health News,* 6). What is needed is health education and active health promotion. The World Health Organization (WHO) pledged to bring "Health to All" by the year 2000 by using Primary Health Care (PHC). The WHO believes the world's worst health problems can be tackled, not by training more doctors and equipping more hospitals, but by simple preventative methods and a selection of basic drugs. Eighty percent of all illness in the world is caused by the lack of clean drinking water and sanitation. Diseases can be prevented by training primary health care workers for every community to ensure midwifery services, clean water, sanitation, immunization, and good nutrition (Taylor, 1985, 47). Primary health care focuses on preventing disease and on women, who are seen as bearing the responsibility for their families' health. It is women all around the world who are responsible for feeding children; fetching water and firewood; hygiene; teaching health habits; who bear children and breast-feed them; who care for the sick, disabled and old. Women are seen as a vital resource on whom the world's health depends and whose own health must be preserved. Women in their domestic role provide more health care than all the world's health services put together (Taylor, 1985, 47-50). Training primary health care workers costs less than 2 percent of all the money it takes to train a physician. And these barefoot doctors are effective in reducing death rates. In spite of these facts, there is resistance among physicians and health ministry officials, mostly men, who have power and control budget decisions.

> Three-quarters of the world's health problems could be solved by Primary Health Care. But three-quarters of developing countries' health budgets are spent on doctors and hospitals (Taylor, 1985, 50).

In Canada we have a similar problem. The five leading causes of death indicated above are largely preventable, yet the largest percentage of our health budget is given to complex technological devices to treat the disease instead of preventing it. Instead of financially supporting public health programs, health education, exercise programs, self-help groups, community-based abortion clinics, midwifery and well-woman clinics, we have expensive X-ray machines, heart-lung transplants and machines, mechanical hearts, and thousands of drugs. Currently, one day in hospital can cost up to $2,000.

The women's health movement has been successful in getting a few self-help clinics, limited rights for midwives to practise, rape crisis centres, homes for battered women, alternative psychiatric help through feminist counselling. The movement is now educating the public about the devastating extent and effects of the medicalization of social problems (e.g. tranquillizing overworked house-wives, drugging poverty and powerlessness).

Physicians have been the most powerful group speaking out on health issues, policies, and how the entire health care system should be run. They have continued to gain economic, social, and political status and power at the expense of other health care workers, including nurses. The time is ripe for nurses to announce their autonomy, recognizing their unique contribution to health care. The nursing profession must develop its own field or it will die. We cannot remain in the shadow of medicine. The "handmaiden" is gone. The public needs nurses to develop a strong advocacy role and to continue to develop a vision of health care that focuses on prevention and health and on working *together* with people.

Nursing must become political, not just in a limited way, but in everything we do so we can build a healthy society that values both men and women. Nursing must examine the vast store of knowledge and analyses from feminist literature so that we can first make ourselves aware of and then get rid of ingrained misogynist beliefs and values of the patriarchy that control and oppress us. Nursing, in solidarity with the woman's movement, can become a truly strong, independent, creative force on the side of women, life, and health. We need to build our commitment to each other and establish a community of shared caring.

References

Ashley, Jo Ann, 1980. "Power in Structured Misogyny: Implications for the Politics of Care." *A.N.S.* 2(3): 3-22.

——, 1979. "This I Believe About Power in Nursing," *Nursing Dimensions* (summer): 28-32.

Armstrong, Pat and Hugh, 1982. *The Double Ghetto: Canadian Women and Their Segregated Work.* McClelland and Stewart.

Burstow, Bonnie, 1985. "Women and Therapy," pp 112-115 in K. McDonnell and M. Valverde (eds.), *The Health Sharing Book: Resources for Canadian Women.* Toronto: Woman's Press.

Chesler, Phyllis, 1972. *Women and Madness.* Avon Books.

Coburn, Judi, 1981. "I See and Am Silent: A Short History of Nursing," pp 182-201 in D. Coburn, C. D'Arcy, P. New, and G. Torrance (eds.), *Health and Canadian Society Sociological Perspectives.* Toronto: Fitzhenry and Whiteside.

Cooperstock, Ruth, 1982. *The Effects of Tranquillization: Benzodiazepine Uses in Canada.* Ottawa: Health and Welfare Canada.

Corea, Gena, 1977. *The Hidden Malpractice: How American Medicine Treats Women as Patients and Professionals*. New York: William Morrow.

Curtin, L., and J. Flaherty, 1982. *Nursing Ethics, Theories and Pragmatics*. Prentice-Hall.

Cust, Kenn, 1986. "Assault: Just Part of the Job?" *The Canadian Nurse*. (June): 19-20.

Dreifus, Claudia (ed.), 1978. *Seizing Our Bodies: The Politics of Women's Health*. New Hork: Vintage Books, Random House.

Ehrenreich, Barbara, and Deirdre English, 1973. *Witches, Midwives, and Nurses: A History of Women Healers*. New York: The Feminist Press.

——, 1979. *For Her Own Good: 150 Years of the Experts Advice to Women*. Doubleday.

Finkelstein, Joanne, and Patricia Clough, 1983. "Foetal Politics and Birth of an Industry," *Women's Studies International Forum*. 6(4): 395-400.

Gilligan, Carol, 1982. *In A Different Voice: Psychological Theory and Women's Development*. Cambridge: Harvard University Press.

Harding, Jim, 1981. "The Pharmaceutical Industry As a Public-Health Hazard and as an Institution of Social Control," pp. 274-291 in Coburn, David, Carl D'Arcy, Peter New, and George Torrance (eds.), *Health and Canadian Society Sociological Perspectives*. Toronto: Fitzhenry and Whiteside.

Illich, Ivan, 1976. *Limits to Medicine, Medical Nemesis: The Expropriation of Health*. London: Rorion Boyais.

Kalisch, Beatrice and Philip, 1982. *Politics of Nursing*. Philadelphia: J.B. Lippincott.

Lee, Anthony, 1979. "How Nurses Rate with MDs: Still the Handmaiden," *R.N.* (July): 21-30.

Leininger, Madeleine, 1970. *Nursing and Anthropology: Two Worlds to Blend*. Chapter 5. Toronto: John Wiley.

Lexchin, Joel, 1984. *The Real Pushers: A Critical Analysis of the Canadian Drug Industry*. Vancouver: New Star Books.

Melosh, B, 1982. "The Physician's Hand," *Work Culture and Conflict in American Nursing*. Philadelphia: Temple University Press.

Miller, J.B, 1976. *Toward a New Psychology of Women*. Boston: Beacon Press.

Muff, J. (ed.), 1982. *Socialization, Sexism and Stereotyping: Women's Issues in Nursing*. Toronto: C.V. Mosby Co.

Rickles, Nathan, 1971. "The Angry Woman Syndrome," *Archives of General Psychiatry*. 24 (June): 91-94.

Roberts, Heklen (ed.), 1981. *Women Health and Reproduction*. Boston: Routledge and Kegan Paul.

Ruzek, Sheryl Burt, 1978. *The Women's Health Movement: Feminist Alternatives to Medical Control*. Toronto: Praeger Publishers.

Scully, Diana, 1980. *Men Who Control Women's Health: The Miseducation of Obstetrician-Gynecologists*. Boston: Houghton Mifflin Co.

Seaman, Barbara and Gideon, 1977. *Women and the Crisis in Sex Hormones*. Toronto: Bantam.

Smith, Dorothy, and Sara David, 1975. *Women Look at Psychiatry*. Vancouver: Press Gang.

Taylor, Debbie, 1985. *Women: A World Report*. London: Methuen.

Tellis-Nayak, N. and V., 1984. "Games That Professionals Play: The Social Psychology of Physician-Nurse Interaction," *Social Science Medicine* 18 (12): 1063-69.

Thorne, B., C. Kramarae, and N. Henley (eds.), 1983. *Language, Gender and Society*. Rowley, Mass.: Newbury House Publishers.

Vance, C., S. Talbott, A. McBride, and D. Mason, 1985. "An Uneasy Alliance: Nursing and the Women's Movement." *Nursing Outlook* (Nov.-Dec.): 281-85.

Weitz, Don, 1985. "Shock Survivors." *Goodwins* (spring): 20-23.

West, Candace, and Don Zimmerman, 1983. "Small Insults: A Study of Interruptions in Cross-Sex Conversations Between Unacquainted Persons." In B. Thorne, C. Kramarae, and N. Henely (eds.), *Language, Gender and Society*. Rowley, Mass.: Newbury House Publishers.

——, 1986. *Healthnews*. University of Toronto Faculty of Medicine. 4(4)(summer).

Chapter 3

For Her, Or Against Her?
The Power of Religious Metaphor
Marymay Downing

Madonna and the Paradox of Modern Religion
The Video
Remember the 1985 video version of Madonna's popular song *Like a Virgin?*
Madonna reclines seductively in the prow of a Venetian gondola. She wears a
slinky black dress. While she moves her body in sensuously suggestive gestures,
she sings about how her lover arouses in her such intense excitement that she's
reminded of being "touched for the very first time." She is patently no innocent
virgin now. There is even a touch of the whore about her. But this man, she croons,
makes her feel as if she were a virgin again:

> You make me feel shiny and new
> Just like a vir - r - rgin...

Another scene conjures up the image she has in mind. It is set with a marriage
bed and features Madonna demurely veiled in a pure white wedding gown. We
watch the groom carry his bride toward the bed. The groom has an animal's head,
we notice. Is it a symbol of his anonymity? Is he just another lover in a stream of
faceless lovers? Or does this particular lover, ostensibly her first, have an
animal's head to symbolize the so-called "animal passions" to which she is about
to succumb in losing her virginity?

The video proceeds by juxtaposing these two scenes of seduction, one in a
gondola and the other in a bridal suite, until the song fades. Then, as the gondola
glides down the canal into the distance, a lion steps into the foreground, silently
stalking among the marble pillars of the city.

Did you notice how the dramatic tension in Madonna's act draws on an
underlying religious theme? Her performance succeeds in capturing your attention in part because of its frank sexuality, but especially because it treats a
particular religious symbol in a naughty, sacrilegious manner. She is, as her name
purposefully announces, Madonna. You are supposed to think of the original
madonna, of course. If you live in Canada, or anywhere else where Christianity

is the dominant religion, you probably know the intended Christian symbol behind Madonna's name. She is the Virgin Mary, the mother of Christ, the Mother of God. In Canada we all recognize the Virgin Mary, regardless of our own religious affiliation or lack of one. Widespread official celebrations and public holidays each Christmas and Easter effectively ensure a general public recognition of most Christian symbols. Now, if you know the intended symbol, Mary, the Holy Virgin, then you also know (even if only at a subliminal level) that in *Like a Virgin* this sacred symbol is being mocked. Indeed, it is being intentionally profaned.

I think it is fair to say that Madonna's whole professional persona, in fact, has been carefully designed to function as an impious parody of her namesake's symbol. She is undoubtedly a very talented performer. The real excitement of her act, however, does not depend on her personal talents alone, considerable though they may be. The quality that makes Madonna's act really stand out and command your attention depends to a much greater extent on her skillful manipulation of implicitly insolent and irrelevant mockery of the Virgin Mary. That is the quality that ensures people will notice her. That is the quality that makes her a huge commercial success in a very competitive market.

How does Madonna mock the symbol of her namesake? She plays with ambivalence. In *Like a Virgin* she summons up the original madonna's sacred virginity through her name, her white bridal dress, the title and repetitious lyrics of her song. At the same time, however, she contrasts this image with its opposite, calls it into question, subtly undermines it. We discover that "like a virgin" does not mean that she *is* a virgin. Attended to closely, the lyrics imply that she is quite the opposite. She is precisely *not* a virgin, merely *like* one in the arms of this particular lover. The revealing black dress, the seductive postures, the animal likeness, all these visual elements also insinuate that she is, instead, the experienced seductress.

So, Madonna conjures up the archetypal Christian ideal of chaste womanhood, she leads us to expect the Virgin Mary, and then she presents us instead with Eve. We all know this biblical figure too, even if we haven't actually read the Bible. Eve (the first woman) enticed Adam (the first man) to disobey God by eating the forbidden fruit from the tree of the knowledge of good and evil. She is the first seductress, the archetypal seductress, the one who brought sex (which is a sin, according to the Christian view) into the world. Madonna presents herself as just such a sexually alluring seductress. She behaves like the infamous Eve. But she knows there would be no impious mockery and no real excitement in her act if she were to call herself Eve. After all, it wouldn't be shocking for Eve to behave like Eve. It would be expected. Such seductive behaviour is shockingly sacrilegious, however, in one who bears the name of the Mother of God.

And that, as Madonna correctly judged, is bound to catch your attention.

The Paradox of Modern Religion

Madonna's act capitalizes on a paradoxical quality of contemporary Christianity, one that holds particular significance for women.

One the one hand, Madonna demonstrates that it is no longer actually dangerous (as it once was) for a woman to taunt the church or to ridicule its sacred symbols in full public view. Near the close of the twentieth century, Madonna can broadcast an irreligious point of view over the public airwaves and make a tidy profit in the process. The most that offended Christians can do in protest is to switch off their own receivers in their own homes (or tune them into evangelical channels). Perhaps they might forbid their teenage daughters and sons from attending Madonna concerts. (I've no doubt some do.) But Madonna need not fear that people who take offence at her act will, say, lynch her physically or anything like that.

Only a few short centuries ago, however, Madonna would not have escaped with her life. If she had dared to offer her performance in Europe during the sixteenth and seventeenth centuries, she undoubtedly would have shared the fate that was suffered then by thousands, possibly millions, of women. Zealous church officials would have tried her for being a heretic and a witch and would have punished her accordingly, probably by torturing her and then burning her at the stake. During this horrific period of European history (known by some as "the burning times") wide-spread executions of women were given official justification, indeed direction, by the church, especially through a 1486 publication called the *Malleus Maleficarum (Hammer Against Witches)*, written by two Dominican Inquisitors.[1] These authors reasoned that, "All witchcraft comes from carnal lust which is in women insatiable." Surely Madonna would have seemed to them a perfect example.

Over the next two centuries the *Malleus Maleficarum* was, for women, fatally influential. Today, though, five centuries later, only a tiny minority has ever heard of the book, and few know much about the persecutions and slaughter it inspired. In Canada in the late twentieth century we don't often witness religious intolerance mixed with misogyny (the hatred of women) on a scale anywhere comparable. True, a few instances of women's censorship arising from religious objections have occurred recently in Canada; but such instances are relatively rare, and they pale in comparison to the persecutions of "the burning times." For example, in the late 1970s a coalition of traditionalist Roman Catholic groups in Montréal temporarily managed to obtain injunctions prohibiting sale of the controversial feminist play *Les Fées Ont Soif* (literally translated as *The Fairies are Thirsty*.[2] The coalition was incensed by the play's "sacrilegious" portrayal of the Virgin Mary. Occasionally you see committed defenders of the faith picketing particular films, such as *Hail Mary!*, for similar reasons. But, on the whole, our age is more characterized by the absence than the presence of censorship based on religious grounds. As the aphorism says, nothing is sacrosanct anymore. Nothing is immune from satirical scrutiny. Traditional religion itself is fair game. It has lost its former power to retaliate, whether through persecution or censorship. Madonna is proof. She is able to make her living satirizing her Christian namesake. She is not publicly censored. And she can sleep soundly at night, with no fear of painful repercussions.

On the one hand, then, Madonna shows us how relatively weak and vulnerable traditional religion has become in the late twentiethth century. She is an indicator of the secular era that we live in.

On the other hand, Madonna is able to profit from religious satire now precisely because traditional religion does persist, at least in some respects, as a significantly relevant, potent force in our lives. Even though the power of the church as an institution may be at a low ebb historically, obviously the power of its symbols of womanhood, at least, has not completely drained away. For if these traditional religious symbols were truly irrelevant to the modern mind and genuinely peripheral to our central concerns, then religious satire like Madonna's would not work. It would have no bite. It would be limp and insipid fare, holding little interest for the audience and earning less money for the satirist.

Thus Madonna's successful marketing of Marian sacrilege reveals an apparent paradox about modern Christianity. Ours is a relatively secular era (when headlines announce declining attendance rates in most Canadian churches[3] and religion seems increasingly insignificant in many people's lives). Sacrilege like Madonna's goes unpunished, even uncensored. Yet even so, it hardly goes unnoticed. Far from it, in fact. Madonna's commercial success shows us that the blasphemous treatment of Christian symbols of womanhood seizes our attention. It still possesses the power to shock, or at least to startle, to titillate, to entertain. Madonna demonstrates, then, that the Christian symbols of Mary and Eve still resonate in our collective psyche. Her act reveals that Christian symbols of womanhood still have a strong hold on the public consciousness, even in the midst of our relatively secular era.

There is a lesson in this paradox. Women in Canada[4] who think that Christianity doesn't really affect them should probably think again. The institution may be but a shadow of its former self. Its power to exert social control over women directly (through persecution or censorship) may be minimal. Nonetheless, Christian symbols of womanhood are evidently alive and flourishing in our popular culture where they continue to affect us all whether we are members of a church or not.

From Satire to Analysis

Now, instead of a music video, imagine a section of bookshelves that bears the subject heading "Women and Religion" or "Women's Spirituality." You might find this section in a university library or in a women's bookstore. I have been browsing around in this section of libraries and bookstores for more than a decade now, building my own personal collection of favourites in the process. As I have watched over the years, the literature published on the topic of women and religion has grown from a collection of five or six volumes of ground-breaking studies in the field[5] to several shelves full of books and scholarly journals. Add popular magazines, too, and you could easily fill a whole bookcase, maybe more. Clearly there is currently a great deal of interest in this subject.

What is in all these books? Why does the topic of women and religion elicit such a flood of words? Primarily, these books contain analysis. They contain analysis that, in its own way, can be as merciless as Madonna's satire, taking full advantage of traditional religion's modern vulnerability to uncensored public scrutiny. The authors analyze Christianity and other religions around the world from women's perspective. That is, they examine women's participation, or lack of it, and how each tradition impinges specifically on women's lives. Many bring an explicitly feminist perspective to their analysis, not hesitating to be critical of religious beliefs and practices which they judge to be harmful to women, nor to praise those they believe to be beneficial to women.

Viewed as a whole, there are two distinctive approaches to the subject that stand out in the literature today.[6] They are distinguishable mainly by the concept of divinity that is common to the group of religions that each approach examines. One approach focuses on analyzing monotheistic systems that are based on one deity which is symbolized as male (i.e., "Our Father, who art in heaven..."). Christianity, Judaism, and Islam are the main religions examined here. The other approach focuses on traditions which symbolize divinity as female, or as both male and female. These are usually polytheistic systems which honour several deities of both sexes. Hinduism and the religion of the classical Greeks are two examples of the traditions examined by this second approach.

Each of these approaches has produced its own body of literature, with the result that the bookcase holding all the recent literature on women and religion today divides naturally into two sub-sections. For this paper I have titled these sub-sections "The Critique of Traditional Religion" and "The Renaissance of Female Polytheism."

In the following pages, I'm going to give you a more detailed picture of some of the ideas presented in each of these approaches to the feminist analysis of religion.

The Critique of Traditional Religion

In this first approach, the traditional religions are probed for indications of having sanctioned sexism or misogyny, whether ritually, symbolically, philosophically, or in any of the myriad ways religion finds expression. Each scrap of sexism, every vestige of misogyny, is duly being dug up out of its history and dragged before our critical gaze. It might help to make these observations more concrete by considering a few brief examples drawn from the feminist critique of Christianity, the dominant religion affecting us in Canada.

The Gateway of the Devil and the Handmaid of the Lord
The Bible contains several culpable quotations that have been pitched at women from pulpits and judges' benches over the centuries. Among them are these favoured formulations by St. Paul (these and all subsequent biblical quotations are taken from the Revised Standard Version):

> As in all the churches of the saints, the women should keep silence in the churches. For they are not permitted to speak, but should be subordinate, as even the law says. If there is anything they desire to know, let me ask their husbands at home. For it is shameful for a woman to speak in church (1 Corinthians 14, 33-35).

> Wives, be subject to your husbands, as to the Lord. For the husband is the head of the wife as Christ is the head of the church, his body, and is himself its Saviour. As the church is subject to Christ, so let wives also be subject in everything to their husbands (Ephesians 5, 22-24).

> Let a woman learn in silence with all submissiveness. I permit no woman to teach or to have authority over men; she is to keep silent. For Adam was formed first, then Eve; and Adam was not deceived, but the woman was deceived and became a transgressor. Yet woman will be saved through bearing children, if she continues in faith and love and holiness, with modesty (1 Timothy 2, 11-15).

For nearly two thousand years, passages such as these have been intoned authoritatively as sufficient reason for confining women to a second-class status in the family and in every other social institution as well. The laws of Canada and other Christian countries were originally drafted on the basis of such biblical precepts.

In Canada nowadays we are trying to extricate our legal system from the influence of any particular religion, for the laws of the land apply to everyone, of all faiths and of none, in a society that is increasingly pluralistic. The principle of the separation of church and state is generally affirmed. Nevertheless, in several instances this principle is not followed. The Constitution Act of 1982, for example, recognizes the "supremacy of God" along with "the rule of law." The Charter of Rights and Freedoms prohibits discrimination based on religion; but the Supreme Court of Canada has upheld the Ontario Government's constitutional right to finance Roman Catholic separate schools although it does not finance the separate schools of any other religious group.[7] And cases of judges who rule against women on the basis of well-ingrained Christian maxims do still occur... Even as I write this, in fact, my radio broadcasts news of Judge Bartlett in Nova Scotia who was dismissed from the bench for applying his fundamentalist Christian views in court. An official complaint was filed by women who reported that the judge "quoted passages from the Bible that he said meant they should be subservient to their husbands."[8] This is hardly an appropriate response to give women seeking protection against abusive husbands.

Today it is no longer lawful for husbands to assault their wives, nor for judges to mix religion and law, but obviously both practices will take time and effort to eradicate. In the meantime, many women will undoubtedly continue to suffer indignities, and worse, in the name of one biblical passage or another.

The Bible has certainly contributed its share to women's suffering. But other literature produced by the church over the course of Christian history has also served to fan the flames of misogyny. For example, one of the early Church Fathers, Tertullian (ca. 160 - 220 C.E.),[9] left us this oft-repeated gem:

> You give birth, o woman, in pains and anxieties; and your desire goes to your husband, and he will lord it over you. And do you not know that you are Eve? God's judgment over this sex continues in this eon; its guilt must also continue. You are the gate of the devil, the traitor of the tree, the first deserter of divine law; you are she who enticed the one whom the devil dare not approach; you broke so easily the image of God, man; on account of the death you deserved, even the Son of God had to die (Tertullian, *De cultu feminarum*, I, 1).

You will remember another infamous church document that I mentioned earlier, the *Malleus Maleficarum* (1486), which helped spread an incendiary mixture of religious zeal and misogyny resulting in the deaths of thousands, possibly millions, of women during the sixteenth and seventeenth centuries. Does not Tertullian's statement foreshadow the later holocaust? At heart it expresses the same potentially explosive blend of attitudes, the same religious reasons for hating women. Note how Eve focuses Tertullian's hatred, but it is a hatred that encompasses all women.

Feminist analysts use a variety of sources in their research. These sources include the Bible, other church literature, and historical records of relations between church and state that have had repercussions for women. These, though, are the relatively easy sources. They contain comparatively obvious data, leading to interpretations that are disputed by few. Christians themselves—for many of these scholars are Christians—acknowledge with deep pain and sorrow what the data from these sources reveal about the history of their church's treatment of women.

The world of religious symbols and rituals is a whole other source of data for the analysts. It is a more difficult source, one that produces more debatable interpretations. For it is impossible to speak with certainty about what effects religious symbols and rituals have on people's psychology and behaviour. Yet there is little doubt among scholars of religion that they have some effect, probably a significant one, so they cannot be ignored. No analysis of the myriad ways in which religion sanctions sexism could be even close to complete if religious symbolism and religious ritual were ignored. Intrepid analysts have, therefore, not let themselves be daunted.

As they remind us, Christian symbols of divinity are exclusively male: the Father and the Son. The most important female symbols in Christian history have been Eve and Mary, neither of whom represents divinity.

Eve, not surprisingly, is identified by most feminist analysts as a symbol that probably promotes misogyny. For Eve has come to represent the idea that women are by nature essentially disobedient, sexual beings, responsible for seducing men into sinfulness. Put simply, Eve symbolizes the idea that women are to blame for men's sufferings. Many believe this makes women easy targets whenever men need a scapegoat for their troubles.

Mary, at first, may seem to represent ideal qualities in women, the goodness in women, reasons why women should be admired rather than despised. However, these very qualities, under closer feminist consideration, are exposed as problematic, or unreal. For example, Mary's submissiveness is proverbial: "And Mary said, 'Behold, I am the handmaid of the Lord; let it be to me according to your work'" (Luke 1, 38).[10] But is submissiveness what we need? How can you expect a woman who speaks so submissively to believe in her own self-worth, to stand up for her rights, to resist the historical weight of sexism? Mary's other notable quality is her ability to fulfill the highly valued function of motherhood (woman's redeeming virtue, according to St. Paul)[11] while miraculously retaining her virginity and thus avoiding any taint of sex, which Christianity considers sinful. Obviously this is an impossible act for ordinary women to emulate (at least it was, until artificial insemination gave new meaning to the phrase "the immaculate conception"). Ordinary mothers, conceiving in the normal way, remain tainted and despicable by default. The Virgin Mary does not represent them. Thus, it seems that Mary either symbolizes women who mutely, even obsequiously, accept second-class status (the handmaids), or else she symbolizes phantoms and not real, flesh-and-blood women. In either case, the symbol contributes to sexism, if not to the more virulent problem of misogyny. It affirms only the women who will not affirm themselves, while by implication reproving all women who lead sexually active lives.

Neither symbol, according to this feminist analysis, is free of serious sexist flaws.

When rituals (such as the Eucharist, baptisms, weddings, funerals, etc.) are examined, they are found to be similarly devoid of adequate female representation. Some Christian denominations still refuse to allow women to lead church rituals as ordained members of the clergy. Some refuse to allow any females inside the sanctuary at all, considering the female presence there to be a cause of pollution and profanation.[12]

Let these be enough examples of the ways Christianity has been accused of sanctioning sexism. I think you can get an idea from them of the degree to which Christianity is susceptible to the charge of having treated women with less than full human dignity. (Important recent additions have been made to this analysis. Please see Brown and Bone, 1989 and Miles, 1987 in bibliography.)

The Debate: Reform It or Abandon It?

The question naturally arises: Is Christianity irredeemably sexist? This question is at the centre of considerable debate among its feminist critics. Books and articles devoted to this debate occupy a fair amount of space in the bookcase.

On one side of this debate you can find authors who will admit the undeniable atrocities, yet argue that they were anomalies and not representative of true Christianity. These authors assert that Christianity in its unadulterated essence bears the message of equality among women and men. They, too, cite the Bible:

> There is neither Jew nor Greek, there is neither slave nor free, there is neither male nor female; for you are all one in Christ Jesus (Galatians 3, 28).

They point out that in the Gospels it was women who were the first to witness the risen Christ. They call our attention to the often ignored women who ministered to foundling congregations in the first century, such as Phoebe of Cenchreae (Romans 16, 1-2), or who became great abbesses during the Middle Ages. They offer reinterpretations for the key female symbols of Eve and Mary, emphasizing their inquisitiveness, independence, and courage. And they search out new, more congenial, but previously neglected female symbols, such as the biblical Sophia. Finally, they remind us of dramatic changes occurring in the modern church such as the ordination of women in some Protestant denominations and inclusive language in prayer,[13] and they optimistically predict further changes in the future. In short, they think Christianity *can* be reformed and that it *is* redeemable for women.[14]

Opponents of this view counter with charges of mere tokenism and naïve optimism. Based on the dominance of male symbolism in the Holy Trinity and other features of the Christian story, critics on this side of the debate conclude that the tradition is inherently and unalterably damaging to women.[15]

As this debate about Christianity proceeds, it adds several new volumes each year to the bookshelves.

The critique and debate concerning Christianity is one sub-section in the first approach to the feminist analysis of religion. If we were to look at the other sub-sections concerning Judaism and Islam, we would find similar critiques and parallel debates.[16]

Yet all this literature still represents only a partial picture of everything that has recently been published on the topic of women and religion. We've only looked at half the bookcase so far. In women's bookstores and in my personal library, there is a whole other focus of analysis that occupies at least as much space on the shelves as the critique of traditional religion.

The Renaissance of Female Polytheism

To give you an idea of the contents in this part of the bookcase and its specific focus of analysis, I'm going to do something a little different. I'm going to begin with a personal story.

Return to Demeter: One Woman's Story

To Demeter
Of Demeter, the lovely-haired and august goddess, and of her daughter, the fair Persephone, I begin to sing. Hail, O goddess! Keep this city safe, and guide my song — from *The Homeric Hymns*, trans. Apostolos N. Athanassakis (Baltimore: Johns Hopkins University Press, 1976)

My grandfather was a Methodist minister, and his daughter, my mother, contin-ues to be a faithful member of the United Church of Canada. I, at the third generation, made the decision to stop attending any church as soon as I gained my independence. Before that I seized every opportunity to avoid having to go to church.

I remember as a young child being disturbed by the jealous, vengeful God I encountered in Sunday school. As a teenager I chafed under innumerable irritants, from hypocrisy detected in some member of the congregation to just the fact of being cooped up for an hour and a half every Sunday morning. I felt suffocated and oppressed by the vast expanse of dead air that hung heavily under the vaulted ceiling, before the equally lifeless body of the crucified Christ glimmering in the large stained-glass window of the sanctuary. I yearned to be outside in the fresh air and sunshine, with the birds whose cheerful chirping could occasionally be heard between sonorous peals of the organ. Many years later I identified immediately with an Ojibway woman I met who remarked that she felt oppressed by the imposition of Christianity on her people partly because, instead of holding their church among the trees of the forest, Christians cut down the trees to build their church.

Thinking back on the times when I did experience those ineffable feelings that I call religious—those moments of heightened awareness of the universe, of life, and of consciousness, in all their awesome wonder—I remember that they always happened to me outside the confines of church walls. The church, its rituals, and its symbols made me feel uncomfortable and out-of-place, but not inspired. I found those moments evoked instead by the blinding dazzle of sunlight on the blanketed white slopes where I skied; or by the thrilling, throbbing lilt of a loon's song reverberating across the satin-black, moon-lit surface of the lake where I spent many summers; or even by the exhilarating flights of the mind induced by a good philosophy book. I did not experience them in church.

By the time I was a young woman independently earning my way in the world, Sunday mornings had become precious because they were the only mornings it was possible to sleep late. Religion, certainly as it was institutionalized by the church, was something I paid very little attention to, and thought less about.

Trying to earn my living and to cope with life as a woman brought something else to the forefront of my concerns. My experiences as a young adult taught me that sexism was a far more crippling problem than I had previously appreciated. The sexual "double standard" that I had bitterly railed at in high school emerged as but the tip of the iceberg. With the little money I earned (as a teacher, then a secretary, a waitress, and a computer operator) I bought nearly every feminist book I could find when they started appearing on the bookstore shelves in Toronto and Montréal during the late sixties and early seventies. I devoured these books, trying to figure out how to wrestle with the problem of women's oppression as it was tangibly affecting my own life.

In those early feminist books there was a fair amount written about how traditional religion sanctions sexism, but the religious factor didn't seem very important to me personally by that time. I was vaguely aware that Catholic women faced condemnation, indeed damnation, for using contraception; but I wasn't Catholic, or even a practising Christian anymore. Believing that the Christian church no longer affected me, I dismissed the whole religious factor, prematurely, as it turned out. I erroneously assumed that it was not pertinent for explaining my personal situation, my personal set of oppressions, or for helping me to cope with them. I might have never discovered my narrowness of view if I hadn't taken advantage of half-price youth fares one year to embark on a trip to Europe. My trip turned into a fateful voyage of discovery.

For nine months in 1973-74 I lived in a sleepy little Greek town, a sun-bleached collection of whitewashed houses by the sea on the Mediterranean island called Crete. While hiking among the craggy Cretan peaks, through silver-green olive groves, lush orchards of orange trees, and vine-laced hillsides, I literally stumbled across the ancient, weathered remains of a prehistoric civilization. Archaeologists call it the Minoan civilization. By their accounts, the Minoans inhabited Crete from around 8,000 B.C.E. to approximately 1,200

B.C.E., before the period of the classical Greek civilization. What immediately caught my eye about the Minoan archaeological record in the local island museum was the dominating presence of female images. It would be an understatement to say that it totally captivated my interest from that point on.

When I returned to Canada I did some preliminary research on the Minoans. My first, untutored impressions were confirmed. Everyone who had worked with the archaeological data had been impressed by the unusual female imagery. It was commonly concluded that many of the female images represented goddess figures. I was entranced by this idea. Suddenly, the religious factor in women's oppression took on new importance. It became interesting, at least for theoretical reasons. I was filled with a thousand consuming questions about what a religion that focused on the Goddess, rather than on God, might have been like. How did it affect the social status of Minoan women?

I enrolled in a university because I was concerned with doing quality research on questions like this. I was fearful that my obvious feminist bias might lead me to ignore those things I didn't want to see. So I took philosophy courses to ensure that my research methods would stand the test of rigorous criticism. And I took Greek courses to acquire the necessary research language and historical perspective. (The Minoans were immediate predecessors of the Greeks, and some of the written documents they left are in an early form of Greek.) It was gruelling, often tedious labour. Reading classical authors in the original Greek meant interminable hours of flipping through the onion-skin papers of my Greek lexicon, reciting the Greek alphabet backwards and forwards as I hunted down new vocabulary, and slowly, painstakingly, pieced the sentences together.

Fortunately, I began to reap benefits very early on, and so was motivated to continue. There were innumerable references, direct and indirect, to the conflicting social relations between men and women in ancient Greece. I discovered among them some intriguing nuances of meaning, nuances which had been invisible in translations by previous male classicists. I eventually came to appreciate how apt it is for the attitude of hatred toward women to be conveyed in English by the composite Greek term "misogyny" ("miso-" from the verb "to hate" and "-gyny" from the noun "woman" [Cf. "gynaecologist"]). For misogyny is an attitude that finds frank expression in several of the Greek texts I read. So even though the difficult process of learning Greek and studying Greek culture was merely preparation for doing research on Minoan goddess symbolism, for me it turned out to be rewarding in itself. It cast light on the historical pattern of sexism and misogyny, which I desperately wanted to better understand.

I didn't realize until near the end of my preparatory undergraduate program that one discovery in particular was turning out to be very important to me in a deeply personal way, not just for its theoretical value. That discovery, I suddenly saw one day, was quietly, almost imperceptibly, changing my life. Let me explain.

In the course of reading so many Greek texts, I naturally met the full roster of gods and goddesses in the polytheistic, ancient Greek religion. I met Zeus, "father of gods and men"; and his wife, Hera; the twins Apollo and Artemis; wise Athena, patron goddess of Athens; Poseidon, who ruled the sea; Aphrodite, the goddess of love; Hermes, the messenger god; Hades, King of the Underworld; Demeter, in whose honour the famous Eleusinian Mysteries were held; ...and so on. I read hymns in their praise as well as epic poems and theatre scripts in which the personalities of these divinities star as larger-than-life, immortal characters, who dramatically affect the lives of humans, mere mortals. Each goddess and each god became a distinctive personality for me. Each name resonated, pregnant with meaning; while yet remaining tinged with mystery, beckoning further exploration. Anyone who has had the pleasure of really getting to know the various gods and goddesses of ancient Greece will tell you the same story about how they can come alive for you. Western artists have drawn inspiration from them down through the ages. So, if they also came alive for me, that in itself should be no surprise. Perhaps that is why it took me several years to recognize, and finally acknowledge, that it was the Greek *goddesses,* in particular, who had come alive for me, with an amazing power that really seemed to be transforming my life.

My life had taken some unexpected and, in hindsight, tell-tale turns since returning from Greece. To support my studies I took various jobs over the years (factory work, cocktail waitressing, office work). One day while on a factory job, I found myself in the boss' office, daring to ask for equal pay for equal work. He laughed. (I will never forget his laughter.) Later he fired me, under other pretences. Instead of dropping the matter there and swallowing my rage, I found two feminist lawyers to help me get the back-wages due me. That task took five years. In the process I had to summon the personal resources to be ever more daring, ever more self-confident. It even became necessary in the end to take the Ontario government to court for unjust administration of its equal pay legislation.[17]

Have you ever imagined yourself taking the government to court? Or giving public speeches and holding press conferences? I certainly had not. I doubt very much that under normal circumstances I would have been able to sustain the sheer nerve that taking precedent-setting legal action demanded of me. Certainly I could not normally have borne it along with the demands of my philosophy and Greek studies, the frequently demeaning "women's jobs" I was holding down to get by on, as well as the strains of various other personal trials during those years. Normally my self-confidence would have crumpled under such weight. I can only think it abnormal that, on the contrary, my self-confidence kept growing stronger. My material and personal circumstances were as precarious as ever;

but, strangely, my life felt richer, more meaningful, more worthwhile in spite of its oppressions. Why?

In retrospect, I attribute the inward changes I was undergoing during this period, and my growth in self-confidence, to much more than the normal processes of maturation. I attribute them to the gradual empowering effect that I was experiencing from the Greek symbols of female divinity that I was studying. For countless times over this period I found myself invoking the different goddesses, calling on the appropriate one by name. I would inaudibly, unnoticeably (even to myself at times) summon the name of her whose powers I needed, depending on the situation.

Themis, goddess of righteousness, and Athena, patroness of Athenian law courts, for example, helped me to brave the intimidating halls of our Canadian justice system. They gave me confidence in the justice of my equal pay claim. Athena lent another of her attributes, wisdom, to my academic efforts as well. Her august demeanour encouraged my will to defy any philosophers, or philosophy professors, who pronounced women incapable of reason. Athena's additional strategic prowess in war seemed to undergird my own stratagems for prevailing as a woman against the historical weight of sexism and misogyny—the war against women—as I encountered it inside academia, in the job market and, increasingly, in myself.

I felt the presence of another goddess, Demeter, most strongly in the spring and summer when I cultivated her special gift: the earth's bounteous harvest. Together, it seemed, we worked the rich brown loam in my city-plot garden, sowed the seeds, and waited with anticipation while the moon waxed. Together we rejoiced in the symbolic return of her long-absent daughter, Persephone, with the arrival of the first, fresh, bright-green seedlings dripping with dew on a misty April morning. Persephone, Queen of the Underworld, led me down into another underworld: the depths of my consciousness. Both goddesses helped me to weed out the internalized forms of misogyny that I found there, just as mercilessly and as lovingly as we weeded and thinned rows of lettuce and Swiss chard as the season progressed.

Yet another goddess, Hestia, goddess of the hearth, puttered around my home with me, making it a haven of warmth and charm in spite of poverty's drabness. She and the other two so-called "virgin" goddesses,[18] Artemis and Athena, supported my choice to live independently and to pursue my own special interests rather than marriage or motherhood. (Meanwhile Hera, the wife,[19] and Demeter, the mother, lingered on the periphery, ready to bless wifedom or motherhood, or both, if ever I might need it.) Artemis, who was also the skillful huntress, transported me to the bracing breezes of her wild woodland haunts when the city smog fogged my senses too much. She tested my physical mettle and smiled on solid, strong muscles that a fashion photographer would be more likely to snigger at.

And still another goddess, Aphrodite, causer of coupling, whispered to me about her province of love and passion. She taught me to respect my woman's body, its awesome procreative powers and sensual pleasures. Aphrodite helped me to reject the dishonour and abuse that I had only known how to endure before her symbol gave me a vision of a better alternative...[20]

The examples could be multiplied indefinitely to cover virtually every aspect of life and death. One goddess symbol or another came to be there for me to call on, to contemplate, to draw strength from in my need. As I continued with my studies over the years, in addition to these Greek goddesses I have found that Minoan goddesses, and subsequently Amerindian goddesses too, have enriched still further the store that I can draw from.

I don't mean that I now believe in goddesses and the myths about them in the same literal way that the church once asked me to believe in God and the story about Christ's immaculate conception, crucifixion, and resurrection. I believe in the Goddess only in the sense that I have come to recognize the power of sacred symbols, and the force of religious metaphor, to give meaning and purpose to life. And I believe that the femaleness of the Goddess symbol, compared to the maleness of the God symbol, immeasurably enriches the ways that I as a woman can tap the power of symbol to serve my distinctively female needs.

If I don't want to, I don't have to use goddesses from other cultures or times. Theoretically, I could create completley new goddess identities, and stories to accompany them, that would better reflect the realities of modern Canadian women. Maybe some day I shall. In the meantime, I am happy to continue learning about the goddess symbols of other cultures and other times and to keep drawing from them many new, personally empowering depths of meaning and affirmations of purpose that are applicable to my life. In this story I have barely begun to describe all the new depths of meaning and purpose with which I feel my life has been blessed by these goddesses. But I hope I have managed to convey some small measure of the degree to which I feel them transforming my life.

My story has been about my changing relationship with religion, especially religious symbolism, as a factor affecting my personal experience of oppression as a woman. Before I knew anything about the concepts of sexism or mysogyny, I had already left the church. Consequently, when I learned through early feminist critiques of traditional religion about how it sanctions sexism, I paid little attention, convinced that at least religion was no longer as destructive a factor in my own case because I no longer attended church or accepted its dogma. What I could do to minimize the negative impact of religion on my life I believed I already had done. Then my chance discovery of goddess symbolism showed me that it was possible to do much more than merely minimize the negative impact of religion. I found out that meditating on life using female-validating forms of religious symbolism provided me with a way to maximize religion as a positive, beneficial factor. Through the support I derived from female symbols of divinity, I gradually found myself becoming more sure of my own worth as a woman, less plagued by crippling self-hatred and other internalized forms of oppression, and surprisingly more confident in my ability to survive and to prevail against all oppressive obstacles.

In my view, my story has a happy ending. For this my gratitude naturally goes to the Goddess.

Return to Demeter, Artemis, Isis, Shekinah, Kali, Yemanje, Sedna, and...

My purpose in telling this story has been to introduce the second approach to the feminist analysis of religion. The first approach, you will remember, focuses on a critique of traditional religion and the debate concerning its reform versus its abandonment. The second approach focuses on what could be called a renaissance in female polytheism, or a resurgence of interest in goddess symbols, usually a plurality of goddess symbols.

Having heard my story, several features of the literature following this second approach should now be more readily comprehensible. The following skeletal sketch should be adequate to convey a fairly full picture of what you find in the books and articles in this section of the bookcase.

First, much of the research component in this case centres on ancient examples of female polytheism. I am not the only one who has been fascinated enough to research and write about Greek and Minoan goddesses, for example.[21] Several authors have written about the history of goddess symbolism among the Greeks, the Minoans, and in several other ancient European and Near Eastern civilizations as well. Drawing on the work of archaeologists and historians of religion, these authors trace a history of goddess symbolism back through an awesome length of time. Some of the earliest evidence dates back to about 25,000 B.C.E. The history of Western male monotheism dwarfs in comparison to the many millennia during which goddess symbolism was normative in Europe and the Near East.[22]

My own research has recently broadened to include Aboriginal Amerindian goddess figures of Canada, but the scope in the literature now available is even more comprehensive still. It encompasses the full range of non-European civilizations, past and present, and their amazing array of goddesses and female heroine, or saviour, figures. Among these you'll find Hindu goddesses (e.g., Kali), African goddesses (e.g., Yamanje), and Amerindian goddesses (e.g., the Inuit sea-goddess, Sedna), to identify a mere three.[23]

In addition to this research component, the analysis of female polytheism includes a debate on its contemporary relevance for Western women. Again it appears that I am not alone. Apparently several researchers have experienced similar new sources of meaning and personal empowerment through their work with female polytheism from other times and cultures.* Some authors have written personal accounts of their experience in much richer detail than I have presented in my story here.[24] Others have written more abstractly, framing their argument in more general terms. These authors claim that the discovery and reclamation of female polytheism by Western women bodes well for the future of feminism. Against the background of my story, their argument should be relatively easy to follow.[25]

Roughly speaking, their argument holds that for Western women, whose inherited traditions contain exclusively male symbols of divinity, there are significant psychological advantages in reclaiming a female polytheism. Through reverently contemplating a variety of female likenesses, a full range of female experience and desire, we can learn to honour ourselves as female human beings in a way that is not available to us through the male monotheism we have inherited. The Father and the Son are not enough. We need the Mother and the Daughter, and all our Sisters too, if we are truly to see our female selves, to know our female will, and to believe in it enough to act on it, despite any obstacles. The argument continues by pointing out that goddess symbolism can be protective: a source of psychological protection against being too frequently battered and bruised by the violence of women's oppressions. It can be healing: a tool for psychological surgery, permitting women to cut out of ourselves our disrespect for ourselves, our internalized forms of oppression. Having thus helped to excise some oppressions, and to blunt the damage from others, goddess symbolism can then buttress our resolve and nourish our inner resources to deal with the oppressions that remain. As a result, the argument runs, an individual woman who has recourse to goddess symbolism can better tap her personal powers for a fulfilling life. And collectively, such personally empowered women might be able to engineer significant social and political changes as well.

Obviously, my personal experience leads me to see some merit in this argument.

Conclusion

I began this paper with an observation about Madonna's successful use of Marian sacrilege as a way to capture people's attention. For Madonna it works very well in the last few decades of the twentieth century. But will an act like hers continue to work as well in the twenty-first century too? Or has Madonna come along at precisely the right moment, after any danger of persecution or censorship is over, but before the symbols of Mary and Eve lose their monopolistic claim on the public consciousness?

It is impossible to say what the future holds for these Christian symbols of

---

*A significant number of articles, books, and films on goddess symbolism have appeared since this article was written. A selection is included in the bibliography following.

womanhood. Today they are being challenged by the re-emergence of alternative symbols of womanhood in the form of various goddesses. The symbol of the Goddess has already found its way into feminist music, art, and poetry, apparently sparking a surge of creative expression among women. For many women who have left the church but felt a spiritual void, goddess symbolism has begun to fill that void. For others still struggling to reform the church, female symbols of divinity serve an iconoclastic function. They are helpful for shattering former rigidly patriarchal patterns of theology, making it possible for new interpretations, more relevant for today, to emerge.

For centuries traditional Christianity has reinforced women's oppression with its sexist symbols. Whether or not that condition will continue very long into the future, however, has become very much an open question.

Notes

Acknowledgements: I wish to thank several women who offered their comments on this paper while it was in draft stage, namely: Eve Gaboury, Sherralee Galey, Naomi Goldenberg, Deborah Gordon, d.i. huron, Rosalie Martin, Suzanne Pilon, and Kelley Raab.

1. The Dominion Inquisitors Heinrich Kraemer and Jakob Sprenger obtained a papal bull in 1484 authorizing them to extirpate witchcraft. They published the *Malleus Maleficarum* as a handbook for Inquisitors. Its vituperative attack on women, in particular, resulted in an overwhelming proportion of female victims during the subsequent witch-hunt period. Clark and Richardson report:

   The historical circumstances occasioning such a brutal outburst against women are still disputed, but the character and object of the attack are not. The ratio of women to men accused of witchcraft ranged anywhere from 20-1 to 100-1. In some cases almost the entire female population of a village was killed.... It is hard for us to imagine the immensity of the victimization. Estimates range from a low of 50,000 deaths to a high of over a million. Not merely in numbers of those killed, but also the systematic character of their selection and persecution resembles the modern destruction of the Jews (1977, 116).

   For an even more disturbing account of the European witch-hunt, and how it has been erased by history textbooks, see Daly, 1978, 178-222.
2. In 1981, while I was attending Concordia University, a fire destroyed the set in the campus theatre where an English version of this controversial play was being staged. The fire was not officially attributed to arson. (See "Concordia Blaze Destroys Set of Controversial Play," *Montréal Gazette,* January 30, 1981, 3. Also see "Québec Judge Bans Sale of Playscript," *Montréal Gazette,* December 5, 1978, 1; "Ban Extended on Montréal Play *Les Fees Ont Soif,*" *The Globe & Mail,* January 16, 1979, 2; and "Appeal Court Ruling: Catholics Unable to Ban Play," *Montréal Gazette,* November 20, 1979, 3).
3. Most of the established churches in Canada have experienced dramatic declines in attendance rates since the Second World War. On average, 2 out of 3 Canadians regularly attended church in 1946, whereas only 1 out of 3 did so in 1986. (Bibby 1987,

11) "From the high of 60 percent attendance for Conservative Protestants, weekly churchgoing stands at about 35 percent for Roman Catholics, 20 percent for Presbyterians, and around 15 percent for United Church, Anglican, and Lutheran affiliates" (Bibby, 1987, 106).

4. Given Madonna's success in Canada, I think this lesson applies here. Even though her act is not a Canadian cultural creation, it is part of the Canadian cultural experience.

5. Six of these early texts include: Daly, 1968, 1973; O'Faolain and Maritines, 1973; Ruether, 1974; Stone, 1978; Clark and Richardson, 1977.

6. It is noteworthy that, while there are these two approaches evident in the literature available on the subject, often they are not both equally represented on reading lists for the few courses on women and religion that have so far managed to eke out a precarious place in Canadian universities and theological schools. With a few exceptions, courses and campus libraries tend to focus on the first approach I describe, if they include any feminist literature at all.

7. Even though this decision might be considered discriminatory against other religious groups that don't receive public financing, the court decided it was more important to preserve what it calls "a fundamental compromise of Confederation in relation to denomination schools." See "RC Scheme Upheld As Right Promised At Confederation," *The Globe & Mail*, June 26, 1987, 9.

8. See "Nova Scotia Fires Fundamentalist Judge," *The Globe & Mail*, January 16, 1987, 1.

9. I use C.E. instead of A.D., and later in the article B.C.E. instead of B.C. People who prefer not to employ the dating conventions from any one religion often use these terms. C.E. stands for Common Era and B.C.E. for Before the Common Era.

10. A modern work of fiction that explores the oppressive potential for women in this biblical theme is Margaret Atwood's novel, *The Handmaid's Tale* (1985). It is a disturbing, futuristic account of an America ruled by religious extremists in which the protagonist is a *Handmaid*, the class of women forcibly enlisted to bear children for the elite.

11. See the quotation from 1 Timothy: "...Yet woman will be saved through bearing children..." (quoted previously).

12. The United Church of Canada, the largest Protestant denomination in Canada, ordained its first female minister (Rev. Lydia Gruchy) in 1936. Half of its candidates for the ministry are now women, and a few notable women have even made it to the very top of the church hierarchy. For example, the Very Rev. Lois M. Wilson, winner of Canada's Pearson Peace Medal in 1985, is a former moderator of the United Church of Canada (1980-1982). She was also the first woman president of the Canadian Council of Churches [1976-1979], and subsequently became one of the first women presidents of the World Council of Churches [1983-1990]. And Dr. Anne Squire, who was made moderator of the United Church in 1986, was the first lay woman to achieve that position. Another major Protestant denomination, the Anglican Church of Canada, agreed to leave the decision of women's ordination up to the discretion of individual bishops in 1976. Over a decade later, at the time this article was written, not all Anglican bishops had given their permission. For example, there were no women ordained as yet in the Anglican diocese of Fredericton. However, since that time two women have been ordained in the Fredericton diocese. A more dramatic development came in November, 1992, when the synod of the Church of England decided to permit women to serve as priests by a two-vote margin. "Making history, the Church of England voted narrowly for women priests last week. But with Anglicans still split and

Catholicism and Orthodoxy resisting any change, feminism is emerging as the faith's most vexing issue." ("God and Women: A second Reformation sweeps Christianity." *Time,* Nov. 23, 1992.) The Roman Catholic Church in Canada, as elsewhere, continues to restrict the priesthood to men. It prohibits girls and women from serving at the altar in lesser roles, too. In June 1987 the archbishop of Toronto, Emmett Cardinal Carter, made headlines for refusing to permit an altar girl to participate in an anniversary mass at a Toronto church even though she had already been serving there as an altar girl for four years. Despite charges of unfairness, Emmett Cardinal Carter chose to hold to the letter of current Church law, which the local priest had been stretching by allowing altar girls in the first place. (See "Girl Not Allowed To Help At Altar At Cardinal's Mass," *The Globe & Mail,* June 19, 1987, 7.) The Eastern Orthodox Churches in Canada, as elsewhere, also restrict the priesthood to men. The Greek Orthodox baptismal ceremony is different for girls and boys: the baby boy is carried inside the sanctuary, but the baby girl is not.

13. "Inclusive language" is the label for new terms that do not explicitly or implicitly exclude the female sex (or, alternatively, terms that do not imply *any* sexual identity, whether male or female). "Good will among men" becomes "good will among people." "Our Heavenly Father" becomes "Our Heavenly Father and Mother" or "Our Heavenly Parent" (or "Our Heavenly Creator"). Christ, of course, being a historical personage, remains "the Son." For some women the maleness of Christ presents no problem; while for others it is one of the reasons they feel irreconcilably alienated from the Christian tradition.

14. The following are examples of books and articles that defend Christianity as essentially egalitarian, though in need of drastic reform: Fiorenza, 1979; McLaughlin, 1979; Reuther, 1974, 1976, 1985; Reuther and McLaughlin, 1979; and Trible, 1979. Daly, 1968 also presents a reformist argument; however a later edition of this work (1975), and Daly's other subsequent books, argue against the possibility of reform and espouse abandoning Christianity altogether.

15. The following books and articles are among those that conclude Christianity is essentially sexist: Christ, 1978; Daly, 1975, 1978 (a highly provocative book); Goldenberg, 1979; and Stone, 1978.

16. The feminist critique of Judaism, for example, exposes misogynist statements in the tradition, such as: "May the words of the Torah be burned, they should not be handed over to women" (T.J. Sotah, 10a, 8). The debate among Jewish feminists is clearly articulated in two articles by Ozick, 1983 and Plaskow, 1983.

17. See: Re Downing and Graydon et al. (1977), 17 *Ontario Reports* (2d) 26, Ontario Divisional Court; and Re Downing and Graydon et al. (1978), 92 *Dominion Law Reports* (3d) 355, Ontario Court of Appeal.

18. For the ancients the term "virgin" did not have the same narrow connotation of sexual inexperience that it bears today. It had the broader sense of an unmarried woman, or a woman who was independent of male manipulation in a psychological sense. This idea finds some contemporary currency, as well, in the interpretation of Hestia, Artemis, and Athena as representations of "the virgin archetype" in female psychology. Bolen explains:

> These three goddesses personify the independent, active, nonrelationship aspects of women's psychology. Artemis and Athena are outward- and achievement-oriented archetypes, whereas Hestia is inwardly focused. All three represent inner drives in women to develop talents, pursue interests, solve

problems, compete with others, express themselves articulately in words or through art forms, put their surroundings in order, or lead contemplative lives. Every woman who has ever wanted "a room of her own," or feels at home in nature, or delights in figuring out how something works, or appreciates solitude, has a kinship with one of these virgin goddesses. The virgin goddess aspect is that part of a woman that is unowned or "unpenetrated" by a man—that is untouched by her need for a man or need to be validated by him, that exists wholly separate from him, in her own right. When a woman is living out a virgin archetype, it means that a significant part of her is psychologically virginal (1984, 35).

19. Although archaeological records suggest Hera was originally an independent and highly revered deity, classical Greek mythology portrays her as the symbol of the unhappy, jealous wife. In the myths, she is married to Zeus. He ruled over all the gods and goddesses and behaved like the paradigmatic patriarch, imposing his will though force and indulging his sexual appetite with whomever he desired, much to Hera's discomfiture. Hera's lot as a wife is hardly appealing; but as a symbol of wifedom under patriarchal conditions it certainly seems apt.

20. A francophone Canadian, Paris writes with insight about the advantages of reclaiming pagan deities like Aphrodite. She asks, for example:

Has the loss of our Goddesses changed our status from that of a sacred object to that of a domestic convenience? Many young men are more excited by their first car than on the day they first make love; others are truly proud and moved when they receive a promotion or experience a new gadget, but are tense, distraught, ambivalent as soon as they engage in a love relationship, witness the birth of a child, or participate in the events of family life (1986, 58).

21. See my article (Downing, 1985).

22. Some of the sources you might like to consult include the following: Barstow, 1978, 1983; Ferguson and Nemani, 1983; Gimbutas, 1974, 1982; Graves, [1961] 1971; Grigson, 1978; Patai, 1967; Pomeroy, 1975; Rohrlich-Leavitt, 1977; and Stone, 1978. Some books consider the persistence of female imagery even into ostensibly male monotheistic traditions. The biblical Asherah and Queen of Heaven (e.g., Jeremiah 44), and the emanation of God, or the feminine presence called Shekinah, are examples from the Jewish tradition that are highlighted by Patai's book (1967). In the Christian tradition, Berger, 1985, traces the persistence of a pagan female agrarian figure. Another group of authors writes about the remnants of goddess-worshipping traditions that persisted alongside Christianity, eluding the Inquisitors. For accounts of the Wiccan (or Witchcraft) tradition and its modern feminist version, see Adler, 1979 and Starhawk, 1982.

23. See, for example, the encyclopedic works by Stone, 1979 and Monaghan, 1981. Nonetheless, the need is still there for more detailed studies on non-European goddesses. Inadequate appreciation of non-European goddesses mars the work of some white feminist authors who have written about women recovering their ancient goddess heritage. A prominent black writer, Audre Lorde, has pointed out how it may even reflect a form of racism. After reading Daly's *Gyn/Ecology*, 1978, Lorde responded with "An Open Letter to Mary Daly" (reprinted in Lorde, 1984, 67-69). In it she says:

Your words on the nature and function of the Goddess, as well as the ways in which her face has been obscured, agreed with what I myself have discovered

in my searches through African myth/legend/religion for the true nature of old
female power. So I wondered, why doesn't Mary deal with Afrekete, Yemanje,
Oyo, and Mawulisa? Where were the warrior goddesses of the Vodun, the
Dahomeian Amazons and the warrior-women of Dan?... I began to feel my
history and my mythic background distorted by the absence of any images of
my foremothers in power... Mary, I ask that you be aware of how this serves the
destructive forces of racism and separation between women—the assumption
that the herstory and myth of white women is the legitimate and sole herstory
and myth of all women to call upon for power and background...

A more recent publication that looks at one of the African goddesses Lorde mentions
is Gleason, 1987. For a study of Native American goddesses see Hultkrantz's article
in Olson's anthology, 1983, a book that also contains chapters on a number of Asian
goddesses and another African goddess, Oshun.

24. See Christ, 1987 and Downing, 1981.
25. For variations of this argument see Daly, 1978; Christ, 1979, 1987; Paris, 1986; and
Spretnak, 1982, xi-xxx.

Note
*A significant number of articles, books and films on goddess symbolism have appeared
since this article was written and a minimal selection is included here.*

References
Adler, Margot, 1979. *Drawing Down the Moon: Witches, Druids, Goddess-Worshippers,
and Other Pagans in America Today*. Boston: Beacon Press.
Atwood, Margaret, 1985. *The Handmaid's Tale*. Toronto: McClelland and Stewart.
Barstow, Anne, 1978. "The Uses of Archeology for Women's History: James Mellaart's
Work on the Neolithic Goddess at Catal Hüyük." *Feminist Studies* 4 (3): 7-18.
——, 1983. "The Prehistoric Goddess," pp. 7-15 in Carl Olson (ed.), *The Book of the
Goddess Past and Present: An Introduction to Her Religion*. New York: Crossroad.
Berger, Pamela, 1985. *The Goddess Obscurred: Transformation of the Grain Protectress
from Goddess to Saint*. Boston: Beacon Press.
Bibby, Reginald W., 1987. *Fragmented Gods: The Poverty and Potential of Religion in
Canada*. Toronto: Irwin Publishing.
Bolen, Jean Shinoda, 1984. *Goddesses in Everywoman: A New Psychology of Women*.
New York: Harper and Row.
Bridenthal, Renata, and Claudia Koonz (eds.), 1977. *Becoming Visible: Women in
European History*. Boston: Houghton Mifflin Co.
Brown, Joanne Carlson, and Carole R. Bohn (eds.), 1989. *Christianity, Patriarchy, and
Abuse: A Feminist Critique*. New York: The Pilgrim Press.
Christ, Carol P., 1978. "Heretics and Outsiders: The Struggle Over Female Power in
Western Religion." *Soundings* 3 (61): 260-280.
——, 1979. "Why Women Need the Goddess: Phenomenological, Psychological, and
Political Reflections," pp. 273-87 in Carol P. Christ and Judith Plaskow, (eds.),
Womanspirit Rising: A Feminist Reader in Religion. New York: Harper and Row.
——, 1987. *Laughter of Aphrodite: Reflections on a Journey to the Goddess*. San
Francisco: Harper and Row.
Christ, Carol P., and Judith Plaskow (eds.), 1979. *Womanspirit Rising: A Feminist Reader*

in Religion. New York: Harper and Row.

Clark, Elizabeth, and Herbert Richardson (eds.), 1977. *Women and Religion: A Feminist Sourcebook of Christian Thought*. New York: Harper and Row.

Culpepper, Emily Erwin, 1987. "Contemporary Goddess Theology: A Sympathetic Critique," pp. 51-71 in Clarissa W. Atkinson, Constance H. Buchanan and Margaret R. Miles (eds.), *Shaping New Vision: Gender and Values in American Culture*. Ann Arbor and London: U.M.I. Research Press.

Daly, Mary, 1968. *The Church and the Second Sex*. New York: Harper and Row.

——, 1973. *Beyond God the Father: Toward a Philosophy of Women's Liberation*. Boston: Beacon Press.

——, 1975. *The Church and the Second Sex: With a New Feminist Postchristian Introduction by the Author*. Second, enlarged edition, with a new preface and introduction. New York: Harper Colophon.

——, 1978. *Gyn/Ecology: The Metaethics of Radical Feminism*. Boston: Beacon Press.

Dexter, Miriam Robbins, 1990. *Whence the Goddesses: A Source Book*. The Athene Series. New York: Pergamon Press.

Downing, Christine, 1981. *The Goddess: Mythological Images of the Feminine*. New York: Crossroad.

Downing, Marymay, 1985. "Prehistoric Goddesses: The Cretan Challenge." *Journal of Feminist Studies in Religion* 1 (1): 7-22.

Ferguson, Heather M., and Tsipporah Nemani, 1983. "Patriarchy & Goddess Worship." *Canadian Woman Studies/les cahiers de la femme* 5 (2): 66-67.

Fiorenza, Elizabeth Schüssler, 1979. "Women in the Early Christian Movement," pp. 84-92 in Carol P. Christ and Judith Plaskow (eds.), *Womanspirit Rising: A Feminist Reader in Religion*. New York: Harper and Row.

Gadon, Elinor W., 1989. *The Once and Future Goddess: A Symbol for Our Time*. San Francisco: Harper and Row.

Gimbutas, Marija, 1974. *The Gods and Goddesses of Old Europe, 7000 to 3500 B.C.: Myths, legends and Cult Images*. London: Thames and Hudson; Berkeley: University of California Press.

——, 1982. "Women and Culture in Goddess-Oriented Old Europe," pp. 22-31 in Charlene Spretnak, (ed.), *The Politics of Women's Spirituality: Essays on the Rise of Spiritual Power Within the Feminist Movement*. Garden City, N.Y.: Anchor Press/Doubleday, Anchor Books.

——, 1989. *The Language of the Goddess*. San Francisco: Harper and Row.

Gleason, Judith, 1987. *Oya: In Praise of the Goddess*. Boston and London: Shambhala Publications.

Goldenberg, Naomi, 1979. *Changing of the Gods: Feminism and the End of Traditional Religions*. Boston: Beacon Press.

Goodison, Lucy, 1990. *Moving Heaven and Earth: Sexuality, Spirituality and Social Change*. London: The Women's Press. Especially chapters 1-3.

Graves, Robert, [1961] 1971. *The White Goddess*. Reprint edition. London: Faber and Faber.

Grigson, Geoffrey, 1978. *The Goddess of Love: The Birth, Triumph, Death, and Return of Aphrodite*. London: Quartet Books.

Heschel, Susannah (ed.), 1983. *On Being a Jewish Feminist: A Reader*. New York: Schocken Books.

Hultkrantz, Ake, 1983. "Religion of the Goddess in North America," pp. 202-216 in Carl

Olson (ed.), *The Book of the Goddess Past and Present: An Introduction to Her Religion*. New York: Crossroad.

Journal of Feminist Studies in Religion 5., no. 1(1989). See the following four articles in this issue: Mary Jo Weaver, "Who is the Goddess and Where Does She Get Us?" pp. 49-64; Jo Ann Hackett, "Can A Sexist Model Liberate Us?: Ancient Near Eastern 'Fertility' Goddesses," pp. 65-76; Howard Eilberg-Schwartz, "Witches of the West: Neopaganism and Goddess Worship as Enlightenment Religions," pp. 77-95; and Margot Adler, "A Response," pp. 97-100.

Lorde, Audre, 1984. *Sister Outsider: Essays and Speeches by Audre Lorde*. Trumansburg, N.Y.: The Crossing Press.

McLachlan, Bonnie, 1992. "Sacred Prostitution and Aphrodite," *Studies in Religion/Sciences Religieuses* 21(2): 145-162.

McLaughlin, Eleanor, 1979. "The Christian Past: Does It Hold a Future for Women?" pp. 93-106 in Carol P. Christ and Judith Plaskow (eds.), *Womanspirit Rising: A Feminist Reader in Religion*. New York: Harper and Row.

Miles, Margaret R., 1987. "Violence Against Women in the Historical Christian West and in North American Secular Culture: The Visual and Textual Evidence," pp. 11-29 in Clarissa W. Atkinson, Constance H. Buchanan and Margatet R. Miles (eds.), *Shaping New Vision: Gender and Values in American Culture*. Ann Arbor and London: U.M.I. Research Press.

Monaghan, Patricia, 1981. *The Book of Goddesses and Heroines*. New York: E.P. Dutton.

O'Faolain, Julia, and Lauro Martines (eds.), 1973. *Not In God's Image*. London: Temple Smith.

Olson, Carl (ed.), 1983. *The Book of the Goddess Past and Present: An Introduction to Her Religion*. New York: Crossroad.

Ozick, Cynthia, 1983. "Notes Toward Finding the Right Question," pp. 120-151 in Susannah Heschel (ed.), *On Being A Jewish Feminist: A Reader*. New York: Schocken Books.

Paris, Ginette, 1986. *Pagan Meditations: The Worlds of Aphrodite, Artemis, and Hestia*. Translated from the French by Gwendolyn Moore. Dallas: Spring Publications.

Patai, Raphael, 1967. *The Hebrew Goddess*. New York: KTAV.

Plaskow, Judith, 1983. "The Right Question is Theological," pp. 223-233 in Susannah Heschel (ed.), *On Being a Jewish Feminist: A Reader*. New York: Schocken Books.

Plaskow, Judith, and Carol P. Christ (eds.), 1989. *Weaving the Visions: New Patterns in Feminist Spirituality*. San Francisco: Harper.

Pomeroy, Sarah B., 1975. *Goddesses, Whores, Wives, and Slaves: Women in Classical Antiquity*. New York: Schocken Books.

Rohrlich-Leavitt, Ruby, 1977. "Women in Transition: Crete and Sumer," pp. 35-59 in Renate Bridenthal and Claudia Koonz (eds.), *Becoming Visible: Women in European History*. Boston: Houghton Mifflin Company.

Ruether, Rosemary Radford (ed.), 1974. *Religion and Sexism: Images of Women in the Jewish and Christian Traditions*. New York: Simon and Schuster.

——, 1976. *New Woman/New Earth*. New York: The Seabury Press.

——, 1985. *Womanguides: Readings Toward a Feminist Theology*. Boston: Beacon Press.

Ruether, Rosemary Radford, and Eleanor McLaughlin (eds.), 1979. *Women of Spirit: Female Leadership in the Jewish and Christian Traditions*. New York: Simon and Schuster.

Spretnak, Charlene (ed.), 1982. *The Politics of Women's Spirituality: Essays on the Rise of Spiritual Power Within the Femiminst Movement*. Garden City, N.Y.: Anchor Press/ Doubleday, Anchor Books.

Starhawk, 1982. "Witchcraft as Goddess Religion," pp. 49-56 in *The Politics of Women's Spirituality: Essays on the Rise of Spiritual Power Within the Feminist Movement*. Garden City, N.Y.: Anchor Press/Doubleday, Anchor Books.

Stone, Merlin, 1978. *When God Was A Woman*. New York and London: Harcourt Brace Jovanovich. Originally published in Great Britain under the title *The Paradise Papers*. (London: Virago, in association with Quartet Books, 1976).

——, 1979. *Ancient Mirrors of Womanhood: Our Goddess and Heroine Heritage*. 2 Volumes. New York: New Sibylline Books.

Trible, Phyllis, 1979. "Eve and Adam: Genesis 2-3 Reread," pp. 74-83 in Carol P. Christ and Judigh Plaskow (eds.), *Womanspirit Rising: A Feminist Reader in Religion*. New York: Harper and Row.

Films

Goddess Remembered 1989; *Burning Times* 1990; *Full Circle* (working title) 1993. Donna Reed, Director. Montréal: National Film Board of Canada.

Chapter 4

Gender, Sex, Image, and Transformation in Popular Music

Susan G. Cole

Political activists yearn to be part of a movement that is popular, a movement that will touch people, speak to them and resonate with their experiences and desires. As a feminist writer, I have yearned for a mainstream voice, one that could reach out to all kinds of women (and men), no matter where they are. Actually, I wish that radical change could be as appealing as popular music. Pop music: those simple songs, employing sometimes just a three or four chord structure that provides the basis for melodies that career through our stubborn brains. (How many times do people complain that they can't get songs out of their heads?) Pop music: the kind that drives people onto the dance floor. Pop music: for which young people are particularly voracious. Pop music: if only it could be politicized, we would have our revolution.

It was precisely this last sentiment that led me to form an all-woman rock band in 1979 called Mama Quilla II. The band, without me and with a male drummer, went on to record a wonderful extended-play album which is now a collector's item. I was not involved in the project because I had become a part of a second band, called No Frills, which played throughout Toronto, Ottawa and Montréal, but which never managed to secure what every rock group needs in order to survive: a recording contract. This essay describes the hows and whys of that situation. It is about who women are in popular culture, how they are seen, and how these roles and values are regenerated through the products churned out by the record and media industries.

This essay is divided into four parts. The first discusses women's situation in popular music and how gendering* takes place on both the administrative and artistic levels. The second section describes the practical problems of trying to succeed in a male-defined context and in venues that are male-controlled. The third section addresses the products of pop culture that regenerate this dynamic of gendering. My method is part research, part experiential. The No Frills band was in for a rocky ride through the pop music industry because we broke almost every stereotype promoted by pop music, by the society that constructs its

---

*What I mean by this will be explained later.

meaning, and by the industry that promotes it. I understood this problem because I began my explorations of pornography at almost exactly the same time. As a result, both my research and my experience are woven closely into theories and perceptions I began to develop about pornographic culture and the way it unremittingly relegates women to the status of object, the body to be exploited, and the body and soul that cannot be empowered within the social frame to which women are confined. What we will discover is a system that is close to perfect, infinitely adaptable, able to devise or appropriate technology and devices to perpetuate patriarchal values to new generations and markets.

But the system is not entirely impervious to change, and so the fourth section of this essay celebrates those intrepid musicians whose work and art seem to transcend the brutal strictures placed on women in the business. These artists help make change. Their art is inspiring and it makes the horizons look not nearly so bleak. A warning, though. The examples of female empowerment in pop music are not offered as proof that any woman can make it and that a woman once down is guaranteed to survive. The road to pop stardom is littered with women who have been used and discarded. Exceptions do not belie the systematic discrimination women experience as musicians, nor do they wholly obscure the sordid attempts of record producers to turn good art into ersatz plastic. While women have become more visible and influential, conditions for women in the industry continue to be dreadful and the consequences for female consumers who learn to emulate their heroic sex objects can be devastating.

As you read this critique of pop music, try not to confuse it with those attacks on the industry which are launched from other quarters, especially those of right-wing activists. They undertook a concerted campaign in 1985, for example, to hound record producers about satanist lyrics, sensational violence and rock music's anti-authority stance. So impressive was the right-wing challenge, and so well situated—the wives of several United States senators were especially vocal—that a U.S. Senate Committee conducted hearings to assess whether stricter controls should be placed on the distribution of some types of rock music.

I mention these developments because there was an interesting parallel between what happened at those hearings and the way the discourse on pornography used to be shaped. Until anti-pornography feminists redesigned some of the terms, the pornography debate featured right-wingers (usually men) arguing it out with pornographers (usually men) for the right of consumers (usually men) to masturbate. Feminists began to notice that within this framework, those portrayed in pornography (usually women), and other women who believe that this portrayal has something to do with their own lives, were consistently left out of the discussion. The feminist critique of pornography also challenged the right-wing anti-pornography assertion that pornography threatened the social order and formulated another analysis that identified pornography as propaganda for sexism and male dominance.[1] At the same time, feminists insisted that women did not share in the freedom pornographers claimed to defend.[2] Pornographers were not liberators, they were pimps.[3]

The same disinterest in women was evident at the U.S. Senate Hearings investigating the impact of rock and pop music. The wives of conservative senators bemoaned the negative influence of rock music on their children, while rock musicians and their lawyers scoffed at the prudery and authoritarianism of the right wing. Defenders of the music industry complained that the industry's critics were using scare tactics reminiscent of the repressed fifties which saw ministers raging from the pulpit against the then new "satanic" rock and roll. At the same time, those rising to pop music's defence conveyed their views that rock musicians challenge the social order with their creative dissidence, in particular with their increasingly sexually explicit imagery. Thus the senators heard a great deal about the value of the family in society and the future of our children on the one hand, and more about the integrity of dissent and the importance of freedom of expression on the other.

While children and male artists had their champions, no one spoke for women. It is fascinating to note that while male pop stars (Frank Zappa's testimony was especially memorable)[4] streamed into the Senate chambers to argue for rock's salutary influence on kids and the dangers of interfering with creativity, not a single woman musician or performer took the stand on behalf of the industry. Women were absent not only because male voices tend to carry more weight and credibility: plainly, women in the industry could not bring themselves to say under oath to members of Congress that everything in the industry was fine.

Gendering in Pop Music

Gender is a term usually used by theorists, and because it has been used in differing circumstances and for different purposes, I want to make clear what I mean when I use it. Gender describes a social dynamic through which members of both sexes take on prescribed sex roles through a socialization process. Note that the process is social and not natural. By this I mean that my use of the word gender does not encompass physical sex differences, body size, for example, or genitalia. Those are sex differences found in biology. Gendering, by distinction, is a social process.

Perhaps an example will help. I complimented my three-year-old niece on her new shirt. She looked at me disapprovingly and told me it was a blouse, not a shirt. The distinction is a social one: she is already becoming intensely gendered; she is *not* revealing her natural inclination to be feminine. Rather, she knows the difference between male and female and is absorbing the social meaning and demands of those terms. If she is a girl, she wears a blouse, period.

The process of gendering has several aspects. One of them is the social separation of roles, activities, qualities, and behaviours according to male and female categories. Thus, according to typical sex roles, women are nurturent caretakers while men are active doers. But the gendering process does not stop with this "difference." It gives different value and status to those male and female qualities. So, the active qualities in males are considered more valuable than the qualities of nurturence that are ascribed to females. Crucially, the discrepancy between how men and women are valued shows up in circumstances where the same quality is valued differently, depending on the sex of the person being talked about. Thus the aggressive woman is villified while the assertive (note the change in terminology) male is celebrated. Women who take care of their children are considered cultural angels, while new fathers who have "discovered" parenting are suddenly being lionized. For centuries, women have been changing diapers, blowing noses, and preparing three meals a day for their children, and it was assumed that it was mother's natural duty to do this not particularly difficult work. But as soon as men started parenting, they became heroes battling the domestic winds of change.

All these dynamics of gendering—gender roles, gender values, and changing values depending on sex—occur in one way or another within the context of popular music. Let's start with the gender roles that are promoted through popular music culture. Cast your mind on what a rock band looks like. Doubtless you envision mostly men. If there are women in the picture they will be either singing or dancing. The instrumentation in rock and pop music is quite obviously gendered. Women almost never play electric guitars and can be found behind a set of drums even less often. In fact they seldom play any instruments at all. This is consistent with the stereotype of the technologically-impaired female, incapable of mastering or even handling machinery. The ultimate in gender reinforcement occurs in the person of the go-go dancer who is invariably a woman and who is there as an object to be watched if the band is not very interesting visually.

It is worth noting that the genre of classical music, although more traditional and conservative than pop music in other ways, is less restrictive when it comes to expectations of what instruments women will play. Many of the world's great concert artists are women. They play pianos, flutes, cellos, and the otherwise-gendered double bass. However, in a study prepared for Status of Women Canada, one of these bass players felt compelled to say that even though women do play the double bass, there is not a single woman occupying the principle chair for double bass in a Canadian orchestra.[5] In addition, compared to men, women seldom compose or conduct, but they have been given permission to be virtuoso concert performers. As far as I know, only once has a female dancer been brought in to enhance a performance, and that occurred at the premiere of Ravel's *Bolero* in Paris.[6]

With the introduction of intricate keyboard synthesizers, more women are appearing in bands—in Arsenio Hall's house band, for example. We can measure some progress here, although the image of woman as keyboardist is consistent with the image of women as typists. Usually, though, women in popular music are singers. This is the one field in the pop music world where women are encouraged to shine, either singly or in the so-called girl-groups of the sixties—the Shirelles, the Chiffons—whose smooth back-up vocals were so intoxicating that they were able to dominate the record charts. As singers, women have high visibility and some status and they may even be the front person for the band, the one with whom the audience relates when listening to the music. Often though, this female visibility is not accompanied by control or even shared input into the band's creative process. This is readily apparent simply by reading the music classifieds in the newspaper. A notice advertising the position of female lead singer is an invitation for a woman to front a band whose musical and business approach has been established long before she appears for her first interview.

Men, on the other hand, usually occupy positions of power in the music industry. Wherever you can locate power, you can count on there being a noticeable absence of women. The most powerful people in the pop music world are the major record company owners, none of whom are women.[7] This is not all that surprising and only echoes the data gathered throughout the corporate world. But leaving aside the key issues of capital, profit, and who controls both, the way the music itself is produced reveals the deep influence of the gender dynamic. For example, in Canadian branch plants, there is not a single woman heading up an Artists and Repertoire (A&R) department,[8] where a company decides which new musicians to record.

In music production, the record producer has the most clout. *He* is the one whose vision shapes the way the music sounds, the one who has the last creative word, who chooses which songs to record, how they should be arranged, where echo belongs, which track should be kept—in short, how the record will sound. With the extraordinary strides that recording technology has made, especially with digital capacities, producers (except when dealing with rock royalty, like Mick Jagger, and more recently, Madonna, who produce their own records) have more creative power than ever before.

They are almost always paid more than the performers, albeit sometimes with good reason. (Peter Asher became wealthy and much more powerful as a producer than he was as part of the performing duo Peter and Gordon.) A performer's career can be transformed by a producer who finds the sound that clicks with an audience and who, for so doing, is often hailed as the brains behind the project. Michael Jackson was close to becoming a forgotten commodity until he teamed up with producer Quincy Jones for his *Thriller* album in 1983. Juno winner Rita MacNeil, the Cape Breton singer/songwriter, used to release flat recordings of wonderful songs. She received little attention outside her home communities, let alone any radio airplay, until she was produced by the high-priced David Foster (also a Canadian). There are still those who claim the Beatles would have sounded like any other band had it not been for the brilliance of their producer George Martin (often referred to as "the fifth Beatle"). Producers have administrative and creative power. They are seldom women. The ones who are, like Canadian composer Trish Cullen, are the exception and usually exert total control over a project only when the material is their own.

As singers, women fit a particular sex role. We live in a society where women make more money than men in only two professions: modelling and prostitution. We also live on a continent where pornography is multi-billion dollar enterprise that depends on the sale and appropriation of women's bodies. Pop music, too, depends on the sale and appropriation of women's bodies. Smart performers like Madonna and Tina Turner know this and combine dance with their performance (thus reducing the need for dancers on the stage). It is no coincidence that women's most valued musical instruments—voices—are part of their bodies. Generally speaking, men play instruments and women play their bodies as instruments. Men also play women's bodies as instruments and their instruments as if they were women's bodies. (Jimi Hendrix's sexualization of his guitar is infamous.) The centrality of this sexual relation to rock music is evident in rock videos (see further) in which the camera plays over women's bodies while the music plays on. Male performers manage to stay separate and sometimes distressingly aloof from the source of their music, yet when women perform, singing and dancing, they give much more away: they give away a part of themselves.

Women's Sexualization in Pop Music

The No Frills band, whose life spanned the years 1979 to 1982, was originally an all-female band, but eventually had to succumb to the pressures of gender: we could not find a permanent female drummer. Finally we accepted a male drummer, leaving us with four women players. Despite the male member, the band's composition was very unusual. There were three writers, three lead singers, a bass guitarist, a lead and rhythm guitarist, and two keyboard players sharing four keyboards. The three women in the band, other than myself— Sherry Shute on guitar, Catherine MacKay on bass, and keyboardist Evelyne Datl—had all been in the music business for close to ten years. They had survived almost unbearable conditions while touring through the hinterlands of Ontario in bands like Otherwise and Lady. Sherry Shute, in particular, was already becoming a legend, playing rock and roll guitar in a style few had seen a woman undertake.[9]

No Frills played original music that covered the vicissitudes of our emotional lives and expressed a need for social change. We had a strong local grassroots following and were particularly delighted with the fact that the band had become interesting to a large number of under-twenty-year-olds. This pleased us because we had always been aware of our potential as role models for young women who are very influenced by pop music but who recognize that women are presented in pop music in very narrow ways.

In 1980, after a full year together, we decided to pay a visit to what was then called a rock consultant, someone whose brain is picked for suggestions as to how a rock group could find success. Our consultant did not mince words as he predicted complete failure for the No Frills band. We were doing everything wrong, he said. We had to be aware that the major market for pop and rock music was men between the ages of eighteen and twenty-five, single men with disposable incomes.[10] We were, according to the consultant, everything that would alienate these men. This group of buyers is attracted to bands that produce heroes for them—bands like Van Halen, Foreigner or Styx. A guitar player is a hero, he said, but only when the guitar player is a man. When the player is a woman, he went on, she represents the listeners' failure to play the instrument as well as she does. These buyers don't like that. We would never get their interest. And by the way, he added, if we were interested in breaking through to these markets, could we go a little heavier on the make-up and skimpier on the costumes?

We were astonished by the consultant's rigidity and challenged his notion that there was only one market. We suspected that the market was fragmenting and there was no longer only one major population to pursue. There were thousands of people over thirty who would be interested in our kind of pop music, and thousands of teenaged women who would like us. The problem was with record executives who could perceive only one identifiable large market to sell to. Ultimately (but much too late for us), we discovered that we had been right. In the latter half of the 1980s, the most powerful pop music stations (even CBC AM) altered their formats to appeal to the group between the ages of twenty-five and forty, known sociologically as the "baby boomers." The eighteen to twenty-five-year-old male market had lost its buying profile.

Naturally, we were outraged by the consultant's comments about our physical appearance. But the consultant was there to give us business advice, not a pep talk. In fact, we should have taken into account what audiences expect women to look like and how they expect us to behave on stage. Male pop musicians—Phil Collins, Joe Jackson, Elvis Costello, all of whom were popular at the time—could look however they liked but female performers had to comply with conventional standards of beauty. Some women with only minimal talent but plenty of appeal could come and go and so their names are not that familiar—they could have hit records. We watched the market situation change, but the demands for women to be sexually appealing did not decrease very much. (We had never counted the odd-looking men who had become commercially successful or noticed that we could not find similar numbers of un-glamorous women in the pop music industry.)

As we continued to toil on the circuit, the pressure to conform was intense.

There were two factors which made our lives particularly difficult. One of them was *not* the content of our songs. We had learned long before that rhythm was the key to pop success. Lyrics were sometimes wholly inaudible, and besides, if inanities like shoo bop de bop and sha na na na could survive over pop's magnetic beat, then political lyrics would do just as well.

No, the first factor is that pop music is performed, especially in the formation stages for bands, in bars, venues that are male-dominated and male-defined. No Frills was happy doing benefits in our own community, but in order to make a living we had to go outside these friendly confines into extremely hostile environments. Bars are not hospitable places for women, let alone feminists, and let alone feminist rock bands. The owners are men, and so are their customers. Most women who venture in, unless they are regulars, or unless they are accompanied by men, are perceived as having invaded men's space, or as looking to be picked up. There never seems to be any in-between. The atmosphere, permeated with alcohol, is also charged with the energy for sexual foreplay. Fights often break out between men vying for a woman's attention, while other male customers fight to assert sexual control over their female partners. The combination of violence, alcohol, and sexual tension makes bars sexual battle-grounds where female submissiveness and male power are played out.

The entertainment is generally for the men in the audience: this was the second factor that contributed so much to our struggle. Because the entertainment was for men only, it was expected that as women we would be sexually entertaining for the male viewers. This was confirmed by the *On a WIM* study in which the majority of respondents reported some kind of sexual discrimination or harassment. One woman put it simply: "A lot of people see it that if you play in a club, you double as a prostitute."[11]

We learned this through our worst—and most instructive—experience in a bar in Barrie, Ontario. We arrived in the late afternoon to set up lights and equipment, but the bar manager said that we would have to wait until after the floorshow, a depressing strip extravaganza that drove us out of the place. When we returned, the stage had not yet been struck and the manager insisted we do it. This was an extremely demoralizing experience, but not nearly as devastating as the playing itself. After the strip show, the No Frills band was a deep disappointment to the audience, and the entire room seethed with anger.

On a consciousness-raising level, though, the Barrie experience was something of a revelation, for we had never thought there was a connection between ourselves and the women who took their clothes off there every day. We needed the juxtaposition of our sister strippers with our own band to see that we had in common the fact that we were women, and that as women we were expected to be sex for men, and sex only. By thinking we could parachute into male-controlled spaces and change everything in them—the atmosphere, as well as audience expectation—we had underestimated the power of socialization and the rigours of gendering, for through those processes women are transformed into objects for men to look at. While men read *Playboy* to gain a sense that they deserve Scotch, cars, and women, or that women are there to be looked at and thus owned, women will buy *Seventeen* or *Vogue* to learn how to make themselves appealing enough that men will look at them. Since men owned the bars, and at least according to our consultant, were doing the greater bulk of the buying of pop music, our female rock band simply could not avoid the syndrome of sexual objectification.

We were objects on the Barrie stage, but more important, we were sexual objects. No matter what we were doing, we were seen as the sex those men wanted. We discovered that rock music had its place on a spectrum of cultural products that existed to provide men with access to female sexuality. Pornography is the most extreme and explicit example and is on one end of the spectrum, but advertising also plays this role, displaying women's bodies on cars, doing their toilette, and in beer commercials, so that men will get some pleasure. Rock videos (see further) have found their niche among the spectacles designed to maintain women's status as sexual objects. In all of these cultural genres, men's bodies are not displayed in the same way or as often.

In the early 1970s, feminists and lesbians began to resist the role of sexual object in rock culture by forging their own recording studios, distribution networks and performance venues. Olivia Records, based in San Francisco, was the most ambitious of these efforts and was founded expressly to provide support for female musicians outside the male-dominated framework. In addition, Olivia provided training for women in tasks usually assigned to men—engineering and producing, in particular. American artists like singer/songwriter Chris Williamson, composer/pianist Kay Gardner, and singer/drummer Linda Tillery began to develop audiences in the politicized context of what became known as women's culture. Other independent companies, like the California-based Redwood records, began to work with women-controlled outlets, mostly women's bookstores continent-wide, to distribute artists like Holly Near and Canadian singer/songwriter Ferron, while concurrently, women's music festivals in Michigan and Indiana began promoting these recording artists, providing them with listeners eager for their women-positive messages. These initiatives have acted to support systems for consumers who have turned to the music to raise their own feminist consciousness and to fortify their emerging lesbian identities.

But this women's music scene could never fall comfortably under the rubric of popular music. For its appeal is specific, not general, and its range for distribution cannot possibly compete on turf closely controlled by the larger, established record labels. Holly Near understood this, and after a long-term commitment to Redwood Records, decided to move to Attic Records, a more mainstream label with a wider distribution potential. She was unhappy to learn just how true it was that the women's music network was not "popular" when Attic refused to deliver to the Toronto Women's Bookstore for distribution because the store was "too small."

While female artists try to figure out where they belong, male artists do not worry as much about escaping the mainstream because they do not experience anything that compares to the performer-as-sex syndrome. This is not to say that men are never perceived as sexy, but only that when male pop stars convey sex, they are not reduced to sex, but rather elevated to positions of power. When women used to throw hotel room keys on the stage while crooner Tom Jones performed, they weren't trying to dominate Jones but asking that Jones dominate them. Prince's performance is hypersexualized, but there is a close connection between that sexual energy and the image of him tossing his girlfriend into the trashcan in his first film, Purple Rain. Madonna was scorned as "just sex" for years, until she managed to transform that put-down into something powerful for herself. All of this illustrates that aspect of gendering in which a particular quality is valued, depending on the gender of the person talked about: male sexuality is powerful, female sexuality is submissive and a source for ridicule.

There is really nothing men experience that compares to the way women are reduced and used for their bodies. Liberal commentators have tried to find parallels, however. The organized sports establishment is often cited as an invidious exploiter of (mostly black) men's bodies for the profits generated by sports-crazed fans. But the salaries men receive as professional athletes are exponentially higher than that which women are paid to be sexual objects in pornography or in pornography's imitators in mass media.* And athletes are lauded for their achievements, admired for what their bodies can accomplish, not made less valuable because of how their bodies are used. Ex-football player Burt Reynolds highlighted the contradiction between jock and sex object when he posed as Cosmopolitan's first male centrefold. He maintains that it almost ruined his chances in Hollywood. Ex-baseball pitcher Jim Palmer, now a baseball broadcaster, had to break through the stereotype to pose in underwear ads, and associates who believe he lowered himself by modelling the jockey shorts still pepper their broadcasts with sarcastic comments.

When women pose for lingerie ads, they are told that they have found their appropriate place, but when women want to play rock and roll they are told that they might do better at something else, something more suitable, like putting on more makeup and going for skimpier costumes, as our rock consultant put it. How does an artist who wants to be taken seriously succeed when her gender role of sexual object is incompatible with art? or with seriousness? With no female corporate support, so few role models, and the non-negotiable demands from producers and venue operators for women to be sex and nothing else, it is a wonder that so many women keep trying.

---

*See Helen Lenskyj in this collection.

Regenerating Gender

Gendering is a social process. In order for the process to be complete, boys and girls must be educated when they are young about which gender they are and how they are supposed to behave. The gendering process, as we discussed earlier, begins at birth. Many hospitals still provide male babies with blue blankets and female babies with pink blankets, thus establishing the gender colour scheme when babies are but a day old. Sex role modelling also helps to institute the rigours of gender. Feminist psychologists developed the concept of modelling in the early seventies. Children, they said, were very sensitive and aware. When daddies work outside the home and mommies do the bulk of the childcare and housework, children tend to grasp the difference in roles and assume that all women are supposed to stay home while all men should support the home financially. They then behave according to their gender prescriptions.

The products of culture play a key role in regenerating gender values.[12] Fashion magazines that convey impossible standards for female beauty promote the notion that women must make themselves physically attractive, and they encourage women to spend the majority of whatever money they have on the cosmetics and clothes that will make them appealing to men. Men's sporting magazines advertise the virtues of male physical freedom and provide photographic features of women in bikinis so that men will want to look at the women who make themselves appealing for them. Advertising, too, has its conventions that promote rigid gender distinctions and often turn women into sexual objects to sell products. What is important to understand is that such advertisements sell not only the product in question but also the gender values implicit in the advertisement. If the ad implies that if you buy the car, a woman comes with it, the message is that women are easy to get: that they, like cars, are objects that can be bought and owned as commodities. Or if you assess how many times women appear significantly less clad—usually to make them sexy—than the men in the same advertisement, you can begin to see how women learn that they are supposed to be sexually available to men and men learn that they have the automatic privilege of sexual access to women. The essence of gender identity is that women equal sex, men equal power. Pop music and its cultural artifacts—song lyrics, record jackets and now rock videos—are also implicated in this gendering process.

In the late 1970s, the pop music industry went into a sag that sent record executives into a virtual panic. There were decidedly fewer records being sold. The culprit was the audio tape cassette player which was making it possible for listeners to tape music from borrowed recordings, thus getting the music for the cost of an audio tape without purchasing the record itself. This was putting a significant dent in industry profits, but just when it looked as if the business might not recover, a new phenomenon developed that would salvage the future of the pop record business—rock videos, those three-minute advertisements for popular songs that have completely restructured pop music marketing.

Before rock videos became a commercially viable product, promotions executives had only radio airplay to count on for stimulating record sales.[13] Rock videos added powerful imagery to the usually hypnotic rock beat, and the combination was overwhelming. Rock videos were so appealing that entire television stations were founded, and now flourish, solely devoted to rock video play. This has created a promotional vehicle like no other, since unlike television advertising, the record companies which release the videos along with the records do not have to pay for the airtime which rock videos receive on either MTV in the United States or MuchMusic here in Canada. In fact, if there is a tilt in any direction, it is toward paying the record company for permission to use the videos for television play.

In other words, rock video has revolutionized the music and television industries. But while the record companies gloated over their corporate coup, they were quite surprised to discover who was their prime audience for rock videos. It was not that tirelessly cited group of men between the ages of eighteen and twenty-five with disposable incomes. It was kids aged nine to thirteen who were watching videos, and these preteens were mostly female. With this new piece of information, culture watchers began to scrutinize the content and style of rock videos, analyzing more closely the extent to which rock video was promoting specific values. Feminists in particular intensified their investigation of the music industry, an investigation whose roots could be traced to a San Francisco protest of a billboard ad for the Rolling Stones' album *Black and Blue*. The billboard featured a woman partially clothed, chained, and bruised with the caption: "I'm black and blue from the Rolling Stones and I love it." It was a classic example of how media products promote the notion that women are sexually submissive and men are powerful and in control.

Turning now to rock videos, Women Against Pornography (WAP) in Vancouver, surveyed scores of rock videos to determine whether there was a pattern to the messages they conveyed. The group discovered that rock videos seemed to harp on three values: the value of conspicuous consumption (rock musicians are often depicted in their videos as living preposterously high lives); the thrill of violence (a popular element of heavy metal—guys and guitars— videos is assault and battery); and of course the prescriptions for gender.[14] The WAP survey is important because it identifies the important role played by the products of the rock industry in the socialization process and the regeneration of traditional gender differences.

To understand how rock videos in particular contribute to the gendering process, we have to combine the concept of gendering and the social construction of sexuality with many of the issues feminist film critics have examined in their discourse on representation and film.[15] The first stage of that discourse asked specific questions about the actual content of film, or in this case, video. Which gender, male or female, dominates the scene? How are men and women portrayed? Is there any violence in the scenario? Who are the perpetrators? The victims? Taking his cue from these primary questions, Robert Kaplan, at the University of Akron, conducted his own survey of 139 videos and concluded that men were more visible than women, had more major roles, were typically older than the women depicted in the same videos, and were significantly more dominant and more positively portrayed. There were also, according to Kaplan's calculations, 10.18 acts of violence per hour of viewing. Kaplan goes on to suggest that this portrayal of women and men is consistent with the way women are portrayed throughout mass media.[16]

However, analysis of content is only the first step in the feminist critique. The second stage focuses on the construction of the image itself, leading to questions like: How are the characters lit? Do they face the camera? Is the camera recording or intruding? Who is assumed to be looking at the image, a man or a woman, and to what extent does that make the camera the masculine eye?[17] This is an analysis of form rather than content.

Let me use an example from a classroom where I teach media studies to illustrate the distinction between the two. In a series of sessions, I showed students three different videos. The first was a video by Motley Crue, a typical product of the heavy metal genre, featuring men singing about the apocalypse while wearing leather and playing their guitars as if they were machine guns. Together, the class and I undertook our own content analysis, scanning the video for acts of violence, assessing who the perpetrators were, and who the victims were, establishing the sometimes degrading depictions of women, and discussing the culture meanings and messages of wearing leather. It was a useful exercise.

The next time I saw the class, I showed them another video, this one called "Shake You Down," performed by Gregory Abbott. The song is a soothing rhythm and blues account of how the very good-looking singer imagines his soon-to-be sexual partner. There is no violence in the video and the song itself is apparently about love. When I asked the class what they saw, they were baffled. The first exercise had been straightforward: look for violent acts and degrading portrayals. The second video was tougher to analyze because it did not give off those obvious signals of female *oppression*. But there were other and different elements of the video that conveyed male *dominance*. To begin with, the camera trained on the singer's object of desire as if intruding on her privacy. She was significantly less dressed than her male partner throughout the clip, and the process of getting her into a near-total state of undress was typical of the way women are constructed as sexual objects to be looked at. Imbedded in the discussion was some insight into the way images construct sexuality as male dominance and female submission,[18] although some of these issues were beyond the range of this high school class. Still, they did begin to see the deeper levels of meaning conveyed through the construction and not just the content of an image.

The last sample for the class was a rock video featuring Bruce Springsteen singing a song called "Fire." Springsteen is one of pop music's most durable pop stars. From the inception of rock video, he tried to avoid having to make one. Eventually his absence on MTV became too much of a marketing liability and he finally agreed to appear in videos, provided they were of concert sessions only. This approach is eschewed by other video producers who prefer that scenarios or art concepts accompany the presentation of the musicians, but Springsteen was adamant and, as of this writing, has released only a short series of videos of his stage performances in conjunction with the release of an album he recorded live.

The class watched the video of "Fire" and were again miffed. There was no violence, no degradation, and no reason to use the sophisticated tools of analysis they had learned from analyzing the second tape. There was only Bruce Springsteen in blue jeans, lit by a spotlight, playing guitar. I confessed to the class that I had cheated them a bit and that I wanted to return to the fundamental criticism feminists had developed of the songs themselves and the lyrics. What were the lyrics for "Fire"? A young man leaped up and dutifully recited "I'm driving in my car? You turn on the radio? I'm holding you close. You just say no? You say you don't like it? I know you're a liar? 'Cause when we kiss, fire."

Since so much of pop music is about love and sex, the lyrics are a splendid reflection of what the sexual landscape is like for men and women. The Beatles sang "Little Child," and no one seemed to notice that either the song was a paean to pedophilia, or more likely, it was typical of the way men infantalize the objects of their desire. Women sing "Stand By Your Man" in ways that encourage other women to remain in abusive relationships. When Pat Benetar sang "Hit Me With Your Best Shot," she seemed to be reinforcing, in a perverse way, the appeal of being battered. Generally speaking, men sing about pursuit, women about pain and suffering. In fact, many of the lyrics for pop music songs give love and sex a fairly repulsive reputation.

The song "Fire" was originally performed in a sultry manner by the Pointer Sisters, but it is utterly transformed when Springsteen sings it. The students in the class got the point immediately. What happens when a man says to a woman "you know you're a liar and like it"? "He's raping her," came the reply, so swiftly that I was taken aback. "What does no mean?" "No means no," they answered.

Plainly this was not a typical class of high school students. In fact, the consciousness level of the class had been profoundly affected by the sex education sessions offered to them at this alternative school. Having learned something about violence and having access to media literacy initiatives,[19] they had come a long way toward perceiving sexual violence in the products of popular culture and to understanding more completely their meaning. This two-pronged strategy—sex education and media literacy—is to my knowledge the only viable method of subverting the regeneration of gender through the products of culture which play such an important role in the socialization process. The pop music industry is an especially important target for analysis. Making young people aware of how these products are made, the way these products deliver messages, and the extent to which teenagers themselves are their targeted market are the tactics that may ultimately eliminate the market for sexist mass media.

Transformations in Pop Music

Marketing pop stars depends on creating an indelible impression on an audience. In order to do this, pop stars must have easily-identifiable personnae, traits, costumes that trigger recognition. Oh, a fan might say, she's wearing a cross around her neck. That's Madonna. Or she's black and wearing a teased-out blonde wig. That's Tina Turner. Or they wear scarves around their legs and on their heads. That's Loverboy. Album covers, posters, rock videos, and the entire array of marketing tools keep a face and an image front and centre in mass consciousness. This is how public relations personnel in the pop music industry create icons.

The successful creation of these icons denies the truth of the matter, which is that pop stars are actually human beings, and that as human beings they experience change and growth. The changes promoted by the industry are usually only cosmetic: Michael Jackson shed his single sparkly glove for black leather from head to toe; David Bowie drops eye make-up and dyes his hair blonde. These are changes in image, not real changes in these artists' lives. The actual biographies of pop stars, on the other hand, help to convey the truth about real change to students of media literacy or to others, even feminists, who have been seduced by the power of the pop icon image. Noticing how female performers change can make us believe in the possibility of political change in the longer run and in the larger picture.

The experience of women in pop music is like the experience of women everywhere. It is one of survival. In the same way that assaulted women move to escape the abuse and take charge of their own lives, many female pop performers start off in one mode and then transform their own conditions to gain more control of their personal and professional lives. Then again, some pop stars are wife assault victims themselves. Over twenty years ago, Tina Turner was married to Ike Turner and was a member of his band, The Ike and Tina Turner Revue. Throughout their marriage, Tina Turner had been abused, physically assaulted, denied money, and kept in prison-like conditions. She dropped out of sight within the industry after she escaped from her husband, then resurfaced in the late 1970s to perform duets on stage with Rod Stewart. Between that time and 1985, when she released her comeback album *Private Dancer*, she told her story to the most influential magazines in the United States, including *Rolling Stone*.[20] She came out as an assaulted woman. *Private Dancer* went on to make her one of the most popular female performers of the 1980s. Listen to the song "You Better Be Good to Me," and you can see how real experience can be conveyed and shared in the powerful medium of pop music.

Pat Benetar used to appear as a leather-clad sex object in spiked heels. Her first Top Ten recording, released in 1979, was a song called "Hit Me With Your Best Shot," a not-very-ambiguous invitation to an assaultive boyfriend. But Benetar did not remain static. In 1985 she recorded a song called "Love is a Battlefield" and with it released an extraordinary video featuring Benetar as a prostitute spearheading a prostitutes' revolt against a pimp operating out of a bar. In the video, the women escape from the bar and walk off into the sunset hand in hand. In 1986, Benetar progressed even further with a song promisingly entitled "Stop Using Sex as a Weapon." Her video for the song fulfilled the promise, offering a satire on the way advertisers use sex and women to sell products. From "beat me if you like," Benetar moved through prostitutes' advocacy to the lofty stance of cultural critic.

Madonna too has transformed. She began as a "boy toy" out to please men, a sexual rebel who was considered a joke by industry insiders. Now she is a powerful influence in pop music. She is someone who understood that sex would have to be exchanged in order to get work, and many of her producers doubled as her sexual partners. She was also viciously abused in sex when Bob Guccione published nude photographs of her without her consent. Ultimately, however, she kicked and clawed her way to the top so that she would no longer be used. Mention of her name in the classroom immediately divides the room into two camps: those who love her and those who revile her as a tramp. And she inspires a great deal of ambivalence among feminists, too. But Madonna, who used to be so casual about sex, now preaches safe sex from the concert stage and is obviously changing, shedding her rebel stance for responsibility to her audiences. Her first film appearance in *Desperately Seeking Susan* showed her willingness to be part of an overtly woman-positive project. The film, written, directed, and produced by women, is about female suburban ennui.[21]

Other pop performers have been fortunate to have the confidence and support to challenge the assumptions of patriarchal interests. She may not use the word patriarchy, but Annie Lennox has always challenged the prevailing social order with her gender-bending antics. She was wholly androgynous in the video for "Sweet Dreams" and then went all the way by appearing in full tuxedoed drag at the 1985 Grammy Awards show. But she is not just one face with one approach. Her androgynous presentation was swiftly followed up in videos where she appeared in full party dress and crinolines, as in "Would I Lie to You," in which she appears to be walking out on her boyfriend while playing guitar on stage.

Chrissie Hynde, lead singer for the British band Pretenders, has always presented herself as a strong woman in control of her music and her life. She seldom wears make-up, even in performance, wears clothing to increase her mobility rather than emphasize her sexuality, and is the main artistic force behind her band. Cyndi Lauper's feminism has been overt. At a Toronto press confer- ence held in 1985, she discussed how difficult it was to be female and intelligent in the pop music industry, and when questionners taunted her with the label feminist, she did not argue and accepted the tag.

The Canadian music industry has made room for a number of musicians who resist the standard formulas for gender. Carole Pope's band, Rough Trade, brought satire and humour onto the pop music stage, something especially unusual among staid Canadians. Pope's "High School Confidential" was a parody of teen love that caught the confusion of adolescence. Wearing leather and telling audiences "I want to have your child," she was decidedly sexual but never submissive. She may be one of the few performers who has been able to convey sexuality and control at the same time. Jane Siberry's music has a probing wit, and her videos create a colourful wash and gentle energy that contrast sharply with the hyper-sexualized products emerging from almost every other corner of pop culture. And the Parachute Club always had an impressive female presence. Their rock videos, especially "At the Feet of the Moon," in which the women in the band dance joyously with each other, manage to convey female empowerment in a world where the term barely has any lived meaning.*

These women have stretched the restrictions of gender, compelling audiences to consider women as more than sex and as intelligent artists. Every one of these breakthroughs is politically important, for they show how radical politics could be popularized without being diluted. There may be a future for female popular music performers after all, and there may yet come a generation of listeners able to absorb their influences and create their own political transformations. But in order to create that future, we must resist the stricture of gender, understand how media work, and recognize that pop culture and music are powerful social forces. When more women control those forces, the world will be a very different place.

Notes

1. The anti-pornography perspective has been expressed in a number of places. See Lederer, 1980, Dworkin, 1979, Cole, 1985 and "Pornography, Civil Rights and Spech," in MacKinnon, 1987.
2. See Cole, 1984 and "Not a Moral Issue," in MacKinnon, 1987.
3. Myrna Kostach puts it this way in Kostach, 1982.
4. Daniel Richler reports in the New Music, City TV, September 28th, 29th, 1985.
5. *On A Wim*, a study of Women in Music (WIM) in Canada, prepared for the Status of

---

*The success of k.d. lang, with an unconventional stage persona and now an open lesbian identity, suggests that transformation on the music scene is possible.

Women Canada by Lorraine Segato, Interim Report unpublished, p. 11.

6. The performance took place at The Paris Opera in 1928.

7. None of whom are Canadian for that matter. The Canadian music business is essentially a branch plant of the American music industry, which in turn creates hardships for all Canadian performers, no matter their gender. Note that Eleanor Kowalski (formerly Eleanor Sniderman) has established a distribution company that may assist women's projects.

8. *On a Wim*, p. 11.

9. Sherry Shute has released her own album. It is self-titled and can be purchased by contacting Lois Carrol Music, 151 Tyndall Ave., Toronto.

10. Singer/songwriter, Nancy White describes almost exactly the same experience in *On a Wim*, p. 15.

11. *On a Wim*, p. 13.

12. See Tuchman et al. (ed.), 1979, and Davies et al. (eds.), 1987 for a survey of some of the feminist work on women and image.

13. It is also worth noting that records have to be heard in order to be bought. Radio airplay, even with the rock video boom, is a very important force for promotion. Of 213 radio stations surveyed for the *On a Wim* study, only one had a woman president and only 44 music directors were women.

14. The study and the tape that illustrate this are available by contacting the Association for Media Literacy in Toronto.

15. There is a large volume of work discussing these issues. For a good introduction, see Kaplan, 1983, especially the Introduction.

16. Kaplan's study was presented at the 1987 *Conference on Popular Culture*.

17. For the best background in these issues, consult the groundbreaking essay "Is the Gaze Male," in Kaplan, 1983. For parallel perceptions of the art establishment, see Parker and Pollack, 1983.

18. See Finn, 1985 and 1986.

19. Consult Masterman, 1985 for what is referred to by teachers as the "bible" on media literacy. Also, the Ontario Ministry of Education together with the Ontario Teachers Federation have prepared a resource book on media literacy for Kindergarten to grade 13 that is very useful.

20. *Rolling Stone*, October 11, 1984, # 432.

21. I've deepened my analysis of Madonna and now believe her public persona mirrors her experience as a child sexual abuse survivor. See *Now Magazine*, Vol. 12, No. 9.

References

Berger, John, 1972. *Ways of Seeing*. London: Penguin.

Cole, Susan G., 1984. "The Practice of Pornography," *Broadside* 5(110).

——, 1985. "Review: Women Against Censorship," *Canadian Journal of Women and the Law* 1(1).

——, 1992. *Pornography and the Sex Crisis*. Toronto: Amanita. Second Story, 1992.

Davies, Cath, Julian Dickey, and Teresa Stratford (eds.), 1987. *Out of Focus, Writing on Women and the Media*. London: Women's Press.

Dworkin, Andrea, 1979. *Pornography: Men Possessing Women*. New York: Perogee.

Finn, Geraldine, 1985. "Patriarchy and Pleasure: Man's Pornographic Eye/I from Pygmalion to the Present." *Canadian Journal of Political and Social Theory*, 9(2).

——, 1986. "Against Sexual Imagery, Alternative or Otherwise," *Parallelogramme* 12(fall).

Kaplan, E. Ann, 1982. *Women and Film: Both Sides of the Camera.* New York: Methuen.

Kostash, Myrna, 1992. "Whose Body, Whose Self," in Connie Guberman and Margie Wolfe (eds.), *Still Ain't Satisfied.* Toronto: Women's Educational Press.

Lederer, Laura (ed.), 1980. *Take Back the Night.* New York: William R. Morrow.

MacKinnon, Catherine A., 1987. "Not a Moral Issue," *Feminism Unmodified.* Cambridge, Mass.: Harvard University Press.

——, supra. "Pornography, Civil Rights and Speech," *Feminism Unmodified.*

McLuhan, Marshall, 1964. *Understanding Media: The Extensions of Man.* McGraw Hill.

Masterman, Len, 1985. *Teaching the Media.* London: Comedia.

Ontario Ministry of Education, 1987. Resource Book on Media Literacy, with OTF.

Parkin, Rozsika, and Griselda Pollack, 1983. *Old Mistresses: Women, Art and Ideology.* London: Routledge Kegan Paul.

Root, Jane, 1984. *Pictures of Women.* London: Pandora Press.

Rolling Stone, an interview with Tina Turner, October 11, 1984. # 432.

Tuchman, Gaye, Arlene Kaplan Daniels, and James Benet (eds.), 1978. "Hearth and Home: Images of Women," *Mass Media.* New York: Oxford University Press.

Chapter 5

Objectivity and Control: Where Television Technology Meets Pornography

Peggy Kelly

In 1987 I wrote an essay for Geraldine Finn's course, "Science, Technology and Gender" at the University of Ottawa. In that essay I described the systemic discrimination I had discovered during my career as a female technician in the Canadian broadcasting industry. In 1988 I studied "Philosophy for Feminism," also with Professor Finn. The paper I wrote for this last course focused on pornography because that year I found myself forced to confront the complexities of pornography and feminism in my work as a member of the Ontario Film Review Board (OFRB), a provincial agency which classifies films and videos. At the OFRB headquarters in Toronto, Ontario, I had the dubious privilege of screening a large number of pornographic videos and films. During this process of studying and working, I came to see a connection between pornography and technology. In this paper* I will attempt to explain this connection. I intend to describe the characteristics which I believe are common to pornography and technology and offer work-related experiences as examples.

One simple connection between pornography and technology is the physical one: pornography depends on technology for its production and dissemination. In the nineteenth century, pornography was available in books and periodicals. At that time the printing press was high technology. Today pornography is still distributed in printed material, but a great deal is also available on videotape and film, both of which are produced through high technology processes. There is *no doubt* that pornography and technology are intimately related.

In addition, both technology and pornography make similar demands of their producers and consumers, such as specialization and objectivity. Anyone in touch with technology today must possess specialized knowledge or experience in order to understand the tools. For example, an x-ray technician uses a camera to produce an x-ray, but s/he would be unqualified to handle a television studio camera. The intimacy of technology and pornography transmits this demand for specialization to the pornography consumer. For instance, a simple

---

*The privacy of all employees and management discussed herein has been respected through the use of fictitious names.

purchase or rental of a pornographic video presupposes awareness of the format distinction: a VHS videotape cartridge is too large for a BETA playback machine. Most men are aware of this elementary distinction because they form the majority of producers and consumers of video equipment and productions. Women are not welcome in this technical arena.

The main requirement for entrance to the realm of technology is objectivity, which technology reveres. Technology is applied science, and science is one of the sources of our partriarchal culture's reverence for objectivity. In the sixteenth century, Francis Bacon, the father of modern science, wrote to his students, all of whom were male, that science must dominate nature: "...bind her to your service and make her your slave" (Fox-Keller, 1985, 37). We are all familiar with the phrase "harnessing nature," for example, through building a hydro-electric dam or using nature's secrets to improve our standard of living.

Scientific experimentation is the model used "to plumb nature's secrets." To produce valid "objective" results, scientists attempt to remain aloof from an experiment's goal. In high school chemistry, students learn to record the objective and the method of each experiment. Standard experimental methods are rigidly enforced in the scientific community in the name of objectivity. But how can one remain aloof from her own work? Simply by choosing a subject on which to experiment, the scientist reveals a personal connection to it.*

Pornography, technology, and objectivity are all linked to women in this way: woman is seen as the other, the object, by the male experimenter or viewer, and the object as woman. That is, pornography and technology have a common attitude towards women: objectivity and separation. To be a successful technologist, one must take an objective approach to the world. I say this because separation and objectivity are inherent in the work performed by and for technology. For example, quality control of the television picture is achieved through use of wave-form monitors. The technician does not rely only on his or her visual evaluation of the image on the television screen. Instead, he or she watches a small screen which is connected to the videotape playback machine. Luminance, chroma, white and black levels are all trans-lated into wavelength interpretations on a scale. If the wavelength conforms to accepted criteria, the videotape is cleared for broadcast. If not, the technician will adjust the image through the videotape recorder as far as the machine will allow. The technician depends on machinery for judgement of the image which will be watched by millions of humans. This separation of mind from body through machinery is imposed on every technician. I believe this process is insidious and largely unnoticed by technologists, technicians, and scientists themselves.

It is this objectivity, this forced separation of nature from culture, mind from body, and male from female that is clearly visible in pornography. There, woman

---

* For more on this see Marilyn MacDonald's essay in this collection.

is obviously an object. Her body is revealed naked for the viewer, who is assumed to be male. The female-object is looked at, devoured, consumed by the viewer of pornography. There is no interaction between the viewed object and the viewer, who is a subject. The viewer is in control whereas the viewed person is vulnerable. Since vulnerability is connected to mortality, the position of the viewed object is an undesirable one. Geraldine Finn believes that men take the viewer's role in order to remain separate and autonomous.

> The desire to view, which is incited in the subject-Man from all directions in our "society of the spectacle" not only by pornography and publicity, but also by science for which "objective observation" is absolutely constitutive—is really a desire for the condition of viewing i.e., for the "ontological status of separation," of Sovereignty. For the viewer is essentially external to the world-viewed and therefore unaffected by it (Finn, 1985, 88).

Women are equated with nature in the scientific mind because of our fecundity. Before the seventeenth century, men had no accurate knowledge of their role in conception. Early scientists, called natural philosophers, portrayed the pregnant woman as an incubator or receptacle for the fully-formed, miniature foetus which was deposited into her during sexual intercourse. Today men are fully aware of their essential, yet relatively minor, role in the physical reproduction of the human race. Perhaps due to an unacknowledged sense of helplessness in the presence of female reproductive power and unrecognized feelings of powerlessness in the face of death, men have tried to separate themselves from nature through a forced objectivity. By assuming the role of the rational, analytical producer of life-supporting *things,* men have chosen to repress the emotional, nurturing characteristics of their *bodies.* These characteristics have been relegated to the female sex.

> [This] has enabled men, the knowers, to falsely abstract themselves from nature, as if they were not themselves historical, material, organic and social beings. This abstraction of men from the rest of nature, and from women, is the root at one and the same time of both their power, for they can be ruthless with others with whom they feel no identification, and of their alienation from the world, each other, and themselves (Finn, 1985, 88).

The traditional man, who may appear non-conventional in his dress and lifestyle, maintains a clear-cut separation between his mind and his body. He is socialized to reject vulnerability in himself; instead, he looks to women for love, emotional support and satisfaction of his daily physical needs: sexuality, food, cleanliness. This is the basis of the rigidly gendered roles to which feminists object so fiercely.

If this hypothetical man (who is alive in real bodies all around us) were to accept his own vulnerability, he would come face-to-face with his own mortality: a painful process which demands a self-admission that he, too, is part of nature. In our culture, nature represents dirt and death: earth, feces, the aging process. Nature is regarded with fear and loathing by those who deny their own natural bodies. "She" is the other, the "not-I." Since nature has been portrayed as feminine for centuries, it's not surprising that women have been treated with contempt for just as long.

That women are viewed with contempt is clear in pornography, the locus of women's role as sexual servants. Just as nature is expected to reveal her secrets to scientists, women are expected to cater to men's sexual desires. This assumption is made flesh in the most frequently represented form of heterosexual intercourse in pornography: fellatio. The woman kneeling in front of the man suggests his domination of her and his control of their situation.

In the television station where I worked for eight years, certain male employees were involved in a private pornographic exchange library. The station received several daily satellite feeds from around the world. There is a lot of violent, hard-core pornography available through this system. One technician would record the pornography from the satellite and another would re-record or "dub" the original onto home videocassettes during the slow hours of the midnight shift. One morning, as I was preparing to record the day's commercial reel, I came across one of these pornographic videotapes and I was offended by its objectification of my own sex. Sexuality and women's bodies are revealed explicitly in pornography, but the individual woman is negated by the constant use of close-ups of erogenous zones. There is no individual reality in the detail we are offered in pornography: it is "unspecific," that is, generalized to all women as objects. I believe this is what Cavell meant when he defined pornography as "combining the absolutely explicit with the completely unspecific" (Cavell, 1979, 55).

I reported this incident to the woman member on the station's sexual harassment committee because I didn't feel comfortable talking to a man about it. She discussed it with the only other member of the sexual harassment committee, a man who was also the General Manager of the television station. This manager was thankful that the pornography had not been broadcast by mistake with the commercials! If that had happened, the Canadian Radio and Television Commission (a federal regulatory agency) could have either issued a severe reprimand (at the least) or revoked the station's broadcast license (at the most).

However, no concern was expressed by anyone about the use of company equipment to record pornography. I heard through the grapevine that one of the company's top executives regularly attended the pornography screenings held by male technicians. I suspect this is common practice in television stations around the world. Fear of detection and interference with this practice could partly explain the cold reception female technicians have encountered in television. Men who frequently view women in a pornographic context, that is, as objects or body parts, could experience difficulty in accepting individual women as co-workers.

In 1985 I was a videotape recorder operator in the on-air department of this television station. My duties included regular shifts as a technical producer in master control. I was the only woman in the department and the first female technical producer to be employed by that particular television station. I experienced a great deal of hostility from my male colleagues in that job. I believe I was perceived to be a threat because my proven ability to work in technology cast doubt on the value of the work itself, on its claim to superiority. If an inferior person such as a woman could perform well in a "man's job," what was so special about it? A female technician's ability to give birth and nurture others contaminates technology in the misogynist mind.

Many men who work with technology presume that their technical aptitude flows naturally from their gender. The unconscious, deep-seated belief that the words "masculine" and "technical" belong together by nature is based precariously on men's claim to a superior level of objectivity. If women represent nature, how can we be objective or scientific? Many men see the phrase "female scientist" as a contradiction in terms. We *are* nature, so we aren't *able* to stand back and study ourselves, and what's even worse, we will become emotionally involved with our work. The results of our labours will necessarily be tainted, because we represent earth, dirt, death, and pain. According to this double standard, men's own personal involvement in their work is harmless because they, and they alone, possess an innate ability to be objective.

For a short time in 1988 I worked in the x-ray department of a hospital. Most of the fifteen x-ray technicians were women; three were men. Although each technician developed x-rays in the darkroom immediately after exposing them, there were a significant number of copies which had to be made for other hospitals or doctors in private practices. The photographic development of all copies was performed by two of the three male radiographers. The female radiographers' time was devoted to interacting with patients and performing technical tasks only insofar as they related to patients. Why was this? Since the women technicians developed x-ray films every day, they were certainly capable of developing copies of these same films.

I believe the reason was an unspoken acceptance of the fallacy that women do not belong in technical occupations. Women are tolerated as long as their technical knowledge is combined with human caring and interaction, tasks which emphasize a woman's mothering role. In *Machinery of Dominance,*

Women, Men and Technical Know-How, Cynthia Cockburn writes that, although male x-ray technicians in a British hospital were in the minority, they achieved management positions more readily than their female colleagues.

Women in television are faced with the same frustrating scenario. Capable, committed women are channelled into the lower-paid clerical areas of work regardless of their technical experience. Promising young women are continually turned away from technical jobs in spite of their technical education. At the same time, young men are privy to the four-century-old apprenticeship system: they are hired without education or experience and taught on the job. Their steady career progress is perceived to be as natural and acceptable as the ghettoization of women in the television service occupations: production assistants, make-up artists, wardrobe assistants, programming clerks, and secretaries.

Besides having more opportunities for advancement open to them, men in television are favoured by the existing male hierarchy. I had a personal experience with favouritism toward a male co-worker in television. I'd like to outline this incident here.

Guy and Dave were friends who worked side-by-side as film editors before Guy became supervisor of the film department. After Guy's promotion, they continued to go drinking together two or three times a week at the pub next door to the television station. Through his friendship with Guy, Dave had a direct line to Roy, the executive producer in charge of several departments, including film. By the time the film department was closed down in 1985, Roy had become the company's vice-president. I was not surprised to see Dave receive preferential treatment during that crisis.

The film department was being phased out to make way for the new technology: videotape. I was hired in 1978 as a film librarian. As a film editor, Dave prepared movies and programs for broadcast and broke them down for return to the distributor. When he was too busy, I performed the break-down editing as well as the library duties. As videotape was gradually introduced, fewer movies arrived at the station on film. Guy trained Dave to edit the news in an effort to provide him with more work. Guy also instructed me to share the film library work with Dave, but Dave had been employed by the television station three years longer than I and he took this change in our work relations as a setback. I believe he grumbled about doing library work because he, and others, saw it as "woman's work."

I asked Guy to train me in news editing, but he refused and said the job was too stressful for a woman. I had to insist on receiving the same assistance he willingly offered Dave. Guy said that I should remain a film librarian because I was a good researcher and he would have a difficult time replacing me. Patronizing attitudes towards women workers are widespread and I'm not the first woman to experience benevolent discrimination. Male employees are never expected to forego career advancement for the convenience of their employers.

The demise of the film department was rumoured for several years before it actually took place. As early as 1979, two film editors, Judy and Tom, were moved to other areas of the television station. Judy chose a regression in her career rather than a transfer to the operations department where she would have been trained in videotape, because operations employees worked on a system of rotating shifts and Judy was concerned about the potential negative impact on her family life.

The other editor, Tom, was happy to accept a transfer to operations because he saw a bright future there, and his wife assumes his home responsibilities when he's working odd shifts. Tom became a videotape recorder (VTR) operator, which is an entry-level position in operations. The operations supervisor, Dan, told Tom that all new staff in operations had to start as VTR operators. However, Tom knew that when he advanced to a videotape editor job, his film editing experience would provide a good background. Tom received on-the-job training in the new technology and became a videotape editor a few years later.

I remained in the film department. In 1983 I began training as an electronic news gathering (ENG) editor while continuing as the film librarian. ENG is videotape in the industrial half-inch videocassette format. That year, the newsroom was in transition from film to video and both media were used. News editors such as myself had to switch from film to video daily. This change made my job four-fold: editing news on-call in film or video, break-down editing (as needed), and film library research. Guy called me the ideal floater because I was versatile.

In 1984 I applied for a videotape editor job in the operations department because I was concerned about my future in the film department. I heard the same story that Tom had heard four years before: everyone entering Operations must start at the junior level of VTR Operator and work up to videotape editor. The difference was that Tom had no previous video experience when he had entered Operations and I had plenty. However, Dan was consistent and appeared to be treating everyone in operations equally, so I accepted this set-back, rationalizing that the extra video training would support my next application for a videotape editor job.

I was the first woman VTR Operator in the operations department and the atmosphere was hostile. When I walked into master control, the room suddenly became silent: I was not welcome. One sympathetic man said that all my co-workers had expressed unequivocal unwillingness to work with a woman. He added that they often criticized me unfairly behind my back. I began to notice that when I reported a broken machine, it was not repaired. A man's report of the same malfunction received prompt attention. If a machine did not work during my shift, the men assumed I was at fault. But if it broke down while a male VTR operator was working, there had to be something wrong with the machine. Cynthia Cockburn tells us that this deeply embedded male prejudice is common throughout the working world.

> For many men it is unthinkable that women could possess a technical competence equal to their own. Women would have to be paragons of competence to be accepted by male colleagues (Cockburn, 1985, 188).

A year and a half passed. It was a difficult phase because I worked the graveyard shift (midnight to 8 a.m.) three-quarters of the time and I was unable to develop a supportive social life. On the job I was isolated from my colleagues.

During that time, the film department was completely dismantled and absorbed by operations. Dave (the film/ENG editor I had worked with in film) was transferred to a videotape editor job in operations. The position was created especially for him to avoid a lay-off. He made the lateral transfer I had requested and been refused.

By then, Tom had become involved with the union, the National Association of Broadcast Employees and Technicians (NABET). He agreed that the situation was grossly unfair and offered to help me file a grievance. Three weeks later Tom said "We're on shaky ground." He had broached the subject at a meeting of the NABET executive and the president, Joan, had suggested we try to "shame management" into following established policy instead of filling a grievance. The NABET staff representative, Steve, was instructed to speak to management. Nothing happened.

Ten days later Tom approached the company's vice-president, Roy, and the general manager. He told me they were defensive and refused to discuss the situation. In Tom's words, "there was no admission of injustice or remorse. They simply said, 'That's the way we did it'." The vague terminology of the union contract supported the company's actions. NABET lawyers claimed that all points could be argued in favour of management, and the union executive was reluctant to file a grievance.

A month later I had a meeting with Dan, the supervisor in operations. He said that his policy of starting all operations employees as VTR operators had been over-ruled by the company vice-president, Roy (formerly the executive producer in charge of film), and the general manager (formerly the director of the news department). Dave and I had both worked for these men when we were film department employees.

When I began working in operations, the entire staff was comprised of men, ninety-five percent of whom acted as if they were being invaded by a foreign species. The ideology embedded in their daily work told them that I was out of place in technology. They were used to seeing women in front of the camera and on the screen: that is, consumed and objectified by themselves, the viewers. In their midst, I was in control of the machine: that is, in the male role.

Our society's adherence to rigid role-playing, such as the division of labour according to sex, mirrors the mind-body separation evident in pornography. Objectivity and the artificial division of nature from culture are characteristic of both technology and pornography. These two fields bolster one another. The body control evident in pornography, that is, the domination of women and the denial of men's vulnerability, is matched in television technology by men's control of machines and space. From comments I overheard, I know that some of the men with whom I worked in television saw me purely in pornographic terms: "a piece of moisture" or "a bitch." Their need to separate my knowledge and abilities from my sex succeeded in alienating me and motivated them to rationalize my talent as an aberration.

I suffered from reduced self-esteem and my physical health was damaged. The stress of daily confrontations took its toll: I succumbed to burn-out. My doctor ordered a month of rest, but the company was unwilling to grant disability benefits even though I had contributed through pay deductions.

I cannot say that I would encourage young women who are entering the work force to fight their way through this morass of male hostility which is entrenched in the world of television. Is it fair to expect other women to suffer the heavy toll I did? Perhaps by working in technology, women risk expressing their tacit acceptance of the artificial dichotomy of mind/body and nature/culture. Would we be co-opted by those who believe that the public and private spheres can and must be separated? Many feminists believe that entering the technological workforce requires a decision to live by the patriarchal code.

Other feminists would argue that technology can be "humanized" through the inclusion of female professionals in scientific and technical fields. In time, a balanced work environment could be developed and the mind/body, nature/culture split would be healed. On the other hand, by assuming that the presence of women in technical and scientific professions will ensure the recognition of emotions, nature, and spirituality as important aspects of human life, are we not subscribing to the ideology which relegates these "soft" characteristics to women exclusively? Are we implicitly agreeing that women are responsible for the state of all human relations?

In fact, there are signs that this humanizing process is beginning to occur in the field of medicine. Traditionally, medical students, interns, and residents have studied and worked in conditions of high stress, high levels of competition, and severe sleep deprivation. Gruelling work schedules deprive interns and residents of their compassion for sick people. Patients appear to be enemies instead of needy human beings.* A critical movement within the Canadian medical establishment is challenging this dehumanizing educational system. Is it merely

---

* For more on this, see Rosemary Murphy's contribution in this collection.

a coincidence that change has begun just as more women are entering and graduating from medical schools? Perhaps this transformation of our educational system for physicians offers hope for the future improvement of other male-dominated professions.

References

Barry, Kathleen, 1981. *Female Sexual Slavery*. New Jersey: Prentice Hall.

Burstyn, Varda (ed.), 1985. *Women Against Censorship*. Vancouver: Douglas and Macintyre.

Cavell, Stanley, 1979. *The World Viewed*. Cambridge, Mass.: Harvard University Press.

Cockburn, Cynthia, 1985. *Machinery of Dominance, Women, Men, Technical Know-How*. London: Pluto Press.

Dworking, Andrea, 1981. *Pornography: Men Possessing Women*. New York: Putnam.

Faulkner, Wendy, Erik Arnold (eds.), 1985. *Smothered by Invention, Technology in Women's Lives*. London: Pluto Press.

Finn, Geraldine, 1982. "Women and the Ideology of Science," *Our Generation* 15(1)(winter)

——, 1984. "Masculinity, Technology and Power," draft, March.

——, 1985. "Patriarchy and Pleasure: The Pornographie Eye/I," *Canadian Journal of Political and Social Theory*, 9(1-2).

——, 1986. "The Politics of Sex," *The Canadian Forum*, April.

——, 1986. "Sexual Representation and Social Control," *Perception*, 9(4), (March/April).

——, 1986. "Women Against Censorship–A Critical Response," *Canadian Dimension* 20(4) (July-August).

——, 1986. "Against Sexual Imagery, Alternative or Otherwise," *Parallelogramme* 12(1).

Fox-Keller, Evelyn, 1985. *Reflections on Gender and Science*. New York: Yale University Press.

Griffin, Susan, 1981. *Pornography and Silence*. New York: Harper Colophon.

Houston, Beverle, and Marsha Kinder, 1980. *Self and Cinema: A Transformalist Perspective*. Pleasantville, N.Y.: Redgrave.

Kuhn, Annette, 1985. *Women's Pictures, Feminism and Cinema*. London: Routledge and Kegan Paul.

Mackinnon, Catharine A., 1987. *Feminism Unmodified, Discourses on Life and Law*. New York: Harvard University Press.

McIntyre, Sheila, 1987. "Gender Bias Within a Canadian Law School," *Canadian Association for University Teachers Bulletin*. (January):7.

New York University Review of Law and Social Change, 1978-1979. "Colloquim–Violent Pornography: Degradation of Women Versus Right of Free Speech," 8(2).

Ontario Institute for Studies in Education, 1987. "Women and Philosophy," *Resources for Feminist Research* 16(3)(September).

PART TWO

The Politics of Science:
Keeping Women in Their Place

Introduction

Peggy Kelly's essay on "Objectivity and Control: Where Television Technology meets Pornography," chapter 5, started life as a term paper for a course I taught in the winter of 1987 on "Science, Technology and Gender" for the Women's Studies Program at the University of Ottawa. Another student in the same course produced a video for her term "paper," of grade school children talking about science, for which she interviewed each child individually and in private. When asked to describe a scientist, all of these children without exception, including the one or two girls intending to become scientists themselves, described scientists as men: always as "he" and more often than not with beards. This was even though, and again without exception, all of them said "yes" when subsequently asked whether women could be scientists, too. The essays in Part Two of this collection explore the effects and implications of the indisputably masculine face of science and the very real domination and control of its contents, methods, and directions by men. The control extends not only to the theories and practices of science itself but also to the lives of women who are excluded from the knowledge and power base of science. They reveal how the institutions, languages, and methods of "science"—of both the "natural" and the "social" sciences—function to exclude women and women's experience, knowledge, and concerns from the scientific agenda and thereby from the social, political, and economic agenda of what is considered *bona fide* knowledge and research, planning, and development. They show, for example, how the rhetorical commitment of "science" to "objectivity" and "neutrality" masks the political rationality of its practice, which systematically—not accidentally—assumes the standpoint of the powers-that-be and reproduces its hierarchies in its discourses and methods and would-be "objective" research results (hierarchies of rich over poor, man over woman, white over black, reason over emotion, First World over Third World, etc.).

Heather Menzies, in chapter 6, describes how she discovered this for herself in the course of her research into the effects of the *new communications technologies* on women in the paid work force in Canada. She began her research,

116

as any good researcher would, by assuming the appropriate "scientific" approach to the reality she wanted to investigate and developing an appropriate mastery of its language, methods, and tools. And she was successful. She got "good results": respectable and respected "scientifically" sound results which hit the headlines of Canada's national newspapers and earned her a place as "expert" at international conferences dealing with similar issues. It was not until some time later that she "regained consciousness," as she says, and realized what, in fact, she had done by assuming the so-called "objective," "value-neutral" methods of "science" in her research. She had betrayed the women whose interests had originally motivated her research. She had assumed the standpoint of the technological establishment itself, the standpoint of power and "masculinity" rather than and *over against* the standpoint of the women whose experiences and values had been the original focus of her concern. She had been seduced, that is, by "science" and the requirements of authorized speech into situating herself and her knowledge *with the men* at the "centre" of economic and political power and against the workers, the women who remained in their proper place (the place proper to them in our economic system) on its "margins": as its instrumentalities and objects and not as its agents and beneficiaries. Heather describes precisely how this worked in her case and what its consequences were for her research and the workers in question, and she concludes her essay with a discussion of feminist initiatives presently under way in the development of alternative studies and technologies, which draw on the knowledge, values, and expertise of those on the margins of power rather than those at its increasingly dead centres.

Jill Vickers tells a similar story in chapter 7 with reference to her own relationship to the academic discipline of *political science,* showing how it colludes with the patriarchal state in maintaining exclusion of women's interests and concerns and women themselves from the centres of institutionalized power and its communities of authorized knowers. She shows how the very "paradigm" of Political Science, its understanding of what constitutes "politics" and "science," renders both women's specific relationship to political power and feminist interventions in it invisible and/or irrelevant to the political science community. Political science, Jill tells us, did not emerge as a specific intellectual discipline until after World War II in the U.S. It was, and remains, primarily concerned with the institutionalized *processes* of decision-making within and between *states,* rather than the substance and content of those decisions or the actual distribution of political power and privilege within society as a whole. Similarly, it is concerned with the "maintenance of the current order through the management of violence, threats of violence, rewards and ideas" rather than with developing critiques or creative transformations of that order. Women's experience of politics and the environments within which women live their lives are, therefore, invisible to political science with its single-minded focus on the politics of the "public" sphere of the "state," abstracted from, and considered other than, the "private" sphere of home, family, work, school, sexuality, religion, and leisure.

The desire of the political science community to be "scientific" reflects its desire to be perceived as a neutral, non-partisan, non-ideological, non-political community of "objective" experts on the processes of the state. But this appearance is belied, as Jill explains, by the reality of political science's assumption of the standpoint of the state and the perspective of its power-holders in its actual "scientific" practices which serve to confirm and legitimize the "givenness," the "naturalness," of the patriarchal state which the methods of political science do not permit it to question. Jill argues that the political science paradigm is constitutively, and not just accidentally, patriarchal and incapable, therefore, of either absorbing women into the political arena on equal terms with men or of accommodating, or changing in response to, feminist criticisms and interventions in the discipline. She sees political theory as a more hospitable site for the development of feminist alternatives to patriarchal political science and the politics of the patriarchal state(s) it serves, and she reviews some of these feminist possibilities at the end of her essay.

Martha MacDonald, in chapter 8, is a little more optimistic about the possibilities of integrating women's interests and experiences and feminist interventions and alternatives into the scientific paradigm which shapes the priorities and practices of *economics* despite the fact that economics is the most "purely" scientific and the most abstract and mathematical of all the social sciences, as well as the most male-dominated. Like political science, economics assumes the public/private division of experience, knowledge, values, and labour and situates itself unambiguously in the "public" sphere, adopting the standpoint of its power-holders in its approach to the economy: their language and their economic presuppositions and priorities. Like political science, therefore, and the technologies discussed earlier by Heather Menzies, economics takes abstract man (men, that is) as its norm of humanity: "public man" abstracted from the concrete social, emotional, and physical context of what is then called "personal" or "private" life. Economists, like political scientists, only "see" women when women appear and behave like men in the "public" sphere: do the same kinds of jobs as men in the paid work force, create the same kind of economic demands and values. Otherwise, as far as economists are concerned, what women do has no relevance to the economy. Economic activities and concerns specific to women located in the so-called "private" sphere and "non-productive" service sectors—things like domestic labour, childcare, shopping, cooking, volunteer work, and demands for pay equity or welfare rights, for example—are invisible to economists and thus excluded from their calculations of the GNP (The Gross National Product) and their determination of national economic policies and priorities. As a result, women's specific economic behaviours, interests, and demands have no presence in and no reality for the academic discipline of economics, just as their specific political behaviours, interests, and demands have no reality for or relevance to the academic discipline of political science. Little wonder, then, that these two disciplines continue to be so thoroughly dominated by men.

Because women's relationship to the economy is mediated through their location in what men call the "private" sphere and through their perceived status as adjuncts of men's "personal" lives, women's economic activities still do not appear in "public" consciousness as appropriate issues for the nation's economic and political agendas. On the contrary, they appear on the "public" agenda as "social" or "personal" problems peculiar to women and better suited to the attentions of professionals like psychologists, social workers, lawyers, and educators than economists or politicians. Thus, the problems women have with an economy which does not take them into account become problems the economy has with women, who must therefore be adjusted to it with the help of an array of welfare services devoted to this end. (Nancy Guberman and Michèle Bourgon say more about this in their essay on feminism and social work, in chapter 17.)

Martha describes the dominant neoclassical economic paradigm in her essay and shows how its singular focus on the model of the economy as a marketplace in which rational individuals exchange goods and services for money and make free but constrained choices to maximize their own well-being and interests leaves women out and renders economics incapable of understanding women's relationship to the economy if and when they do appear. The best classical economics can do, for instance, is explain the wage inequalities between men and women in terms of the domestic division of labour and women's responsibility for "reproduction" in the home and the domestic division of labour within the home in terms of wage inequalities between men and women in the paid work force! She believes the alternative marxist economic paradigm (which she describes) holds out more promise for getting feminists' and women's concerns onto the economic agenda because it does, at least, recognize the political contexts within which individual economic choices are made and the politics of the family in particular. She comments, however, that most of the useful work in this area has been done by sociologists rather than economists and is more likely to appear in interdisciplinary Women's Studies courses than it is in the regular curricula of either economics or sociology departments. Martha concludes by calling upon the women's movement to take on economists and the economy directly: to master their jargon and confront their experts with the realities of women's absolutely indispensable contribution to the "public" economy and their stake in its research and development; and thereby to transform both the economy and the would-be "science" of economics so that they take into account the full economic picture, including the full participation of women in the economy of the household and the various "informal" economies, along with their activity in the more restricted "economy" of the marketplace.

The next essay in this section, chapter 9, addresses the question of the *sexism of science* more directly. It takes the form of an imaginary letter from the writer Marilyn MacDonald to her niece, Lisa, who is about to start a science degree at a Canadian university. Through a detailed explanation and analysis of the ideals, methods, institutions, and knowledge of modern science—its commitment to "objectivity," for example: to abstraction, fragmentation, observation, measurement, prediction and control—Marilyn demonstrates how science is sexist to its very roots and not simply in its particular uses and abuses: to its political and historical roots in European imperialism and colonization (of both women and the "world"; the world as Woman and Woman as the world) and its philosophical and conceptual roots in the ideology of Man as Sovereign of the Earth (second only to God). She shows how the ideology informing Science divides Man and Mind from Woman and Nature and simultaneously entitles Man-Mind to sovereignty over both: over Woman as Nature and Nature as Woman.

Against this misogynist and imperialist paradigm of male-stream science (the constitutive details of which closely parallel the requirements of contemporary masculinity: objectivity, abstraction, mastery of body, environment and emotions) Marilyn outlines the possibilities of a feminist alternative: a way of knowing which would aim for creativity rather than control, and co-operation rather than mastery, which would respect and encourage diversity, difference, ambiguity and change instead of reducing all differences to preconceived systems of binary oppositions. Such systems always work to legitimize the domination of one term over another by constituting differences as binary, hierarchical, and exclusive; as man *or* emotion, mind *or* object, etc. Patriarchy relies on such polarities and both reproduces and legitimizes them in the discourses and practices of its various "sciences," as the essays in this section will show. Getting more women into "Science" as it is presently defined and practised will not, therefore, solve the problem of the sexism in Science which, as Marilyn so clearly shows, runs much deeper than the question of its personnel. A much more profound and radical transformation of the ideals, methods, institutions and practices of "science" is required, a transformation both prefigured in and initiated by the essays in this section.

The final contribution to Part Two of this collection, chapter 10, anticipates a not-too-distant future—the turn of the century, perhaps—in which some of these systematic and structural changes in "science" and in the organization of the economy in particular (in how we study and transform it) have already started to take place—not through the wisdom or initiatives of policy-makers and "professionals" at the centre of the economy, whose privilege, power and place in the "public" sphere protect them from the ravages of their own decision-making, but through the practical initiatives of the people on its margins: the women and under- and unemployed men "at home." The narrator of Suzanne MacKenzie's short story, which explores the relationship between *urban design,* economics and the imagination, remembers a time in her past (our present) when "work" and "home," "public" and "private," "social and "personal" life were divided from each other both physically and conceptually. They occurred at different times and places and necessitated a great deal of movement of individuals and populations between the designated sites: from home to work to school to shopping to recreation to places of healing, socializing and so forth. She reflects on how and why these artificial divisions between and within human lives appeared in our history (alongside industrialization) and how and why they came to be associated with differences between men and women—men who "work" in the "public" sphere and women who stay "at home"—as if this reflected some "natural" division of labour, function, tendencies, and talents between the sexes—as if, that is, environment and economy merely adapted themselves to differences between men and women rather than vice versa. The narrator looks back on the deepening economic recession of the eighties and nineties (on our times) and the inability of professional economists to offer any effective remedies as alternatives to it. Alongside this failure of authorized knowers and planners, she describes the emergence of creative, co-operative, collective, localized non-market economies among the under- and unemployed, invisible to the official politicians and economists. These alternative economies are based on exchange and barter, collective ownership and control, and the sharing of resources and skills, and effectively bridge those gaps between "public" and "private," "personal" and "political," "work" and "recreation" which determine not only the shape of our present and failing economy but also the configuration of our environments, social relations, consciousness and imagination, as well as our very particular oppression as women.

Suzanne's short story shows how environments reflect economic prescriptions and priorities and limit our ability to imagine or even desire alternatives. It also shows how the environments we live in will have to change in response to feminist understandings of the structures and conditions of women's subordination, exploitation, and oppression. The alternative integrated economies she anticipates, for example, entail a rather thorough reorganization of buildings and environment: the knocking-down of walls within and between private homes and properties which nobody can afford to keep anymore, and their transformation, along with abandoned garages, car parks, shopping precincts, and apartment and office buildings into communal gardens, nurseries, schools, libraries, health centres, laundries, kitchens, sports facilities, etc. Her story also demonstrates just how and why Women's Studies is and must be inter- (or anti-) disciplinary in its approach to producing both knowledge of and effective interventions in patriarchal social reality and the specific and complex relationships of women to it. At the same time, it illustrates how and why feminism as a politics and a movement is not "just" about "women's" issues, narrowly defined, but about the whole of society in all its various forms, contents, and structures, starting from and in relation to the position, experience, and knowledge of women but not restricted to it. These aspects of feminism and women's studies are discussed in greater detail in a number of different contexts in Part Three, which focuses on the politics of knowledge in general and the difference feminism makes to its contents and methods in particular: to what counts as literature and literary criticism, for example, the appropriate duties and responsibilities of social workers, the proper subject and method of sociological investigation.

Chapter 6

Home on the Margin: Toward a Feminist Understanding of Technology

Heather Menzies

TECHNOLOGY. Webster's dictionary describes it as the application of scientific knowledge to commere and industry. Funk and Wagnall's defines it as applied knowledge, particularly in industry. The Oxford Dictionary talks about a discourse, particularly about the industrial arts and crafts.

The images that spring to mind are of factories and assembly lines, not bathtubs and rolling pins; patentable knowledge, not baby-weaning advice passed on by word of mouth.

If the dictionary definitions were more open and inclusive, simply saying technology is "applied knowledge" or "know-how," these other senses of technology might have come through. But the dictionaries emphasize one type of know-how over the others: specifically, techniques and other knowledge applied for the purpose of industrial production within a capitalist market economy. One of the values running this economy is control through domination and an attendant hierarchical ranking from the centre to the margins. Whether or not this value preceded industrialism, its application in the rise of the industrial market economy corresponded with the marginalization of women in society as well as the denigration of women and of the social characteristics commonly associated with women. The two have reinforced each other from generation to generation through the structures of industrial society, showing up even in such seemingly value-neutral media as dictionaries.

Consulting these dictionaries, women are directed by the definition provided there. This first means adopting its view that industrial technology is the most important and that any other technologies the women might know about—everyday know-how to do with food or fitness; birth-control devices such as the pill or IUD; or medical technologies such as valium and other drugs, if they qualify to be called "technology" at all—are obviously pretty marginal, pretty unimportant in the larger scheme of things.

Adjusting first to the dictionary's perspective that only industrial technology counts, women then adjust to its organizational structure. If they want to

Thanks to Marilyn MacDonald for valuable advice and inspiration.

influence technological choices, they have to individually overcome the histori-cal exclusion of women from industry, master the masculine-identified skills associated with it, and work their way up the career ladder to where technological choices are controlled.

But of course, only so many can make it to the centre, and these are likely to be the most competitive, the most adept in technical skills and thinking. The systemic discrimination latent in the dictionary definitions then fulfils its prophecy. Women, marginalized in the dictionary definitions of technology, are equally marginalized in the practical application of technology as well. And women reproduce that marginalization every time they adjust themselves to technology on its terms: at the level of authoritative definitions as well as computer systems installed in offices, factories, hotels, and nursing homes.

That, in a nutshell, is why technology is an urgently feminist issue. But to reverse the trend of women being adjusted to the central conceptions of technology, feminists must first understand how that trend is effected through the centre-margin ranking built into the formulations. Only then can we begin to reform the conception of technology from within and rehabilitate a broader, more inclusive, more open-ended technology before a sense of other possibilities is extinguished. That sense and those other possibilities are fading fast as more and more women and life activities are adjusted out of the value set of the old home- and community-centred economy and assimilated into the mainstream industrial model with its centre-margin mechanisms of rationale and control.

Most of this chapter will deal with the mainstream industrial technologies, especially computerization in office work and how it marginalizes and excludes women at the levels of both perception and daily experience. Following this "de-construction" critique, the chapter will end by sketching in some of the feminist efforts toward a positive re-construction of technology as flexible, participatory, and democratic. In the words of Dr. Ursula Franklin, paraphrasing Fritz Schumacher, "technology as if people matter" (Franklin, 1984). Technology as if women and children matter!

Turning back to the dictionary definitions, there are a couple of things missing, even from the definition of technology as narrowly "industrial." For instance, there's no reference to social structures: to institutions and the people in them who control which technologies will be developed, how they will be used, and, of course, how they will be written up in dictionaries to frame the public discourse and perception of technology.

The definitions portray technology at the level of tool, implying that people are free to use technology as they wish. Yet most modern technology operates at the level of system, through complex social structures such as governments and corporations which institutionalize certain applications of technology; for exam-ple, roads structured as an urban freeway system with its limited exits and entrances and built-in trade-off of flexibility for speed. Paralleling this, it also operates as "discourse," through the established knowledge systems of dictionaries, conferences, and the like which are associated with the public portrayal of technology. What technology will be developed, as well as how it will be portrayed and perceived publicly, these are decided at the centre of the technological system, with little control available at the margins, which is where most people, and certainly most women, experience technology. One buys into the freeway system with its built-in choices and priorities almost at the point when one buys a car. Yet the public perception of cars—as liberty and freedom—obscures this.

Women don't have problems with technology at the level of tool. What technophobia we have can usually be quickly overcome. Witness Rosie the Riveter[1] and her counterparts who womanned the machinery of the war-time economy while the men were away fighting. Witness, too, the joy of liberation around women graduating from simple computer-literacy workshops. They laugh and shout with glee: "I can do it; I can do it."

Of course women can do it, given the chance to control the technology, given the power to use it as a tool, as an extension of their bodies, minds, and values. The problem lies with the chance to be in control. By and large women don't get it, for it's locked away within the structures associated with technology as system, which pre-frames the choice of what tool will be used, and how.

A good portion of women's experience of technology is of this sort, on the receiving end of technology as a system designed and decided on by others. The control women exercise using technology (computers) in the office, consuming it (chemically-sprayed vegetables) in the kitchen, and even "choosing" it (the pill or the IUD) in the bedroom is often a highly limited one. Choice often translates as the equivalent of the A, B, or C options on a multiple-choice questionnaire. Sometimes the choice—the birth-control pill or unwanted pregnancy, *in vitro* fertilization or infertility—seems to offer no choice at all. The technology seems even to reduce women's control over the situation, in this case control over our own bodies, given the nature of the choices offered. But the language used to describe these technologies (the pill as "sexual liberation," and *in vitro* fertilization as "solution" or even "salvation") steers women's perceptions away from this. In effect, the rhetoric accompanying the technology marginalizes women's own private perceptions and installs the established public perception in their place.

I experienced this myself—essentially having my perceptions restructured by the technology—when I began back in 1980 to research women's worries about technology in the workplace. I began by taking the dictionary definition at face value and the advice of a friend who suggested that what I wrote would carry more weight if it were published by a research institute with established credentials in the international debate on technological change. In case I didn't realize it, Canadian policymakers were taking their cues from this international debate, so if I wanted to influence their thinking I had to position myself within this official discourse—within their field of vision, so to speak.

It hadn't occurred to me that there was such a debate going on and that I should try to be part of it. My concern about technology had stemmed from something concrete and quite local to Canada: as computers and sophisticated telecommunications equipment were being installed through the corporate economy and as information was moving from paper to electronic form, companies with branch plants in Canada were exploiting the capacity to move electronic information cheaply over telephone wires and were centralizing a lot of their information-processing work into their U.S. head office. The phenomenon was called "trans-border data flows" or international data services, and it was indicative of the immense power of the new computer-communications technology to restructure information work. Restructuring, from the perspective of the senior managers in the central office, meant rationalizing operations around the globe for maximum efficiency, productivity, and central control. From the perspective of the local secretarial and administrative staff on the receiving end of these new technologies, it often meant wrenching change. From having had some measure of control over paper-based files of information and steady, if not always challenging work—typing, filing, and organizing the flow of information through the local office—these women (and some men) were seeing their jobs being de-skilled, downgraded, and even disappearing. Yet over a third of working women in this country depend on this sort of work (clerical work, administrative-support work) for employment.

I was determined to sound a public alarm about their situation, and to do so effectively. I vowed to adjust myself to whatever forum had already been established for authoritatively warning that alarm bells should be rung. I took my friend's advice and approached a prestigious research institute, the Institute for Research on Public Policy.

There, the director of research directed my attention to the established discourse, i.e., a pile of research reports, conference papers, and books which stood nearly as tall as myself. At first the words blurred; the discussion seemed to have nothing to do with the women I had talked to. I'd sit there reading about "innovation," "productivity gain," "diffusion rate," "reduced manpower content," and "social impacts," and I'd hear the women's voices inside my head telling me, as in one instance where a regional office was closed altogether: "They treated the machines better than they treated us."

Eventually my perspective swung around. Instead of trying to find words and frames of reference which would fit what the women had to say, I adjusted the women to fit the words and established frames of reference. The women's voices—their experiences as they experienced them—began to seem out of place in the discussion, and they faded away.

At the time I didn't even notice. I was completely immersed in the established discourse, what I would later come to understand as a technological system in its own right, a mirror image of the one under discussion and particularly faithful in reflecting its priorities, not just in its framing of the issues and thus its phrasing of the policymaking agenda, but even in the rational language used in the discussion.

I slipped unthinkingly into the established grooves and pigeonholes for discussion. The women I had interviewed became X number of "clerical workers." Just as their existence in the workplace was recognized only in terms of their usually restricted function there—not running the place, but executing one pre-specified operation as a teller, typist, or telephone operator—so I went along with naming them in the discourse only as "statistical units in sociological categories" (Smith, 1974).

I only realized later how much I'd helped to marginalize the women by adopting this language, by participating in the "conceptual imperialism" (Smith, 1974) built into the language of the official discourse. It was only later that I understood that imperial administrations and contemporary technological systems are variations on very similar themes. The margins being defined around, and only in relation to, the central concerns of the discourse parallels the metropolis-hinterland phenomenon of imperialism. In this case, the economic, social, and even cultural life of the hinterland, or colonies, are redefined according to the values and priorities of the imperial metropolis or power: material priorities such as fur, fish and timber, and values such as the Protestant ethic promulgated by, for instance, the Family Compact of Upper Canada.[2]

I also found parallels between the "colonial mentality" associated with the inability to define oneself outside the limits of what would accommodate the powers that be and the consciousness-shaping powers of technological systems. Marshall McLuhan teasingly called this technology's "power to massage you," to "work you over" (McLuhan, 1967). It's the power to fine-tune your mind-set like a TV, to bring your thinking into harmony with the values and priorities of technology, and those who own and control it; or at least to mute any dissonance.

I didn't realize at the time how much I was adjusting myself as well as the women I was concerned about: abandoning the authority of my own authentic perceptions and impassioned reactions to adopt the perception-lens and voice— that is, abstract concepts and proper methodological grammar—of the official discourse. Then, I felt all the élan of a young woman having mastered the techniques of flirting: simply delighted at knowing how to play the game, to speak the language. I could talk "redundancies," "de-skilling," and "displacements of clerical workers" with the best of them, spouting statistics on long-term unemployment prospects big enough for banner headlines.

As I wrote up my research, I congratulated myself for my maturity. I'd overcome the quirky habit of structuring my writing any old way that seemed appropriate to what I had observed and, in observing, felt. Now, having familiarized myself with what the established authorities on technological change were saying, I positioned myself within their frame of reference—the better to speak their language, then to be heard, recognized and invited into the discourse myself.

The frame of reference had long been established as a market-economics one. Technology was officially understood, by government and business leaders alike, as a key to innovation and labour-saving productivity, and both were crucial to economic growth. Growth being progress, and progress being a *Good Thing*, technology came to be synonymous with progress. The words automation and modernization were even used interchangeably in the literature. Efficiency was another popular word: efficiency in modern technological society was seen as a *Good Thing*, a value in and of itself, quite divorced from the social context.

This frame of reference was the forum at which messengers from the social context began to appear. But if they were to be let in and recognized within the established discourse, that is, if they were to be invited as speakers and delegates to the big international conferences sponsored by such prestigious bodies as the Organization for Economic Cooperation and Development (OECD), these more socially and sociologically-oriented people had to speak the same language. They had to fit into the agenda set by the organizers (generally economists with established credentials in the international discourse and the big international institutions sponsoring it) and the themes set out by the keynote speakers. These, too, tended to be economists; for example, Dr. Christopher Freeman of the Social Policy Research Unit at the University of Sussex in England whose first major (as in "recognized") work on technological change was sponsored by the OECD. Those who were invited to speak at conferences and to contribute to government reports, etc., were those who adapted themselves to the built-in biases of the economic frame of reference and talked not of the social uses of technology but of the social "impacts" of the economic uses of technology (impacts as in after-the-fact and secondary to the main point, side-effects marginal to the main economic effect). In other words, technological innovation for economic growth; any social effects were incidental. The centre-margin bias was built into the debate.

It was taken as given that "typically, technological decisions are also economic decisions" (MacKenzie & Wajcman, 1985, 14), i.e., that economics is the axis around which technological decisions and related discussions shall turn. An IRPP report to which my research, *Women and the Chip*, was billed as a sequel concluded that "women...are expected to bear the brunt of the impact..." (Zeman, 1979).

A review of *Sociological Abstracts* demonstrated the pattern. Sociologists had been writing for years about women's participation in the labour force in terms of the labour force not in terms of the women themselves. For example, the theory of "intermittent labour-force attachment" (Barnes & Jones, 1974) talked about women's tendency to have jobs—typist, teller, telephone operator—rather than careers and for those jobs to require relatively little preparatory education. The explanation offered was that women's family responsibilities caused them to move in and out of the workforce intermittently through their adult lives. Accordingly, they didn't have the time or the inclination to make a huge "investment" in career preparation nor commitment to a career which required taking initiative and shouldering a lot of responsibility.

Women returning to the workforce weren't defined as bringing immense managerial talents from the home- and community-economies into the industrial economy but only in relation to the industrial economy. With that economy at the centre of the definition, these women were described therefore as "re-entry women."*

Mainstream sociologists merely carried on the tradition of defining social experience from a perspective other than the one of the people experiencing it. They wrote about the "social impacts" caused by technological change and the "social adjustments" required of women by it. The assumption that women should adjust to technology, and not technology to women, was built into the structures of the discussion. The idea of challenging technological change itself never came up, or wasn't allowed into the official discourse; not even in sociological journals. For sociologists learn "to think sociology as it is thought, and to practise it as it is practised... The boundaries of enquiry are thus set within the framework of what is already established, by men" (Smith, 1984, 8). The framework works like a cookie cutter, channelling thoughts as effectively and seemingly innocuously as the pastry cutter. If you want to be recognized, if you want to be published, then you adjust to the system of that established discourse. If you don't get published in the journals associated with the official discourse, then you don't get taken seriously, you don't get recognized, and you don't get tenure as an academic; you're silenced and forgotten on the sidelines.

My contribution to the sociological aspects of the economics-centred discourse on technological change (officially phrased as the "long-term social impacts of technological change") was to express women's problem as a function of their concentration in dead-end clerical job ghettos—teller, typist, telephone operator—and to call for retraining and occupational bridging schemes. I suggested that this apply not just to women in the workforce now but also to "re-entry" women as well. Again and again, I adjusted women to the existing categories, themselves a rendering of the centre-margin dynamic in the organization of work. The point wasn't women's experience as women, but as abstract support workers being redefined into redundancy by technological innovation for productivity gains and economic growth; then, in turn, they would be redefined into cases of techno-phobia or candidates for re-training. The women

---

*Martha MacDonald analyzes women's 'invisible' relationship to the 'economy' in this collection.

as women, as people, had never entered into it. They were defined only in relation to the workplace and its technologies. By definition, therefore, they and their point of view were secondary, marginal, and therefore a side-issue.

The compromise of confidentiality (un-named sources) in return for co-operation in the research process, plus the pressure to generalize for the sake of making sweeping statistical predictions, took me further from the particular context, not just from specific towns and specific companies but from the biases and values of the specific people who were designing and introducing techno-logical change in very particular ways. These people—primarily engineers, primarily men—were the subjects, the agents, of technological change; the women were the objects.

Instinct told me that it would be appropriate to include the response of the personnel manager in one company when I asked what he planned to do about the hundreds of clerical workers made redundant by the automated information system being introduced at the time. He shrugged his shoulders and said offhandedly: "I guess they'll go to wherever redundant clerical workers go."

His indifference seemed an important research finding. But then, I myself had used the abstraction "clerical worker" with its built-in indifference to a real, live person.

In the end, I adapted myself completely to the established technology—largely simply by having adapted to its language—for establishing knowledge in the official discourse. I stripped away all references to context and absolved or "abolished" all agency (Vickers, 1982). Blithely I climbed the ladder of gener-alization and abstraction to predict that up to a million women (existing and would-be clerical workers) could be unemployed by 1990 if nothing was done to help them: specifically, to help them adjust to technology on its terms.

At the time I didn't feel I'd betrayed the women by helping to marginalize them in the discourse. I'd brought them into the discourse at least, albeit on the terms set down by the discourse rather than their own terms. But I didn't feel accountable to the women. I didn't even particularly feel for them. They had become this amorphous hysterical abstraction. (One million unemployed by 1990!!! In 1981, it made headlines all across the country.) As real women living in a particular place and time, they had disappeared, along with their subjective statements and my subjective response to them. If I was accountable to anything beyond a front-page headline, which would confirm the success of my attempt to sound an alarm, it was only to the gatekeepers of knowledge at the research institute which made me an overnight "expert" and "authority" on technological change by publishing my report. Their *"Good Housekeeping"* seal of approval seemed to satisfy the various government bodies, unions, and professional groups who convened conferences on technological change over the next few months and years and who breathlessly asked my advice on how women could adjust to high technology and avoid an ignominious future as redundant clerical workers. A gratifying array of microphones, as well as invitations to conferences and attendant honoraria, seemed to confirm that the answers I provided were both authoritative and appropriate.

When I regained consciousness, as Segeant Renfrew of CBC Radio's Airfarce would say, I discovered that if I hadn't actually sold out, I had certainly served as an accomplice in my own hostage-taking. The discourse had drifted into a limbo of futures speculation, with the official "jury" still "out" on what the long-term employment effects of technological change would be. There was money to be made continuing to research the social impacts of technological change, but the exercise was beginning to smack of "make-work." The social question of technological change had fulfilled the prophecy inherent in its having been cast in terms marginal to the main economic questions and had marginalized both the people raising the question and what they were trying to say.

As I sat there wondering what had happened, the worst was knowing that I had contributed to this marginalization by abandoning my own centre, my own sense of what the point of the discussion was all about. In adjusting myself to gain credibility and recognition within the official discourse, I had lost my own sense of the main points, the important issues.

Thinking back, I could recall many instances where what I'd wanted to say hadn't fit smoothly into either the language or the structures for portraying it. Then I'd interpreted these as my inadequacy in the discourse rather than the discourse's inadequacy. Now as I talked to other women with similar stories to tell, I joined them in faulting the discourse, its rigidities, and biases. I even began to take these dissonances as clues to the existence of another perspective, a possible feminist discourse on technological change which would radically transform mainstream technology and its agenda.

As one example, when I'd give a speech on the social impacts of technological change, the flow of the speech took me from an analysis of women's concentration in clerical job ghettos through an explanation of how automation was gutting employment in those ghettos and on to a shopping list of measures for adjusting women to a more promising future in high-technology. The logic of the speech somehow prevented me from addressing the physical effects of low-level radiation associated with computer terminals: in addition to chronic headaches, backaches, and blurred vision, there was the traumatic experience of birth defects in children born to women who operated computer terminals while pregnant (de Matteo, 1985). It took years before some conclusive proof linked fetal defects and even deaths to computer-related radiation (Roseman, 1987). Meanwhile, women were left with the burden of proof, the technology was given the benefit of the doubt, and the whole issue was marginalized by being labelled a "health and safety" issue to be considered by experts in such matters, separate from the main issue of long-term job and productivity effects associated with technological change.

Similarly, in a speech treating jobs as numbers and abstractions, it was hard to work in more than a mention of de-skilling (the computer controlling more of the work process) and computer monitoring (the computer keeping track of how fast you worked, when you took a break, and for how long, through the automatic functioning of its electronic memory). The former issue was officially phrased as a loss of skills, to be solved through retraining. The latter was given the official name of "loss of privacy," to be solved through privacy codes etc. However, if these issues hadn't been sidelined into the question-and-answer period or separate workshops; if all the effects of technological change had been considered—the unintended as well as the intended—and if they had remained concrete instead of being abstracted under side-lining labels, a very different understanding, and a different agenda, might have emerged.

But the point is, that never happened. At conference after conference, the format was the same; the result was the same.

Now, feminists with many shared experiences of exclusion from or marginalization in mainstream academic conferences, of being told that the inadequacy lies with them—that their data isn't objective or their theory not firmly grounded in the discourse—are beginning to understand why they can't get their points across. The problem is not with women as academics but with the academic discourse which isn't open enough to women's perspectives. The product of what is said is controlled through the discussion process: the structures, the rules, the language of the established discourse. To open up the possibilities of other perspectives, other knowledge, other understandings and other social agendas, we must first open up the discourse. To do that, to break the cookie-cutter moulds, we must show how they work. That's the "de-construction" work.

As I began to deconstruct my own experiences of being worked over by technology, I discovered others doing similar work. Elaine Bernard has held up history to challenge the rhetorical ribbons in which computers and word processors are presented to women as "liberating" them from the "drudgery" of retyping. A century ago, the self-styled "father" of the typewriter, Christopher Shoales, thought he should be thanked for "liberating" women from the drudgery of manual copying (Bernard, 1984). Yet the progressive promise of word processors and office computers for women shows signs of remaining unfulfilled, just as Shoales did a century ago, and for the same reason: the women operating word processors and typewriters have not been free to use the technology as they wish any more than the women before them were free to use their quill pens for anything more creative than manual copying. The restrictive job descriptions, and attendant wages, continue to limit women's use of the modern technologies to tasks or to choices defined by others. The marginalization of women is re-enacted in a computerized setting because the marginalization is built into the organizational structures and the scientific management that controls it, centralizing the power of decision making and marginalizing the work of supporting and executing those decisions (Braverman, 1974).

Anne Pappert is among other feminists critiquing technologies by demonstrating how their rhetorical packaging structures or pre-conceives our perception of them. She has unearthed history's comment on the "side effects" of using the inter-uterine device (IUD): pelvic scarring and even sterility. According to her research (Pappert, 1986), when the IUD was introduced in the early 1900s, its association with pelvic infection quickly led to its rejection. But the technology was rehabilitated in the 1960s, largely by the New York-based Population Council who held conferences hailing the IUD as the perfect tool for population control in the Third World. "(O)ne conference participant, the esteemed gynecologist, Robert Wilson, told the conference, 'if we look at this from an overall long-range view—these are things I never said out loud before and I don't know how it is going to sound—perhaps the individual patient is expendable in the general scheme of things, particularly if the infection she acquires is sterilizing and not lethal'" (Pappert, 1986).*

Ruth Schwartz Cowan has plumbed the mystery of why women still spend about the same amount of time on housework today as their foremothers did before all the modern "labour-saving" technologies associated with housework were invented. The reason is that the imagery surrounding the technology subtly imposed on women higher and higher standards in cleaning, baking, household decorating, etc. (Cowan, 1983). When women buy a Cuisinart, they buy into the gourmet standard of home eating, which it helps make easier to achieve but nonetheless, subtly imposes.

Other writers point out that when the economy was more life-centred rather than market- and military-centred as it is now (Mumford, 1966), women were recognized as major shapers and users of technology: for cheese and beer-making, soap and candle making, and so on.

Pat Armstrong has integrated an understanding of women's marginal role in industrial-age production work with that of their dependency in reproductive work (the work entailed in having children and looking after them). She argues that the segregation of women in the work world can best be understood as a function of the subordination of women in a patriarchal society[3] (Armstrong, 1984). This would suggest that the centre-margin dynamic built into technological systems is a function of a larger societal dynamic of control expressed universally as domination-subordination through gender relations.

Through what has become a network of friends and friends of friends around the world, I've learned more about the material construction of technology. For instance, Dr. Ursula Franklin has shed some interesting historical light on the social forces shaping the evolution of technology through her pioneering work

---

* See also *Side-Effects*, a dramatic exploration of the uses and abuses of women by the pharmaceutical industry.

opening up the new inter-disciplinary science of archaeological metallurgy. She's discovered that the escalation of metalworking from hand-craft scale to the mass scale associated with metal manufacturing, for example, in the case of bronze work in early China, virtually required a large, centrally-organized and controlled labour force (slavery) for the labour-intensive and dangerous mining and smelting work involved; metal manufacturing didn't just appear (Franklin, 1983).

Today, computers are often presented as a given, purely a technical artifact. Yet they don't spring fully-formed from the backrooms of computer stores and trade shows. They come off a dirty, noisy electronic assembly line in free-trade zones in "under-developed" countries such as Indonesia, Malaysia, and the Philippines, where under-paid and often under-nourished young women work for nine and ten hours a day. Their work consists of bonding chips onto circuit boards with a soldering iron, while peering down a microscope for several hours at a stretch; coating these circuit boards with an epoxy resin and baking them; and testing the finished board in a chemical bath, which burns the skin while the vapors burn the lungs. For this they are paid as little as 35 cents (U.S.) an hour. The working conditions are dangerous and the living conditions, in barracks where the women rent bed and cupboard space supplied by the companies, aren't much better. Attempts to unionize are either forbidden or, at times, brutally put down. The women usually only last in these jobs for a few years, by which time their eyesight has deteriorated, as has their general health (Ehrenreich, 1982; Shriad, 1982).

My journey out to the margins was completed when I retrieved the perception that women are involved in technology everywhere. It's only the structuring of technology and our perceptions of it that makes them disappear or become marginal, not central enough to be significant.

Now, in a feminist discourse centred on women's experience of technology, the women have come clamouring back into the picture: those in impoverished countries of Southeast Asia making advanced electronics; those in history, manufacturing soap and cheese; those processing information in computerized office buildings all around the world; those in biotechnology research labs scraping petri dishes; and those in "infertility clinics" executing the operations involved in *in vitro* fertilization; those in the factories, the hotels, private houses, and public nursing homes.

The feminist discourse includes the human-scale, often hand-powered technologies such as maize-shelling devices, water pumps, and solar dryers, which women still use in subsistence economies of the so-called Third World. While these are ignored in the mainstream discourse or are side-lined under the label "low technology," they are called "social technologies" in the feminist discourse (R. Sandhu and J. Sandler, 1986).

The term aptly applies to the pre-industrial technologies which women developed around home-based bread-making, cheese-making, beer-making, spinning, and weaving. In researching the history of cheddar cheese-making in rural Ontario, I've found evidence that women pioneered many techniques and tools in dairying and cheese-making long before the industrialization of the craft moved the work off the farm into factories and turned the work into a business run by men (Oxford County Board of Education, 1979). Yet women's role and women's technology aren't mentioned in any of the official histories of dairying and cheese-making in Ontario, such as that of Canada's pre-eminent economic historian Harold Innis who grew up on a dairy farm in Oxford County, Ontario, where women played a formative role in the cheese industry (see Innis, 1947).

The historical record serves as final proof of the gender biases built into technology and discussions about it. It also serves as a reference point for restructuring technology around broadly social goals. Retrieving women's historical experience with technology, learning from it, and applying its lessons is therefore a vital part of the feminist discourse.

Reconstructing the present discourse on technology means letting women out of the conceptual boxes of "clerical worker," etc. in which they have been shut up and sidelined and letting them speak for themselves. In some cases, this has taken the form of film, heretofore a structure of knowledge and information banned from consideration as part of the "discourse." Yet the participatory documentary film called *"Quel Numero/What number?"* by Sophie Bissonnette (Bissonnette, 1985) contributes authentic perceptions of technology and its present practice (and malpractice).

The film helped send me back to some of the telephone operators whose jobs disappeared when Bell Canada automated long-distance telephoning, centralized its operations, and closed its switchboard at Midland, Ontario. Listening to them, I found that an entire conception of telephone service had been silenced with the closure. Although the company defined them and paid them only as switchboard operators, the women, as women living in a particular community with a particular social reality, defined themselves as providing a community information service. Forgetful old ladies dialed "0" when they couldn't remember where the beauty parlour was. A blind man called for help in finding local numbers.

As these women described their vision of telephony, I could imagine a very different evolution of telephone technology had their conception of community information and referral service been allowed influence (Menzies, 1989, 229).

Centering myself in a sense of solidarity with all the people on the margins of technology—in Southeast Asia and in Canadian homes and workplaces—I can also imagine that a policy on how technology should be organized in society, based on the perspective of all these people, would not be one based on ranking. Its perspective would be that of margins without centres, democratic and pluralist in the best sense of the words.

But having initiated a feminist discussion on technology, how does one move this from the sidelines to empower social change at the centre?

So far only this much is clear. Feminists are at once exiles ("ontological exiles," Vickers, 1982) within the existing technological society and immigrants (Franklin, 1984) carrying the sparks of other possible conceptions of technology, much as immigrants carry the customs, language, and values of homeland in their hearts. To achieve more than a ghetto status for those conceptions, feminists must return to the official discourse, to reform its technology from within.

As one possible example of this, I will end with the story of a graduate student at Carleton University, Ottawa. Knowing the dangers of assimilation into the mainstream language of the official discourse, Suzanne Bastedo Renaud committed herself to the women whose experiences she wanted to represent authoritatively in a Master's thesis. This thesis looked at women's attitudes towards technology and employed a multiple-choice questionnaire as the "research instrument." Users of such questionnaires are advised to tabulate the box scores and process them through complex statistical analysis and to ignore any marginal comments. But Suzanne couldn't ignore the marginalia: the voices of the women kept bursting out of the directed choices to say, just by doing so, that these were inadequate, that they gagged the women and misrepresented their views and experience. As we talked one day, she began to re-think her perception of the questionnaire as neutral, objective methodology and recognize it as technology operating as system: directing and controlling creation of knowledge from within the information-generating device of the multiple-choice questionnaire. Tugged toward and finally determined to be accountable to what these women had scribbled in the margins, bearing witness to the directedness of the multiple-choice research instrument, Suzanne declared that the marginalia had been as significant as the X marks in the boxes. She described what she'd done— moving the marginalia out from the shadows and into the centre of the discussion—as "transformed technology" (Renaud, 1986). And she got her degree.

The feminist discourse continues to grow, opening like a flower.

Notes:

1. Originally the name of a song written during World War II to glamorize women working in factories as part of the war effort, "Rosie the Riveter" has more recently become the title of a movie which goes on to note that when the boys returned from overseas, the women were pushed out of these jobs and have been excluded from industrial technology to a greater or lesser degree ever since *(A Feminist Dictionary)*.

2. The Family Compact was an elite group of church administrators, business and military officials who informally directed affairs in the early nineteenth-century colony.

3. A patriarchal society is one governed by a narrow set of values stressing control and competition over co-operation and reconciliation; these values are designated as "masculine" traits and therefore tend to be assimilated more by boy children than girls.

References

Armstrong, Pat, 1984. *Labour Pains: Women's Work in Crisis*. Toronto: Women's Press.

Barnes, W.F., and E.B. Jones, 1974. "Differences in Male and Female Quitting," *Journal of Human Resources* 9 (fall): 439-451.

Bastedo, Suzanne, 1986. "Between a Rock and a Hard Place: Asking Some Women Questions About Technology," M.A. Thesis, Canadian Studies. Ottawa: Carleton University.

Bernard, Elaine, 1984. "Science, Technology and Progress: Lessons from the History of the Typewriter," *Canadian Woman Studies/les cahiers de la femme* 5(4).

Braverman, Harry, 1974. *Labour and Monopoly Capital: The Degradation of Work in the Twentieth Century*. New York: Basic Books.

Cowan, Ruth Schwartz, 1983. *More Work for Mother*. New York: Basic Books.

de Matteo, Bob, 1985. *Terminal Shock: The Health Hazards of Video Display Terminals*. Toronto: NC Press.

Ehrenreich, Barbara, 1982. "MNCs Exploit Women in Global Assembly Line," *AFSC Women's Newsletter*. Philadelphia: American Friends Services Committee.

Franklin, Ursula, 1983. "On Bronze and Other Metals in Early China," in B.N. Keightley (ed.), *The Origins of Chinese Civilization*. Los Angeles: University of California Press.

———, 1984. "Will Women Change Technology or Will Technology Change Women?" *Knowledge Reconsidered: A Feminist Overview*. Ottawa: Canadian Research Institute for the Advancement of Women.

Freeman, Christopher, 1974. *The Economics of Industrial Innovation*. London: Penguin Books.

Innis, Harold, 1947. *The Dairy Industry in Canada*. Toronto: Ryerson Press.

Mackenzie, Donald, and Judy Wajcman (eds.), 1985. *The Social Shaping of Technology*. Open University Press.

McLuhan, Marshall, 1967. *The Medium is the Message: An Inventory of Effects* (with Quentin Fiore). New York: Bantam Books.

Menzies, Heather, 1981. *Women and the Chip: Case Studies of the Effects of Informatics on Employment in Canada*. Montréal: The Institute for Research on Public Policy.

Mumford, Lewis, 1960. *The Myth of the Machine* (1). New York: Harvest House.

———, 1989. "The Voice With a Smile Goes Digital," (229) (forthcoming). *Saturday Night Magazine*.

Oxford County Board of Education, 1979. *Outstanding Women of Oxford County*. Oxford County, Ontario.

Pappert, Ann, 1986. "Bell Tolls for IUD But is it the End?" *The Globe and Mail*.

Roseman, Ellen, 1987. "VDT Radiation is Cited in Mice Fetal Deaths," *The Globe & Mail*, August 22, p. A-4.

Sandu, R., and J. Sandler, 1986. *The Tech and Tools Book: A Guide to Technologies Women are Using Worldwide*. New York: International Women's Tribune Centre.

Shriad, Sharon, 1982. "Life in the Free Trade Zones," *Priorities*.

Side-Effects, 1985. Play, written and performed by Women's Health Interaction, Ottawa. Video available for rent or sale from Inter Pares, Women's Health Interaction, 58 Arthur Street, Ottawa, Ontario.

Smith, Dorothy E., 1974. "Women's Perspectives as a Radical Critique of Sociology," *Sociological Inquiry* 44(1): 7-13.

Vickers, Jill McCalla, 1982. "Memoirs of an Ontological Exile: The Methodological Rebellions of Feminist Research," in Miles A. and G. Finn (eds.), *Feminism in Canada*. Montréal: Black Rose Books.

Zeman, Z.P., 1979. *The Impacts of Computer-Communications on Employment in Canada: An Overview of Current OECD Debates*. Montreal: The Institute for Research on Public Policy.

Chapter 7

Sexual Politics and the Master Science: The Feminist Challenge to Political Science

Jill Vickers

When the Supreme Court made its landmark decision on the unfairness of Canada's abortion law in January of 1988, a young friend told me that, for the first time, she understood that the state could influence her life as a woman in a significant and intimate way. A male colleague, viewing the same decision, told me that the process had been unfair because Madam Justice Bertha Wilson had been on the Court panel as part of the majority against the old law. To him, the process had been unfair because a woman had taken part. He assumed that Wilson was biased because she was not detached from the circumstance of experiencing an unwanted pregnancy. Both of these observations tell us something very important about politics, the state, and how we live them. To many women, politics only rarely seems to be about things that matter to us. One of the reasons for such alienation from the politics of the state among women is revealed in my colleague's view that the institutions of the state, such as Parliament, the Courts, the bureaucracy, and the military, are properly dominated by "objective" male persons as has been the case historically since the creation of the very first states more than five thousand years ago (Lerner, 1986).

Long before I was a feminist, I was trained as a political scientist. I was expected to operate as an intellectual male, viewing politics through a very particular paradigm.* I was taught to identify some things as political and others as personal and therefore *not* political. I became an insider, a member of a community of experts who knew how the political system worked and could voice sound views about its strengths and weaknesses. The price of admission to this cognitive community (Douglas, 1986) was to accept its basic world view and

---

I am using the term "sexual politics" in the sense employed by Kate Millett. It refers generally to the relationship between sex/gender and political power. It refers to issues surrounding sexual intercourse only when specifically identified in the text. Millett sees sex "as a status category with political implications" and politics as "power structured relationships" (Millett, 1969, 32-3).

* A paradigm is a set of concepts and theories which scholars in a field accept and work with. The scientific paradigm, for example involves basic units such as atoms, and basic laws such as the law of gravity (Kuhn, 1962).

to check my sex at the door. Even so, very few women were admitted then or are admitted now to the confines of the master science.*

It strikes me now as inconceivable, but it wasn't until after I had received the degree that certified me as an "expert" that I discovered that many of the "truths" I had learned didn't apply to me because of my sex. I discovered the ancient democracy of Athens would not have included me because of my sex. I discovered that women hadn't always had the right to sit in Parliament, to vote, to be judges, to own property, or to serve on juries. I also learned that generations of women had struggled to be admitted as citizens and that some women had died for the vote as a symbol of our legal emancipation. Now, your doubts to the contrary, I was not usually dim. As part of a community which saw no connection between my sex and the great issues of politics, I simply didn't notice. In much the same way, I hadn't noticed the absurdity of Joan Crawford abandoning her hard-won career for a frilly apron and a hairy man in the old movies I loved. I certainly didn't notice the disdain with which women's political behaviour was discussed (when it was) in the texts of my trade. I know I read those texts because I still have them in my library, with the "evidence" carefully underlined. Women were described in those texts as apathetic, uninformed, naïve, moralistic and reactionary. I simply didn't notice and I certainly didn't apply those judgements to myself. In order to *be* a political scientist, I had to become an abstract, detached person who didn't notice contradictions between my own experience and the "received wisdom" of my professional community.

Unlike most of my colleagues in political science, I happened also to be interested and increasingly involved in the practice of politics. I was a member of a political party. I worked on behalf of a candidate during elections, and I worked within my political party to achieve specific policy goals. This practical experience meant that I had to painfully unlearn many ideas taught by political science about the nature of politics. I also developed a feminist perspective as a result of sharing women's struggles within my political party and finally began to notice that my discipline rarely took women into account in its analyses. I began to re-orient my research and teaching toward women. Others whose experiences were similar were also taking tentative steps in the same direction.

That was over a decade ago, and I should find this assignment of describing feminist approaches to political science relatively easy. In fact, it is a profoundly difficult task because no genuinely feminist approaches exist within political science. That leaves me the task of explaining why the "master science" remains almost immune to feminist approaches. Certainly, a subject-matter best described as the study of women-in-politics has existed for the past decade. Indeed,

---

* The notion that the study of politics is the master science comes from the twenty-five hundred year tradition of political theory. This "pride of place" and sense of superiority is an unexamined part of the paradigm. Certainly it reflects a view of politics from the perspective of the powerful, not the powerless.

I have been involved in the elaboration of that subject-matter. This tentative sub-field, however, has not provided the basis for a feminist approach, although most of its developers are themselves feminists. As Joni Lovenduski observed, "in what is one of the major tragedies of contemporary scholarship, an absorption of a rather constrained branch of women's studies [women-in-politics] by a one-dimensional academic discipline [political science] has taken place" (Lovenduski, 1981, 83).

In this chapter, I will explore the possibility that the very nature of the discipline of political science is such that the development of distinctively feminist approaches within it is not possible. In and of itself, such an assertion could be considered of little importance. If, however, the political science paradigm accurately reflects characteristics of the political system itself, my hypothesis is of much greater importance. If, for example, institutions studied by political science, such as the state, have never existed except in a patriarchal form, developing feminist approaches within the paradigm would be very difficult indeed. In order to explore this proposition further, four things are required. First, we need to know more about political science, its theories and methods of study. Second, we also need to know something about feminism as a way of seeing the world, its theories of politics, its methods of study, and the nature of its challenge to political science. Third, we will need to ask why women don't fit into the paradigm within which political science works. Finally, we need to consider why feminism has been unable to have any perceptible impact on political science and whether this is a temporary condition, as some would argue, or a permanent stalemate, as I have suggested. This last question will require us to examine the role of political scientists as legitimizers and even propagandists for patriarchal states.*

The "Master Science": A One-Dimensional Discipline?

Academic disciplines shape what their initiates can "see" in the world they are to understand and explain. In human terms, they are cognitive communities (Douglas, 1986, Ch. 2) whose members interact with one another through a common set of ideas about their subject matter. Each new generation is socialized into the discipline's world-view. In fact, most of the certification process involves replicating this world-view or paradigm. In this section, I want to present some ideas about the general characteristics of the world-view of political science.

Political science is a new academic discipline which emerged in its current

---

* I define patriarchy as institutionalized male dominance such that men hold power in all of the important institutions (the legislature, the courts, the bureaucracy, the military, the media, the economy, etc.) and the balance of power between men and women in the other institutions and organizations tends to favour men (see Lerner, 1986).

form in the United States just after the World War Two. Bernard Crick has described the predominant mode of doing political science as "the American Science of Politics" (Crick, 1959). Certainly people studied government and politics in other ways previously. But the desire to be as scientific (and well-funded) as the natural sciences while studying political phenomena has its origins in the Cold War politics of the most powerful country in the world. In the 1950s, when the discipline was emerging from the older "field" of the study of government, the McCarthyite* environment made statements or observations about politics especially dangerous. The cloak of science made the study of politics apparently non-ideological and therefore safe. This evolution of the discipline as an apparently scientific and ideologically-neutral field reflects its origins in American society as part of its legitimizing knowledge system.

Prior to the 1960s, politics was studied in departments of history and in departments of government in Canada. The study of political institutions and of the history of political events, therefore, dominated. The imported American-style political science was the "master science" in the sense that its paradigm reflected the ideas of people who believed their nation was at the centre of the world. Some Canadians have accepted this world view and, of course, the large number of U.S. emigrés to Canada has an impact too.** Although the American-style scientific paradigm currently prevails in Canada, there are schools of rebellion as well. The political economy paradigm, which rejects the abstraction of political processes from economic causes, is a nationalist tradition re-invigorated by several critical strains of analysis, primarily of marxist inspiration. The other school of rebellion looks to a universal and eternal tradition of political philosophy and rejects the scientific pretensions of the American school. Each, however, accepts many of the elements of the dominant paradigm dealt with below.

As an academic discipline, political science operates within the intellectual division of labour in our bureaucratized universities. This division of intellectual labour fragments the natural and social worlds in which we live. Political decisions are about things as diverse as family policy, environmental controls, and free trade. Political science, however, is often not about the content or substance of those decisions but about the *processes* of political decision-making in government, bureaucracies, lobbying, elections, or courts. This reduction of subject-matter comes in part from political science's late arrival on the scene with most of the substance of political questions already the province of other social sciences, especially economics. In part, it also reflects the intense desire to be scientific in an ideologically detached way for the reasons suggested earlier.

---

* Senator Joe McCarthy led a witch hunt in the U.S. against suspected communists, leftists, socialists, etc.
** The rapid expansion of our universities in the 1960s involved the hiring of many U.S. professors, especially in the social sciences.

Finally, in a democratic era, there is some presumption that substance of political questions is properly "left to the people" to decide. Each of these forces helps to explain what Lovenduski has called the one-dimensional character of political science.

Despite the recency of the discipline's origins in its current form, political science traces its ancestry to the "master" theorists in a twenty-five hundred year tradition of political ideas, beginning with Plato and Aristotle in classical Athens at the beginnings of the ancient state (O'Brien, 1981). It is also from this tradition that the notion of politics and its study as the "master science" is drawn. The claim comes from the fact that the subject matter studied in the tradition, i.e., governing and other activities of the state, *are* master in the sense that those who occupy the institutions of the state enjoy a monopoly on the coercive power of courts, the military, and the police which allows them to enforce compliance with their policies. Similarly, those who occupy the institutions of strong states can impose their policies on the inhabitants of weaker states. This traditional heritage is believed by some political scientists to distinguish their discipline from the other social sciences because of its grander or more inclusive theory. In fact, the discipline's paradigm shaped both by its recent origins and by the tradition on which it draws has a more narrow focus than most of the other social sciences.

Political science, despite its name, does not deal with all of the class of activities we might normally describe as political. It deals with political activities if and only if they occur within a particular class of structures called states or if they occur between states. This focus leaves to anthropology the study of political interaction among those peoples who did not develop the institution of the state. It leaves to sociology the study of political interaction within societal institutions "under" the state because they do not have the capacity to compel the compliance of their members. It has traditionally left to psychology or sociology political interaction within the family. And as I have already noted, it generally leaves questions concerning the substance of state political decisions to others as well. It is, therefore, little wonder that feminist observers such as Joni Lovenduski have described political science as a one-dimensional discipline since it is primarily concerned with maintenance of the current order through the management of violence, threats of violence, rewards, and ideas.

This realistic meaning of the "master science" was well reflected in Canadian women's dilemma before the Supreme Court's decision concerning the abortion law. Those in charge of the institutions of the state (legislators and judges, especially, in this case) had decreed only very limited circumstances under which women with unwanted pregnancies could obtain abortion services. They enjoyed a monopoly over the coercive power to punish those who disobeyed. Our actions as women were also constrained by the ideas surrounding the issue. Only the power holders could determine whose ideas concerning abortion would be contained in the laws and even whether or not there would be a law. Political science, in viewing this issue, would be led by its world view to do so from the perspective of the power-holders concerned with the legitimacy of state power. Its practitioners would have little interest, as political scientists, in the substance of the issue or its potential impact on the politics of the family.

To summarize, political science is a compartment of the social sciences which emerged in the United States during the Cold War Era but which is also influenced by a twenty-five hundred year-old tradition of political theory. The discipline's commitment to study state politics scientifically has led it to abstract state politics from other political and social processes and to leave most questions of substance to the experts of other disciplines or to the democratic process. It reflects the approach of people who consider their country to be the world's most powerful and whose focus is primarily on the mechanics of state politics.

I have spent some time outlining the background of political science as a cognitive community because it can help us to understand the prospects for the development of feminist approaches within that community and its paradigms. It is natural that we would begin by supposing that a community of scholars would receive with enthusiasm our statements that their current knowledge system was inadequate for incorporating issues of sex/gender as a category of analysis. In fact, we know from the work of Thomas Kuhn, 1962; Mary Douglas, 1986; and Evelyn Fox Keller, 1982, that the cognitive communities represented by academic disciplines do not simply accept such challenges and alter their world views to accommodate new facts, categories, concepts, or theories. Kuhn, who developed the concept of paradigm to capture the notion of a world-view within which natural scientists are trained to "see," argued that things which don't "fit" the paradigm are more commonly ignored by the community than used as the basis for revisions which advance knowledge. It is his view that changes in the paradigm are resisted and the knowledge on which alterations might be based is repressed.* Eventually, enough "deviants" may exist to constitute an alternate community to rebel and substitute its paradigm.

These ideas support my view that feminist approaches will only be able to grow to sufficient maturity to be able to have an impact in cases in which the feminist challenge to the discipline's paradigm is relatively mild. In particular, this is a possibility where the categories of knowledge in a feminist approach are not so deviant that accepting them would ultimately require abandoning the paradigm. The paradigm with which anthropology works, for example, conceptualizes power, the family, the political system, and the state in ways which make feminist approaches relatively non-threatening. The same appears to be the case in sociology** and history with their rather eclectic and inclusive paradigms. By contrast, it is my view that the lack of fit between feminist views of politics and the paradigms central to

---

* Heather Menzies describes her own efforts to fit women's experience of technology into the dominant paradigm in this collection.
** See Marilyn Porter's contribution in this collection.

or tolerated by political science is so extreme that only a major revolution in conceptual terms could admit a feminist approach to the discipline.

As Kuhn has shown, the usual reaction by an academic community to a threat to its paradigm is resistance and repression. We must not assume, however, that this is somehow just a perverse reaction of timid academics. The knowledge generated by our institutions of learning constitutes part of the symbolic order which legitimizes society's dominant institutions. Political science, in this context, is central to the forces which maintain existing political arrangements, just as economics produces the ideas which maintain ideological support for the free enterprise system.* In the remainder of this chapter, I will attempt to demonstrate these links, especially as I explore in more substance the nature of the paradigm with which political science works.

Why Political Science Can't "See" Women

We are all familiar with "trick" pictures in which an image is invisible from most vantage points but is revealed when our line-of-sight is precisely right. Understanding why the paradigm of political science leads its practitioners to be blind to women unless the line-of-sight is precisely right is our next step. It is important to note that many of the grand theorists from whom political science claims part of its lineage were able to "see" women, even if they usually considered it appropriate to exclude them from the politics of the state (Clarke and Lange, 1977; Okin, 1979). Why, then, are women invisible when viewed through the paradigm of contemporary political science?

Modern political science is mainly about the state, that specialized set of institutions within which decisions are made for a whole society, taxes are collected, programs administered, disputes decided, and enforcement of compliance ensured. Although there are many definitions of the political, in practice political scientists study activity within, by, and aimed at these institutions of the state. In brief, political science assumes a division between the private and the public realms and studies those specialized institutions which make up the state in the public realm.

This division of intellectual labour has meant that "the family remained invisible or was seen as part of that vast consensus-making machinery necessary to a stable, well-run political society" (Elshtain, 1982, 1). In fact, political scientists sometimes study the impact of the state on the family and the impact of the family on the state, especially in relation to the socialization of family members towards the political system. What political science excludes, however, are studies of the relationships *within* the family, which are defined as not being political relationships.

While the exclusion of within-the-family relationships as not political will

---

* See Martha MacDonald in this collection.

be the aspect of most concern to us, it is important to realize that many other relationships are also defined as not political in character. So while such things as the impact of people's religions on their voting behaviour are of interest to political scientists, relationships within religious institutions and psychological states of faith or loss of faith are not. This process of abstracting *political man**

from sexual man, religious man, athletic man, or artistic man is the essence of the modern social science paradigms of which political science is but one example. The lead example is the construction of homo economicus, the rational calculator of marginal utility constructed by classical liberal economic theorists from the sixteenth century on. The process of abstraction is considered the key to developing scientific theories of economics or politics. This, in turn, is considered the key to men controlling their social environment as natural science seems to allow them to control their physical environment. This desire to understand, in order to control, marks the modern social science mind-set. In the political realm, of course, those in power have the greatest interest in controlling the social environment and will use the experts in political science to understand how to do this.

In fact, the private/public split and the abstraction of political man from his non-political aspects also has roots in the political philosophies of Western civilization. Not all political philosophers ignored the family, but the trend has been towards invisibility of the environments in which most women lived out their lives. This reflects the fact that the history of political thought begins with the formation of the state in the city states of Greece.** As Mary O'Brien demonstrates, its paradigm assumed the subordination of the family and kinship to the new territorially-organized political system and the incarceration of women in the "private" sphere of the family, except for some sacred duties and ceremonies (O'Brien, 1981, Ch.1).

In the classic ancient statement of a paradigm for political study, Aristotle defines the family as inferior to the polis or political community. The rule of men over women, children, servants, and slaves in the family, Aristotle asserted, was qualitatively different from political rule of free men by free men. This was in part because he viewed those ruled in the family as natural inferiors and in part because he believed the sexual, reproductive, and economic activities of the family to be inferior because they were dictated by necessity rather than by the choice of the political realm. For him, only free and independent men, who don't have to face the sweaty reality of physical labour or be subject to such physical dictates as pregnancy, can be political beings.

This theme, in general outline, continues in the modern discipline. Over the centuries, elements of it have changed. For Machiavelli, writing of the militarist

---

* I use man deliberately here and I will return to the problem of abstracting political woman.
** Fifth century B.C.

origins of modern states in the sixteenth century, the moralities of private life were necessarily different from the values of public life. But, in at least an outward nod to Christianity, he assigns private life, religion, and friendship a positive value. Liberal thinkers like John Locke in the seventeenth century firmly asserted the status of families and churches as private associations and recast the political realm as an arena in which the enforcement of contracts creating and regulating private associations occurred (Elshtain, 1982).

Since the sixteenth century, the private realms and especially the family have been more highly valued, and the institutions of the state are seen more in utilitarian than moral terms. The family as a retreat or a "Haven in a Heartless World" (Lasch, 1977) and religion as a consolation from, rather than as a guide to, political life are familiar modern themes. Nonetheless, there has been wide agreement among the men who shaped the paradigm that the family does not involve political relationships. Their rule over wives and children was "natural" and not to be evaluated in terms common to other forms of rule. Hence, if we were to try to abstract political woman from woman in general, that abstraction historically would contain very little, given women's legal exclusion from the politics of the state until quite recently. The right to participate was denied to women, except for the odd female monarch, until our own century (Lovenduski, 1986).

For the twenty-five hundred years of the recorded history of political thought, the same basic set of political arrangements prevailed. Territories within the rubric of Western civilization were ruled by states or state-like structures which were patriarchal. Gerda Lerner has demonstrated that the apparent stability of the patriarchal state forms, as we now observe that history, is misleading. It had taken a prior period of almost twenty-five hundred years to invent and make stable the patriarchal state (Lerner, 1986). Given this almost incomprehensible time frame, it is not surprising that most political scientists act as if the patriarchal state is as natural as the law of gravity. Feminist approaches, by contrast, are impossible unless the patriarchal state is understood as man-made and consciously treated as such.

Modern political science works with a functionalist paradigm shared in part with the other social sciences. The paradigm was also developed primarily in the period after World War Two, but it bears an uncanny resemblance to the Aristotelian paradigm introduced above with regard to women (Okin, 1979, Ch. 1). Basically, this paradigm assumes that the arrangement of things in our societies, such as the assignment of women to the "private" realm of the family, exist because they serve a basic value or fulfil a basic function. Aristotle's paradigm assumed that the ultimate moral values could best be achieved by women and slaves freeing men to act as autonomous political actors in the public realm. More than two thousand years later, our modern functionalist paradigm "presupposes a stable congruity or fit between the modern industrialized economy and the nuclear family" (Elshtain, 1982, 1). Unlike Aristotle's rather bald justification of the patriarchal state with the declaration that women, slaves, workers, and foreigners were properly excluded because of their natural and inevitable inferiority, the modern version pins the same basic structures on a division of labour and men and women's "suitability" for performing different functions. It assumes that women's "nature" best fits us to perform the nurturant, expressive roles in the private realm [mind the kids, do the housework, and keep hubby sweet when he comes home from work]. Having these functions performed and having them performed by women is seen as necessary to the system functioning. In other words, it assumes that a world in which men struggle in the public realm and women nurture children and men in the private realm is good for society and good for people.

While many contemporary political scientists would reject the notion that they are functionalists, the discipline's paradigm as a whole is functionalist in its underlying presuppositions and categories. Most political scientists, while not claiming that the state, the family, and the private/public split are natural, believe them to be necessary, functional, and treat their broad arrangements as given. In particular, the "splits" between politics and non-politics and between public norms of behaviour and private morality are "seen as necessary to maintain politics, law, order, justice, and sovereignty on the one hand and to protect the innocent and helpless, preserve the home and its private virtues, and provide succor for those [men] seeking respite from the public world on the other" (Elshtain, 1982, 56).

It might seem logical that granting women the vote and the right to hold public office, in most cases decades before this paradigm gelled, would have had some noticeable impact on how the discipline "saw" women. The fact that as late as the 1960s it could still view public institutions as if women didn't exist at all tells us something very basic. The legal freedom for women to participate in the public sphere and to compete for power in state institutions had very little impact on the nature of political systems or on political science. Women didn't need to be taken into account because the conditions to empower women politically did not exist; only *legal* emancipation was possible.

It did set the stage for many men and later a few women to ask Professor Henry Higgins' question, "Why can't a woman be more like a man?" The way in which societies governed by patriarchal states are structured is based on the lives of elite men and the ability of those men to abstract themselves as political men from those whose material and emotional support make that abstraction possible. In political science such male behaviour is the norm. Any such female behaviour is regarded as deviant and this is borne out by the basic definitions of the paradigm.

To make these points more concretely, the paradigm assumes that men are "free" to participate in state politics in terms of having the time, money, energy, and support to do so. In fact, the paradigm has now made political actors unisex, but as soon as we ask the question "Who is minding the kids?" it becomes quite apparent that relatively few women are "free" in this way. Some may not have children and a man to provide support for, but how many women enjoy the support of a wife? Obviously, voting doesn't require a great deal of time, money, energy, and support, but most other political activities do. Just as Aristotle's paradigm assumed the citizen must be free of sweaty labour to participate, the current paradigm assumes the actor in the public sphere has "someone" in the private realm to provide the material and emotional support to allow him to participate without worrying where his next meal is coming from, if his shirt is ironed, and if his kids are being looked after. The basic world view assumes the normal political actor is male in the sense of having a male "right" to abstract himself from the necessities of everyday life. The expectations of the elite man's life circumstances then constitute the norm, even if not all men and few women can ever enjoy such expectations.

Once women achieved the right to vote, those not active in the public realm were assumed to be apathetic, incompetent, or unsuccessful competitors. The possibility that, by its very nature, the political realm could not admit women as actors on the same basis as men was inconceivable. The fact that many women felt this to be the case was largely undetected by the discipline. As a result, the only possible approach to the study of women within the dominant paradigm of political science was the constrained enterprise I will describe as the normal integration model of women-in-politics.

What Political Science Can See

The normal integration model within which some political scientists have studied women in politics assumes that women can be integrated into the politics of the state as it exists and occupy all of its roles and offices on the same basis as men. Such work concentrates on exposing sexist interpretations of data in the discipline's research and examining the barriers to women's integration into the existing political system (Bashevkin, 1985; Brodie, 1985; Sapiro, 1983; Vickers and Brodie, 1981). The development of a specialization studying women within political science reveals clearly what its paradigm permits us to "see" about women. The approach, which has focused largely on liberal democracies* like Canada, the U.S., and Great Britain, assumes there is nothing intrinsic to the nature of political systems to keep women out on a permanent basis and that any barriers which now exist can be overcome in time. This approach lets us "see" women acting where they *have* been integrated into the existing system on the

---

* Liberal democracies have a competitive system of elections for filling some decision-making offices with at least two political parties. They also include a free-market sector of the economy and a rule of law, often with a basic, written constitution.

same basis as men. We can "see" women's voting behaviour, tap some of their political attitudes, and see them playing low-level support roles in many political institutions. Most easily, however, we can "see" the very few women who have "made it" at the elite level by being elected to parliament, appointed as judges, or achieving high-level bureaucratic positions.

In fact, the faces of state institutions (legislatures, courts, the upper bureaucracy, the police, and the military are all male-dominant institutions) remain overwhelmingly male more than half a century after women's legal emancipation. The normal integration approach, therefore, can only focus on what is there and explore barriers, presumed to be subject to remedy, to women's integration elsewhere. A time-lag thesis is presumed to explain the slow pace of women's integration into key state institutions with the assumption that full integration will eventually occur.

Limited though the normal integration approach is, it has constantly been on the verge of "kicking over the traces" and escaping the paradigm's constraints. The work of U.S. scholar Virginia Sapiro rejects the normal method of always comparing women to the male norm (Sapiro, 1983). Sapiro compares some women to other women in terms of their willingness to be available for integration. She identifies some women's acceptance of the ideology of privatization (acceptance that their familial roles are key) as a major factor in limiting their availability for political activity. The fact is, of course, that most women are *not* available for state politics except as voters and support personnel because they are assigned major responsibility for *species-essential* work in the family. Sapiro finds that those who accept their privatization are less likely to be uncomfortable with their exclusions from politics. Accepting limitations on women's political role as appropriate, however, doesn't make women more available if their time and resources available for politics are limited. The participation costs* for women being "integrated" into existing political structures are shown by research in this vein to be too high to be effectively combined with paid-work, mother-work and house-work (CRIAW, 1987). The abstract political man freed from most species-essential work, therefore, is not paralleled by an abstract political woman unless the woman chooses chastity or commands the wealth to buy substitute labour.

Joni Lovenduski's work on women's role in European politics reveals the fact that their involvement in ad hoc political activity such as demonstrations and in social movements such as the anti-war or ecology movements is high. This may reflect lower participation costs than for involvement in more structured political institutions, but it may also reflect a growing awareness by women that they cannot simply be integrated into existing political systems on the same basis as men (Lovenduski, 1986). American research on the gender gap which shows

---

* Participation costs involve travel to the location of the political institution, time off work (few women have secretaries to "cover" for them), childcare substitute, etc.

women holding quite different views on some political issues than men, appears to offer the hope that women can be mobilized to use their voting clout to achieve improvements in their life conditions. Despite ongoing scholarly and popular interest in gender gap research, however, the forces which move the American ship of state seem as impervious to the threat of this "normal" political behaviour by women (the development of a voting bloc) as European political systems have been to the revealed potential of their female citizens for ad hoc, radical, and even violent political acts.

Useful though the work done within the normal integration approach has been in describing the characteristics of women citizens constrained by male-centred and male-dominated state institutions, it cannot help but lead to frustration and, as Lovenduski has described, eventual absorption into the political-science-as-usual engine. If politics is understood as being about things which can be changed, the deep barriers to women's integration on the same basis as men still seem unchangeable. Moreover, the research may be said to point to an escape hatch for some women to be integrated on the same basis as men into the political system as it is, even if most women remain firmly marginalized. Political science is interested in the stability of existing states and their stability is aided by the integration of a few women who do not fundamentally challenge the status quo.

These exceptions of women who do gain significant power within the state (the Mrs. Thatchers) are increasingly taken to mean that the barriers to women's involvement can be scaled. One result of the normal integration research, therefore, may be to enhance the notion that political systems are neutral devices for performing societal functions and which recruit on an equal opportunity basis. This reassuring notion may make political science less, rather than more, willing to examine feminist views that existing political systems can never admit women, *qua* women, on the same basis as men.

This is not to suggest that those who have studied women-in-politics within a normal integration framework are somehow not "genuine" feminists. Nor would I suggest that our research findings are useless for the achievement of feminist goals. Rather, I would argue that *the failure to explore the links between sex and power in the family and in the state* has cut the approach's practitioners off from the radical challenge of feminist theory. Moreover, the absence of insights from feminists within political science, beyond the normal integration research, has weakened the growth of feminist theory in relation to its grasp of the nature of the state.

Feminism's Challenge to Political Science

Within the dominant paradigm of political science, we are led to accept the question-setting agenda of the paradigm. That is, we mostly ask the wrong questions. Moreover, until the last decade, most feminists attempting to develop woman-centred knowledge have been engaged in debates with the male "greats" who created the paradigms which inhibit our insight. As Gerda Lerner wrote (Lerner, 1986, 227), "We each hold at least one great man in our heads." Learning to ask the right questions to give us the ability to "see" women in relation to the subject-matter of political science is a very difficult process. Nonetheless, the framework with the greatest potential to put women fully and finally into focus comes from some elements in radical feminist theory and from feminist history. In this section, I will outline the character of this challenge and attempt to show why political science can neither cope with it nor even recognize it for the challenge it is.

In previous political thought, the state was understood as an association which was *sui generis* with the goal of achieving virtue for men in the ancient world or aimed at achievement of the protection of life, liberty and property in the modern world. Even Marx, who predicted the eventual demise of the state, also saw it as an instrument to protect property and to supervise the oppression of those whose labour produced its value. How then does modern radical feminist thought differ? First, it sees the state as part of the technology of patriarchy. That is, it sees control of women's sexuality, reproductive and nurturing capacities, and the manipulation of women's consciousness about these capacities as a central purpose of the state and its institutions. Second, it rejects the notion that the state involves a unique association with rules of operation different from or superior to those of other associations. In the slogan, "the personal is the political" moreover, it challenges the assumption that supposedly "private" relationships, especially in the family, are not-political. Finally, it presumes that women (as women as distinct from a few token women or honorary men) cannot be integrated into existing political systems but that those systems must either be transformed in their fundamental character or that women must separate themselves in all senses from men and male institutions.

Using the powerful concept of "sexual politics," Kate Millett conceptualized patriarchy as a system of government in which men rule women and older men rule younger men (Millett, 1969). In this conception, the family is the key arena for sexual politics. For her, state institutions per se are secondary arenas engaging in damage control when the forces of male dominance in the family are threatened. "Personal" relationships are understood as power relationships, and the centrality of force or threat of its use in rape, battering, compulsory heterosexuality, etc. are seen to be the same as the backdrop of state force in laws, prisons, police, or military.

Although several other elements of this challenge remain to be outlined, I will first provide more depth to this basic picture. Although the cognitive communities described as liberal-feminism and marxist-feminism do not, on the surface, share in all of the elements of this challenge, which is at once a theory of politics and a theory of the links between sex and power in both the state and the family, the agenda to which each has invariably had to respond comes from it. That agenda is both political and an agenda for the radical reconstruction of knowledge. To quote Catherine MacKinnon, "Sexuality is to feminism what work is to marxism..." (MacKinnon, 1982, 515). Some liberal-feminists continue to believe that women can be integrated into the existing public domains, including the institutions of the state, with relatively few alterations. Yet, as Zillah Eisenstein has shown, the process of trying to achieve such integration has moved liberal-feminism more and more into a radical stance and analysis which revolves around a sex-based agenda (Eisenstein, 1981).

Marxist or socialist variants of feminism share some common roots with radical feminism, in particular the outward role of the state. Both are theories of power and its unequal distribution. Marxism and its leftist variants, however, reject the centrality of male attempts to control women's sexuality. Leftist feminists have also had to respond to the powerful political agenda constructed by women out of their experience of their "personal" lives. The marxist paradigm shares with political science notions of private and political which are similar. That is, each means much the same thing by "state" and "family," both naturalize* sexual relations and the sexual division of labour in reproduction and nurturance.

While the revolutionary understandings of politics outlined above are, then, not fully shared by all variants of feminism, few feminists would reject the centrality of "private" sexual "issues" to their agenda. That is, each recognizes that her powerlessness is manifested daily in relation to her sex. She may also identify powerlessness manifested in relation to work, to faith or to intellect, but would not doubt that she would enjoy more power if she woke up tomorrow morning as a man.

Two further elements have been added to this challenge to all male-centred paradigms of politics. They have emerged from women's political and intellectual practice but have become central to the paradigm of challenge. The first lies in the distinctive method of agenda-setting and knowledge-construction called consciousness-raising.** The second involves the political practice of rejecting the inevitability of formal leadership and hierarchy in the practice of feminist groups. Each moves the radical feminist paradigm further away from sharing any common ground with political science.

The issue of method is of profound importance in understanding the problem of finding any common ground between the political science paradigm and the

---

* Assume that sexual relations are governed by natural instincts and are not historically shaped and that women nurturing children is "natural."

** Consciousness-raising involved self-directed groups of women who got together to discuss issues as diverse as who initiates sex to who cleans the toilet. The process politicized "private gripes" as women saw that they *shared* common problems and perceptions.

radical feminist paradigm. To quote Catharine MacKinnon, "Consciousness raising not only comes to know different things as politics; it necessarily comes to know them in a different way. Women's experience of politics, of life as a sex object gives rise to its own method of appropriating that reality: feminist method" (MacKinnon, 1982, 535). Remembering the titles of feminist manifestos in the 1960s and 1970s makes MacKinnon's point clearly: the San Francisco Redstockings—"Our Politics Begin with Our Feelings" (Rosak and Rosak, 1969, cited in MacKinnon, 1982, 536). This disaffection from the kind of objectivity demanded by all social science paradigms "locates" the radical feminist challenge as part of some "lunatic fringe." As we will see shortly, however, many of the key insights of the radical feminist paradigm are supported by the work of feminist historians. (History, with its greater tolerance for conceptual and methodological deviance, clearly provides a more productive venue for the maturation of the radical feminist paradigm. This serves to confirm my argument that it is the degree of "fit" between a disciplinary paradigm and feminist approaches which determines how much relative success the latter will have in terms of making an impact.)

The political practice of radical feminist groups in the conduct of their politics provides the second area in which radical feminism has, over a decade and a half, shifted further and further away from any potential common ground with political science. Although not unique in attempting to develop collectivist, egalitarian organizations which embodied anti-hierarchical, anti-leadership values in practice, many thousands of grass-roots groups pursued this course with considerable creativity and mobilization as the result. From the perspective of political science, whose practitioners believe implicitly in the iron law of oligarchy in which at least leadership, if not elite domination, is seen as inevitable, this stance seems naïve at best. As this set of political practices became elevated to the level of theoretical precepts, moreover, many negative aspects of traditional political institutions were simply attributed to male nature. Thus, what to political science is a natural feature of political institutions it is to radical feminists an evil attributable to the male nature.

Gerda Lerner, one of the first grand theorists in feminist history, has begun the work of providing an historical basis for the radical feminist paradigm. In her work, *The Creation of Patriarchy,* she attempts to remedy the fact that many elements in this challenging paradigm were speculative by drawing on the history of the formation of archaic states, on an analysis of their symbol systems, and on the contemporary, comparative work of feminist and non-feminist anthropologists. While I will not attempt to summarize all of her findings, several are key for our analysis. First, based on her evidence concerning the formation of the archaic states, she finds that all were organized in the form of patriarchy "thus from its inception the state had an essential interest in the maintenance of the patriarchal family" (Lerner, 1986, 9). She finds that "women's sexual subordination was institutionalized in the earliest legal codes and enforced by the full power of the state" (Lerner, 1986, 9). Women's co-operation was ensured by privilege to reward compliance and the obliteration of empowering symbol systems and rituals of solidarity. Her analysis concludes that an identifiable, historical process lasting over 2500 years was involved in establishment of the technology of patriarchal government and that its central, if not exclusive, purpose was to enable men to appropriate women's sexual and reproductive powers.

Lerner's grand synthesis is, of course, not the first. Mary O'Brien, in the *Politics of Reproduction,* achieved a similar, ovarian text. What Lerner's work does is to offer concrete historical evidence that the state has only ever existed in a patriarchal form. This confirms that the radical feminist paradigm leads us to ask some of the right questions and establishes some of the right categories. Certainly, if we do not explore the relationships between sex and power and the role of the state in establishing male rights to appropriate female reproductive powers, we will never begin to understand the riddle of women's systematic exclusion from all societal institutions of power in modern states. The political science paradigm, which accepts the proposition that by definition sexuality and reproduction are private and not political, can never alone direct us to frame that central question.

Can Feminism Have an Impact on Political Science?

"Women have been systematically excluded from the enterprise of creating symbol systems, philosophies, science and law" (Lerner, 1986, 5). In a few disciplines or cognitive communities this is changing. Feminist paradigms are being allowed to develop to maturity and are having an impact. In the social sciences, history and anthropology have been the most open because the cognitive "fit" is less threatening of disruption. Established sub-disciplines have developed in sociology and psychology. Even in geography the analysis of the relationships between gender and space is developing in a promising way.* Why, then, have I expressed such pessimism concerning the possibility of developing to maturity a feminist paradigm within political science?

First, the subject-matter of political science, like that of law and economics, matters to those who hold and exercise power within the state. The cognitive community of political science involves risks and rewards. Writing too openly about power holders can bring punishments; writing admiringly can bring jobs and reputation. It is much easier to write and speak about those safely dead or in distant locales. This leads to a greater defence of paradigm and scientific method. The claim to being scientific keeps the political scientist safe. Information about

---

* Suzanne MacKenzie discusses this in her chapter in this volume.

how to manipulate existing systems is likely to be rewarded; arguments which appear to challenge arrangements seen as legitimate to the ruled are risky. Accepting the feminist challenge would mean questioning the fundamental elements of the patriarchal state.

It is unlikely that a mature, feminist paradigm will emerge within political science proper in the foreseeable future. Nonetheless, the prospects are much brighter within political theory. Although the study of political theory in recent decades has been largely a rather arid, scholastic field, the norms of the grand tradition are flexible enough to permit the exploration of some key questions. And although they have as yet had little impact with the field, such original theorists as Mary O'Brien, Zillah Eisenstein, Jean Bethke Elshtain, Susan Moller Okin, Nancy Hartsock, and Carol Pateman have emerged from it. Each has had a profound impact on the feminist cognitive community, limited impact within the sub-field of political theory, and virtually no impact within the dominant scientific paradigm. Nonetheless, each is exploring some aspect of the feminist paradigm I have outlined in this paper. Moreover, the rise of the New Right, which bases its attack on feminism and the welfare state on an understanding of the centrality of sexuality and reproduction to politics which is almost a mirror-image of the feminist understanding, provides opportunities as well as profound risks. Although on different sides of most issues, Radical Feminism and the New Right share the view that the political *includes* the family and sexuality.

In fact, political science has almost as much difficulty understanding the New Right as it has understanding feminism. It is, however, more likely to be affected by the New Right framework than by the feminist paradigm. For that reason, if for no other, it is crucial that we not abandon political science to its patriarchal paradigm. Joan Kelly's concept of the need for a "doubled vision" best expresses my view of the necessary course (Joan Kelly, 1976). We cannot simply accept the normal integration model or the private/public split. Nonetheless, we can advance our understanding of the mechanics of patriarchal government. Framing the questions to develop a mature feminist theory, however, will require extensive work within political theory and outside of the discipline all together; work which must be both interdisciplinary in nature and based on feminist method.

Clearly the "master science" is too central to the forces maintaining patriarchal government to abandon the task of developing a feminist paradigm which can have an impact. In the end, however, it will be by making sexual politics fully visible in the world of "doing" politics that will create the need for a fundamental revision. Until political scientists can "see" women in the realms they recognize as political, it is unlikely that our paradigm based on an analysis of patriarchal government and sexual politics will prevail. Perhaps to be tolerated as domesticated deviants would in fact be the worst fate.

References

Abzug, Bella, 1984. *Gender Gap*. Boston: Houghton Mifflin Co.

Bashevkin, Silvia B., 1985. *Toeing the Lines: Women and Party Politics in English Canada*. Toronto: University of Toronto Press.

Brodie, M. Jannine, 1985. *Women and Politics in Canada*. New York: McGraw-Hill Ryerson.

Canadian Research Institute for the Advancement of Women, 1987. "Women's Involvement in Political Life: A Pilot Study," CRIAW Papers, Nos. 16 and 17.

Clarke, Lorenne, and Linda Lange, 1977. *The Sexism of Social and Political Theory*. Toronto: University of Toronto Press.

Crick, Bernard, 1959. *The American Science of Politics*.

Douglas, Mary, 1986. *How Institutions Think*. Ottawa: Cornell University Press.

Elshtain, Jean Bethke (ed.), 1982. *The Family in Political Thought*. Mass.: University of Massachusetts Press.

Eisenstein, Zillah, 1981. *The Radical Future of Liberal Feminism*. Longman.

Harstock, Nancy, 1981. *Money, Sex and Power*.

Keller, Evelyn Fox, 1982. "Feminism and Science," *SIGNS* 7(3)(spring): 589-602.

Kelly-Gadol, Joan, 1976. "The Social Relations of the Sexes: Methodological Implications of Woman's History," *SIGNS* 1(4)(summer): 809-824.

Kuhn, Thomas, 1962. *The Structure of Scientific Revolutions*.

Lash, Christopher, 1977. *Haven in a Heartless World: The Family Besieged*. New York: Basic Books.

Lerner, Gerda, 1986. *The Creation of Patriarchy*. London: Oxford University Press.

Lovenduski, Joni, 1981. "Political Science" in Dale Spender, *Men's Studies Modified*.

——, 1986. *Women and European Politics: Contemporary Feminism and Public Policy*. Mass.: University of Massachusetts Press.

MacKinnon, Catharine A., 1982. "Feminism, Marxism, Method and the State: An Agenda for Theory," *SIGNS* 7(3)(spring): 515-554.

Millett, Kate, 1969. *Sexual Politics*. Ballantine Books.

O'Brien, Mary, 1981. *The Politics of Reproduction*. Routledge Kegan and Paul.

Okin, Susan Moller, 1979. *Women in Western Political Thought*. New York: Princeton University Press.

Pateman, Carol, 1970. *Participation and Democratic Theory*. Mass.: Cambridge University Press.

——, 1980. *The Problem of Political Obligation*. New York: Wiley.

San Francisco Redstockings, 1969. "Our Politics Begin With Our Feelings," in Betty and Theodore Roszak (eds.), *Masculine/Femine*. New York: Harper and Row.

Sapiro, Virginia, 1983. *The Political Integration of Women*. Chicago: University of Illinois Press.

Smith, Dorothy, 1978. "A Peculiar Eclipsing: Women's Exclusion from Man's Culture," *Woman's Studies International* Quarterly 1(4): 281-296.

Vickers, Jill, and M.J. Brodie, 1981. "Canada" in Joni Lovenduski and Jill Hills (eds.), *The Politics of the Second Electorate*. Routledge Kegan and Paul.

Chapter 8

Becoming Visible:
Women and the Economy
Martha MacDonald

Think about the economy. What issues come to mind? Perhaps you think of inflation rates, free trade, unemployment, the budget. Think of these issues as they are discussed on TV. What is the sex of the economist giving an analysis of the issue? What is the sex of the unemployed worker being interviewed? What is the sex of the finance minister giving the budget speech? The bank director or stockbroker explaining trends? The chief negotiator in the free trade talks?

Think of flying, reading the inflight magazine. What sex are the executives in the ads? The flight attendant (a woman?) comes along passing out magazines. Who gets offered Business Week? Think of a political party you may have been involved with. Who sat on the economic policy committee? Who spoke up at conventions on economic issues? I expect you answered "men" to virtually all these questions. The economy and economic discourse, it would seem, are the domain of men.

Now, think of some other images. TV ads for floor cleaners, diet pop, clothes, houses. Who are these ads aimed at? Who knocks on your door collecting for charity? Who are the secretaries, nurses, cashiers you see every day? Who in your family cooks the meals, mends the clothes, does the laundry, often after a full day of paid employment? Odds are you answered "women" to virtually all these questions: women as consumers, paid workers, volunteer workers, houseworkers. Isn't that part of the economy?

Think about the issues you associate with the women's movement. They probably include improved child care facilities, reproductive rights, equal rights, pay equity, welfare rights. These are usually characterized as social issues. The professionals who argue for them tend to be social workers, sociologists, lawyers, educators. But aren't these issues also economic? To the extent that economics enters the discussion, it is usually in opposition. "That sounds like a good idea, but we simply can't afford it." "That would interfere with the market." Women are ridiculed when they dare threaten to intervene in the economy with policies such as pay equity or childcare, and their issues are labelled social. Their issues are also identified as being special interest group issues, whereas jobs (for men), unions (of men) are considered general issues.

So far, we have three conclusions from our images.
1. Economics and the economy are associated with *males* in our society.
2. Activities of women seem to be important to the economy too, though ignored in the discourse.
3. The women's movement is labelled as *social*, not economic.

Let's consider these three points in more detail. In doing so, we will discover more about economics and its treatment of women, we'll think about what a new feminist economics would look like, and we'll discover how crucial it is that women and the women's movement set an *economic* agenda and make a claim on economic policy.

Economics — A Male Preserve

If you study economics at university, you have over 80 percent probability of having a male professor. It's the most male-dominated of the social sciences. One reason for this is that economic theory has become very abstract and mathematical and girls fall far behind boys in their math skills in our present school system. Another reason is that it is considered to be a science about the "economy," the public domain which, in our political economic system, has traditionally been seen as a male sphere. Having women pronounce on the economy is considered inappropriate. Who would take their advice seriously?

Obviously, many of the men who pronounce on the economy—from journalists to cabinet ministers—are not professionally trained economists who have jumped through the necessary mathematical hoops. Yet they assume a right to an opinion on the economy that most women would not presume. You will quickly notice in your economics classes that the male students are more likely to voice an opinion than the female students. Female students will only speak up based on what they have learned in formal economics courses. They have no "natural" right to economic discourse, as do the male students.

The heavy male dominance of the discipline, the policy arena, and the discourse pose obvious barriers for women: students and interested citizens alike. It is important to think about why this dominance is so strong and how it functions to exclude and discourage women even in this modern era. This question is a key part of a women's studies program. You would not address this question in an economics course, but an understanding of it from other women's studies courses would certainly help prepare you to deal with the barriers as you tackle economics.

The content of economics, as traditionally practised, influences and is influenced by the gender composition of the profession. Economics claims as its domain the whole of production, distribution, and consumption in society: the use of resources (human and physical) to meet human needs. Such a broad definition should include women. However, in fact, economics has had very little to say about women. Like philosophy, history, and political science, which also claim universal coverage, economics is essentially about male experience or a male view of the world.

First of all, economics has overwhelmingly concentrated on the public sphere, on the buying and selling of goods in the market, and on the production of these goods for sale and hence on the buying and selling of inputs, including labour used to make goods. This focus on market prices means that much of what women do is ignored in the analysis. Examples include the work women do providing services to family members, caring for children, and doing volunteer work in their communities. This is partly a result of the methodology, but it is also a reflection of the real invisibility of women's labour in the market economy. Rather than revealing the true relation between the unpaid work of women and the more visible, paid market transactions, economics replicates and reinforces the separation of the market/non-market spheres in the real world.

The classic example of this orientation is in the measurement of the aggregate output of the economy, Gross National Product (GNP). GNP records market values of final goods and services produced in a given year. All production in the home is excluded unless it is sold. The standard joke is that if a man marries his housekeeper, GNP goes down because the housekeeper-employee's production is counted while the same work done by the housekeeper-wife is not.

As Marjorie Cohen points out,[1] ignoring the productive activity in the household "raises questions as to what we know about how effectively the system allocates resources," and the issue of resource allocation is key in economics: evaluating how efficiently our economy uses its resources to produce what people want. Similarly, analysis of concepts such as unemployment and inflation suffer if a part of each household's "economic" activity is totally ignored. This has been gaining recognition recently in the study of economic development in the Third World, although more by sociologists than by economists. Development efforts in many countries which focused on paid employment and cash income have been shown to leave many families, and particularly women, worse off, for the non-market sources of production and consumption were often undermined. For example, food production may become totally export-oriented, destroying the subsistence crops of peasants.

We have mentioned the severe under-representation of women in the economics discipline and the invisibility of women in the overall economic analysis. The economy, as studied in most fields of economics, does not include the unpaid work activities of women. There is not even a recognizable fringe field in economics devoted to the study of women's economic contributions.

Obviously, no field as broadly defined as economics can ignore women completely. There are areas in economics where women have been a topic of interest. However, much of the economic work with "women" as a focus ranges from frightening and anti-feminist to simply boring and elementary compared to the general level of feminist scholarship.

In examining the work on women in economics, explicit account must be taken of the context of this work in the major paradigms of the discipline. Feminists are extremely sensitive to the fact that all science and research is based on a conceptual framework or paradigm; that is, a way of looking at the world. Every framework makes assumptions about the nature of society and about human motivations and behaviour. Each chooses aspects of reality on which to focus and abstracts from others. Each framework shapes the question asked, defines the concepts employed, and the research methods to be used. They are "perceptual glasses" with which the scientist views the world and identifies problems. The framework can bind or restrict possible topics of inquiry and possible policy outcomes.

Neo-Classical Economics

In economics there is a dominant paradigm which is referred to as neo-classical, or orthodox, or mainstream economics. The cornerstone of this paradigm is that decentralized, individualistic decision-makers act in their own best interests and in so doing determine the observed economic outcomes. The primary unit in neo-classical analysis is the individual person or the individual firm. The methodology analyzes rational choice to maximize satisfaction (consumer) or profits (firm), given constraints such as incomes and prices. For example, the consumer decides how best to allocate her/his income among possible goods, to gain the most satisfaction, given prices and income. This methodology of analyzing constrained choice has generally been confined to market-related phenomena: the public domain. What combination of eggs and clothes should a consumer buy? How much capital and labour should a firm employ? However, economists have long claimed that the tools of neo-classical analysis are also suited to any social behaviour where choices must be made. Virtually every aspect of life is a potential subject for this kind of analysis. In recent years this potential has been explored with vigour by a group of economists studying non-market behaviour such as choice of marriage partners, fertility, and time use. This expansion out of the price system lands one in women's sphere. This work, like that of the more market-oriented mainstream, still abstracts from the sociological, political, and organizational aspects of the problem. No attention is given to the nature of conflict, the use of power, or the basis of attitudes. In this framework there is no systematic, structural basis for inequalities or discrimination or the sexual division of labour, as we shall see later. They are all attributed to accidental outcomes of people's rational free choices.

Radical Economics

In contrast, the radical paradigm, with more or less explicit roots in the marxist tradition, emphasizes factors beyond the control of individuals, focusing on the structural forces in the economy that limit and shape the choices people have. Only a small minority of professional economists in North America work within the radical paradigm.

The marxist literature has traditionally focused on the relations of production and class, i.e., workers and capitalists, rather than reproduction* and gender, i.e., women and men. The economy which was studied was the same money economy as in neo-classical economics. The disagreements between the paradigms are for the most part disagreements among men. The methodologies of each are both in the tradition of scientific rationalism, a tradition that has been criticized by feminists as being male-biased, reflecting male values of logic and rationality.** It is argued that this method fails as a way to understand human behaviour.

The marxist tradition, however, has always paid some attention to the unpaid work of women. For example, the framework incorporated a relationship of the work of women in the home (called domestic labour or reproductive labour) to the moneyed economy, in that the value of labour and the amount of surplus value or profit created, were affected by the costs of sustaining the labour force and raising the next generation of workers (called reproduction of labour power). There were also predictions about the development of capitalism and its impact on the family and the sexual division of labour. Marx's view of the labour process also drew attention to the creation of divisions among the workforce as a tactic by capital to maintain control over labour and lower wage costs.

In these ways gender relations are more visible in marxist economics, though they have traditionally been of only peripheral interest to the main development of the paradigm. There has been an emphasis on class relations (between capitalists and workers, for example) over gender relations and a tendency to pursue most economic analysis without reference to women. As in neo-classical economics, women have been introduced in certain fields such as labour economics as a topic, but the overall radical paradigm has not been altered and most fields proceed to study economics for and of men.

The work done in all of economics related to women is concentrated mainly in labour economics and falls into two broad categories: *family economics*— looking at labour force participation decisions and market/non-market economic activities; and *wage inequality*— looking at discrimination, occupational segregation, and segmentation. A brief discussion of each will give the reader a sense of the work done by both radical and neo-classical economists on the subject of women.

---

* Having babies and looking after them; looking after others.
** See Marilyn MacDonald in this collection.

Family Economics

In terms of family economics, there has been considerable work done in explaining changes in labour supply. Why do people enter the labour force and how much time do they spend at work? This is the major area of economics that looks at non-market activity, since decisions about whether to enter the labour force are related to other uses of time and resources. The specific issue of determinants of female participation in the labour force has been of interest for many years in both paradigms. In the neo-classical paradigm, this took the form of standard labour supply analysis, based on individual choice between leisure and work (income). The individual faces certain constraints (such as available wages), has certain preferences about how s/he values income and leisure, and makes a choice of whether to work outside the home and how many hours to work which will maximize her/his well-being (utility).

In recent neo-classical work, the allocation of the time of various family members between market and non-market activities is analyzed as a matter of optimizing overall *family* (as opposed to individual) well-being. The "rational" choices families make, of course, turn out generally to leave women in the home or in secondary labour market activity, while men are the main family income earners. This is due to the lower expected wages women face in the labour market.

The analysis is useful for describing how a system perpetuates itself: how market wage differences for men and women lead to a household strategy of labour allocation which makes women secondary earners and which in turn perpetuates the market wage differences. It may well describe the choices rational people make in the present economic and social context. However, the analysis does not address the origins or development of the current gender and economic relationships. The constraints families face in the theory—such as lower market wages for women—are the real topic of interest, and these are passed over in the theory as "givens." As we shall see, neo-classical economists explain wage differences, ultimately, as a function of the gender division of labour in the home, and the division of labour ultimately as a function of wage differences. Most women make lower wages than their husbands, and therefore if one parent is to stay home with small children, it makes sense for it to be the mother. But if women tend to have interrupted careers because of their childcare responsibilities, then employers will not pay them as much or promote them as much. Thus, the neo-classical analysis aptly describes the vicious circle women experience, but it does not explain its existence or function. Furthermore, as an analysis of domestic activity, it does not go beyond the benefit of this activity to the individual family. Again, this productive activity in the home is not related structurally to market productive activity. How does the "economy"/company/male worker gain from this domestic activity? How does the organization of domestic labour tie in with market production? What forces move production from one sphere to another? How are market dollar values—prices, wages, profits—affected by what occurs in the non-market sector? These questions are not addressed in this framework.

These issues are more central in the marxist economic work on the family. There have been two lines of development in this. One begins from the wage labour side and the other begins from the domestic labour side. The former analyzes historically women's differential participation in the labour force, linking it particularly to the marxian analysis of the "reserve army of labour," which argues that a capitalist system creates and needs surplus labour and that women have served this function: available for paid work when needed and sent home when not needed. The latter approach focuses on the household sphere of reproduction, examining its relation to profit-making in the economy and its changing relationship to the sphere of production. These two lines of development in the literature are meeting each other, for the reserve army literature has had to develop an analysis of domestic labour and the domestic labour literature has had to examine the meaning of the movement of production (and labour) in and out of the wage-labour sphere. Economists working on these issues have, by and large, begun from a wage-labour market focus and then extended the analysis into the household. Most of the marxist-feminist work starting from the household has been done by sociologists rather than economists. Women's studies offers the opportunity to bridge these discipline boundaries and grapple with the total literature.

The analysis of women's labour force participation in the marxist literature focuses on historical changes in the economy and on the function of domestic labour in the external economy rather than focusing solely on the decisions of the individual woman and her family, as in neo-classical analysis. Capitalism's changing needs for labour as the market expands into new products and new services draw women into the workforce. For example, almost all clothing is commercially made now, and women who used to sew at home now work in textile factories and retail clothing stores. Of course, the economy of individual households is also important in this framework, but the questions asked differ. For example, why do more and more males not earn enough to support families? When one examines marxist-feminist work on the nature of the family and resource allocation within families, a very different image of the family emerges from that of the neoclassicists. The family is a locus of unequal power, conflict, and dependence. It must be emphasized, however, that marxist work on these issues is so marginal within economics as to be virtually invisible. Most PhD economists would never have encountered it. This means, of course, that most students in economics will not be exposed to this research. Such work is, however, part of a women's studies curriculum.

Wage Inequality

The other major area in economics where women are a focus, of course, concerns their experiences once they are in the labour force: in the public, priced economy. Here their experiences can be dissected and compared with all other members of the formal workforce. In this regard they present an interesting problem to economists in terms of wage inequality with men and occupational segregation. Full-time women workers earn approximately 66 percent of what male full-time workers earn. Even in identical jobs there may be striking wage gaps. Most women, however, don't work in identical jobs as men. Over 60 percent of women workers work in just three occupations—clerical, sales and service. Their labour force experience, all in all, is quite distinct, and economists have paid some attention to this.

In the neo-classical paradigm, worker wage inequality must be integrated into a general model of wage determination which emphasizes that competitive market forces tend to create wage equality for workers with equal skills, i.e., equal treatment of equals and wage equalization. If women were cheaper, everyone would want to hire them and their wages would be bid up. Of course, if there are restrictions on competition, then wage differences may exist and persist, though they serve no purpose in the economy. Unions might restrict membership and protect their jobs from competition with "cheaper" labour. Or large companies might pay higher wages than the going market rate to avoid unionization or to ensure loyal employees. Neo-classical economists also tend to emphasize discrimination that occurs *outside* the labour market rather than *inside* the labour market. A lot of emphasis is put on social attitudes or on discrimination in the education system.

Another direction taken by neo-classical theory has been the focus on *unequal* productivity, using human capital theory. Human capital is the productive ability a person brings to the labour market. Investment in education, health, and work experience all increase a person's human capital. In this work, the lower earnings of women are not viewed as unjust but are attributed to women's smaller investments in human capital and their resultant lower productivity, i.e., they are less valuable to employers. It is argued that, given the sexual division of labour at home, women *expect* to spend less time in the workforce, therefore get less education and training, and therefore earn lower wages.

However, empirical research has found that less than half of the average wage difference between men and women can be attributed to human capital (education and skill) differences. Over half is due to occupational segregation or pure discrimination in wages. These are not easily explained in the neo-classical framework, as we saw above.

The radical paradigm in economics has less problem explaining wage inequalities. The paradigm *emphasizes* economic inequality and conflict as key to the functioning of the capitalist system. A lot of attention is paid to the conflict between capital and labour or firms and workers. As part of this conflict, divisions are created among workers which help employers control workers and therefore increase profits. If male and female workers, or black and white workers, are kept in separate jobs or pitted against each other, then they are less likely to realize their common interests and to struggle for a greater share of profits. Radical economists expect to see divisions in a capitalist economy by race, ethnicity, and sex. However, little attention has been paid to the differences among these groups and how they fare in the economy. This approach, which can be labelled the "women and other minorities" approach to inequality, does not really address the particular nature of women's oppression and their contribution to the economy.

Women's Contributions to the Economy

It is to this question of women's economic role that we now turn. We have seen that economics as a discipline pays very little attention to women's contributions. We have seen that it perpetuates the invisibility of their work and does little to explain why they are in an unequal position in the paid labour market. The economic studies of women do little more than describe and measure the inequalities that exist. They do not examine their function in the economy or their origin.

There is a great need to develop an analysis of the full economy—an economy which includes women. This economics must, by necessity, be different from economics as it is now studied, taught, and practised. It must be interdisciplinary. It must not focus exclusively on price relationships. It must go beyond the surface phenomena of our economic system, where women indeed *are* invisible, to uncover the underlying relationships. It must include the economy of the household as well as of the market place, the informal as well as the formal economy. This work is only just beginning in economics.

The current mystification of the economy serves to perpetuate an economic system where women are subordinated in terms of opportunity, status, and power, at the same time as their labour remains essential to the maintenance of the whole system. It is common to talk of how women are marginalized in our economy, that they are unequal, discriminated against, and so on. But the other side of that picture is that we are extremely important to the economy—that our subordination is the source of much profit, that our services are indispensable. The work of women, as we all know, stretches paycheques, provides cheap labour, absorbs unemployment in communities, and cushions the blow of government cut-backs. When men lose their jobs, they are visibly unemployed. When women lose their jobs, they often disappear back into the status of "housewife." When there is unemployment in a family, it is the woman who stretches the few dollars, who may sell crafts, babysit, or take in boarders to help make ends meet. When the government cuts back nursing care for the elderly, who picks up the burden? Women, of course. The resistance women meet in struggles for equal opportunity underscores how important their contributions are to the status quo.

A handful of women, inside and outside the economics profession, is beginning to try to reconstruct an analysis of the economy. The task is formidable, but nowhere is it more important for changes to be made, given the power of the discipline in shaping public discourse on issues vital to our well-being.

The Women's Movement — Taking on the Economy/Economists

So powerful is male control over economic discourse that women have been silenced in their demands for equality by the admonition that they don't understand the "economic implications" of their demands or by having their issues labelled as social, not economic. These demands include better childcare, equal pay laws, housing, equal rights in the constitution, and a host of others that women's groups have mobilized around over the years. It is very important that we enter the economic debate, that we learn to take on economics and economic issues. Part of taking on economics means being confident in our economic arguments in support of policies like better childcare, pensions, maternity leave, education, and equal pay. Taking on economics also means tackling more general issues of economic policy such as free trade, industrial development strategies, and monetary policy. We must understand changing economic conditions and how they affect women, and we must get directly involved in economic policy debates. Women have begun to take up this challenge with regard to the impact of technological change and the trend towards increased part-time, low wage work at the expense of full-time work. Women are lobbying for policies to ensure benefits to part-time workers and equal wages for part-time and full-time work.

It is more important than ever that women students study economics and master the jargon so they can enter the current debates. At the same time, the ultimate goal must be to alter the terrain and shift the nature of the economic discourse, as discussed above.

Women's groups have suffered from abandoning economics to the men. While they have been busy focusing on particular issues directly relevant to women and even making gains in some areas, economic changes or policies in other areas continue to have negative effects on women, often indirectly. The right hand of government makes some gestures to improve the status of women while the left hand of government continues with policies which systematically perpetuate a worsening status quo for women. For example, Canada Employment and Immigration has set up special women's employment centres but has eliminated training programs that might enable women to move into better jobs. The federal government passed employment equity legislation at the same time it was negotiating free trade which affected thousands of women's jobs in textiles, food, and beverage industries. Free trade is generally not thought of as a women's issue, but it is, as are all economic policy issues (see Cohen, 1988).

Another general economic issue is the development strategies of provincial governments. Women are noticeably absent from the debates on development. There is no concern in most provincial development strategies about providing jobs for women. In fact, the more male-oriented the jobs, it seems, they more "real" they are in the government's score card. But women are unemployed and women are supporting families. Where are jobs for women? And why does nobody care?

Another example comes from debates in Nova Scotia about fishery policy, something that is certainly not thought of as a women's issue. The actors in these discussions always seem to be the companies, the fishermen, and the government. Where are fish plant workers, the majority of whom are women? The fishing industry runs on the unpaid and low paid work of women: as wives of fishermen, helping to outfit the boat, sell the fish and cook for the men; as fish plant workers doing the most tedious, low-paid jobs; and as workers in the service sector earning enough to enable their husbands to keep fishing for low returns. For example, there was much debate about the introduction of factory freezer trawlers. Most of the concern was with the threat to onshore fishermen and the net loss of processing jobs. Even without a net loss of jobs, however, there is a substitution of male freezer trawler jobs for female plant jobs. Women need to address this issue and examine the barriers that prevent them from access to these jobs. More importantly, this is a good example of jobs which are against the interests of women, no matter *who* has the job. These jobs assume someone (a woman) is at home to manage childcare and the household for weeks on end while the worker is at sea. Most "good" (i.e., male) jobs assume the person is free to work sixty-hour weeks, relocate around the country, or go to sea for two weeks at time. Equalizing childcare and housework is impossible in such a world. Both women and men must demand that employers recognize the work done in the home. This is a very radical demand and underscores how fundamental to our economy is the assumption that there is a sexual division of labour.

These are just a few examples of the desperate need for women to take action, to take on the economy and the economists. We all need to be able to talk about the economy. Only by doing this will women become visible. Only then will some of the economic realities reflected in the images mentioned at the outset begin to change.

Afterword, 1992

There is much more interest and activity in feminist economics now. Since this essay was written (1987), the Women Economist Network of the Canadian Economist Association has been established, as has the International Association for Feminist Economics. Nevertheless, feminist economics remains marginal to, or absent from, university economics curricula, and the representation of women in economics has seen no dramatic improvement.

Notes

1. Marjorie Cohen, "The Problem of Studying 'Economic Man'," in Angela Miles and Geraldine Finn (eds.), *Feminism in Canada* (Montréal: Black Rose Books), 1982, 92.

References

Amott, Teresa, and Julie Matthaei, 1991. *Race, Gender and Work: A Multicultural Economic History of Women in the United States*. Boston: South End Press.

Amsden, Alice (ed.), 1980. *The Economics of Women and Work*. London: Penguin Books.

Bakker, Isabella, 1992. *Engendering Macroeconomic Policy Reform in the Era of Adjustment and Restructuring: A Conceptual Overview*. Ottawa: North-South Institute (June).

Becker, Gary, 1981. *A Treatise on the Family*. Cambridge: Harvard University Press.

Beneria, Lourdes, 1981. "Conceptualizing the Labour Force: The Underestimation of Women's Economic Activities," *Journal of Development Studies* 17:3.

——, 1982. "Accounting for Women's Work," *Women and Development: The Sexual Division of Labour in Rural Societies*. New York: Praeger.

Beneria, Lourdes, and Martha Roldan, 1987. *The Crossroads of Class and Gender: Industrial Homework, Subcontracting and Household Dynamics in Mexico City*. Chicago: University of Chicago Press.

Beneria, Lourdes, and Gita Sen, 1981. "Accumulation, Reproduction and Women's Role in Economic Development," *Feminist Studies* 8(1)(spring).

Bergmann, Barbara, 1974. "Occupational Segregation, Wages and Profits When Employers Discriminate by Race or Sex," *Eastern Economic Journal* (April-July).

——, 1986. *The Economic Emergence of Women*. New York: Basic Books.

Bettio, F., 1988. *The Sexual Division of Labour: The Italian Case*. Oxford: Clarendon.

Blau, Francine, and Carol Jusenius, 1976. "Economists' Approaches to Sex Segregation in the Labour Market: An Appraisal," *SIGNS* (spring) 1:3.

Blau, Francine, and Marianne Ferber, 1986. *The Economics of Women, Men and Work*. Englewood Cliffs, New Jersey: Prentice-Hall.

Brown, Claire and Joseph Pechman (eds.), 1987. *Gender in the Workplace*. Washington: Brookings.

Cagatay, Nilufer, and Gunseli Berik, 1991. "Transition to Export-Led Growth in Turkey: Is There a Feminization of Employment," *Capital and Class* 43.

Cohen, Marjorie, 1982. "The Problem of Studying Economic 'Man'," in Angela Miles and Geraldine Finn (eds.), *Feminism in Canada: From Pressure to Politics*. Montréal: Black Rose Books.

——, 1985. "The Razor's Edge Invisible: Feminism's Effect on Economics," *International Journal of Women's Studies* 8(3): 286-298.

——, 1988. *Free Trade and the Future of Women's Work*. Toronto: Garamond Press.

Connelly, M.P., 1978. *Last Hired, First Fired*. Toronto: Women's Press.

Day, Tanis, 1992. "Women's Economic Product: Unmeasured Contributions to Measured Output, or the Perils of Woman-Blindness," presented at the Canadian Economics Association Meetings, Charlottetown, P.E.I. (June).

Elson, Diane, and Ruth Pearson (eds.), 1989. *Women's Employment and Multinationals in Europe*. London: MacMillan.

Elson, Diane, 1991. "Gender Issues in Development Strategies," paper presented to the Seminar on Integration of Women in Development, Vienna.

—— (ed.), 1991. *Male Bias in the Development Process*. Manchester: Manchester University Press.

Ferber, Marianne, and Carole Green, 1983. "Housework vs. Market Work: Some Evidence of How the Decision is Make," *Review of Income and Wealth* 29(2)(June).

Ferber, Marianne, and Julie Nelson (eds.), 1993. *Beyond Economic Man: Feminist Theory and Economics*, forthcoming. Chicago: University of Chicago Press.

Folbre, Nancy, 1982. "Exploitation Comes Home: A Critique of the Marxian Theory of Family Labour," *Cambridge Journal of Economics* 6(4).

——, 1986. "Cleaning House: New Perspectives on Households and Economic Development," *Journal of Development Economics* 22.

——, 1986. "Hearts and Spades: Paradigms of Household Economics," *World Development* 14(2).

Folbre, Nancy, and Heidi Hartmann, 1988. "The Rhetoric of Self-Interest–Ideology of Gender in Economic Theory," in A. Klamer, D. McCloskey and R. Solow (eds.), *The Consequences of Economic Rhetoric*. Cambridge: Cambridge University Press.

Goldin, Claudia, 1990. *Understanding the Gender Gap*. London: Oxford University.

Goldschmidt-Clermont, Luisella, 1982. *Unpaid Work in the Household: A Review of Economic Evaluation Methods*. Geneva: International Labour Office.

Grapard, Ulla, 1992. "Who Can See the Invisible Hand," presented at the First Conference on Feminist Economics, American University (July).

Harding, Sandra, 1986. *The Science Question in Feminism*. Ithaca: Cornell University Press.

Harding, S., and Jean O'Barr (eds.), 1987. *Sex and Scientific Inquiry*. Chicago: University of Chicago Press.

Hartmann, Heidi, 1976. "Capitalism, Patriarchy and Segregation by Sex," *SIGNS* 1:3 (spring).

——, 1981. "The Family as the Locus of Gender, Class and Political Struggle: The Example of Housework," *SIGNS*, 6:3 (fall).

Humphries, Jane, 1977. "The Working Class Family, Women's Liberation and Class Struggle: The Case of Nineteenth Century British History," *Review of Radical Political Economics* 9(3)(fall).

——, 1990. "Enclosures, Common Rights and Women: The Proletarianization of Families in the Late Eighteenth and Early Nineteenth Centuries," *Journal of Economic History* 2(1)(March).

Humphries, Jane, and J. Rubery, 1984. "The Reconstitution of the Supply Side of the Labour Market," *Cambridge Journal of Economics* 8.

Keller, Evelyn Fox, 1982. "Feminism and Science," *SIGNS* 7:3 (spring).

MacDonald, Martha, 1984. "Economics and Feminism: The Dismal Science?" *Studies in Political Economy* 15(fall).

Manser, Marilyn, and M. Brown, 1979. "Bargaining Analysis of Household Decisions," in Lloyd, Andrews and Gilroy (eds.), *Women in the Labour Market*. New York: Columbia University Press.

Matthaei, Julie, 1982. *An Economic History of Women in America*. New York.

McCloskey, Donald, 1985. *The Rhetoric of Economics*. Madison: University of Wisconsin Press.

——, 1989. *Some Consequences of a Feminine Economics*, Project on Rhetoric of Inquiry. Iowa: University of Iowa, Iowa City.

McCrate, Elaine, 1991. "Rationality, Gender and Domination," Working Paper, Women's

Studies Program and Department of Economics, University of Vermont.

McElroy, M.J., and M.B. Horney, 1981. "Nash Bargained Household Decision-Making," *International Economic Review* 22.

McFarland, Joan, 1976. "Economics and Women: A Critique of the Scope of Traditional Analysis and Research," *Atlantis* 2(1)(spring).

Michael, R., H. Hartmann, and B. O'Farrell (eds.), 1989. *Pay Equity: Empirical Inquiries*. Washington: National Academy Press.

Nelson, Julie, 1992. "Gender, Metaphor and the Definition of Economics," *Economics and Philosophy*.

——, 1991. "Value Free or Valueless? Notes on the Pursuit of Detachment in Economics," *History of Political Economy*, forthcoming (manuscript August).

Palmer, Ingrid, 1991. *Gender and Population in the Adjustment of African Economies: Planning for Change*. Geneva: ILO.

Phillips, Paul, and Erin Phillips, 1983. *Women and Work*. Toronto: Lorimer.

Pujol, Michele, 1992. *Feminism and Anti-Feminism in Early Economic Thought*. Edward Elgar.

Robb, Roberta Edgecombe, 1991. "Gender and Economics: Some Issues," presented at the Canadian Economics Association Meetings, Kingston, Ontario (June).

Rubery, Jill (ed.), 1987. *Women and Recession*. London: Routledge and Kegan Paul.

Schultz, Theodore, 1974. *Economics of the Family: Marriage, Children and Human Capital*. Chicago: University of Chicago Press.

Sen, Amartya, 1990. "Gender and Cooperative Conflicts," in I. Tinker (ed.), *Persistent Inequalities: Rethinking Assumptions About Development and Women*. New York: Oxford University Press.

Sen, Gita, 1991. "Macroeconomic Policies and the Informal Sector: A Gender Sensitive Approach," Working paper No. 13, Vassar Department of Economics.

Waring, Marilyn, 1988. *If Women Counted*. San Francisco: Harper-Collins.

Williams, Rhonda, forthcoming. "Race, Deconstruction and the Emergent Agenda of Feminist Economic Theory," in Marianne Ferber and Julie Nelson (eds.), *Beyond Economic Man: Feminist Theory and Economics*.

Wilson, G., 1991. "Thoughts on the cooperative Conflict Model of the Household in Relation to the Economic Method," *IDS Bulletin* 22(1).

Woolley, Frances, 1991. "The Feminist Challenge to Neo-classical Economics," Working paper CEP 91-13, Department of Economics. Ottawa: Carleton University.

Chapter 9

On Sexism and Science
Marilyn MacDonald

September 15, 2002

Dear Lisa:

Thanks again for your hospitality—nothing like a surprise visit from your relatives, especially when you're studying for an exam the next day! It was good to see you and to catch up on how things are going in your second year of university. I'm sorry that we didn't have a longer talk about your science courses, and that we only got started on a discussion of sexism in science.

It's hard for me to put myself back twenty-five years to my first year in university. I remember how exciting it all seemed, living away from home, in a small town, in residence with women who would become friends, acquaintances, enemies. It's even harder to separate my love of science from the people I knew, the atmosphere of the place, and just being young and free to learn. Like all memories, that time is a collection of incidents—convincing my mother that switching from Fine Arts to Science was a good idea because in art you had to have something to say, while in science you could find out what there was to say; having a two-hour discussion of a book by Koestler on the similarity of creativity in science, art, and humour; taking part in work-ins, sit-ins, and demonstrations because it was the sixties and the world could be changed; and, above all, picking Biology over Math, Physics, or Chemistry because it was fascinating, and incredible to get an inkling of how so dynamic an interplay of systems, from chemicals to biosphere, could develop and maintain themselves. I felt like, and was, part of a privileged few. Other incidents from that time took longer to be appreciated—the cell biology course in Home Economics that was far better than that offered by the Biology department but was not quite as "legitimate;" the only woman teaching in the Science/Math faculties, who was not offered tenure and left when her probationary period ended. I spent twenty years studying ecology in graduate school working as an ecology consultant, with the government in research and development contracting, and being involved in various groups (environmental law, anti-nuclear, and so on). In those twenty years, I went from loving science and the pursuit of knowledge through feeling inadequate and lost in the competitiveness and the irresponsibility of "the system," to coming to terms with what is lovable about science as we have envisioned and created it and what is not lovable. There are two things that epitomize those twenty years for me. The first is a poem I wrote when things had started to come together again, when I'd stopped taking responsibility for the alienation I'd felt in the system of science and started looking for alternatives.

I cannot believe that I can sit here missing you,
Recalling the way that your body moves or stays,
And the things that we've said or understood.
After all the years of being alone,
You've given me back my mind.

I can remember when every morning was a time of dread
That I would have to live until evening;
When everything that I knew was childish, counterproductive
And the result of mid-Victorian oppression.
So I learned that the way to knowledge was not through compromise and love,
But through overpowering the opposition—
The Vince Lombardi ethic raping poor vestal virgin thought.
We have our own mythology for chaos—
A Faustian hope for recognizable patterns;
Oedipus' fate, seen all too clearly;
And the mirror-doom reality of the Lady of Shallott.
The ancient healers learned all too well
That the dangers of knowledge lie in possession.
Transcending sight,
We cannot see reality.

Yet I've been a scientist for too long now;
And separation is such an easy act
To share. I cannot write this down without desiring recognition;
Publisher or reader to parse and praise, or tell me how it stands
In relation to current theory on the meaning of the soul
And life.

Life. In any form sacred.
Yet now the poor are genetic load, and Skinner holds
The cards of our minds.
A human trinity of dilemma—
That somewhere between fate and freewill lies an unrecognized alternative.
Remember when you were young, and time was a thing
That could be turned back, if you could find the right moment?
Something kept now with the feeling that you could fly,
Or that parents knew everything.
Leaving the cobwebbed toys of the growing mind,
Do all our rites of passage only mark our growth away
From deeper truth?

Please wait. Don't listen to my defences.
Probably none of this is true; more to be taken with a grain of salt
To melt away on my blue Mondays.
And I'm old enough now to wonder at my foolishness
In letting even one moment pass involved in triviality
Instead of what matters. And it is true
That I sit here missing you
And the way your body moves or stays.

The second thing is the death of a friend of mine. He was an epileptic on medication to control the seizures. The medication made him drowsy, and, under the pressure of finishing his graduate degree and getting good enough results to get post-graduate support, he stopped taking the medication. He choked to death one weekend, working overtime—he had a seizure when nobody was around. It was such a needless death and is wrapped up, for me, in all the other needless deaths and cruelties and disastrous side-effects of a science practised at the limits of endurance rather than within a web of positive support.

So, was my experience just a run of bad luck (better than some, worse than others)? Or were/are there fundamental problems with science? If there are problems, do they result from sexism? I'm always tempted to use facts to point out that sexism exists—that men and women have different success in science; that women drop out of science courses at a younger age than men; that women who stay in science have a harder time finishing graduate school, getting science-related jobs in university, government, or industry, and accumulating the publication/funding merit points necessary to reach positions of power; that women studied by scientists are often victimized in those studies; that men and women do not differ enough on either cognitive or personality bases to account for the disparity between male and female success in science. However, all those facts have been "done to death"—if you want a list of references I can send you one. (Some of them are included in the bibliography.) Suffice to say that this disparity is not innate. What does sexism in science entail?

I think the effect of sexism on science was best explained in a psychology text by Atkinson, Atkinson, Smith and Hilgard. The authors were discussing the tendency that people have to obey authority. The example that they used was an experiment in which people thought they were giving lethal shocks to other people. Over three-quarters of the people studied gave the shocks, even though they felt bad about doing so. As the authors said,

> A belief in the primacy of "scientific research" is the ideology that prompts individuals to relinquish their personal moral authority and to voluntarily subordinate their own independence to goals and purposes of a larger social organization (Atkinson et al, 1987, 613).

My argument is as follows:

1. people create stereotypes to make life easier. They have models of what should be and mould reality to fit those models;
2. people are transient and live in an unpredictable world of pain, poverty, and death. Any system that provides or seems to provide, a bulwark against these forces of chaos would be welcome;
3. people grow through stages from an uncritical acceptance of authority to an ability to make their own moral decisions;
4. given the above, a sexist science will have control over chaos as an ideal and this ideal will be seen as masculine;
5. a feminist science will involve integration and relations and would not have an ideal, being pluralistic and diverse;
6. there is strong resistance to the idea that science is anything other than an objective way to ultimate truth, because too many other things are involved (like power, wealth, control, and so on).

So where do I begin to argue against the new religion? Let's start with the nature of science and sexism.

In a sexist science, women and men believe that women are inferior to men in the performance of science and that the values of science are more properly male. Part of the feminist impact on science is a change in that belief system. Women can do mathematics, study science, and work in laboratories as capably as men. But that is only part of the impact, because it does no good to have more women entering into a destructive system. There are basic changes needed in our ideal or model of science. This leads to the obvious question: what is science?

To answer that question, let's first look at science as a function (how it is done, what it does) and then at science as it is perceived (dictionary definition, expectations, and so on). As I eventually realized, there is quite a gap between the two, and the cause of the gap is sexism.

Science is essentially the evaluation of creativity. That is, someone has a flash of insight and then finds out if that insight is true in a few or in many situations; if it is part of other insights; and so on. For example, Archimedes (so the story goes) was looking for a way to measure the volume of things. As he got in the tub to take a bath, he watched the water rise. Eureka—a body (philosopher) submerged in a liquid (bathwater) displaces an amount of said liquid which just might equal the volume of that body. How to check it out? Submerge a lot of bodies of known volume and measure the amount of bathwater displaced. After several weeks in the bathroom, Archimedes had a new scientific principle.

This method of evaluating creativity is a way of looking at the world that people have used for four hundred thousand years. The first woman who envisioned a scraper (wedge) in a flint pebble, or a digging stick (lever) in a branch tested her theory by science. We use science to form theories about ourselves and others, in the ways that we organize our perception of our surroundings, in our acquisition of language, in our cognitive moral and social development. The flash of insight may be luck or the result of years of observation or anything in between, but it is creative, personal, and necessary to the scientific process. Then, through observation, experiment, and discussion, through generalization and discrimination, we try to fit the insight into our overall understanding of the nature of things. If the insight is significant, either alone or with other insights, then we may be forced to change that overall understanding of things.

Science is both a private and a public act. Archimedes had a flash of insight which he rushed out to share with his students and with other philosophers. The principle of constancy of volume displacement lasted beyond Greece and 200 B.C. because other people accepted the principle, made use of it, and passed it on. The public function of science in evaluating creativity is the legitimizing of knowledge—what deserves to be kept and what is best dumped and forgotten. Therefore, the nature of the society will affect the science that is carried out. For example, if the members of a society are afraid of tampering with their social store of knowledge, they will then restrict access to knowledge to only a few people, or they will limit the ways in which knowledge can be presented and preserved, or they will develop rituals to ensure that the purity of knowledge is maintained. These measures lead to inequity because the people controlling the knowledge have power over the ones who don't, whether in deciding when crops should be sown, or what cure is needed for an illness, or if a genetically engineered human should be patentable. So why argue that science is sexist rather than classist or racist or any other of the "ists" which act to maintain a fortunate few at the expense of many?

First, stereotyping according to gender is one of the first distinctions that we make. Second, the habit of discrimination which one gets into with sexism can be readily generalized to include race, class, or any other criterion. During the sixties, many women dropped out of civil rights, back-to-the earth, environmental, and other movements and into feminism because they realized that they'd still be support staff the day after any given glorious revolution. Third, much of the authority granted to science rests on its association with masculine ideals. To support these three points, I have to make a clarification that at first may seem to add more confusion than anything. That is, what I've been calling sexist should be called genderist (but that just isn't as catchy a word).

Sex is something that we take for granted as a distinction among people. We ask if a baby is a boy or a girl; we use forms of address that identify an individual's sex; we carry birth certificates and driver's licenses and fill out job applications that have a little space for F or M (picture doing the same thing for race or class—we've become much more overt about those issues!).

However much of what we consider a function of sex is really a function of gender. Sex is the biological basis. That is, people are born with one or the other (or occasionally both) of two sets of reproductive equipment which determines the individual's sex; i.e., male, female, or hermaphrodite. Gender is learned thereafter. A child is taught a gender role from the moment of birth on; that role generally conforms to the biological sex but need not. It is a socially-imposed identity, acquired by children in their first three years of life. Although reproductive activities are the basis for gender identity, other activities are added on which are considered appropriate (or inappropriate) for each gender. Yet of these other activities, on a world-wide basis, there are none that are done solely by one or the other sex. If sex were the determining factor, then women would do the same thing from culture to culture (as would men).

Given that gender is a socially constructed identity, what does our culture (whatever that is) consider appropriate for men and women? I've culled the following from some first year psychology texts:

Female	Male
dependent	independent
supportive/nurturing	aggressive/competitive
emotional/affective	rational/cognitive
intuitive	logical
verbal	spatial/mathematical
simultaneous (no time)	sequential (time sense)
passive/gentle	active/rough
relational	linear
repetitive	innovative
immanent	transcendent
experience	argument

In essence, this stereotyping causes some people (say 52 percent of the population) to repress their competitiveness and their innovation in order to appear dependent and nurturing. "Boys don't make passes at girls who wear glasses;" "You have to let him win at tennis/chess/work or he won't feel like a man;" "The hand that rocks the cradle rules the world." Other people (say 48 percent of the population) repress their emotions and their verbal communication of relationships in order to appear logical and independent. "Dolls are *girls'* toys, don't be a sissy;" "Big boys don't cry;" "Real men don't eat quiche;" "That's an old wives' tale."

How does this stereotyping relate to science? It has the greatest impact when the private act (of evaluating creativity) is made public. There are three main aspects of this:

1. methodology: how the private act is made public, and how the public act is carried out;
2. body of knowledge: what is accepted as valid, and maintained and transmitted;
3. institutions: the formal (e.g. schools, universities, associations, societies) and informal (e.g. family, networks) ways in which the first two are carried out.

As I said earlier, science is sexist when women and men are perceived as unequal performers thereof. That is, science is sexist when the methodology unrealistically embodies only masculine ideals; when the body of knowledge does not include women's realities or includes them only as deviations from the male norm; and when the institutions exclude women from making decisions about and taking part in science.

Before expanding on those three points, let me go back to the gap I'd mentioned between science as a function and science as it is perceived. I've argued that science is insight followed by evaluation. Does that view fit with the normal view? The Oxford Dictionary defines science as:

> ...a branch of study in which facts are observed and classified, and usually quantitative laws are formulated and verified; involves the application of mathematical reasoning and data analysis to natural phenomena.

As my father would say, "If that thing shit, it would smell like roses." This definition contains the ideals to which we expect science to conform. It is much too methodical, too predictable, too omniscient to account for the real thing. For example, it took a power failure at a Maryland greenhouse (and the subsequent flowering of some plants) for us to realize that daylength affects flowering. Teflon resulted from a mix-up while looking for a different product altogether. Lyell, who publicly announced that he's been wrong and that Darwin was right, is held up as a shining example of a good scientist because so many others are too pig-headed to change their minds. How does this dictionary definition, this normative standard, embody sexism? Let's go back to the three points of methodology, body of knowledge and institutions.

Methodology

In the evaluation of creativity, there are certain steps to be taken, namely:
- flash of insight: formation of a tentative explanation for some event (i.e., hypothesis)
- evaluation: carrying out the scientific method from designing a crucial experiment (which will support only one of any of the possible hypotheses); through carrying out the experiment and analyzing the results; to discussion, conclusions and submission of the whole thing (from hypothesis to conclusion) to public review and duplication.

There are a number of ideals involved in that scientific method such as empiricism, objectivity, openness to question, determinism, and progressiveness. I've drawn up a table giving some of the reasons for and against the likelihood of attaining those ideals.

Ideal	What is it?	For	Against
Empirical	knowledge is based on observation; derived from experience rather than theory ("facts are observed")	continually checking theories against reality, getting new observations	limited by the range of our senses; ignores the theories we use to decide on which observations to make in the first place
Objective	knowledge is gained by removing the consciousness (perception, thought) of the subject; presenting what is external to the personal mind ("involves the application of mathematical reasoning and data analysis")	seeks to remove biases and presuppositions	by the time people do scientific research, they have so many hidden beliefs and biases that they can't recognize them let alone remove them; when we reduce ourselves to only the intellectual exercise, we remove the necessity to act morally or ethically (other than doing "good" science)
Openness to Question	results have to be obtainable by anyone under the same conditions; results have to be defensible against anyone's scientifically valid tests; results have to be "public" ("usually quantitative laws are formulated and verified")	the knowledge gained in science is continually checked against new information; everyone has a chance to contest a theory's validity	experiments take more time and money than most people (including researchers) have, so most work is not redone; most scientific results are tied up by commerical confidentiality, security or specialist jargon; there often is a significant time lag between the statement of a theory and its rejection

Deterministic

knowledge has predictive value because cause-effect relations can be found; implies that natural phenomena will behave according to laid-down patterns

("laws")

allows one to deduce consequences and therefore to test theories; means that science is useful in making sense of the future

causality is difficult to define because we are not sure we've found the ultimate cause or even just a relationship; most complex systems are not deterministic (chance has a large effect on outcomes)

Progressive

because it is constantly checked, objective and empirical knowledge is added together as we move towards ultimate truths

("phenomena become facts which become laws which become ever more general laws")

errors which we made in the past may not be repeated; we have a broader understanding by synthesizing many areas of knowledge

doesn't proceed in a linear fashion but more in stages or revolutions; may be unable to accurately reflect reality because it is limited by our senses, our cognition, our creation of categories

I've dissected that Oxford definition in detail because I've looked in vain therein for the human creativity that is the basis of science. All the fact-gathering, law-making, and mathematical reasoning apparently could be done with exactly the same results by either people or computers. But, if you equipped a robot with eyes, ears, and touch, and set it down someplace to gather facts, it would still be gathering them centuries later, no closer to doing science then than now. It would need some prior reason for selecting from the infinite number of sensations, for deciding on one small aspect of reality, for picking one particular crucial test to see if it was right or not. We go to a great deal of effort, strenuously ignoring reality, to pretend that science transcends the human. Even mathematics, so often cited as the ultimate abstraction, is subject to the whims and foibles of its human creators. The Athenian philosophers were limited in their numbering system because they found some types of numbers distasteful and so they wouldn't use them. There are similar fads in various mathematical systems today. But why do we put so much effort into their idealization?

We have created a stereotype of science where truth is reached only if we allow free competition (verification of theories), logic and reason, and a separation of cognitive from all other mental and physical efforts. In addition, truth is reached by separating from a complex reality the simplest of its component parts, and then testing that part in a linear sequence (if I change this, what happens to that?). In other words, if you look back at the comparison of feminine and masculine gender traits, you can see that we have endowed our model of science with everything we hold to be masculine in our gender stereotypes. Even though the actual practice of science is a blend of the masculine and feminine, we edit out what we'd associate with the latter. For example, the creative insight that is the basis for scientific discovery is often intuitive, yet it is ignored in our description of science. Similarly, the linear, independent laboratory experiment (in which one factor is studied while all others are held constant) is inadequate to explain the real world's complex interactions. Yet all the evidence we have of "side-effects" are ignored or down-played. The North Sea is dying? No problem, we'll find a technological solution.

I think this masculinization of science has been a two-way street. Over three or four hundred years, as we've worked out an ideal for science, we've also worked out one for the masculine. The result is that scientific knowledge has an authority above and beyond its actual value, and the masculine gender is perceived as more naturally having access to that authority. Thus, knowledge which came from science was held to be a true reflection of reality (because it was gained by observation, by logical analysis, by competitive evaluation, and because it was truely independent of human belief). Anyone who doubted the authority of science was shown the blunders of Ptolemy (who thought the Earth was the centre of the universe), of the witches (who thought peasant medical knowledge was useful), and of numerous other subjective fools who threatened to pollute the pool of knowledge. Only men were thought able to meet the rigorous intellectual demands of such an authoritarian pursuit.

Some feminists have argued that sexist science is simply bad science. They cite non-random samples (e.g., Piaget using only boys to make claims about girls' and boys' cognitive development), overgeneralization (e.g., the U.S. National Institute of Health monitoring the effect of AZT as a treatment for AIDS but refusing to allow women into the test program, and only in December 1992 even acknowledging that women had unique symptoms of AIDS—the acknowledgement meaning that women dying of the disease could now be officially diagnosed and get the right medical help), poorly-formed hypotheses in which unidentified assumptions about women's/females' biological role are not separated from the way the data are gathered (e.g., anthropologists who study other cultures' "technology" and ignore cooking, childcare, and vegetable gathering as non-technological women's work), and any of the other errors which flesh and logic are heir to but can be cured of. Some feminists have also argued that women need to stay in science and in mathematics, from public school to public policy-making. But above and beyond that, it is necessary to change our fundamental ideals of science. We need to bring our understanding of science more in line with reality, to reincorporate the feminine with the masculine ideals, and to look at curbing those aspects of our human nature that make us such a difficult species with which to share a planet. Next on the list after "methodology" in looking at how science goes from a private to a public act is "body of knowledge."

Body of Knowledge

People have an insight, evaluate it, and find it worthwhile. If they don't have access to our culture's institutions (discussed later), then the chances are that the insight will not be preserved. The body of knowledge, then, is not so much the private information which a person accumulates in a lifetime, but the shared information which we write down, pass around, teach, and mark for approval. How does this relate to gender?

First, there is a tendency to grade scientific knowledge by its tumescence. Physics/chemistry, with their precise and expensive equipment and isolatable simple systems, produce "hard" data. Biology/psychology/anthropology with their complex interrelations, their subjects' "free will" and their diversity, produce "soft" data. (While "exact" and "fuzzy" might seem more accurate terms, there is a hidden association of the more logical/masculine end of the continuum of the sciences with a state of manly arousal and the other end of the continuum with flacidity: either femininity or a lack of arousal.)

Second, there is a tendency to spend more on aggression (whether it is military research or tearing knowledge from nature by force) than on nurturance (whether it is healthcare or seeking insight into the ways in which life is expressed and interacts). That is why Canada spends $4 billion on military helicopters and $10 million on breast cancer research. As an interesting exercise, you might look up the spending done by various countries on research. On a world-wide basis, a lot of it goes into the military, and a lot of what is left goes into high-priced laboratory equipment. We spend more on high tech medicine than we do on preventative health care. We spend more on pesticides, mechanization, and fertilizers than we do on marketing and minimizing ecological damage. What we know is based on what we've spent time and money on, and, unfortunately, most of the effort has been directed at power over others rather than on coexistence.

Thirdly, there is a tendency to oversanctify scientific knowledge, to assume that it is purified of human content. However, it is as much a mistake to argue that science is progressive (i.e., that it moves over onward and upward, apparently unaffected by human concerns) as it is to argue that men are unswayed by emotion in their practice of science. Scientists are as consumed by jealousy, need for recognition, curiosity, love, hate, fear of death/failure/job loss as anyone else, and those emotions affect their work.

Scientists form cliques, accept someone's dubious results based on their position in the discipline's hierarchy, and don't have enough money or time to duplicate others' experiments or to read more than the abstracts of many of the papers being published in their fields. Some scientists cheat, lie, steal each other's results, run around on their spouses, use graduate students or technicians as slave labour. All those behaviours are part of the human condition (maybe not necessarily, but for now). If we accept this vulnerability of scientific knowledge of emotional influence, then we may have a more realistic, albeit less cocksure, approach to using that knowledge.

Fourthly, scientific knowledge is overloaded with information about men, the male and the norm. From research studies that ignore women, or that treat them as deviant men, through history that forgets women and their contributions, to whole areas of knowledge that are trivialized because they are seen as feminine, the scientific body of knowledge on which our culture depends is sexist. Unfortunately, it is like the situation in the little verse (pronouns changed as required):

> Last night I met upon the stair
> A little woman who wasn't there
> What she can want, I cannot say
> But how I wish she'd go away.

In other words, scientific knowledge cannot be considered unbiased or representative until all "sides" are heard from. In addition, scientists cannot fall back on the "fear" motivators such as, "if you try to control the direction of research (i.e., cut off funding), then you could be the reason we don't find a cure for cancer and solve world problems." Obviously, political decisions are made all the time about what research is carried out and what problems are or aren't important. That's why the U.S. has an "orphan drug" law: pharmaceutical companies have to spend some research money looking for cures to diseases where there aren't enough sufferers to make such research "worthwhile." To better understand the basis of the knowledge so far created, we should look in detail at how that knowledge is kept and passed on.

Institutions

Every society has customs and practices through which certain activities are carried out. These may be either formal or informal. For example, scientific activity is carried out in formal organizations such as clubs, universities, research laboratories, and so on; and through informal, socially recognized roles, norms, and agreed-upon paradigms. In the informal institutions, there are expectations carried within these roles or norms to which individuals such as professionals are expected to conform. Taken together, formal and informal institutions control human behaviour and the realization of human potential.

Feminist criticism of science has dealt with both the formal and informal institutions and the ways in which women are excluded from positions of power and influence in them. The fourth century A.D. Alexandrian mathematician, Hypatia, was murdered at the instigation of the Christian Church, to which she appeared (as a learned woman) blasphemous. Universities in Europe came into their own as centres of learning in the eleventh century A.D., yet women could not attend that type of institution until the 1800s. In the United States, some universities opened their doors to women, not because they had a change of heart about women's ability to become professionals, but because some women and men had put together a convincing argument for scientific motherhood (that is, training in the domestic sciences). Such Home Economics disciplines included biology, chemistry, physics, and so on, but the people who worked in them and the publications about their research were trivialized by the men in the more mainstream institutions. As women acquired training in the sciences, they looked for jobs. They moved into support positions as technicians, research assistants, and wives or daughters of researchers. The existence of women who could learn to do science but who could go no further than assistant or teacher in an academic backwater casts doubt on claims of science's objectivity and openness to question.

The awareness of victimization followed from the first two areas; once feminists knew that women's contributions had been ignored and that strong social barriers existed to keep them out of science, then they began to look for more widespread and subtle evidence of victimization. Victims are people (or other living things) that are hurt because they get in the way of someone else or some other circumstance. Women are victims of science when their lives are affected by decisions over which they have no control. Since women have only recently had the vote, had access to education, and been recognized as adults in the law, and are still engaged in struggles with men for equality of freedom to define ourselves, there are many examples of such victimization.

At present, women do not have the same access that men do to the pursuit of the profession of science. Women's child-bearing years are from about age fourteen to age fifty; in our society, the average age for first birth is twenty-five and the average number of children per woman is under two. Thus, procreation and career come into conflict at the time when job mobility and job devotion are paramount in the "typical scientist's" life cycle. The typical scientist's academic career begins in kindergarten (for a child of four or five years of age) and runs straight through to a doctorate degree (age twenty-six to thirty), with post-doctorate research (another five years) and a career path in industry, government or university that proceeds from one level to the next, year by year and job by job. This pattern is planned for men's and not women's life cycle. A more egalitarian society would have daycare, co-parenting, continuing education, parental leave, job-sharing, and many of the other changes sought by women who want or need to work outside the home.

Women are left out or are subject to the biases of male researchers. Women have difficulty convincing the existing research establishment that opportunities to know more about women's lives are worth funding, or even considering. Creative insights which women may have on health, reproduction, peace, and so on are rarely carried further than the individual can afford. For example, although men and women have been working outside the home in industry for over one hundred years, the Canadian Department of Health and Welfare, in 1986, launched a study of occupational-related sickness in men. The assumption seems to be that women are a version of men and that the results found for men can be transferred to women. Unfortunately, women's occupations and life cycles differ enough from men that this could be a life-threatening assumption.

One of the easiest ways to verify this resistance to granting women's issues any validity is to suggest in class or at work that you would like to see some research done on, say, male contraceptives (and why they aren't being used); or job re-entry programs for scientists returning to work at age thirty onwards; or women's contribution to the development of science (given that the universities, societies, and guilds which formed the network for the Scientific Revolution of the 1600s were closed to women), and to see if it's taken seriously and in a supportive way.

In summary, science is a private act made public, relying on methodology, a body of knowledge, and institutions. A closer examination of each of these reveals bias due to gender. First, the ideals of the scientific methodology correspond closely to the masculine ideals of independence, competition, rationality, logic, linearity, and transcendence beyond the human. The ideals, however, of the feminine stereotype—of support, intuition, simultaneity, relation, dependence, and acknowledgement of our realities—are as much a part of the actuality of science but are downplayed to lend authority to the knowledge gained by science.

Second, that body of knowledge is flawed because large areas of experience are left out and because much of the knowledge is wrapped up in hidden assumptions, unwarranted credence, and other subjective biases. Because science has been considered progressive and open to question, the exclusion of women has been justified on gender-based grounds, supported by the argument that the methodology is too masculine for women to handle and by the demonstrated fact that much of the knowledge is masculine.

Third, such arguments have been furthered by the formal and informal institutions of our society which concentrate the power of science—the power to find control over others—in the hands of a few.

Our definitions of masculine and feminine gender roles create a relationship of control, with the masculine as leader and the feminine as follower. Yet throughout life, men and women encounter situations which require them to display attributes from both gender roles. Essentially, then, a feminist science requires a rethinking of gender roles towards a more fulfilling realization of human potential.

A feminist science also requires a rethinking of social roles as defined by class, race, or other parameters. If we consider individual human development, then a feminist science is liberating because it will provide people with the ability to make their own cognitive and moral decisions and to have confidence in their creativity.

Finally, a feminist science requires a shift in the values of our society, away from the desire for power over others (and the need to clearly define such others), and towards a realization of power within (and the strength in interrelatedness). It is after such a shift that I can envisage us finally beginning to understand a feminist science.

I've included a definition of a feminist science—some of the concepts are ones we haven't yet named (a small liberty on my part). Let me know if you can guess which ones are which and what they might mean.

It occurred to me that what you will be doing this summer is a feminist approach to scientific research. By studying whales in their habitat(s), by recognizing them as individuals, and by taking care not to intrude, the BIOS research is invaluable. Contrast that with the "research" undertaken by countries which are looking for an excuse to slaughter—like Japan with a kill of three hundred whales.

Anyway, good luck in your exams. See you in August.

Love,

Marilyn

P.S. November 20, 2002
Enclosed is a copy of a page from the latest edition of The Feminist Dictionary. I thought you might find it interesting.

Science—the clarification of relationships; the tying of new creative thoughts of existing human knowledge through syncognition, contextualization, and evaluation; a combination of methodology and institutions (both formal and informal) in which human understanding of the richness of reality is expanded; part of the I-Chaltra cycle of meditative training, including the techniques of critical examination and affective reattachment; an act of love.

—partial word-nest* as follows (for n-dimensional imagery, refer to hologram KR-238)

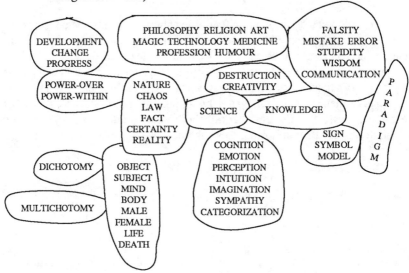

*A group of words of associated meaning, all of which contain common assumptions about the aspects of human experience being described (Feminist Dictionary, 8th ed., 2001, 1045).

References

Albury, D., and J. Schwartz, 1982. *Partial Progress: The Politics of Science and Technology*. London: Pluto Press.

Alic, M., 1984. *Hypatia's Heritage: The History of Women's Science*. London: Pandora Press.

Arditti, R., P. Brennen, and S. Cavrak, 1980. *Science and Liberation*. Montréal: Black Rose Books.

Ardrey, R., 1961. *African Genesis: A Personal Investigation into the Animal Origins and Nature of Man*. New York: Dell Publishing Co.

Atkinson, R., R. Atkinson, E. Smith, and E. Hilgard, 1987. *Introduction to Psychology*.

9th Edition. New York: Harcourt Brace Jovanovich.

Barbour, L., 1966. *Issues in Science and Religion.* New York: Prentice-Hall.

Bleir, R., 1984. *Science and Gender: A Critique of Biology and its Theories on Women.* New York: Pergamon Press.

——, (ed.), 1986. *Feminist Approaches to Science.* New York: Pergamon Press.

Brighton Women and Science Group, 1980. *Alice Through the Microscope: The Power of Science Over Women's Lives.* London: Virago Press.

Bynum, W., E. Browne, and R. Porter, 1985. *Dictionary of the History of Science.* Princeton, New Jersey: Princeton University Press.

Capra, F., 1975. *The Tao of Physics: An Exploration of the Parallels Between Modern Physics and Eastern Mysticism.* Oxford: Fontana Paperbacks.

Carson, R., 1962. *Silent Spring.* New York: Fawcett Crest.

Ching, E. (ed.), 1983. *Proceedings of the First National Conference for Canadian Women in Science and Technology.* Society for Canadian Women in Science and Technology, Vancouver.

Cockburn, C., 1985. *Machinery of Dominance: Women, Men and Technical Know-How.* London: Pluto Press.

Comfort, A., 1984. *Reality and Empathy: Physics, Mind and Science in the 21st Century.* New York: State University of New York Press.

Corea, G., 1977. *The Hidden Malpractice: How American Medicine Mistreats Women.* New York: Harcourt Brace Jovanovich.

Cowan, R., 1983. *More Work for Mother.* New York: Basic Books.

Dinnerstein, D., 1977. *The Mermaid and the Minotaur: Sexual Arrangements and Human Malaise.* London: Fontana

Doern, G., 1972. *Science and Politics in Canada.* McGill-Queen's University Press.

Earman, J. (ed.), 1984. *Testing Scientific Theories.* Minnesota: University of Minnesota Press.

Easlea, B., 1983. *Fathering the Unthinkable: Masculinity, Scientists and the Nuclear Arms Race.* London: Pluto Press.

Edwards, D., 1979. *Drawing on the Right Side of the Brain.* California: J.P. Tarcher Inc.

Eichler, M., and J. Lapointe, 1985. *On the Treatment of the Sexes in Research.* SSHRC Canada.

Faderman, L., 1981. *Surpassing the Love of Men: Romantic Friendship and Love Between Women from the Renaissance to the Present.* New York: William Morror and Co. Inc.

Fee, E., 1982. "A Feminist Critique of Scientific Objectivity," *Science for the People* 14(5-8): 3-33.

Feyerabend, P., 1981. *Problems of Empiricism: Philosophical Papers.* Cambridge: Cambridge University Press.

——, 1985. *Philosophical Papers: The Problems of Empiricism 2.* Cambridge: Cambridge University Press.

Fuller, R., 1969. *Utopia of Oblivion: The Prospects for Humanity.* New York: Bantam Books.

George, S., 1984. *Ill Fares the Land: Essays on Food, Hunger and Power.* New York: Institute for Policy Studies.

Gearhart, S., 1979. *Wanderground: Stories of the Hill Women.* Boston: Alyson Publishers Inc.

Gilman, C., 1979. *Herland: A Lost Feminist Utopian Novel.* New York: Pantheon Books.

Goodman, P., 1962. *Compulsory Miseducation and the Community of Scholars.* New

York: Random House Inc.

Gonatilake, S., 1984. *Aborted Discovery: Science and Creativity in the Third World*. London: Zek Books Ltd.

Gornick, V., 1983. *Women in Science: Portraits from a World in Transition*. New York: Simon and Schuster.

Gould, S., 1981. *The Mismeasure of Man*. New York: W.W. Norton and Co.

Graham, L., 1978. "Concerns About Science and Attempts to Regulate Enquiry," in *Limits to Scientific Enquiry*. Daedalus 107(2): 1-22.

Greenglass, E., 1982. *A World of Difference: Gender Roles in Perspective*. Toronto: John Wiley & Sons.

Griffin, S., 1979. *Women and Nature: The Roaring Inside Her*. New York: Harper and Row.

Gutting, G., (ed.), 1980. *Paradigms and Revolutions: Applications and Appraisals of Thomas Kuhn's Philosophy of Science*. Indiana: University of Notre Dame Press.

Haas, V., and C. Perrucci (eds.), 1984. *Women in Scientific and Engineering Professions*. Ann Arbor: University of Michigan Press.

Harding, A., 1986. *The Science Question in Feminism*. Ithaca: Cornell University Press.

Harding, S., and M. Hintikka (eds.), 1983. *Discovering Reality: Feminist Perspectives on Epistemology, Metaphysics, Methodology, and Philosophy of Science*. Netherlands: Reidel.

Hayden-Elgin, S., 1987. *The Judas Rose*. New Jersey: Daw Books Inc.

Hrdy, S., 1981. *The Woman that Never Evolved*. Cambridge: Harvard University Press.

Hubbard, R., M. Henifer, and B. Fried, 1979. *Women Look at Biology Looking at Women*. Cambridge: Schenkman Publishing Co.

Illich, Ivan, 1983. *Deshooling Society*. New York: Harper and Row.

Keller, E., 1983. *A Feeling for the Organism: The Life and Work of Barbara McClintock*. New York: W.H. Freeman and Co.

——, 1985. *Reflections on Gender and Science*. Mass.: Yale University Press.

Kevles, D., 1986. *In the Name of Eugenics: Genetics and the Uses of Human Heredity*. Berkeley: University of California Press.

Kline, M., 1980. *Mathematics: The Loss of Certainty*. Oxofrd: Oxford University Press.

Koblitz, A., 1983. *A Convergence of Lives: Sofia Kovalevskaia: Scientist, Writer, Revolutionary*. Boston: Birkhauser.

Koestler, A., 1964. *The Act of Creation*. London: Hutchinson & Co.

Kramerae, C., 1981. *Women and Men Speaking: Framework for Analysis*. Mass.: Newbury House Publishers Inc.

Leakey, M., 1984. *Disclosing the Past: An Autiobiography*. New York: McGraw-Hill Book Co.

Lips, H., 1981. *Women, Men and the Psychology of Power*. New Jersey: Prentice-Hall Inc.

Lloyd, G., 1979. *Magic, Reason and Experience*. Cambridge: Cambridge University Press.

Madden, E., 1960. *The Structure of Scientific Thought: An Introduction to Philosophy of Science*. Mass.: Houghton-Mifflin.

Medawar, P., 1984. *The Limits of Science*. New York: Harper and Row.

Merchant, C., 1980. *The Death of Nature: Women, Ecology and the Scientific Revolution*. California: Harper and Row.

Merton, R., 1979. *The Sociology of Science: Theoretical and Empirical Investigations*. Illinois: University of Chicago Press.

Morris, R., 1983. *Dismantling the Universe: The Nature of Scientific Discovery*. New York: Simon and Schuster.

Morison, R., 1978. Introduction. "Limits to Scientific Inquiry," *Daedalus* 107(2) 1-22.

Munevar, G., 1981. *Radical Knowledge: A Philosophical Inquiry into the Nature and Limits of Science*. Indianapolis: Hackett Publishing Co.

Murphy, Y., and R. Murphy, 1974. *Women of the Forest*. New York: Columbia University Press.

Newman, L. (ed.), 1985. *Men's Ideas/Women's Realities: Popular Science, 1870-1915*. New York: Pergamon Press.

Oesterle, J., 1953. *Logic: The Art of Defining and Reasoning*. New Jersey: Prentice-Hall Inc.

Orpwood, G., and J.P. Sorique, 1984. *Science Education in Canadian Schools* 1 of 3. Introduction and curriculum analysis. Background Study 52. Science Council Canada.

Piercy, M., 1976. *Woman on the Edge of Time*. New York: Fawcett Crest.

Prigogine, I., and I. Stengers, 1984. *Order Out of Chaos: Man's Dialogue with Nature*. New York: Bantam Books.

Reed, E., 1978. *Sexism and Science*. New York: Pathfinder Press.

Reiter, R., 1975. *Towards an Anthropology of Women*. New York: Monthly Review Press.

Reynaud, E., 1981. *Holy Virility: The Social Construction of Masculinity*. London: Pluto Press.

Richards, S., 1984. *Philosophy and Sociology of Science: An Introduction*. New York: Schocken.

Rohrbaugh, J., 1979. *Women: Psychology's Puzzle*. New York: Basic Books Inc.

Ronan, C., 1982. *Science: Its History and Development Among the World Cultures*. New York: Hamlyn Publishing Group.

Rossiter, M., 1982. *Women Scientists in America: Struggles and Strategies to 1940*. Maryland: Johns Hopkins University Press.

Sayre, A., 1975. *Rosalind Franklin and DNA*. New York: W.W. Norton and Co.

Schwartz, B. (ed.), 1972. *Affirmative Education*. New Jersey: Prentice-Hall.

Shahar, S., 1983. *The Fourth Estate: A History of Women in the Middle Ages*. New York: Methuen.

Spender, D., 1981. *Men's Studies Modified: The Impact of Feminism on the Academic Discipline*. New York: Pergamon Press Inc.

Sperry, R., 1984. *Science and Moral Priority: Merging Mind, Brain, and Human Values*. Westport, Conn.: Praeger Press.

Starhawk, 1982. *Dreaming the Dark: Magic, Sex and Politics*. Boston: Beacon Press.

Stark-Adamac, D., and M. Kimball, 1984. "A Psychologist's Guide to the Conduct of Non-Sexist Research," *Canadian Psychology* 25(1): 23-24.

Statistics Canada, 1983. *Canadian Science Indicators*. Science and Technology Statistics Division.

——, 1985. *Women in Canada: A Statistical Report*. Social and Economic Studies Division.

Stent, G., 1978. *Paradoxes of Progress*. New York: W.H. Freeman.

Stone, M., 1979. *Ancient Mirrors of Womanhood*. Boston: Beacon Press.

Turkle, S., 1984. *The Second Self: Computers and the Human Spirit*. New York: Simon and Schuster Inc.

Vickers, J. (ed.), 1984. *Taking Sex Into Account: The Policy Consequences of Sexist Research*. Ottawa: Carleton University Press.

Chapter 10
Redesigning Cities, Redesigning Ourselves: Feminism and Environments

Suzanne Mackenzie

As feminism is a politics which involves us in day-to-day change of our lives, it is important to keep in mind visions of possible futures, both those we are building toward and those we are working to avoid. Conventional academic discourse often makes it difficult to talk about imagined futures. Feminist scholars have struggled to overcome this, but the most powerful evocations of our possible futures are novels, utopian and dystopian.[1] Another, less widely recognized source of inspiration, is the study of the built environment, specifically the environments which women have altered and created to meet their needs and embody their visions. Historically, changes in human environments have been an integral part of changes in gender roles, both enabling and constraining choice and creativity. One of the ways of understanding our past accomplishments and failures, and of planning for our futures, is to look at the concrete forms and patterns which people have created in the course of changing their lives and to see these as the resource base upon which future changes will be built. This is essential both to avoid the pessimism and paralysis which result from forgetting our creativity in chronicling our oppression and to build strategies which are both grounded and far-sighted.

This is the story of one woman's attempt to trace some of the ways in which environments have interacted with women's lives, some of the conflicts which the contemporary city poses for women, and some of the ways in which women have responded to these conflicts. This woman talks about how she and other people have altered their environments in the course of altering their lives, and she seems to argue that the environments she and her neighbours are creating "work"; that is, they enable greater choice by providing flexible resources. *She stands some time in the not-too-distant future and looks back at our cities.*

The vision here is incomplete and very open to debate. The details are only sketched out, the outlines are jagged and full of disjunctures. I have added notes to this woman's story which suggest readings to help fill out the picture. But the vision can only be completed, altered or extended by ourselves, by looking around us at our spaces, by talking about them, moving through them, changing them, or preserving them. And although we create the forms and the resources together, there are probably as many visions as there are people to see them.

I remember my mother and her friends talking, those apparently eternal summer afternoons while I sat, a little uncomfortable from my sunburn, exploring textures of wooden lawn chair slats and melting ice cubes with my fingers, smelling heat from the street, not quite hearing the traffic from behind the tall varnished fence. They always had a sense of urgency, those women. Sometimes they argued. But it seemed to me then, as it does to me now, that those women and their words were surfeit with security and confidence. Part of this came from the assurance that there was a functioning microwave inside the kitchen to cook the dinner, that the laundry was being done by a machine somewhere. Part of it came from the assurance that their work was to talk and think and plan and write down their ideas in journals and planning reports. And most of their security and confidence came from the unstated conviction that they, and women like them, could change the world.

They were feminists, those women. They were also geographers, planners, architects; women specialized by long years of training to be conscious of, and in some way responsible for, the natural and built environments in which our lives went on. They felt their feminism as immediate and active, and they felt the environment—the houses and neighbourhoods and paths and factories and office towers—was also immediate. They talked about how these environments affected the ways people could act, how environments funnelled people into moving along certain paths, focused their imaginations into certain channels. They talked about how environments restricted women's actions and movements and imaginations in specific ways.[2] Their talk was full of flashes of startling insight, suffused, I realize now, with blind incomprehension. And I can see, looking back now, how much of the blindness came from the places in which they lived and worked, and the ways these places constrained their vision of alternatives.

My mother worked in two places. One was an office. On the few occasions I went there, it seemed a cold and uninviting place, with few interesting textures or colours or places to move freely. She said this was because it was a place organized for work, not for children. My mother also worked at home, cleaning, cooking, caring for me and my father and the house. Our home was different than her office, full of smells and colours, with rooms for eating and cooking and sleeping and sitting.

I see now that she must often have been tired, moving between these two different places. Perhaps she was often lonely and harassed too, by all this moving back and forth, even when my father was there after one of his business trips. She said movement was the curse of her generation, annihilating space with time until movement took up all the time. She said we could move our ideas instantly over space, by telephoning or talking by computer, but that the people who had those ideas and acted on them could not follow their thoughts so easily. They needed real, concrete places, full of walls and separations, in order to work and live. Moving people required a lot of effort: driving cars over massively expensive freeways in snow and heat and traffic jams, sitting on airplanes, and standing on crowded buses.

She and her friends were always moving, going to meetings and conferences and to shops and, above all, back and forth between work and home. Sometimes I think that all this moving made it more difficult for them to work and think and live. The different parts of their lives—their "work lives" and "home lives" and "social lives"—were all parcelled into boxes, divided into different buildings and separated by space. They worked and lived in a series of spaces which were incomplete, like my mother's office, which seemed to be designed on the assumption that she had no life other than her work, or our home, which had few facilities for doing her "work" and had few places near it for doing shopping or for meeting with neighbours. It was as if these places had been designed in isolation, with no thought for the variety of activities which make up human lives.

We live now in such different spaces, and our time is so different, full of contrast, fluid, and vulnerable. Our time and space hold nothing and no one still. And yet what we have now we built out of those spaces that existed then, sometimes in opposition to them. As the economy underwent the massive upheavals of the 1990s, and as our lives changed in fundamental ways, we used what we had to create new ways of living. And we will create our futures using the resources we have now.

More and more, I want to understand the places I recall from my childhood, before I lose the sense of how important they were to what happened. I've read my mother's books; I've talked with her and with her friends; and in my odd spare moments, I've tried to reconstruct those places and where they came from.

Our house had been built for a particular kind of family—one where someone worked there full time, cleaning, cooking, shopping, driving children to after-school activities—which did not resemble ours. It was obsolete even when I was young. It was built, I see now, by people who wished to make money. They built things as cheaply as possible with little care for flexibility or permanence. Inside these little boxes, which were powered by vast amounts of electricity running incredible numbers of machines, people attempted to create places for meeting some universal human needs—nurture, affection, food, rest—common to all people in all times.

But the places were limiting. All the food, clothing, furniture, electricity for meeting these needs came from somewhere else. And in order to get these things and pay for them, the women and men who lived in these houses had to rush out, to a variety of other limited and specialized places, to make money and to purchase these things.

I knew from reading my mother's books that spaces hadn't always been organized in this way. In the past, centuries ago, people had lived and worked in one place. They had farmed or made pots or woven cloth in their households and communities, with their children tumbling and learning around them. Everyone and everything was there; there was no place else to go. Threatened by hunger, by diseases which are only names now, by capricious wars, they had worked and lived and celebrated. They were tied to their homes and their communities by multitudes of bonds, by the resources they found or created there and used to make a living: soil, tools, neighbours, markets. In those times, being without a household and a place meant you were poor, redundant, cut off from resources.[3]

But slowly, people created a system—industrialism—which meant they had to move away from their places and those immobile resources and long-standing networks. More and more moved to cities where industries were oriented not to local needs and resources but to global markets. And then they moved *within* these cities. Every day, family members left the homes where they ate and slept and talked. One by one they went off to separate places, places owned by someone else, to do a set of activities, such as tending spinning machines or cutting metal or writing figures in columns. These activities were meaningless in themselves. They had no apparent relation to the people's needs for food, clothing, shelter, friendship. And they were often dull and dangerous as well. People did these activities for a specified number of hours which was determined by someone else. At the end of that time, they did not own what they had made or written down. Instead they were given money, itself not inherently meaningful. They took this money to yet other places and exchanged it for things they needed. And those things they took home, to pool together with the things others brought, to sustain themselves.

This altogether odd system took time to establish, especially as there was often a mismatch between what people needed and what they could obtain with what they had earned. There often was not enough money, no matter how people tried, to buy good food and adequate shelter. Often it was impossible for individuals to match their pay with the needs of their households.

There appeared to be many people who were homeless, children who were uncared for, and a lot of sickness. And there appeared, by the late nineteenth century, to be a lot of "reformers," people dedicated to rebuilding the city in new ways because they believed that many of these problems were inherent in that vast, wonderful, awful resource system people had built to house the machines and the people who worked them.[4]

The reformers, and those who found ways to make money by redesigning the city, acted to change the form of the city, to create something wholly new. They worked to create a city where thousands of small individual homes would be separated from the central places where manufacture and trade went on. They built suburbs full of these homes with schools and churches, and sometimes shops. And they rebuilt the centre as a place where work could go on untroubled by crying children, church bells, and other reminders that nurture and other values had a role in life.

The city became separated into places for "work" and places for "life." Work, which had always been part of life, now had a separate place and time. And workplaces and times came to be defined as somehow more important than lifespaces and times. Public planning was primarily concerned with efficiency in the workplace and design of industrial-commercial areas. And people began to organize their lives to fit around work: buy or rent homes to be close to "work," educate their children to be good workers instead of good human beings.

It was not just the space that was separated. As always, the way people created their buildings and resources and paths reflected and affected the way they lived their lives. People's social roles became more specialized and distinct.

Within this separated city, some people became "workers:" they were defined by others and by themselves as people who did specific jobs for pay, as "factory workers" or "clerks" or "managers." Every day they moved from home to places designed exclusively for work, and they did their appointed tasks. These people were generally men.

Other people were "housewives" and "mothers." They worked in the residential areas, moving around their homes and the neighbourhood, cleaning, caring, tending fears and bruised knees, cooking, organizing social services, marketing. These people were generally women.

Other people were "children" or "youth" or "students" and went to special places—schools—to learn the skills necessary to become either "workers" or "housewives" and "mothers."

All of this was possible because the productivity of labour had become higher as each worker used more machinery and produced more goods, and people formed unions to demand higher wages. By the early twentieth century, for the first time in history, one worker could be paid enough to buy the raw materials to meet the needs of other people. Other people worked to turn these raw materials into the necessities of family life: preparing food for meals, sewing material into clothing, cleaning and maintaining household equipment.

But it is not clear why women and men took on these separated, gender-specific roles; why men denied themselves access to the time and resources for life and women allowed themselves to be denied access to the places of work and public life and the resources there. That some men and women resisted this is suggested by the records of the early twentieth century saying over and over that it must be so, it must be natural. But I think their resistance must have weakened. Later, by the mid-twentieth century, the record becomes silent. It is simply assumed that men act this way, that they go out and earn money *because* they are men, and women act this other way, they stay home and care for men and children and take care of "life" *because* they are women.

The written record provides so little evidence, but the city, the landscape which people built, provides much more. The record is there in those homes and neighbourhoods. Those women who worked in them were too busy to write: maybe they had little time to reflect. They moved around their homes, nurturing, creating places where people could be emotional, could love, eat, rest. And because they were there, in those homes and communities where all of this went on, they became seen as naturally suited to this work. Women became associated with all the feelings and activities of the home. They lost much of their individuality as they all came to be seen as nurturant, emotional beings. The problem wasn't the work itself, which was important, usually satisfying work. The problem was that women and men had few choices. All women were defined as naturally suited to being housewives and mothers and nothing else and all men as suited to being wage earners, no matter what the individuals might actually wish to do. It was said that women were unsuited to the market and to public life. Most were denied access to education, apprenticeships, and university degrees, and married women were denied access to most jobs.

Each woman was largely isolated in her individual home, cut off from other adults and the wider resources of society. Each woman expended tremendous amounts of energy maintaining her home and family, duplicating the labour of other women millions of times. And each woman was defined as a "non-worker"; she had no money of her own, no public place in society, no claim to recognition or resources except as a "dependent" of her husband.

Women came to be defined by the space of the home and neighbourhood, circumscribed by it, filled with it, and it filled with them. They did so much there and left such a rich record in their homes and communities, a record we are only now coming to read.[5]

And yet, by the 1950s, the written record begins to talk of a new phenomena. They call it "working mothers and wives." Since it must have been obvious to everyone that those women at home did work, one can only assume that this meant women were entering the public places and times of "work" again. People again seemed to need more than one income to build their homes and provide for their children. There was a flood of studies about this, as if women working was a new thing. The way these mid-twentieth century women worked was perhaps new, because they worked in this new kind of city which separated life and work. They moved between those places set up for life—the home designed on the assumption that someone was working there full time—to those places set up for work—offices and factories—which were designed on the assumption that there was no other work in society.

These women rushed back and forth, feeding their families, cleaning their homes, bearing their children, all in the time left over from canning pet food, scrubbing hospital floors, writing advertisements to sell things to other women. The market seemed flooded with things called "instant"—coffee, meals, ovens—aimed at saving time. Yet in all this dizzying movement, few people seemed to notice that little was done to help with the important things, like good childcare and affordable, efficiently designed houses. No one seemed to think that those places and times designed for work should adapt to the needs of life.

There was a blindness somehow, in this separated city. People seemed to think that the only way to get resources for the home and community was by getting money through work. People talked about increasing profits and productivity as the central aim of nations. At the same time they talked about the human needs which had been met in the home and community—care for children and older adults, ensuring adequate diets and housing—as "drains on resources." The economic system which people had created to meet their needs appeared to have taken on a life of its own and was trampling on the needs of many of the very people who had made it. Because these human needs were being met in places separated from work, no one seemed to realize that they were important, that they created jobs and human wealth.*

Some people, my mother and her friends among them, argued against this. They said we had to plan for an androgynous labour force, one which included both men and women. They said we had to realize workers were also parents and had elderly relatives to care for, and we had to provide things like good childcare and support services and pay equity to ensure that both men and women could make choices about where they would work and could do their paid jobs and home jobs successfully. Because they talked about human beings and their needs, they were often dismissed as a "special interest group" or ridiculed as "utopian" by people who said that national survival depended not on meeting people's needs but on maintaining something called a "competitive edge."

But these discussions were eclipsed by something which was, at first, called a "recession." Later, by the 1980s, people began to call it "restructuring" and said that we were moving into a post-industrial or post-capitalist society. Whatever one called it, it seemed to mean, most immediately, that more and more people lost their jobs and of course began to lose access to many of the resources they needed for survival. And just when they were most needed, many "social services"—health care, housing, social counselling, income support services— were curtailed. People said there was no money to pay for meeting human needs that could not be met by the market. There was certainly no money to meet the demands for pay equity and better education by so-called "special" groups, such as women.

The debates about what to do became more and more heated, as unemployment rates of 20 to 30 percent—once confined to rural areas where people depended on fishing, mining, smelting, farming, and forestry—became the norm in many cities. Access to things like health care and housing and welfare services became more difficult. It became harder and harder to understand what was going

---

* See Martha MacDonald in this collection.

on. There was little news from rural areas or from other countries. The government asserted over and over that things were all right. The newspapers and radio and TV repeated this to us. The discussion about solutions began to crystallize. By the time I was in my early teens, people were arguing and acting from very different perspectives.

Many people had begun to argue that, in fact, it was women who caused the problems. They said that all women should stay home, in those millions of boxes, and each make millions of meals and take on the full care of millions of children and the old and sick, clean millions of ovens and miles of carpet, drive millions of cars to acres of shopping centres. If women did this, they said, there would be no unemployment. Men would find jobs doing what women used to do and there would be no need for social services.[6]

These arguments were oddly reminiscent of the nineteenth century records. Women's activities became defined as the focus of the problem. Changing women's activities, especially changing the places they worked, came to be the focus of the solution. (In many respects, of course, women changing both the ways they worked and the places they worked was the focus of some part of the "solution" but not in the way these people had anticipated). They argued for a strict separation between "home" and "work," with people's space and responsibility and social activity clearly demarcated by their gender. They tried to shore up the early twentieth-century city with its separation of home and work, to recreate or preserve the boxing away of caring, affection, nurture into the household, leaving the market free of the inconvenience of human idiosyncrasy, of unions demanding childcare and pensions, of workers having to tend sick children.

Other people, like my mother, her friends, and women and men like them, said this was not only oppressive—denying both men and women choices about how and where they would work—but that it wouldn't work. Most people couldn't afford to live this way, they said, even if they had two parents in a family, which many did not, and even if they could survive on one income, which was likely to be a very low one if men took over the pay scales as well as the jobs of women. They extended their earlier arguments for bridging services between home and work. They said, more and more forcefully, that we had to alter the economy, the way we worked, the places we worked, to meet the needs of people. They argued about job-sharing and flexible work hours. They said we had to realize that human services like childcare and care for the elderly created jobs. They pointed to examples of specific businesses which had bridged the gap between home and work, providing childcare and flexible time. They pointed to housing projects where social services and childcare were provided or where a variety of age groups and income levels were housed and provided services for each other, allowing people to care for their families *and* do wage jobs.[7]

Yet while people debated on TV screens and in the places of government, everyone seemed to have forgotten those people who were "at home," unemployed or underemployed. No one seemed to ask what they were doing to get by. Having left the market, they became invisible. And yet it was *at home*, in part, that a new way of living and working was being created, sometimes out of desperation, sometimes out of concentrated creative energy, wholly out of the necessity to survive, to keep going by using what one had left.

What people had left when their jobs began to disappear, when there were fewer and fewer resources coming in from the public sphere, were their homes, their communities, their families, neighbours, and friends. While it was no longer possible to go "to work" in a separate, air-conditioned, streamlined place, making or organizing things, it was still possible, in fact it was essential, to do the things that had been done at home: caring for children and adults, maintaining the home and its equipment, trading time and skills and resources. These resources, human and physical, and these jobs, remained.

Somehow, more and more people began, quietly, to create another kind of response, to make a new economy out of what remained to them. Women had always cared for each other's children and other adults. They had always done most of this at home, being paid little or nothing and going largely unrecognized. Now they made small businesses of this, used their homes as childcare centres or as informal centres for the disabled or elderly. Women (and some men) had always made things at home to give, barter, or sell. Now they made businesses of this, setting up workshops in garages and basements, organizing networks to buy materials and to sell things co-operatively. Women and men organized to provide services. They typed, sewed clothing, fixed cars, canned food. Occasionally they were paid for these goods and services; almost always they traded things and time back and forth.[8]

People outside this new, informal economy rarely saw what was really going on here, or, if they did, they dismissed it as "temporary," as a "minor aberration." And yet, as I grew older, this seemed to be the group of people I was drawn to. Often it felt as if the others were clinging to an outmoded system which separated human life from wage work. They were blinded to what went on in the community, often blind even to the physical changes in the homes and neighbourhoods. They seemed, all of them, to assume that the home was a private place and that nothing really significant could go on there.

When I was a child, I had gone every day to the home of a woman who lived and worked near our home, a woman who cared for other people's children along with her own. This woman's house was a rich and noisy place, full of neighbourhood children, toys, books, and other adults. It was her home and her workplace. In addition to caring for us in her home, she and some other women had organized a playgroup, with a toy and book library, in a local church hall. We went there from her house three times a week, and the women met and talked and we played with the sand and water toys made by one of the caregivers and her husband.

Women who were skilled craftsworkers or musicians came to teach us things. I know they had meetings about their work: they invited my mother to speak once. My caregiver also made toys, large soft animals and people, glittering and strong. And she and other women made trips together to buy materials and sell the toys.

I remember one afternoon, in my late teens, when I was helping her, I remarked, half casually, as if I was mouthing accepted wisdom, that unemployment was a problem. "Why?" she asked me, and I looked up from the wooden train I was repairing, startled. I told her it was a problem because people didn't have jobs. "Is that a problem?" she asked. "Some people, like your mother, enjoy their jobs. They would hate to lose them. But most people don't like what they do at work. Much of it is boring, meaningless." "Well," I said, "but if they don't have jobs, they don't have money." She agreed but said that money in itself was meaningless. She said there were two things that were important: the resources people needed to survive and the sense of self-worth and identity, of belonging to a community and doing something worthwhile. In this society, she said, most people assumed they could only get those things by having jobs. But that wasn't true, she told me. "Look around you," she said. "People need resources to survive, people need to be part of society. But there are a lot of different ways to accomplish the that."

As I grew older there seemed to be more and more people "at home." Fewer moved out to work. The jobs people did in the wage sector changed. There were fewer life-long, well-paid, unionized jobs in industry. More and more people were employed in the so-called "service" sector, doing things like working in restaurants and shops, for delivery companies, as clerks. These people often worked on contract or part-time; they were generally badly paid and had little sense of performing skilled or worthwhile work. Many worked under increasingly difficult conditions. Wages and benefits such as pensions and unemployment insurance were cut, safety and health regulations ignored. Even professionals like my mother became increasingly insecure. Many professionals lost permanent jobs and became "private" contract workers, doing the same work for less pay and with fewer or no benefits.

Sometimes it seemed everything was in flux. Families moved around a lot. A growing number of men left the area. Some, like my father, did not come back. Others went away "to find work," sent money, and eventually returned. More and more men began to stay "at home" too, to live and work there. The community still contained a lot of work to be done, and for a growing number of people it became the centre.

The shape of the home and community began to change, including its concrete walls and paths. At first, it was just that things seemed shabbier, the paint peeled, grass grew in deserted supermarket parking lots, the cars were older, there were a growing number of boarded-up buildings. Gradually, the shabbiness became invisible, turned into something else. We put home-made playground equipment in the overgrown parking lots and built a small grandstand in one. People tore down the backyard fences from which the paint was peeling and created block gardens and play spaces. They moved in together, and the whole block used an empty house for a food co-op, play centre, drop-in clinic, and meeting place. People used each other's washing machines and cars. A few years ago, we moved all the washing machines that still worked into one house and took turns doing each other's laundry. We even do some cooking that way now, and we use one house as a workshop to make things that other people need and will pay or trade for. We spend most of our time here, working and living.

Sometimes I feel an affinity with those people, long ago, who lived and worked in one place. I know this is different. We are islands, changeful and vulnerable. Often it feels we are only hanging on, waiting for something. But then, too, it feels that we are hanging on to what really matters.

I spend an afternoon sometimes with my mother and her friends, and we talk. They still have a sense of urgency, often of anger. They admit that the houses and the neighbourhoods had to change, that they were entirely unsuited to the way we live now. They admit we cannot all do everything, that it is easier and more pleasant to share tasks like cooking, cleaning, caring, gardening, earning, getting resources.

But they are not resigned, they never will be, those women. Like many of my contemporaries, they continue to argue that public money and resources should be paying for childcare, health care, housing. I say we are providing those things here, and they nod, and then go on to say we should demand more resources, lobby, refuse to give up. I say we haven't given up. But, I point out, we also have to survive. We cannot wait to feed ourselves and the children or love and comfort each other until someone gives us the resources to do it better. I say we must ask for resources from the basis of what we have built here, an economy built on our immediate human needs. We must extend the resources and the values of serving human needs outwards, to other groups of people, like and unlike us.

Last night my mother said "You are removing yourself from the centre," and I did not know what to say. As I walked home, across the garden, past the co-op apartment and the community garage, I told myself, "No, we have moved the centre back home." Yet I found myself arguing with her invisible presence, with all of those women I remember talking to on those summer afternoons. And I found myself stopping, standing still in the autumn wind, looking around me.

Notes/References

1. Novels of dystopias–negative or oppressive imagined societies–include:
Atwood, Margaret, 1985. *The Handmaid's Tale*. Toronto: McClelland and Stewart.
Fairbains, Zoe, 1985. *Benefits*. New York: Avon
Utopian fiction includes:
Gilman, Charlotte, 1979. *Herland*. New York: Pantheon (originally published 1915).

Kesler, Carol (ed.), 1984. *Daring to Dream: Utopian Stories by United States Women, 1836-1919*. Boston: Pandora.
Piercy, Marge, 1976. *Woman on the Edge of Time*. New York: Fawcett Crest.

2. There is a growing body of literature about the relations between gender and environment, especially about how environments affect women's lives. See, for example:
Andrews, Caroline, and Beth Moore Milroy (eds.), 1988. *Life Spaces: Gender, Household, Employment*. Vancouver: University of British Columbia Press.
Keller, Suzanne (ed.), 1981. *Building for Women*. Lexington, Mass.: Lexington Books.
Little, Jo, Linda Peake, and Pat Richardson (eds.), 1989. *Women in Cities: Gender and the Urban Environment*. London: MacMillan.
Matrix, 1984. *Making Space: Women and the Man-Made Environment*. London: Pluto.
Stimpson, Catherine, Elsa Dixler, Martha Nelson, and Kathryn Yatrakis (eds.), 1981. *Women and the American City*. Chicago: University of Chicago Press.
Tivers, Jacqueline, 1985. *Women Attached: The Daily Lives of Women with Young Children*. London: Croom Helm.
Wekerle, Gerda, Rebecca Peterson, and David Morley (eds.), 1980. *New Space for Women*. Boulder, Colo.: Westview.
Women and Geography Study Group of the Institute of British Geographers, 1984. *Geography and Gender: An Introduction to Feminist Geography*. London: Hutchinson.

3. On the medieval city in Europe and attendent social relations, see:
Laslett, Peter, 1965. *The World We Have Lost*. London: Methuen.
Mumford, Lewis, 1961. *The City in History*. New York: Harcourt, Brace and World.
Tilly, Louise, and Joan Scott, 1978. *Women, Work and Family*. New York: Holt, Rinehart and Winston.

4. On the problems and reform of early industrial Canadian cities, see articles in:
Rutherford, Paul (ed.), 1974. *Saving the Canadian City: The First Phase, 1880-1920*. Toronto: University of Toronto Press.
Stelter, Gilbert, and Alan Artibise (eds.), 1977. *The Canadian City: Essays in Urban History*. Toronto: McClelland and Stewart, 54-91.

On women's activities in this period, see articles in:
Cook, Ramsay, and Wendy Mitchinson (eds.), 1976. *The Proper Sphere: Women's Place in Canadian Society*. Toronto: Oxford University Press.
Kealey, Linda (ed.), 1979. *A Not Unreasonable Claim: Women and Reform in Canada, 1880s-1920s*. Toronto: The Women's Press.
National Council of Women in Canada, 1900. *Women of Canada: Their Life and Work*. Ottawa: National Council of Women of Canada.

On British women and men, see:
Mackenzie, Suzanne and Damaris Rose, 1983. "Industrial Change, the Domestic Economy and Home Life," pp. 155-199 in James Anderson, Simon Duncan and Ray Hudson (eds.), *Redundant Spaces in Cities and Regions? Studies in Industrial Decline and Social Change*. London: Academic.

5. On living in these suburban communities, see:
French, Marilyn, 1978. *The Women's Room*. London: Sphere.

On the record women left in the environment, see:
Hayden, Dolores, 1981. *The Grand Domestic Revolution: A History of Feminist Designs for American Homes, Neighbourhoods and Cities*. Cambridge, Mass.: MIT Press.
——, 1984. *Redesigning the American Dream*. New York: Norton.

6. Some Canadian discussions of people who argue this position are:
Dubinsky, Karen, 1985. "Lament for a 'Patriarchy Lost'?: Anti-Feminism, Anti-Abortion and R.E.A.L. Women in Canada," *Feminist Perspectives* 1. Ottawa: Canadian Research Institute for the Advancement of Women/Institut Canadien de Recherches sur les Femmes.
Eichler, Margrit, 1985. "The Pro-Family Movement: Are They For or Against Families?" *Feminist Perspectives* 4a. Ottawa: Canadian Research Institute for the Advancement of Women/Institut Canadien de Recherches sur les Femmes.

American discussion includes:
Dworkin, Andrea, 1983. *Right-Wing Women*. New York: G.P. Putnam Sons.
Petchesky, Rosalind, 1984. *Abortion and Women's Choice: The State, Sexuality and Reproductive Freedom*. New York: Longman.

7. For some good examples of arguments like this, see the journal *Women and Environments*, an international journal published in Canada. Also, see:
Klodawsky, Fran, and Suzanne Mackenzie (eds.), 1987. "Gender-Sensitive Theory and the Housing Needs of Mother-Led Families: Some Concepts and Some Buildings," *Feminist Perspectives* 9. Ottawa: Canadian Research Institute for the Advancement of Women/Institut Canadien de Recherches sur les Femmes.

8. For some discussions of these kinds of strategies in the 1980s and 90s, see:
Mackenzie, Suzanne, 1986. "Women's Responses to Economic Restructuring: Changing Gender, Changing Space," pp. 81-100 in Roberta Hamilton and Michele Barrett (eds.), *The Politics of Diversity: Feminism, Marxism and Nationalism*. London: Verso.
——, 1987. "Neglected Spaces in Peripheral Places: Homeworkers and the Creation of a New Economic Centre," *Cahiers de Geographie du Québec* 31(83): 247-260.
Also see articles in the Canadian *Journal of Community Development*.

This also goes on extensively in Third World cities. See articles in:
Bromley, Ray, and Chris Gerry (eds.), 1979. *Casual Work and Poverty in Third World Cities*. Chicester: John Wiley.
Redclift, Nanneke, and Enzo Mingione (eds.), 1985. *Beyond Employment: Household, Gender and Subsistence*. London: Basil Blackwell.

PART THREE

The Politics of Knowledge: Feminism Makes a Difference

Introduction

In this section, teachers of women's studies courses and feminist researchers from a number of different disciplines describe and demonstrate the difference feminism has made, and continues to make, to our understanding of the contents and methods of traditional bodies of knowledge like literature and sociology, and established cultural practices, like psychoanalysis, social work and sports. In every case the particular subject matter and the knowledge and methods considered appropriate to it have been completely transformed and revitalized by developments in feminist theory, analysis, and critique. But in every case, those developments continue to be marginalized and, like women themselves, excluded from mainstream/malestream disciplinary definitions and practice, to the extent that an unknowing student can still spend many years in an academic discipline without encountering *any* feminism, except perhaps by way of a dismissive gesture. As Marilyn Porter so aptly expresses it, feminists are still like cuckoos in the disciplinary nests. We "squat" where we can, taking up space and stealing the disciplines' young when we get the chance, but we have not as yet succeeded in "penetrating" and thus transforming the disciplinary species themselves. Our presence in their nests remains, therefore, precarious and insecure. This is one of the reasons we need *Women's Studies,* our own disciplinary nest, where feminism can be developed, encouraged and rewarded, *as well as* a location in the traditional disciplines from which we can challenge and offer alternatives to the distortions and evasions of patriarchal thought which continue to pass themselves off as "general" knowledge.

Pamela Sachs opens this section in chapter 11 with a description of how her own evolution as a teacher and a feminist parallelled the evolution of women's studies as a distinctive approach to *English literature* and then as a discipline in its own right. She identifies four stages of the feminist intervention into literary studies—the stages of critique, recovery, reassessment, and gynocriticism (described earlier in the Introductory essay) and clarifies them in terms of her own development as a feminist and a classroom teacher. The essay is rich in literary detail and illustrations of a variety of feminist approaches to literature. She ranges

203

from a discussion of the relationships between women in Shakespeare's plays to the fate of his imagined sister Judith, and what Gertrude really knew about the death of Hamlet to an investigation of the subversive "subjects" of the novels of Jane Austen and Charlotte Brontë, and a reassessment of the writing of those Canadian women who pioneered the novel in North America: Frances Brooke who wrote the first North American novel, *The History of Emily Montague (1769);* the two sisters Catherine Parr Traill and Susanna Moodie; Martha Ostenso, and Lucy Maud Montgomery. Although the body of feminist literature and critical work reviewed by Pamela in this chapter is still largely ignored by the malestream literary establishment, Pamela believes it represents the only creative, hopeful, and indeed interesting alternative to the current state of literature in academia which, with its sterile and elitist preservation of an established canon of (largely male) writers and critics, is increasingly incapable of defending either its place in the academy or its relevance to the lives and concerns of today's students. She concludes her essay, therefore, with a description of the literature courses from a women's studies perspective which she is presently teaching and of the exciting possibilities for courses in the future which she looks forward to developing.

Both Pamela and our next writer, Pat Smart, comment upon the fact that in Canada we tend to take for granted that our most important writers in both official languages are, in fact, women: Margaret Lawrence, Margaret Atwood and Alice Munro in English-speaking Canada, for example; Gabrielle Roy, Anne Hébert, Marie-Claire Blais and Nicole Brossard in Québec. In chapter 12, Pat Smart discusses this latter group and other Québec writers in the context of their engagement as women and as feminists with *Québec Literature* in general and in its mythologizing of the French-Canadian woman as "mother" in particular.

The strong, silent, suffering, enduring mother/matriarch is a constant figure in Québec literature. Indeed, for a long time, it has been the only configuration available in literature of a "good" French Canadian woman: someone whose self-sacrifice on behalf of family, church, and nation is constituted in the literature as the necessary and essential female gesture holding French Canada together and securing its identity and survival. Any deviation or disaffection on the part of individual women from the ideal of heroic self-sacrificing motherhood has been correspondingly construed, therefore, as treachery; as a betrayal, not just of the local conventions of "femininity," but of French Canada itself: of one's family, religion, culture, identity and nation; as going over to the side of the "enemy," to the "other" side of the conquering English.

Pat Smart contrasts this idealization of the great self-sacrificing French Canadian mother in the novels of male writers with its demystification in novels written by women. Their novels emphasize not so much the heroism and virtue of these women but the pain and brutality of their lives. They likewise show more compassion for the daughters of these mythic mothers, who must choose between the proverbial rock and a hard place: between repeating the pattern of their mother's pain and self-sacrifice or abandoning their French Canadian identity by marrying "up" and "out" into the English. Pat also shows how quickly the idealization of the powerful mother/matriarch in men's writing flips into its antithesis: into a fear and resentment of the power of women in general and Monster Mothers in particular, which she sees expressed in the disturbing increase in the amount of violence towards women which started to appear in novels by French Canadian men in the 1960s and following. During that time Québec women were becoming increasingly and self-consciously feminist and especially so after the victory of the Parti Québecois in 1976. Pat reviews some of this work by Québec women and the controversies surrounding it: Louky Bersianik's feminist science-fiction novel *The Euquélionne* (1976) for example, and Denise Boucher's play *The Fairies Are Thirsty* (1979), both of which confronted Quebeckers with the fundamental misogyny of their culture (which found its most dramatic expression in the massacre of fourteen women by Marc Lepine at the University of Montréal in December 1989.)

There is now a large and identifiable community of innovative and success-ful, and still controversial, feminist writers in Québec seeking a literary voice to speak the truth of women's experience, avoiding the old hierarchies and division of culture and nature, mind and body, self and other, etc. Many of these writers are familiar with the recent theoretical work of French feminists who are exploring the relationship of women/Woman to language and psychoanalysis, and their own novels, plays, poetry, and prose reflect this interest and speak to the same concerns. Writings by these Québec women circulate well beyond the borders of Québec and have become an important voice in a literary conversation among and about women which is going on around the world.

Caryll Steffens examines the relationship of feminism to *psychoanalysis* in greater detail in the next chapter of this section, chapter 13. Her essay begins with a description of Freud's theory of the psycho-sexual development of adult gendered identities: from the "primary narcissism" of the not yet (sexually or otherwise) differentiated infant still wrapped up in its attachment to the mother through its recognition of the father as a rival for the mother's love and the ensuing Oedipus complex to the always conflictual and problematic acquisition of the appropriate adult "masculine" or "feminine" identity. Caryll believes that Freud's theory is neither determinist nor essentialist; that is, that it does not imply, as is so often assumed, that sexual identities are somehow prescribed or determined by one's biology or physiology; by having or not-having a penis, for example, even though having or not-having a penis is central to the dynamics of gendered personality development in male-dominated societies. On the contrary, Caryll reads Freud as offering a useful, if flawed, account of the complex processes and costs of the social construction of gender and of the acquisition of masculine/feminine identities, destinies and values by particular men and women within traditional patriarchal families (that is, families characterized by the traditional division of labour, power, and prestige between men and women whereby men have authority and go out to "work" in the "public" sphere and women stay at "home" in the "private" sphere to "nurture" both them and their children).

Freud did not, of course, escape the effect of his own engendering in such a family, nor the patriarchal "narrative belief system" of his own time and place (in turn-of-the-century Vienna), nor, therefore, its misogynist interpretations of the masculine/feminine difference he struggled to understand. Caryll describes both the explicit and implicit sexism of Freudian theory as well as some of the better known critiques and reconstructions of it by contemporary (English-speaking) feminists. She discusses the work of Dorothy Dinnerstein, Nancy Chodorow, and Carol Gilligan, in particular, all of whom focus on the effects of women's mothering on the development of *unconscious* motivations and personality structures in men and women which lead us to reproduce the patriarchal system even as we try consciously to work against it: motivations towards misogyny in both sexes, for instance (Dinnerstein); towards traditional sexual divisions of "work" and "nurture" (Chodorow); and towards typically "masculine" and "feminine" moralities of competitive individualism, equality and rights on the one hand, and care, responsibility and relationship on the other (Gilligan).

All these theorists conclude that hierarchical, sexist, and misogynist gender differences will not disappear until men share the task of mothering infants equally with women and accept thereby the burden and rewards of the resulting unconscious psychic structures and motivations. While Caryll agrees that "male mothering" may be a necessary condition of our collective liberation from oppressive gender differences, she does not believe it is enough and worries that it may, in fact, only exacerbate the situation it is intended to remedy: the masculine/feminine split in general and the rejection of the "feminine" and of women *as mothers* in particular. She reminds us that the desire for a coherent non-contradictory sexual identity is, after all, a "masculine" desire constructed against the more flexible and fluid boundaries of the "feminine" and of "mother." And she suggests, therefore, that the task of a feminist psychoanalysis should not be the achievement of closure and completion, either in theory or in practice, but an on-going project of systematic destabilization, reflection, and change: a task which will never, that is, be accomplished.

Naomi Goldenberg extends this reflection on psychoanalysis and the unconscious motivation of gender behaviour and personality to a consideration of the symbolic meanings of hockey sticks and hopscotch patsies in her discussion of the *Sexuality of Sports* in chapter 14. Naomi observes that throughout our culture enormous amounts of time, money, energy, emotion, and resources are expended on male stick sports from which women are excluded as players: games like hockey and snooker, for example, in which, as she puts it:

Men take pleasure in competing with one another over the issue of who can best control his stick and sink the largest number of balls into a particular hole.

She interprets these games as "phallic dramas" through which cultural taboos against incest and masturbation (putting the ball/semen into your own goal/hole) are repeated, replayed, and rehearsed. She sees them, that is, as exercises in genital discipline which teach men and boys to focus their sexuality (their sticks and their balls) on the appropriate goals and channels (the "holes" of the "other") according to elaborate sets or rules about who can touch what, when, who, and how. Naomi proposes three sporting categories which share this (mainly hetero-) sexual agenda: stick games like hockey and snooker, soccer, baseball and golf, all of which emphasize competition among men; net games like tennis, volleyball and ping-pong which emphasize (hetero-) sexual exchange or intercourse; and court games like squash, handball and racquetball which emphasize (homo-) sexual exchange between members of the same sex. Though all these sports have a slightly different emphasis, they are all, nevertheless, organized around the cultural and sexual centrality of the phallus/penis and rehearse and repeat society's prescriptions for acceptable sexual relations and activities focused on it. For all of them, "scoring" is a question of hitting the appropriate ball/semen into the appropriate hole or space.

Naomi wonders if there are any non-phallic sports organized around the clitoris and the requirements of female sexual agency and control. She thinks there are and points to the little ball games, bouncing ball games like jacks and hopscotch, which are played by little girls, often between their legs and often to the accompaniment of rhythmic chants and songs. These, too, consist of elaborate rules about the use of space and against improper touch of the jacks or the patsie. But they are noticeably different from boys' games in scope and scale: in their confinement to small movements and spaces and in their negligible price tags. They are often played alone (rather than in teams) and within the confines of domestic, "private" space, and they tend to be abandoned at adolescence. Naomi situates these differences of structure, scope and scale between male and female ball games within the context of the traditional (Freudian) prescription for mature female sexuality: that it transfer its object and its aim from the solitary and female-centred childhood pleasures of the clitoris* to the adult gratification of vaginal penetration in heterosexual intercourse. The domination of our culture by, indeed its obsession with, male stick games repeats and reproduces this prescription for adult female sexuality *ad nauseam:* that it be organized around and subordinated to the competitive desires of the penis (of men) and its (their) over-riding need to "score" against others. This analysis suggests that perhaps women turn to men's sports for pleasure and excitement, as players or as fans, for

---

* See Caryll Steffens in this collection.

the same reason they turn to men for companionship and sex—not because it is the best thing going but because it is, after all, the "only game in town."

The next essay in this collection, chapter 15, reveals just how determining this heterosexual (and thus hetero-sexist) agenda has been and remains for *Women's Experiences of Sport and Physical Activity* in general. Drawing on recent research on the sex-differentiated socialization of boys and girls and her own interviews with three competitive Canadian athletes from three generations: Ethel (basketball, born 1908), Deb (distance running, born 1938) and Chris (judo, born 1960), Helen Lenskyj shows how widespread social prescriptions for appropriate "feminine" demeanour (e.g., domesticity, passivity, subservience, sex appeal to men) continue to fix the horizon and the specific conditions within which women and girls participate in sports. She identifies and discusses five key "sites" of determination which mediate, organize, and reproduce the hetero-sexual (hetero-sexist) agenda of the sporting life; sites in which that agenda can and must be resisted, therefore, if girls and women are to participate in sports and physical activity on equal terms with boys and men. These sites of determination are the family, coaches and teachers, schools, media, and socio-economic conditions. Both the experiences of the individual athletes interviewed by Helen and systematic research show how important family and peer support is to the participation possibilities of girls and women in sports: Ethel's older brothers encouraged and coached her in basketball; Chris' father ran a judo club and her mother and three older brothers were all black belt performers; Deb's husband and all four children are involved in competitive sports.

Although recent human rights legislation now makes it illegal to overtly discriminate against women and girls in schools and organized sports, it has not *required* schools and sports institutions to actively *integrate* women into sports on equal terms with men or, therefore, distribute their resources equally. So we continue to have exclusively male sports at the top of the sports hierarchy, like hockey and baseball for example, and the widespread organization of both professional and amateur athletics into exclusively male or female leagues and teams. This is difficult political territory to negotiate: the integration of women into "men's" sports as currently organized risks simply reinforcing the mascu-line/feminine hierarchy already in place as it leaves masculine privilege and the dominance of male sports intact while creaming off the best female athletes from the women's teams to the men's, thus strengthening their already strong hand. On the other hand, maintaining separate women's leagues, teams, and competitions *as is*—underfunded, undervalued, under-represented and marginalized—merely perpetuates the discriminatory structures and practices of (hetero-) sexism in sports.

Change in the arena of sports, it seems, must be struggled for on all fronts simultaneously, and victories will always be provisional and ambiguous. Corporate sponsorship and media coverage of women's athletics has certainly increased over the last ten years and this has corresponded with an increase in the facilities and opportunities for, and participation of, women in both professional and amateur sports. But, as Helen points out, this "improvement" in sponsorship and media coverage and in women's participation rates in sport and physical activity has been framed and contained by a corresponding increase in the media, in general, and sports coverage, in particular, in the pressure on women and girls to conform to rigid and confining phallocentric prescriptions of femininity. These are defined almost exclusively in terms of physical appearance and demeanour (good looks, charm, figure, face, smile, domesticity, and sex appeal to men) rather than ability, skill, strength, and power. Helen documents some of the ambiguous victories of women within the determining institutions of various sports and the differences they are making to women's access to and experiences of physical activity in general. She leaves us with the challenge of finding ways to preserve and enhance the positive potential of sports for celebrating human vitality, strength, skill, and sociability in an area accessible equally to women and men, while at the same time continuing to work against the traditional institution-alized practices of sport—of exclusivity, hierarchy, heterosexism and male dominance. Quite a challenge!

The next chapter in this section, chapter 16, returns us to academia and to the place of *Feminism in Sociology* in particular. Marilyn Porter chose, in 1971, to pursue graduate studies in sociology in Britain precisely because it offered her an opportunity and a context within which she could produce knowledge for feminism and for the practical struggles of the Women's Liberation Movement. These opportunities were not available at that time in the other, older and more established, academic disciplines such as history, economics, and political science. Sociology was a relatively new discipline then and had not yet congealed into conanical texts and rigid methods. It was, therefore, more open to new methods, like feminism, and new objects of study, like women, gender, and sexuality. Sociologists study how society works and the relationship between the different social groups which constitute society. Students and teachers of sociology had been at the forefront of the various political rebellions and liberation movements of the 1960s and of the events in France in 1968, in particular, from which the current Women's Liberation movement emerged as an independent political movement of women for women. Sociology was, therefore, a suitable home in the 1970s for feminists who wanted to understand more about the specific relationship between women as an identifiable social group and the rest of society, toward creation of desirable change in the status of women in that society. "Sociology of the Family" was already an established (if somewhat staid and stale) area of study in sociology at the time and an appropriate academic site from which feminists could do their research.

Marilyn clarifies the subsequent relationship of feminism to sociology in her essay and the relationship of both of these to Marxism. She grounds her reflections in her own biography as a marxist-feminist-sociologist whose work focuses on understanding the complexities of the intersection of "class" and "gender" in the determination of women's social experience and reality. She reviews the history and development of feminist scholarship within sociology: debates around the social, political and theoretical consequences of applying traditional class analysis to women, for example, whose social and economic "class" position cannot be simply read off from the class position of their husband or male "head" of household—as it had formerly been; and debates around the social, political, and theoretical implications of women's "domestic labour" for a "Sociology of Work" which had heretofore excluded it from its category.

Marilyn believes feminism has done much for sociology, generating exciting new areas of sociological enquiry and creative challenges to its founding theories.* But she wonders what sociology has done for feminism apart from providing it with an institutional home. Feminism remains ghettoized in sociology, as it is in other academic disciplines (like English literature, economics, and political science).** Feminist researchers and teachers in traditional academic departments, even departments as "progressive" as sociology, still feel like "cuckoos" in the nest, therefore, of birds of quite another feather altogether. This is despite the fact that their particular disciplinary specialization—feminism— has experienced unprecedented and sophisticated intellectual growth in its brief twenty-year history, so much so that it has generated its own interdisciplinary "Women's Studies" programs in between and on the margins of the various traditional disciplines. Marilyn concludes her essay with a question: should she flee the nest of sociology, where her feminist commitments throw her sociology commitments into question among "sociologists," for the more hospitable, reciprocal, and supportive environment of Women's Studies? Or, should she remain as a cuckoo in sociology's nest, as a constant reminder of the noisy and growing breed of feminist scholars who have something to offer their young and who are, bit by bit, usurping the territory of the old disciplinary fathers?

In the final chapter of this section, chapter 17, Nancy Guberman and Michèle Bourgon describe the difference feminism makes to *Social Work Theory and Practice,* or, as they put it: "how feminism can take the crazy out of your head and put it back into society." They describe the theoretical premises informing feminist social work intervention and show how this works in practice, by reproducing and analyzing an interview between Michèle and one of her "clients" (a word they are not comfortable with but one for which they can find no adequate substitute). The client is fourteen-year-old Kristy who, after a fight with her father, ran away to a friend's house where she hid for three days. When she returned, her parents forced her to see a social worker; this was the occasion of the interview presented here.

---

* Pamela Sachs makes a similar case for English literature in this collection.
** See Pamela Sachs, Martha MacDonald, and Jill Vickers in this collection.

Nancy and Michèle begin by reminding us that the "helping" professions and their "experts" typically hold women responsible for the problems they or their families encounter in their lives.

> Lisa is told her son's delinquency is the direct result of her inadequate mothering, Mary-Lou that her husband's infidelities are due to her sexual responses, and Beth that her romantic failures all stem from her unrealistic expectations of men.

Readers, I am sure, will add their personal favourites to this list: women don't get promotions because they "fear success," women are raped because they "ask for it." The first challenge of feminism to social work orthodoxy is, therefore, to stop pointing the finger: to take the blame away from women and place it where it belongs—in the social relations which organize and structure our lives, in the dominant and dominated political, economic, and ideological relations between social groups which define a society at a given moment in history.

At the present time, the dominant social relations of our own society are patriarchal and capitalist. This means that they favour white, middle and upper-class, middle-aged (30-45), heterosexual men with no mental or physical disabilities. These men have privileged access to the resources which make life viable in our society: "hard" resources like money, food, shelter, health, and schooling, as well as "soft" resources like attention, respect, recognition, care, and self-worth. Because they have access to the resources which make life viable, such men (white, heterosexual, middle-class) are unlikely candidates for social work intervention. The rest of us, who do not have the same access to the same resources, are: women in general, young and old people, people with disabilities, gay and lesbian people, people of colour, unemployed, low income and working-class people.

One of the first premises of feminist social work theory is, therefore, that the responsibility of the social worker is not to change the client—to make her more "assertive" or "self-confident," or more "realistic" about or "responsive" to the "needs" of her "family," for example, (all deeply ideological prescriptions)—but to procure for her the resources she needs to live her life in good mental and physical health. In practice, this translates into acknowledging *with the client* the very real limits to what any particular social worker can do for any particular client, given that the roots of preventing problems lie in the social, economic, and ideological relations which organize our lives and not in the individuals who must lead them as best they can. It also entails a mutual recognition of the *power* differential between client and social worker and an explicit negotiation of it in the social work relationship. A client's mistrust of social work should not be turned against her, for example, as a sign of her deviance or unwillingness to co-operate or change, but rather should be attended to respectfully, as a realistic and rational response to an objective situation where once again all the "resources" are on the other side. What Michèle and Nancy call "contracting," that is, "coming to a *shared* understanding of why, when and how a social worker and the other person are going to work together and what they are going to work on," is a central feature of the feminist intervention they recommend here, and one well illustrated by their presentation and analysis of Michèle's first interview with Kristy.

While obtaining the resources necessary for a client to lead a healthy and viable life should be "the only goal of a feminist intervention" with individual clients, the practice of feminist social work itself must, according to Nancy and Michèle, extend beyond one-to-one or small group interventions and into the community as a whole. Collective resources must be made available to all women so that individual women will no longer have to seek "help" from "professionals" for "problems" which appear to be "personal" but are, in fact, rooted in the social relations which determine our chances and the failures and successes of our individual lives. Feminist social work practice must extend, that is, into the analysis, critique, and transformation of the patriarchal-capitalist system itself into the political, economic, and ideological relations which are the real origins of what social work institutions continue to regard as women's personal problems.

Chapter 11
Literature and Women's Studies
Pamela Sachs

Introduction

By the time I started to teach, in the early seventies, I knew I was a feminist. This knowledge profoundly affected my sense of myself in the world; it profoundly affected my teaching—it still does. In a way, my evolution as a teacher can be seen as reflecting the evolution of Women's Studies, at least insofar as it applies to the teaching of literature. I've been out there in the front lines, so to speak, almost from the very beginning. It's always been a struggle: feminism has never been either fashionable or legitimate. At first I slipped in only one course with feminist content, but now I'm brazen: all my courses could, with some minor alteration, be part of a Women's Studies curriculum. In this paper I shall attempt to explain what this means and give you an overview of the concerns, the scope, and the development of a feminist perspective with regard to literature. In order to make abstract concepts more concrete, I shall be drawing from my experience in the classroom. I want, above all, to give you some idea of what Women's Studies has added to the literature curriculum and of what happens in a Women's Studies classroom. Where possible and appropriate, I shall do so from the perspective of an anglophone Canadian.

Even though I've been there almost from the beginning of the current phase of the women's movement, which started in the late sixties, I came to feminism, as I did to so much else apart from marrying and having children, rather late in my life. It took a long time for me to come to the knowledge that I was "different," "other," "inferior"... in brief, a woman. I should have suspected it all much earlier: when I was given an education different from that of my brothers; when I got married at twenty-one because I was in a panic about my future and could think of nothing else to do; when, in 1950, immediately after marrying, I emigrated with my husband from England to Canada without asking myself whether that was what I wanted; and finally when I found myself in university in my late thirties, years older than anyone else in the class. But like so many women of my generation, I had been conditioned into complicity; I had been taught not to take myself into account. I was to some extent jolted into awareness when I was told, at the end of my undergraduate career in 1968, that the graduating honours which should have been shared between me and a fellow student (male and younger) had been given to him because he would obviously go on to a career. But even then I did not protest, I thought this was the way things were and the way they had to be.

I realize from the vantage point of the nineties that all of this must seem like ancient history. My students at CEGEP tell me that women have won the battle for equality. I don't believe it; I think we are living in very dangerous times, with a swing to traditional values that tries to put women back in their place—not where the power is. I believe that, although we have made some gains, we cannot be sure of holding on to them; without Women's Studies we would not even know what we stand to lose. Women's Studies are revolutionary because they posit a commitment to a change for the better; they are more important than ever in a climate which is against change.

Women's Studies also holds out a hopeful alternative in the embattled state in which the teaching of literature now finds itself. The crisis in literacy (and the call for more and more "writing" courses) has put teachers of literature on the defensive: they are no longer sure of what they are supposed to be teaching, let alone of what approach to take.

When I was at university in the sixties, things were different. The New Critics[1] were still in the ascendancy, and they were supremely confident not only that everybody could be taught to read a text but also that this was something that every literate and cultured person would want to do. The New Critics regarded the text as a little world unto itself; they taught us to handle terms like "ambiguity" and "irony" and to search for metaphors, symbols, and images. Since we had learned to detach the text from its context, we looked with scorn at the earlier critics who had dealt with the history of ideas and with suspicion at the few contemporary critics who linked literature to politics. Our greatest contempt was reserved for those who made the error of confusing literature with morality.

But all this has now changed. There is no single theoretical approach which holds sway: the New Critics long ago gave way to the Structuralists, who, in turn, were replaced by the Deconstructionists. In addition there are New Historicists, Phenomenologists, Marxists, reader response critics, and psychoanalytical critics.[2] All of these critical approaches afford interesting and innovative insights; the trouble is, they are extremely complicated and rather esoteric and thus not readily accessible to the ordinary reader.

The Feminist Critique of Literature: A Review: Beginnings

In contradistinction to the foregoing approaches, the feminist critique offers a way out (of the critical dilemma) and a way in (to the text). Growing out of the Women's Liberation Movement of the late sixties, it drew upon the experiences of ordinary women who had grown tired of listening to the experts and finding themselves excluded from the discourse. From the first, the emphasis was interdisciplinary[3] and anti-elitist, and from the first it was the pages of literature that seemed to offer the best resource for knowledge as women turned to the past in their search for themselves, only to find themselves excluded from history.

The pages of literature also provided feminists with their own literary critic, who also happened to be the leading woman novelist of this century. Virginia Woolf's *A Room of One's Own* is still the most influential text, the best place to start any exploration of the question of women and literature. Just as modern philosophy has sometimes been called footnotes to Plato, I would venture that most of contemporary feminist literary criticism, and therefore most of what happens in a Women's Studies classroom, may be seen as "footnotes" to Virginia Woolf.

Originally conceived as a series of lectures for an audience of women university undergraduates, *A Room of One's Own* (written in 1928) defines the central issues for feminist critics today: the importance of tradition and, more specifically, the lack of tradition for a woman writer; and the influence of gender upon genre, content, and style. While Woolf is always provocative, her argument is not always consistent: at one point she insists that women writers should write as women[4] and at another she claims that the truly great writer should transcend gender in the possession of an androgynous vision.[5] But most importantly, her essay is revolutionary in that she ascribes the failure of women to achieve artistic greatness not to any innate deficiency but to the constraints of political disadvantage within patriarchal culture. The "room of one's own" becomes the spatial symbol for the minimum independence which is the female artist's due if she is to take herself and her achievement seriously.

The most imaginative and most empowering chapter of the essay is that in which Virginia Woolf fantasizes about what would have become of Shakespeare's sister (had he had one) if she had been born as brilliant and gifted as he. History comes alive as Wolf describes the pitiful reality of the life of the ordinary woman in the sixteenth century. It would have been impossible for Judith Shakespeare to have succeeded as her brother did. Instead, Woolf envisions her tragic death by suicide. The essay's conclusion, when Woolf asks all women to work towards the time when "Shakespeare's sister will put on the body which she has so often laid down" (Woolf, 112), is as inspiring today as when it was first written. Woolf was not only Women's Studies' first literary critic, she was also our first literary polemicist.[6]

Perhaps, in the end, Woolf's greatest contribution to the women who followed her was to give them a distinct and personal feminine voice. The essay's style is a far cry from the magisterial authority of masculine prose. You may at first find its tentative, freeflowing, playful, and provocative tone difficult to follow. Hers is the expressive rather than the expository mode. She gives permission for the experiential history and anecdote which characterizes so much of contemporary feminist writing.

The more recent work which I would (and do) place beside Woolf's essay as being equally inspirational in tone and ground-breaking in content is Adrienne Rich's "When We Dead Awaken: Writing and Revision." Here is another place to start one's thinking about women and literature. Written in the early seventies, Rich's essay celebrates the collective reality of women's awakening and notes that, "It is no longer such a lonely thing to open one's eyes" (Rich, 35). Although far more radical and hard-hitting than Woolf, Rich also shows that when women write, they think back through their mothers. She uses the personal anecdotal mode, pioneered by Woolf, to record the difficulties she had to overcome to find her own voice as a writer.

Rich describes the conflict the woman artist experiences as she tries to balance a job, writing, and family. Recalling her marriage in the fifties and her attempt to cope with three small children, she speaks of "the female fatigue of suppressed anger and loss of contact with my own being" (Rich, 43). How many of my "mature" women students, caught between the different parts of their lives, have responded to those words! Rich chides Virginia Woolf for her attempt at detachment and says that women have to experience their anger in order to save themselves, each other, and even civilization itself.

In her hostility to the patriarchy, Rich goes far beyond Woolf's ideal of cultural androgyny. For Rich the creative energy of patriarchal society is now spent and directed solely towards self-destructive ends. Such statements are bound to elicit a defensive response from male students and readers, but they can also lead to some positive re-examination and questioning. It was one of my male students who made the connection between phallicism[7] and the weapons on which so much of our budget is spent.

The most empowering aspect of Rich's essay is her challenge to women to reclaim the language and take back the power of naming which man has controlled since the time of Adam.[8] She sets the example with her idea of "re-vision" whereby we see the word as if for the first time: "re-vision, the act of looking back, of seeing with fresh eyes, of entering an old text from a new critical direction—is for women more than a chapter in critical history; it is an act of survival" (Rich, 35). This, of course, is exactly what feminist critics do: they review, they revise; they see with fresh eyes.

I have spent some time on Virginia Woolf and Adrienne Rich because theirs is the most eloquent prose. It is worth noting that Woolf was English, Adrienne Rich is an American. I wish I could find a Canadian to put beside them. But the Canadian scene offers a curious paradox: women writers have been represented in Canadian literature since the very beginning, and at present their pre-eminence is such that one male critic went so far as to say that if a matriarchy ever existed it exists now in Canadian literature. Yet we have no comparable novelists or poets who have spoken out for feminism, as Woolf and Rich have done, and no critics of the stature of those American scholars to whose works I shall be referring in the course of this essay and in the bibliography which follows. Perhaps we should be satisfied that at least two of our greatest women writers, Margaret Atwood and the late Margaret Laurence, would not be embarrassed to be labelled as feminists. In the meantime the field is still wide open for the Great American Feminist Critic to take her place beside Northrop Frye.[9]

The Four Strategies

In the fifteen years that have elapsed since Rich's essay, feminist criticism (although still largely ignored by the male academic establishment) has come of age. That is to say, more critics are practising it (men included) and they now seem to have some idea of what it is they are doing and how it all fits into some overarching perspective, with its own criteria and its own terminology. Four distinct stages and strategies of feminist criticism have been charted.[10] Borrowing from current usage, I shall refer to these stages as critique, recovery, reassessment, and gynocriticism. I propose now to explain these four approaches and to show how I have used them in my courses thus far, then to conclude this paper by opening up some possibilities for the future.

Critique

The critique approach is the most developed and also the most depressing. British and American feminist scholars began by exploring the image of woman as she has been presented in the tradition of literature written by men. Only rarely did they find a male author providing a recognizably human portrayal of women. All too often the image was either diminished or exaggerated: a stereotype, either impossibly good or impossibly bad.[11] The critique approach identifies and labels these stereotypes and explores the ways they have been used in literature and society to maintain the patriarchal status quo: the situation of women throughout history as politically, economically, and legally subordinated to men. Goddess or bitch, earth mother or witch, seductress or spinster, woman is always the Other against whom man has to protect himself. The only really safe place for woman in relation to man as depicted in the male-stream literary tradition has been as wife and mother, but here again the stereotypes deride and distort. The Middle Ages set the tradition for the stock portrait of the unfaithful wife, while our own century has contributed the distortion of mother as destroyer and consumer of sons.

In her book *The Resisting Reader* (1975) Judith Fetterley points out that these negative images force a woman reader to identify against herself, and she ends up feeling split and disloyal. It might be well to give a practical example of what I mean by "to identify against oneself." I teach a course called "the Novel and the Family" which explores changing family relationships in a changing literary form: the novel. Until very recently the second book on my reading list was D.H. Lawrence's *Sons and Lovers*. After all, it's centrally about family relationships and Lawrence is unquestionably a great novelist: the book has the added advantage of being about the working class family, which so few novels are. But eventually I found I could teach it only by denying my personal response, which is difficult with this patently autobiographical novel. In the end, if the reader wishes to remain on the side of life (and of Lawrence), she is forced to turn against the most important female character in the novel, the mother, Mrs. Morel. The only way her son, Paul/Lawrence can continue to live is by killing her, and even then the ending is ambiguous: it is not clear that he has freed himself. I'm not saying that I can't accept all this—Lawrence is very persuasive—but I can't do so without a sense of bitterness and self-betrayal.

A secondary concern of the critique approach is the unmasking of gender-biased criticism: i.e., the criticism by men of works by women. Gender-biased critics use various techniques to disparage women writers. They ignore women writers and leave them out of the canon, include them as peripheral and marginal, or are unable to separate the work from the biology of its author. Labelled as "phallic" criticism by Mary Ellman, this use of a double standard was first identified by Virginia Woolf who noted that books are considered important if they deal with war and politics and trivial if they deal with "feelings of women in a drawing room" (Woolf, 74). As we move from the critique approach to reassessment, we discover that perhaps it is not that the works themselves are trivial, but rather that the traditional male criteria of value in literature preclude an adequate and appropriate reading of portrayals of women and their world.

Recovery

The recovery approach also has two main emphases: it recovers works by women writers which were either passed over at the time they were produced or have since fallen into neglect and oblivion, and it validates previously neglected literary forms: diaries, journals, and letters. In the United States the recovery process has resulted in no less than a "feminization" of the bearded and bewhiskered canon. It is no longer possible to assume that no woman writer of any importance ever existed in the U.S.: at least Edith Wharton and Willa Cather have been accorded their places, not to speak of lesser-known writers like Ellen Glasgow and Eudora Welty. In addition, the recovery process has brought forth previously-hidden minority traditions: lesbian literature, working class literature, and black literature. A major testimony to this concerted effort was the publication, in 1985, of the first "establishment" feminist anthology, *The Norton Anthology of Literature by Women,* unequivocally subtitled "The Tradition in English." The whole question of whether or not a tradition of women's writing exists seems to have been settled by this vote of confidence.

In the U.K. the task of recovery has been less urgent. After all, even F.R. Leavis, the patriarchal moralist, acknowledged women writers as part of The Great Tradition.[12] Consequently the major contribution from the U.K. has been the reissue, mostly by Virago Press, of previously forgotten works, mainly by

British writers but also including American, Canadian, and Third World writers. Interestingly enough, among recent reissues has been Susanna Moodie's *Roughing It in the Bush,* (1986) the Canadian classic of settler experience, this time reprinted in its entirety with a foreword by Margaret Atwood.

An encouraging flurry of activity on the Canadian publishing scene suggests that here, too, the recovery process has gathered a certain momentum. The last decade has seen the reprinting of several major works by Canadian women writers, among them one that can proudly be claimed as the first North American novel. Frances Brooke's *The History of Emily Montague* (originally published in 1769), focusing as it does solely on flirtation and courtship against a romantic Québec garrison backdrop shortly after the British conquest, is clearly not a serious contender for any searching feminist critique. Yet it is of real interest for what it reveals about the customs and values of this small group of transplanted gentlewomen still clinging to the genteel way of life of a more established world. The woman's viewpoint gives the reader a different slant on history: it is a refreshing change to read about skating parties near the Montmorency Falls, and there is something reassuring in the references to the enchantments and challenges of a Canadian winter. On a more serious note, there are also some surprisingly progressive observations on male-female relationships.[13]

Of more significance within the tradition of early Canadian women's writing is the work of the remarkable pair of settler sisters, Catharine Parr Traill and Susanna Moodie. Their respective classics, *The Backwoods of Canada* and *Roughing it in the Bush,* have both been reprinted and now some of their minor works have been recovered. Other publications of the 1980s include Traill's children's tale *The Canadian Crusoes,* and a handsome collection of Susanna Moodie's letters, to be followed by those of her sister. In addition, Traill's *The Canadian Crusoes* has recently been reprinted. While these two traditionally proper Victorian ladies would not have much in common with today's feminists, they never lost sight of the fact that they were women and that what they were writing about was women's experience. The startling contrast in temperament between the two sisters adds an extra dimension to a reading of their works; each has her own coterie of admirers. Moodie's emotion-charged response to her experiences inspired Atwood's moving tribute in her cycle of poems *The Journals of Susanna Moodie,* while in Laurence's novel, *The Diviners,* the writer-protagonist tries vainly to live up to the example of sensible competence set by "Saint Catharine."

I would suggest that it is appropriate now to see the two sisters as they saw themselves; complementary rather than opposite. As individual artists, each is somewhat one-sided and restricted; taken together they project an empowering model for the full range of woman's potential: artist and naturalist, right and left brain. Above all they were strong, determined women whose courage, perseverance, and sheer hard work offset the rather pathetic endeavours of their weaker husbands.

A less intimidating role model in Canadian literature has been the heroine of the most spectacular success story of Canadian "recovery." True, the impetus had little to do with feminism and everything to do with dollars, but the success of the televised version of *Anne of Green Gables* proved that Canada's answer to *Little Women's* Jo March can still capture the imagination and that Canadian television need not always be dull. On the face of it, the novel might not seem as central to Women's Studies as *Little Women:* Anne Shirley is not as brusque and boyish as Jo March; she is not as much in conflict with the traditional woman's role. Yet in some ways her image is more affirmative: she is not required to give up on romance as is Jo, and she is allowed at least some measure of academic success.

It is also worth noting that the novel is not claustrophobically centred on the traditional nuclear family: Marilla and Matthew Cuthbert are not the traditional childless couple: they are brother and sister. In addition, the novel abounds with single women who seem to be managing just fine on their own. Although looked upon askance by some rigid academics, *Anne of Green Gables* deserves a place on a reading list for Canadian Women's Studies.

So, too, do a number of later novels which are no longer widely read, including Martha Ostenso's *Wild Geese* and the entire and all too brief canon of Ethel Wilson. However, living as we do, in a disposable, throwaway culture of obsolescence and fads, it is not realistic to talk of any sustained recovery: a relapse into oblivion is far more likely.

So perhaps at this time it is safer to turn to the third phase of critical strategy, *reassessment,* and to the one writer who remains unscathed by the vagaries of fad or fashion: I refer of course to William Shakespeare.

Reassessment

I have decided to restrict the focus to Shakespeare in the reassessment part of this discussion because he is one of the few male writers who can withstand a feminist re-vision. All too often the only way a feminist reader can approach a traditional male-authored text is by having her defences firmly in place.[14] Shakespeare is different: we don't have to label him a misogynist in order to preserve our self-respect.

On the other hand, the new feminist critique has made it impossible for us to continue to accept Virginia Woolf's idealization of Shakespeare as the truly androgynous writer, the writer who burns with a pure incandescent flame, purged of the taint of gender discrimination. Marilyn French, in her book *Shakespeare's Division of Experience* (1981), is the critic who, more than any other, has shown that Shakespeare was, after all, a man and, at that, very much a man of his time. While never denying Shakespeare's greatness and the breadth of his vision, she nonetheless gives a very compelling picture of that vision as firmly based on the traditional Western polarization of masculine and feminine principles, the polarization which informs all the dreary sexist stereotypes. French suggests that at the beginning of his career Shakespeare undervalued the feminine principle and at the end he overidealized one aspect of it—what she calls the "in-law" (legitimate) aspect, that part which softens and humanizes the patriarchal order—but that he never got over his dis-ease with the "out-law aspect," the part linked with pleasure, changefulness, non-goal directed sexuality, darkness, and mystery.

I think French's analysis goes a long way towards explaining our disappointment at the role women play in Shakespeare's tragedies where "good women are often powerless, and powerful women are always threatening and often, in fact, destructive" (Lenz, Greene, and Neely, 1983, 6). For this reason the women in the tragedies are almost always destroyed and hence absent from the new order established at the end of the plays.[15]

The women fare considerably better in the comedies: often they are quite literally the "good guys." The fact that so frequently in the comedies the women put on men's clothes has not gone unnoticed by feminist critics. Dressed as young men, Rosalind in *As You Like It,* Viola in *Twelfth Night,* and Portia in *The Merchant of Venice* are permitted a range of freedom to act, and simply to move, far beyond the constraints of the traditional female role. (Consider, for example, the powerlessness of Desdemona in *Othello* or Cordelia in *Lear.)* In fact, the only times the women in Shakespeare can make any impact for good in the world is when they are dressed as men. Yet at the end of these plays, they resume their women's clothes to marry men who are in may ways their inferiors. No wonder they seem diminished: they are!

What the feminist critique does best in reassessing Shakespeare is to alter our perception of his works by shining the light of attention on a different part of the plays: the woman's part.[16] (Shakespeare himself obviously thought hers to be a lesser part than the man's, since he never allowed a woman to have a whole play to herself; the best she can hope for is to share top billing with a man).

In some cases this deflected light throws into relief some surprising anomalies. One of the most fascinating examples is Rebecca Smith's recent study of Gertrude's role in *Hamlet*. By focusing clearly on Gertude's lines and actions, without allowing herself to become diverted by the obsessed editorializing of either Hamlet or his ghostly father, Smith discovers a timid, living, self-effacing woman, only too anxious to placate her difficult men but hardly enticing them to join her in "incestuous" sheets (Smith, 194-208).

Smith notices that Gertrude, the object of so much discussion, herself says very little. She has fewer speaking lines than any other main character in the play. When she does speak it is to ask questions or to express concern on behalf of some of the other characters. She is the only one who seems genuinely touched by

Ophelia's plight and speaks to her gently. Of course her actions are even more restricted: they consist, for the most part, of acceding to Claudius' request that she leave the scene. If we listen closely to her lines, we hear that she had no prior knowledge of her first husband's murder. The guilt to which she alludes in the lines, "So full of artless jealousy is guilt/It spills itself in fearing to be split" seems pretty free-floating; if anything, she is the still centre of the storm. To borrow a phrase from T.S. Eliot, it would appear that Gertrude is an unlikely candidate as the "objective correlative"[17] to Hamlet's disgust and despair.

Attention to the woman's part, apart from casting new light on the way the women relate to the men in the plays, can also reveal interesting patterns in the way the women relate to each other. Virginia Woolf suggested that no writer until the twentieth century has ever said anything about friendships between women (Woolf, 81). I think that she was wrong and that Shakespeare did so. Other critics have focused on the relationship between Desdomona and Emilia in *Othello* in this regard, but I would prefer to turn to my two favourite comedies: *Twelfth Night* and *As You Like It*.

In *Twelfth Night* there is a great deal of sighing and posturing about love, but it's difficult to take it seriously. The only times we can feel any genuine tension or emotion are in the scenes between Viola disguised as Cesario and Olivia, and I don't think it's only because Olivia fell for the unisex look. I don't want to make too much of this but it's definitely there. It's there also in a different, but no less moving, way in the very real love which Rosalind and Celia feel for each other, a love which makes them cheerfully accept exile as long as they can be together. I think it's no accident that Celia's words to Rosalind, "Say what thou canst, I'll go along with thee," so clearly recall Ruth's words to Naomi in the biblical example of the love between women.[18]

But we have to look hard, even in Shakespeare, for examples of women relating positively to each other or living their own lives with their own feelings and experiences. They are seen mostly in relation to men. This is so because imaginative vision, like all other vision, is filtered through the lens of gender.[19] For this reason most of the energy of the feminist critique has come to be centred on the last of the four approaches, the one that concentrates on writing by women for which Elaine Showalter invented the term "gynocriticism."[20]

Gynocriticism

The first concern of the gynocritics was to determine whether it would be possible to see the works of women writers not as isolated interstices within the masculine canon but as belonging to a tradition of their own. Again, the inspiration came from Virginia Woolf who had proclaimed that "masterpieces are not single and solitary births, they are the outcome of many years of thinking in common... so that the experience of the mass is behind the single voice..." (Woolf, 66). The mid 1970s saw the publication of three of the first major works of gynocriticism. In an endeavour to trace a tradition of women's writing, these works focused on the commonality of women's thinking. It is important to draw them to your attention since they provide valuable background to any literature courses in a Women's Studies program.

The first of these works, Patricia Meyer Spack's *The Female Imagination,* posits a specifically female imagination which is to be found in novels that take seriously "matters more or less peripheral to male concerns" (Spack, 1975, 6). Hers is a tradition of women writers who have more in common with other women writers than with male writers because women write about the same sorts of things: they validate a range of experience often trivialized by men (women's experience and the problems they encounter). The next work, Ellen Moers's *Literary Women* (1977), describes the tradition of women's writing as a movement which can be discerned beneath the mainstream of the masculine tradition. She shows the literary support systems which women writers built for themselves and gives a moving account of how they used each other as sounding boards even when separated by great distance and lack of personal acquaintance.[21]

Elaine Showalter's *A Literature of Their Own* is today perhaps the most influential of these three studies. For me, Showalter's most useful contribution is her identification of three developmental phases of women's writing which she labels as the "feminine," the "feminist," and the "female" (Showalter, 1977, 13). In the "feminine" phase, which she dates from about 1840-1880, women wrote in an effort to be equal to men. They appeared to acquiesce to male dominance and subscribed to male values; in England they even adopted male pseudonyms in order to "pass" with the publishers. You will remember that George Eliot (1819-1880) was really Mary Anne Evans and that the Brontë sisters: Charlotte, Emily, and Anne, invented three Bell brothers: Currer, Ellis, and Acton, as a strategy for coping with the double standard.[22] The "feminist" phase was from 1880-1920, the time of the first wave of feminism and the struggle for suffrage for women. This period saw the emergence, as a character of the New Woman, a liberated Amazon who blazed the trail of political, sexual, and psychological independence for her more timid sisters. Paradoxically, I find that the two best examples of the New Woman occur in novels written by men—Sue Bridgehead in Thomas Hardy's *Jude the Obscure* and Rhoda Nunn in George Gissing's *The Odd Women.*[23] The "female" phase, which has persisted since 1920, rejects both imitation and protest and instead affirms female experience as the source of autonomous art. A "female" novel which I always enjoy teaching is Margaret Drabble's *The Millstone,* one of the first affirmative novels about single parenthood.

A more recent example of gynocriticism also merits attention. First published in 1970, Sandra Gilbert and Susan Gubar's *The Madwoman in the Attic* is gynocriticism at its most probing. The evocative title brings us an allusion to *Jane Eyre's* poor crazy Bertha, locked up in the attic while sane Jane is downstairs with

Rochester. It is not difficult to see the madwoman as a metaphor for the artist. Like Showalter's book, this is a study of the work of nineteenth century women writers, but its thesis is more innovative. Gilbert and Gubar use the phrase "the anxiety of authorship" to explain the situation of the woman writer caught in a contradiction: the need to express her artistic vision, and the desire to conform to the submissive norms of silent dependence. In fascinating, if somewhat quirky, new readings of individual authors and texts, they uncover an "encoded subtext" celebrating the delights of autonomy, assertiveness, and intellectual curiosity beneath the conventional surface.

Since I think it is impossible for the feminist critic and critical reader to ignore Gilbert and Gubar's *Madwoman*, I'd like to look briefly at their discussion of Jane Austen's (1775-1817) six beautifully crafted novels, all centrally concerned with the subject of courtship and marriage in an acquisitive society. At the end of each of the novels, the heroine gets married and presumably lives happily ever after. This sounds like the romantic plot of fairy tale and Harlequin Romance; after all, this is the way we might like things to be. But of course Gilbert and Gubar go further and point out that "All the heroines who reject inadequate fathers are engaged on a search for better, more sensitive men who are, nevertheless, still the representatives of authority" (Gilbert and Gubar, 1979, 154). They conclude that "becoming a woman means relinquishing achievement and accommodating oneself to men and the spaces they provide" (Gilbert and Gubar, 1979, 154).

However, the plot line is the least of an Austen novel; the critical reader reads the novels for the free play of a satirical mind which mercilessly and wittily dissects the follies and foibles of the society she knows so well. This part of the subtext is not too difficult to decode. But Gilbert and Gubar do raise an interesting question. Why does Austen not allow her characters the same freedom she claimed for herself: the freedom to opt out of the marriage stakes and to live alone in autonomous integrity? For example, in *Pride and Prejudice* they see Elizabeth as punished for her spirited imagination and as having to learn the lessons of silence and subordination. According to Gilbert and Gubar, "Authorship for Jane Austen is an escape from the very restraints she imposes on her female characters" (Gilbert and Gubar, 1979, 168).

I think all this may be true, but it's not the only way of reading the novels; it is somewhat tendentious. It is difficult for me to see Elizabeth Bennet as seriously diminished by marrying Darcy: it seems far more likely that she will change him than that he will change her. She is faulted by Gilbert and Gubar for not speaking the whole truth in her final encounter with Lady Catherine when she refrains from telling her that she is not engaged to Darcy, but most readers would cheer her as entirely the victor in that scene.

It is worth staying with the subject of marriage in *Pride and Prejudice* to examine what gynocriticism does best: to ground the novels firmly in the context of the times in which they were written and to use the texts to show the lives and situations of women; to study, in fact, what is left out of history.

What we find out is that women had no way of obtaining autonomy unless they were artists. And even then it was problematical; to some extent, Jane Austen remained dependent for the whole of her life.[24] We also find out that marriage was not quite the norm that we generally suppose: at least one-third of middle-class women did not get married—sometimes that figure is put even higher. However, not to marry was not to be free; rather, it meant that you remained dependent on your parents as long as they were around or had to depend on the charity of your oldest brother (assuming you had one). Without marriage women had no respectable status at all: the only profession open to the more impoverished of Jane Austen's female characters is that of governess. In *Emma,* Jane Fairfax regards this as a fate worse than death and definitely worse than marriage. In *Pride and Prejudice,* sensible, plain Charlotte Lucas is the foil for Elizabeth. She agrees to marry dreadful Mr. Collins because she has little other choice. It's true that Elizabeth had refused him, but she was younger then, and better-looking, and she probably assumed she still had choices.

Taking into account the context of Austen's times, we find that the courtship period was, in fact, the only time in a woman's life in which she was able to exercise some sort of autonomy over destiny: Elizabeth is not forced to marry Collins and she even refuses Darcy the first time he proposes. The courtship period is the one time of true adventure for women. Looked at in this way, the subject of the novels is in no way trivial and transcends the spurious sensationalism of the Harlequin Romance.

Poetry

So far my discussion of gynocriticism has focused solely on novels and novelists. This is not surprising since the novel is pre-eminently the genre with which women have been most associated and on which they have made the greatest impact. At the end of the eighteenth century, which is when women first started to write in order to earn money, they wrote novels, partly because the novel was a new and flexible form and partly because it was a form with a ready-made "captive" audience: the middle-class woman confined within the four walls of her home. But perhaps the main reason was that the subject matter of the novel was within women's knowledge and experience: the domestic scene and personal and social relationships.

Poetry, on the other hand, has had a far longer and infinitely more elevated history. Originally it was associated with priests: poets have to be inspired. As the most demanding and disciplined of the genres, it has always been at the top of the literary hierarchy. It's difficult to write epics about the birth of nations when you're busy giving birth to babies or directions to servants. So poetry and women were deemed incompatible:

I am obnoxious to each carping tongue
Who says my hand a needle better fits,
A Poets pen all scorn I should thus wrong,
For such despite they cast on Female wits:
If what I do prove well, it won't advance,
They'l say it's stoln, or else it was by chance.

Thus wrote Anne Bradstreet, America's first woman poet, in 1650. Had Shakespeare's imagined sister aspired only to be a novelist, she might not have had to commit suicide, but she was "born" too early for the novel. Far closer to our own times, two of the most famous American women poets, Syliva Plath and Anne Sexton, ended their own lives. It seems that they, too, were unable to maintain the balance between the demands of their art and those of their personal lives. On the surface they seemed successful and happy: they were known, they were published, they were married, they had children. Again one is reminded of the words of Virginia Woolf: "who shall measure the heat and violence of the poet's heart when caught and tangled in a woman's body?" (Woolf, 50).

But there are hopeful signs that this tension between being a woman and being a poet is now changing, that it has, in fact, been changing ever since the modern women's movement began. More and more women poets are finding their voices and breaking the silence. They are reshaping the language to suit their needs and inventing a new mythology to replace the negative archetypes of virgin, shrew, spinster, and whore. And finally, they are being recognized by the feminist critics who had previously concentrated only on prose writers. *Shakespeare's Sisters,* a collection of feminist essays on women poets edited by Gilbert and Gubar, came out in 1979, and *Stealing the Language,* an inspiring history of American women's poetry by Alicia Suskin Ostriker, was published in 1986.

In Canada we have been slow to link poetry with gender and to look for our own tradition of women poets, but I think it is worth doing so. For example, in the *Oxford Book of Canadian Verse,* edited by Margaret Atwood, she notes in her introduction that the book "does not contain an equal number of male and female poets" although there *were* some female poets even in the nineteenth century when "a woman Canadian poet was the equivalent, say, of a white Anglo-Saxon Protestant Inuit shaman." She adds that there are many more good ones today. Atwood speculates that for some mysterious reason Canada has "favoured the production of good women poets" more than have other major English-speaking countries. I suspect that the real study of the works of these "good women poets"—what they write about, the language they use, what they have in common—is going on in the Women's Studies classrooms throughout the country. These classes can therefore be seen as providing the grassroots of gynocriticism.

Grassroots: The Classroom

I should like to end this paper as I began it, on a personal note, and to talk about what goes on in my own classroom. Not altogether surprisingly, the first woman-centred courses I taught, several years ago, were called "The Image of Woman in Literature." In my first course I started by lecturing on the history of women in the classical and Judeo-Christian tradition. The actual readings traced the stereotyped images of woman as she appears throughout the literary tradition, starting with the story of Eve. We found that she was depicted as good if she conformed to society's expectations of woman as the "relative creature,"[25] living for others, but bad if she deviated either by living through others (like Lawrence's Mrs. Morel) or for herself (like Chaucer's Wife of Bath).

I found this course thoroughly depressing, and the next year I found a new text and changed the readings, although I did not change the course title. This time the course was far more prescriptive, less historical, and more psychological in approach. Drawing on the Jungian theory of each person having within themselves masculine and feminine aspects and attributes, I focused more on male-female relationships and the search for the "ideal other," which is really a projection from one's own unconscious. In Jungian theory, the truly developed "individuated" personality is one which has integrated the different aspects of the self, so I ended my course with the last part of Woolf's essay, her dream of androgyny as she looks outside and sees a man and woman stepping into a taxi and, presumably, driving off into the sunset, together.

I've given up teaching this course partly because I felt I was trying to do too much and was not doing any of it well enough (the course would have worked better had I been able to team-teach it with an historian and a psychologist,)[26] and partly because I'm no longer sure that I want to end up with androgyny. While I'm not yet ready to dismiss it as contemptuously as does Mary Daly, the feminist philosopher who sneers at androgyny as Raquel Welch and John Wayne glued together, I'm no longer happy with the gender polarization which is the basis of Jung's theories.[27]

My present woman's course is called "The Ages of Woman." It is a course that every woman student can relate to personally because it covers the problems and choices that every woman faces in her life. In addition, we read fewer and longer works. The reading list varies so that I can keep a fresh perspective on the material, but the basic framework remains the same. We trace the different stages of a woman's life from girlhood to old age. Interestingly enough, I could teach this course based entirely on the work of Canadian writer Margaret Laurence. I don't, but I usually conclude with her marvellous novel of old age *The Stone Angel*. The readings vary to include British, American, and Canadian writers.

There is no limit to the possibilities for new courses, ranging from traditional survey courses (only this time it would be a survey of women's writing based on the Gilbert and Gubar text) to different thematic courses. For example, I teach a course called "Alternative Worlds" in which we explore utopian and dystopian visions;[28] I'd like to teach this based entirely on women's visions: Atwood's novel *The Handmaid's Tale* would be one of the readings. As I'm a Canadian and interested in nature, I have recently introduced a course called "Women and Wilderness in Canadian Women's Writing." We will start with the writings of Catharine Parr Traill and Susanna Moodie and perhaps finish with Marian Engel's disturbing novel *Bear*. Along the way we would explore what the wilderness stands for in the writing of Canadian women.[29] Another idea I've been turning over is the proliferation of women mystery writers; there are so many good ones.[30] What is it about the genre that appeals to women? Is their writing any different from that of male writers in the genre?

There is so much to read, to re-read, to respond to, to discover. The special focus of the feminist vision brings new light to bear on any text, and in so doing, brings excitement and "real life" back into the classroom. The climate of the eighties was antipathetic to feminism, but we must not allow ourselves to become discouraged. Women's Studies is here to stay; it makes the world more hopeful and the study of literature a great deal more interesting.

Afterword

Five years have elapsed since I wrote the preceding article; it is now impossible for me to omit, ignore, or merely acknowledge the advent of the intellectual revolution known as "Theory," which has rocked the academy, sent shock waves into mainstream and popular culture, and trickled down into the classroom. For this reason, although my own thinking has been unsettled rather than changed, I have decided to add an Afterword to try to explain what is meant by this term, to discuss its connections with feminist thinking, and to share with you briefly how my practice in the classroom has shifted to accommodate the new perspectives.

I have used the plural form of "perspective" because the term theory is loosely used as a kind of umbrella designation for several diverse and diverging perspectives, the most important of which for feminism, and hence for this paper, are deconstruction, post-modernism, French feminist theory, and reader response theory. What they have in common is "a shared commitment to understanding how language and other systems of signs provide frameworks which determine how we read, and more generally how we make sense of experience, construct our own identity, produce meaning in the world" (McLaughlin, 1990, 1). You can see then how in some ways theory has replaced philosophy as the site for intellectual interrogation, for asking the big questions about truth and the meaning of life.

Theory challenges mainstream humanist thinking by positing that truth and meaning have no prior objective existence in the world outside the text. Language is not transparent, it is not a window through which we can see the real meaning.

It is up to the reader to construct meaning. Although the reader becomes foregrounded (as she does in reader response theory), it is important to remember that the reader, too, is contingent, a product of history, culture, and gender. What kind of meaning you make of your larger world, or of the world of the text, is to a large extent determined by your historical and cultural context and whether you were born male or female.

The feminist response to this new kind of thinking has, on the whole, been quite positive. North American feminists were proud to welcome their trendy French feminist sisters whose persuasive voices were among the first to introduce the heady ideas of the new theory. Suddenly, all feminist theory was taken more seriously; male critics scrambled on the bandwagon, hailing the feminist discourse as the paradigm (model) for opposition and resistance. Nor were feminists much threatened by the challenge to liberal humanism. Inasmuch as the universal eternal truths always seemed to be the prerogative of white males, feminists have, from the first, privileged the particular truths of lived personal experience.

This is not to say that there has not been active and, at times, divisive debate within feminism itself as the voices of women who have been silenced begin to speak out for themselves. The central conflict is around the issue of difference. Does the difference that divides women from men supersede the differences that divide women from each other? Is it even possible to talk about a "woman" let alone a "feminist?" While these questions have not been resolved, they have made for a more inclusive and examined feminism, a feminism more in keeping with the ideas of post-modernism. Feminism is more than ever open to the idea of pluralism and diversity. It's time to add an "s" and use the word in plural form.

What this means for me as a teacher is that I can no longer teach a course called the "Ages of Woman" which assumes that the singular form of the word can stand for all women. The course that I would teach now would be more aware of differences of class, colour, and ethnicity. I would be sure to include readings from minority writers and from writers of different social backgrounds.

But in any case I'm not sure that at present I'm interested in entering the debate about differences between women. Let's not forget that to divide intellectually is to conquer politically. One of the dangers of the new interest in theory is that feminist thinking and Women's Studies will become safely institutionalized within the academy, which is *not* where social changes take place. But the struggle for change must continue; we really have no alternative. It is clear that the old patriarchal ways of doing things seem pretty well played out. So women have to situate themselves beyond intellectual difference in positions conducive to collective political action. There are some hopeful signs that this is happening as women once again reach out to each other when they become politically involved. Maybe Women's Studies will regain its original impetus and make the connection between the classroom and the community.

Notes

1. The so-called New Critics flourished in the fifties. Although this was a long time ago, they are still important because they taught literary analysis as a practical skill accessible to all. It is more than likely that most of your literature teachers use some New Critical technique.

2. It is not necessary that you understand all these critical approaches, but you should be aware that they exist. If you want to find out more about them, M.H. Abrams' *A Glossary of Literary Terms* is a good place to start.

3. This means that "subjects" like literature, history, biology or whatever were no longer compartmentalized. Women could talk to each other across these boundaries.

4. "Writing as women" has become a central feminist goal, although what this means remains a question of healthy but heated debate.

5. The concept of androgyny was in the forefront of ideas a few years ago. The best book on the topic is Carolyn Heilbrun's *Towards a Recognition of Androgyny*.

6. A "polemicist" is someone who argues eloquently and aggressively for a cause.

7. Phallicism" is the cultural enrichment of the male sexual organ as the symbol of potency.

8. In the second chapter of Genesis, Adam names the animals. Naming is the first step to acknowledge and hence to power.

9. Frye is the pre-eminent Canadian critic. His most influential work is *The Anatomy of Criticism*.

10. My particular debt is to Sandra Gilbert and Susan Gubar in their guide to the *Norton Anthology of Literature by Women* (1985).

11. The three classic examples of this kind of criticism are Katherine Rogers' *The Troublesome Helpmate* (1966), Mary Ellmann's *Thinking About Women* (1968), and Kate Millett's *Sexual Politics* (1971).

12. F.R. Leavis was a famous British critic, roughly contemporary with the New Critics. For Leavis, in order for a work to rate as part of his Great Tradition, it had to contribute to the moral life. The works of Jane Austen and George Eliot pass his test; in fact, Jane Austen establishes the tradition.

13. This novel, like almost all early novels, is epistolary–the story is told in the form of letters. Perhaps not surprisingly, the most enlightened letters are those written by the men. Frances Brooke's female characters are disappointingly conventional.

14. Judith Fetterley's suggestion in *The Resisting Reader*.

15. This is certainly true of the three great tragedies: *Macbeth, Hamlet,* and *Lear.* At the end of these plays the stage is littered with corpses but a new and better order will prevail. The women will be absent from this order.

16. A recent collection of feminist essays on Shakespeare is called *The Woman's Part* (see References).

17. T.S. Eliot introduced this phrase in an essay on "Hamlet and His Problems" written in 1919. He meant that there was no concrete, objective series of events to account for Hamlet's gloom and despair.

18. Naomi is Ruth's mother-in-law. When Ruth's husband is killed, Ruth leaves her own people to be with Naomi: "Whither thou goest will I go . . . "

19. There are many other filtering lenses such as class, religion, race, colour, sexual orientation, etc., but gender is surely the most basic (see Afterword).

20. The "gyn" stem signifies women in Greek. Gynocriticism is woman-centred criticism.

21. For example, George Eliot (British) and Harriet Beecher Stowe (American) were

separated by an ocean and were never to meet, yet they corresponded on quite intimate terms (Moers, 65).

22. This term was originally used to refer to two standards of sexual morality–one for men and the other for women. The man had far more license. It is now used to cover any standards which are unequal.

23. The latter is a personal favourite. A heavy 19th century novel but surprisingly contemporary in its viewpoint and the situations it depicts.

24. She was never able to live alone–it is quite posible that she might well not have wanted to.

25. I am taking this term from the title of Francoise Basch's book *Relative Creatures: Victorian Women in Society and in the Novel* (1974).

26. We have recently established a women's studies program at the college where I teach. This should make this kind of interdisciplinary team teaching far more practicable.

27. I don't like calling one set of qualities "male" and another set "female." If you want to pursue this point, it's part of the "essentialist" debate (i.e., a woman in essence is different from a man).

28. A "utopia" is an ideal world while a "dystopia" is a nightmare world.

29. Marian Fowler's *The Embroidered Tent* (1982) and Coral Ann Hwells' *Private and Fictional Worlds* (1987) have blazed the trail in the exploration of this theme.

30. I'm thinking of writers like P.D. James, Ruth Randell, Sara Paretsky, Sue Grafton, and Amanda Cross.

References

Abrams, M.H., 1961. *A Glossary of Literary Terms* 4th Edition. New York: Holt.

Alcott, L.M. *Little Women.*

Atwood, Margaret, 1970. *The Journals of Susanna Moodie.* Toronto: Oxford.

—— (ed.), 1982. *The Oxford Book of Canadian Verse.* Toronto: Oxford.

Austen, Jane *Pride and Prejudice.*

——. *Emma.*

Basch, Francoise, 1974. *Relative Creatures: Victorian Women in Society and the Novel.* New York: Schocken.

Blain, Virginia, Isobel Grundy, and Patricia Clements, 1990. *The Feminist Companion to Literature in English: Women Writers from the Middle Ages to the Present.* London: Yale University Press.

Brooke, Frances, 1985. *The History of Emily Montague.* Carleton.

Brontë, Charlotte. *Jane Eyre.*

Drabble, Margaret, 1968. *The Millstone.* London: Penguin.

Ellman, Mary, 1976. *Thinking About Women.* New York: Harcourt.

Engel, Marian, 1976. *Bear.* Toronto: McClelland.

Fetterley, Judith, 1975. *The Resisting Reader: A Feminist Approach to American Fiction.* Bloomington: Indiana University.

French, Marilyn, 1981. *Shakespeare's Division of Experience.* New York: Summit.

Frye, Northrop, 1967. *Anatomy of Criticism.* New York: Atheneum.

Gilbert, Sandra M., and Susan Gubar, 1979. *The Madwoman in the Attic: The Woman Writer and the Nineteenth-Century Literary Imagination.* New Haven: Yale.

—— (eds.), 1985. *The Norton Anthology of Literature by Women: The Tradition in English.* New York: Norton.

——, 1985. *A Classroom Guide to Accompany the Norton Anthology of Literature by Women*. New York: Norton.

—— (eds.), 1979. *Shakespeare's Sisters: Feminist Essays on Women Poets*. Bloomington: Indiana University.

Gissing, George. *The Odd Women*.

Hardy, Thomas. *Jude the Obscure*.

Heilbrun, Carolyn, 1973. *Towards a Recognition of Androgyny*. New York: Harper.

Howells, Coral Ann, 1987. *Private and Fictional Worlds: Canadian Women Novelists of the 1970s and 1980s*. London: Methuen.

Laurence, Margaret, 1974. *The Diviners*. Toronto: McClelland.

——, 1964. *The Stone Angel*. Toronto: McClelland.

Lawrence, D.H. *Sons and Lovers*.

Leavis, F.R. *The Great Tradition*.

Lenz, Carolyn, Ruth Swift, Gayle Greene and Carol Thomas Neely, 1983. *The Women's Part: Feminist Criticism of Shakespeare*. University of Illinois Press.

Moers, Ellen, 1976. *Literary Women: The Great Writers*. New York: Doubleday.

Millett, Kate, 1970. *Sexual Politics*. New York: Doubleday.

Montgomery, L.M. *Anne of Green Gables*.

Moodie, Susanna. *Roughing It In the Bush*.

Ostenso, Martha. *Wild Geese*.

Ostriker, Alicia Suskin, 1986. *Stealing the Language: The Emergence of Women's Poetry in America*. Boston: Beacon.

Rich, Adrienne, 1979. "When We Dead Awaken: Writing as Re-Vision," in *On Lies, Secrets, and Silence: Selected Prose 1966-1978*. New York: Norton.

Rogers, Katherine M., 1966. *The Troublesome Helpmate: A History of Misogyny in Literature*. Seattle: University of Washington.

Showalter, Elaine, 1977. *A Literature of Their Own: British Women Novelists from Brontë to Lessing*. New Jersey: Princeton University.

Smith, Rebecca. "A Heart Rent in Twain" in Lenz 1983, 194-208.

Spacks, Patricia Meyer, 1972. *The Female Imagination*. New York: Avon.

Traill, Catharine Parr. *The Backwoods of Canada*.

——. *The Canadian Crusoes*.

Woolf, Virginia. *A Room of One's Own*.

Afterword

Work Cited:

Introduction by Thomas McLaughlin, 1990, in *Critical Terms for Literary Study*. Frank Lentricchia and Thomas McLaughlin (eds.). University of Chicago Press.

Chapter 12
Women in Québec Literature
Pat Smart

In this century, women's words will have changed the face of the world
as radically as the technology of the cosmonauts changed the romantic
face of the moon. —Jean Royer[1]

In both English Canada and in Québec, we tend to take for granted the fact that
our most important writers are women. If asked to name some writers from their
culture, most English-Canadian readers would automatically come up with a list
that includes Margaret Laurence, Margaret Atwood, and Alice Munro; and in
francophone Québec a similar list would undoubtedly contain the names Gabrielle
Roy, Anne Hébert and Marie-Claire Blais. As well, those familiar with contemporary Québec writing would certainly mention Nicole Brossard as the most
influential writer of the present generation. Women writers in Québec have been
strong and articulate voices in their culture, and—at least since 1945—their
importance has been recognized. All four of the above-mentioned Québec
writers have won the Governor-General's Award as well as an array of other
prestigious literary awards both in Québec and in France.

But more significant than any list of individual writers we could put together
is the impact that women have had *collectively* on Québec history and culture and
the radical transformation of values that has been taking place through feminist
writing over the last ten or twelve years. In addition to Nicole Brossard, writers
like Louky Bersianik, France Théoret, Madeleine Gagnon and Carole Massé are
among the most visible of this new generation of women who are consciously
writing as women and as feminists. At the same time, feminist literary criticism
has begun to bring a gender perspective to bear on writers of the past and to
analyze the very particular situation of women in traditional Québec culture and
its influence on both men's and women's writing.

Nicole Brossard has summed up the implications of a feminist perspective
for the creative writer in a simple but profound sentence: "To write 'I am a
woman' is full of consequences" (Brossard, 1977). Similarly, to *read* as a
woman, whether one is reading a single work of literature or a whole culture,
opens up new perspectives on old areas of knowledge, like, for example, the
role of women in traditional Québec society. Critics have always insisted on

233

the importance and strength of Québec women in their traditional role of wife and mother and shown how that role is portrayed in literature. A feminist perspective allows us to go further and see how the ideas and myths associated with the struggle for French-Canadian survival within North America came to depend heavily on keeping women in their "proper sphere," and how, by the end of the nineteenth century, the role of wife and mother had become the only allowable one for them. Looking at the literary works produced up until at least the 1940s, we see that male and female writers have portrayed that role very differently.

Women in Québec Society and Literature

Let's look first, then, at the role and image of women in Québec society and literature. There is no question we are talking about a strong woman, very much a part of the traditional value system of family, church, and national survival: she is essential to it, in fact, because of her role as mother and educator. The first important novel in twentieth-century Québec literature is *Maria Chapdelaine* by Louis Hémon, published in 1912 (Hémon, 1975). Its heroine, Maria, a young farm girl from the Lac Saint-Jean area, was made into a model and a symbol for several generations of French-Canadians. By her heroic choice of remaining on the land and struggling for the survival of her people, Maria provides an image of the important role played by women in the continued existence of French-Canadian culture. In her relationships to her three suitors—the *coureur de bois* François Paradis, the Franco-American Lorenzo Surprenant, and the neighbouring farmer Eutrope Gagnon—Maria is in fact a symbol of French Canada and the three "choices" open to it. François, Maria's true love, represents the spirit of adventure and space that presided over the beginnings of French culture in North America, and (like the spirit of French Canada after the British conquest?) he dies, a victim of nature, as he braves a winter storm to travel to her. Bitter and defeated, Maria is tempted to accept Lorenzo's offer of marriage so that she may leave the hard life of the Québec settler for the more comfortable and materialistic life of an American city. But she realizes that to do so would be to abandon her language and culture, and her final decision to marry Eutrope and stay on the land is portrayed as a continuation of her own mother's heroism and self-sacrifice. Women were the "glue" that held French-Canadian culture together against the tremendous pressure of the American way of life, and *Maria Chapdelaine* makes that clear. But without denying Maria's courage or the rightness of her choice, Québec feminists have asked whether she—or at the least the propaganda based on her after the novel appeared—was not also a male-created image of devotion and self-sacrifice used to keep women in their prescribed role. A recent novel by a young feminist writer, Nicole Houde's *La Maison du remous (The House By the Whirlpool)*, published in 1986, shows the life of a character like Maria Chapdelaine from a *woman's* point of view. Houde's vision of the life of her foremothers, the farm women of early twentieth-century Québec, is an angry and almost despairing picture of poverty, annual child-bearing, and male brutality so intolerable that they lead her heroine to madness. The blackness of the novel is relieved only by the solidarity among the female characters against their victimization.

Long before such consciously feminist works, novels by women were showing the reality behind the myth of the strong French-Canadian woman. Rose-Anna Lacasse, the heroine of Gabrielle Roy's *Bonheur d' occasion (The Tin Flute*, 1945), is an example of the mythical French-Canadian mother: strong, capable, and self-sacrificing; surrounded by numerous children; and usually with her husband nowhere in sight. Rose-Anna is expecting her thirteenth child and trying to keep her children fed and clothed and a roof over their heads despite the fact that her husband, a victim of the Depression years in Montréal, has given up on trying to find a job. Somehow she manages to hold her family together through a combination of love and down-to-earth realism, but it is significant that her own daughters (like Maria Chapdelaine before them) dream of a life very different than that of their mother. Florentine, the oldest and a waitress in the neighbourhood five-and-ten store, has (like Maria) only one way to escape: by marrying a man who can offer her a more comfortable way of life. Unlike Louis Hémon however, Roy refuses to idealize the situation of women. Pregnant, unwed, and abandoned by her lover, Florentine is forced to give up her dreams and face reality; and in so doing she discovers in herself the same tenacity that her mother has always displayed. Mothers and daughters in Gabrielle Roy's work seem linked to each other in a vicious circle that has much to do with their reproductive role. But the solidarity and courage shared by women is what gives meaning to Roy's universe and moves it beyond tragedy or absurdity.

The Myth of the Mother

Reading the work of Roy and of the other francophone women writers, one can imagine the difficulties women experienced in trying to conform to ideals preached in French-Canadian sermons and political speeches for well over a hundred years. The identification of women with the traditional role of wife and mother was brought about by the British conquest in 1760, and the consequent retreat of French Canada into a rural way of life centred on family and church. Before the conquest there was the possibility of another kind of strength for women, one that involved freedom and active participation in the public realm. New France was in fact *founded* by women working as active partners with men. Marie de l'Incarnation (1599-1672), the writer and mystic who founded the Ursuline order of teaching sisters in Québec City, Jeanne Mance (1606-73), the founder of Montréal's first hospital, and Marguerite Bourgeois of the Congrégation de Notre-Dame (1620-1700), who was Maisonneuve's advisor and confidante as well as a rebel within the Church hierarchy, are only a few of the adventurous women who fled traditional families and cloistered religious orders in France to come to the New World where they had the freedom to teach, minister to the sick, and participate in public affairs. As well, there were the women known as "Les Filles du Roi" (Daughters of the King), recruited from among the poor, the social outcasts, and the prostitutes of France and forced to go to New France to provide children to populate the colony. It is hard to imagine a more striking example of women being confined to their reproductive role than the stories of these women who were married off to strangers within fifteen days of their arrival in New France, expected to produce a child a year, and usually left to run the farms and raise the children while their husbands worked in the fur trade. The roots of the wandering (and somewhat irresponsible) man and the strong woman that runs throughout Québec literature is a tradition that goes back as far as these couples, the real founding parents of French-Canadian culture.

It was not until the middle of the nineteenth century, however, that the identification of women with the role of wife and mother became an important part of French-Canadian ideology. *Although property-owning women had been granted the vote in the Constitutional Act of 1791, that right was withdrawn in 1849, and women would not regain it until 1940, twenty-three years after women in the rest of Canada had secured the right to vote.* The maintenance of the traditional family and of a high birth-rate were seen as essential to the survival of French Canada, and the belief that French-Canadians could become a majority again through the birth-rate was summed up in the popular slogan "La revanche des berceaux" (the revenge of the cradle). Sermons, speeches, and articles by nationalist church and political leaders insisted on the importance of the mother and the dangers of feminism. A series of articles written by Henri Bourassa, the founder of the nationalist newspaper *Le Devoir* (Bourassa, 1925) attacks the idea of women's suffrage and argues that the mother is the linch-pin holding the entire structure of French-Canadian culture in place. Feminism is an Anglo-Saxon import that has no place in Québec, says Bourassa; and he predicts correctly that if feminism ever does get a "foot in the door" of Québec, the whole structure of its traditional society will come tumbling down!

Women's magazines, often edited by men, were an excellent place to communicate to women these ideas about the glories of traditional motherhood. The "Poem of the Mother," written by a man and published in *La Revue moderne* (the forerunner of *Chatelaine* magazine) in 1924 depicts an image much different than that of the independent women of New France. Its idealization of the mother is linked to the belief that her self-realization will be achieved not only through her child, but through her male child, and it is not hard to see the Virgin Mary and *her* male child behind its imagery. As well, this ability to "create a future man" is presented as women's version of the creativity that men express in art:

No poet, no matter how great, even Homer
Has ever made ...
A poem as beautiful as the mother's:
The child, pure masterpiece of love.

Her life and her fleeting beauty she gives
to the sons who will resemble her ...
To make a child walk and talk — to create a man!
What can man do that is greater?

So that in her son, her glory and her poem
The mother with happiness later
Finding herself entirely in him
Says: "He is my voice, he is my gaze!"[2]

The Mother Demystified:
Anne Hébert, Marie-Claire Blais, Gabrielle Roy

If such ideas contributed to trapping women in the maternal role and discouraging them from daring to write, they also help to explain the *kind* of mother, totally dependent on her son for identity, who will appear later on in Québec literature as the "monstrous" mother against whom both daughters and sons must struggle to exorcise their own demons. The violence against women in novels written by men in the 1960s and 1970s must be understood at least partly in terms of this overpowering figure of the mother in earlier generations. In fact, up until the "Quiet Revolution" (the period between 1960 and 1966 when Québec very rapidly modernized its structures and values), French-Canadian society was often referred to as a "matriarchy" (i.e., a society where power is held by women rather than men). We have already seen that it was men, in fact, who created the image of the powerful mother for their own political and religious purposes, but forced into the "perfect mother" stereotype, many women must have played that role all too well. For example, it was the mother's task to transmit to her children the ideas of traditional French-Canadian catholicism, with its emphasis on sin and suffering and its insistence that the greatest sin of all is that of sexual "impurity." The opening lines of Anne Hébert's short story "Le Torrent", published in 1950, capture a resentment, very common in Québec literature, against this archetypal negative mother. The narrator, an anxious and bitter young man cowering in the shadow of a huge mother figure, begins his story with the following words:

As a child, I was dispossessed of the world. By the decree of a will higher than my own, I had to renounce all possession in this life... I could see the large hand of my mother when it was raised towards me, but I could not perceive my mother as a whole, from head to foot. I could only feel her terrible size, which chilled me (Hébert, 1973, 7).

In her famous 1965 novel *Une Saison dans la vie d'Emmanuel (A Season in the Life of Emmanuel)* (Blais, 1965), Marie-Claire Blais divides the maternal archetype into two parts, showing the family as dominated by the powerful matriarch Grand'mère Antionette who apparently dispenses candies and disciplinary taps of her ruler to the children who swarm around her. The children's mother, however, is shown as thin and silent, exhausted by annual childbirths, the brutality of her husband, and the loss of many of her children through infant death. It is a striking example of the contrast between the myth and the reality of the mother around which so much of Québec literature revolves.

Anne Hébert makes a similar contrast between the grandmother and the mother in her novel, *Les Fous de Bassan (In the Shadow of the Wind)* (Hébert, 1982). What she is suggesting is that the Québec woman, at least before the Quiet Revolution, was only able to relax into a sense of her real power and love of children after her child-bearing years were over and she had become a widow. Or is she talking about *all* women? Felicity Jones, the grandmother, swims every morning with her two grand-daughters, Nora and Olivia Atkins, in the sea by their Gaspé village, and the image of the three women together suggests a female power which combines Eros and freedom and which the men of the village—voyeurs excluded from this source of female power—observe with hate and envy, seemingly needing to destroy it in order to prove their own power. And indeed, during the summer recounted in the novel, the two young girls will be raped and brutally murdered by their cousin, Stevens Brown, in a violence which seems to symbolize that of a whole culture against nature and against the feminine-maternal origin which frightens and enrages it, and which it therefore seeks to control. Women's status as mothers, Hébert is suggesting, is at one and the same time their great power and their great crime in the eyes of patriarchal culture.*

All three of the classic Québec woman writers—Gabrielle Roy, Anne Hébert and Marie-Claire Blais—have given us powerful images of women's reality and have contributed to the destruction of the idea that Québec was a "matriarchy," although they do accord great importance to the mothering role. None of the three, by the way, is or was herself a mother. Both Gabrielle Roy, who died in 1984, and Anne Hébert, a energetic and beautiful seventy-six-year old, have spoken of the need felt by their generation of women to choose between writing and mothering, and both have spoken of their lack of children as the only real regret of their lives. All three writers, however, have created wonderful children characters in their work.

---

* See also Caryll Steffens and Marymay Downing in this collection.

Roy, Hébert and Blais have been read and taught for years as important writers, but it is only in recent years, with the emergence of a feminist perspective in literary criticism, that the similarities in their visions become clear. All three insist on the violence of our present-day culture and speak of the powerless and innocent who are victimized by that violence. All three denounce war and analyze it as a product of dominant cultural values.[3] It is a very different vision from that of Québec male writers of the 1960s, for example, who are seeking *their* identities through Québec nationalism and whose work is filled with violence towards women.[4] Women writers in Québec are not, of course, opposed to the self-definition and growth of Québec culture that emerged in the 1960s and led to victory by the nationalist Parti Québécois in 1976. But they are less inclined than their male counterparts to see that self-definition as dependent on rigid national boundaries and on violence. Michèle Lalonde's poem "Speak White," very popular during the nationalist days of the 1960s and 1970s in Québec, is perhaps a *female* version of nationalism, for it stresses the violence of all powerful, imperialist nations against poorer and weaker ones and the solidarity of all the oppressed nations of the earth:

> Speak white
> from Westminster to Washington take turns
> speak white as on Wall Street
> white as in Watts
> Be civilized
> and understand our conventional answer
> when you ask us politely
> how do you do
> and we mean to reply
> we're doing all right
> we're doing fine
> we
> are not alone
>
> We know now
> that we are not alone. (Lalonde, 1987)

It is similarities like these that suggest there really is such a thing as a "women's way of writing." While all are sympathetic to feminism, none of the above-mentioned women would describe herself as a "feminist writer." Let's look now at some of the Québec writers who *do* consciously write as feminists and the impact their writing has had on modern Québec literature and values.

Feminism in Québec Literature

Because of women's symbolic and real importance as upholders of the national heritage, it seems appropriate that feminism as a force within Québec literature did not emerge until 1976, the year in which the Parti Québécois came to power. It was as if, now that the important work of articulating the national aspirations of Québec had found an expression in political reality, women writers could at last dare to speak of their own concerns *as women.*

Nineteen seventy-six was the year of *La Nef des sorcières* (*The Ship of Witches*) (Brossard et al, 1976), a collective feminist play put on in Montréal and of Louky Bersianik's best-selling novel *L'Euguélionne.* The Euguélionne is a science-fiction visitor from another planet who arrives on earth looking for her "positive planet" and for what she calls "a male of my species;" in other words, she is searching for a world in which females would be treated as human beings and equals of men. That is not, of course, what she finds on the planet earth, and the novel describes the plight of those women the Euguélionne meets in homes and workplaces, women who gradually begin leaving their situations of alienation to follow, as "apostles," this funny and fun-loving female Christ-figure. Bersianik's novel, written in chapter and verse like the Bible, parodies the patriarchal bias of Western culture from Christianity to Freud and his influential French interpreter Jacques Lacan who claims that, "Woman doesn't exist," and that, "the Phallus is the Transcendental Signifier." It calls on women to take possession of language and reality on their own terms and is a good example of a feminist humour which is doing just that. Here, for example, is the description of the Euguélionne's "divine origins," which is clearly a parody of the male "logic" behind the Christian doctrine of the Holy Trinity:

> He said that the Euguélionne was the beloved daughter of the Goddess Wondjina and of the Supreme Brain, and that these three divine persons were in reality only one Goddess: Wondjina, the Eternal Mother; the Euguélionne, the beloved daughter; and the Supreme Brain, the Divine thought which is there to closely unite the Mother and Daughter, to cement them together in a way... One proceeds from the Other. The Mother proceeds from the Daughter, the Daughter proceeds from the Supreme Brain, and the Supreme Brain in this case proceeds from the Daughter... Nevertheless, mysteriously and miraculously, the Mother and Daughter proceed at the same time from the Supreme Brain... (Bersianik, 1981, 50).

Members of the Church hierarchy, if they had read *L'Euguélionne,* would definitely not have been pleased; but feminist novels were unlikely to have been part of their reading material. In 1978, however, a feminist play staged in Montréal hit the headlines and brought out the full power of Church and State in

Québec to block its publication. A little more than fifty years after Henri Bourassa's dire prediction that feminism would be the force that would destroy traditional French-Canadian society, the uproar surrounding Denise Boucher's play (1979) *Les Fées ont soif (The Fairies Are Thirsty)* seemed a striking example of that prediction coming true. The play, centred on three characters — the Virgin Mary, a traditional mother and a prostitute—is a strong attack on the Catholic Church and on a legal and social system which turns a blind eye on rape and violence to women and which, by cutting women off from their own power, reduces them to self-hatred and depression. Its title refers to a legend telling how the fairies of Brittany, female figures associated with pagan and magical powers, refused to kneel in adoration at the arrival of Christ on earth. The play provoked demonstrations and counter-demonstrations for weeks in the streets of Montréal, and its publication was temporarily banned by an injunction granted by the courts to the Catholic diocese of Montréal.

In the play, a character emerges from within a huge plaster statue representing the Virgin Mary and asks the audience to recognize the real woman who has been hidden by the pure and bloodless image of Mary that the Church has created. "I am an image," she says, "I am a portrait... I am she who has no body... No one dares to break my image... Don't I have, somewhere, a daughter who will deliver me?" (Boucher, 1982, 21-22). Together with the mother and the prostitute, who also abandon their traditional roles, she sets out in search of her real self, her body, and new ways of relating to men and to children. It is a revolutionary project, and the play ends with the imagining of a new society based on love among equals:

> And here I stand before myself,
> Ready to love you.
> Carnal, I am, full of brains...
> I will never again be in any part of you
> That means exile for myself...
> Imagine! (Boucher, 1982, 66-67).

Influenced by French theories of psychoanalysis and language, Québec feminist writers have set out in search of a new "language," a new way of writing that would speak women's experience, one that they sometimes describe as emerging from within the "cracks" and spaces in male discourse and through which they seek to recapture an original sense of contact with the body, the mother, and the "feminine" unconscious. Novels like Madeleine Gagnon's *Lueur* (1978), an "archaeological" journey into the collective unconscious of women's history, and Carole Massé's *Nobody* (1985), in which the female narrator seeks to discover her own voice by reconstituting her childhood relation to her parents and through them to a more distant past, are examples of this type of writing.

An important writer of the feminist generation in Québec is France Théoret, the author of several volumes of poetry and of a novel, *Nous parlerons comme on écrit (We will Speak As They Write*, 1982). Théoret's work shares the feminist questioning about psychoanalysis, language, and literary form, but it also sets out to reclaim Québec history for women and to chart the direction in which Québec society is moving today. Her novel is made up of a network of women's voices from past and present, emerging from silence to tell the pain of their reality (fatigue and poverty, a lack of confidence born of generations of fear, of too much gentleness, of submission and silence). "Keep going, don't pay attention to what's being said and done around you, but continue, keep going, it can be done, you can do it" (Théoret, 1982, 67, my translation), says one of the voices, that of a seventy-four-year-old woman who is a constant encouragement and example for the narrator. It is this coming together of women's voices that will make change possible, suggests Théoret, but at the same time there is a sense in the novel that the struggle is only beginning and that there is still a very long way to go before women's and men's voices will come together in harmony.

Henri Bourassa's prediction that feminism would be a revolutionary force for change in Québec society is fulfilled by all of these feminist works which pose a more radical challenge to the traditional value system than any of the (male) writing produced during the Quiet Revolution of the 1960s. The works of that period had *appeared* revolutionary in their demand for a new political order based on Québec autonomy, but they had not challenged the dualistic value system inherited from Christianity which privileges spirit over body, eternity over time, culture over nature, and Man over Woman. Feminists refuse to make those divisions, seeing instead that these apparent "opposites" are inextricably linked. As Louky Bersianik writes: "I tell you that you bear witness to the body, and—as the body is very spiritual—you also bear witness to the spirit" (Bersianik, 1979, 49, my translation). Similarly, feminist writing is collective in spirit and challenges the individualism and competitiveness that has kept writers apart and kept them, therefore, from having any real impact on social reality. These writers quote each other constantly, write introductions to each other's work, meet often at conferences to talk among themselves and with men about the directions they are taking in their writing. As Madeleine Gagnon writes in her preface to Denise Boucher's *Cyprine: Collage pour être une femme:*

> Your words people mine. Understand them. Resemble them... We will tell them about the resemblance that lives in us. How we repeat each other, plagiarize each other, how our writing is becoming collective, how we will no longer be separated in their anthologies, their analyses, their libraries, their literary prizes and contests which divide us... We will say in the face of all that, me too, me too, I could have written it, I will write it in your place and you will write it in mine. And others and others will emerge (Boucher, 1978, 9-10).

It is through this collective spirit, and through their conscious attempt to use feminism to change society and language that these writers differ from precursors like Gabrielle Roy, Anne Hébert and Marie-Claire Blais. But, like their precursors and like their female ancestors going back as far as New France, they are strong Québec women using their "civilizing" role at last to bring about real social transformation.

Notes

1. *Le Devoir*, March 19, 1983, 17.
2. Jean Aicard, "Le poème de la mère," *La Revue moderne*, July 1924, 56.
3. Roy (1945), Blais (1982), Hébert (1982).
4. See, for example, Jacques Godbout (1965), Hubert Aquin (1968), Victor-Lévy Beaulieu (1972).
5. Montréal, Éditions Quinze, 1975.

References

Primary Sources:

Aquin, Hubert, 1968. *Trou de mémoire*. Montréal: Le Cercle du Livre de France. *(Blackout*, trans. Alan Brown. Toronto: Anansi, 1974).

Beaulieu, Victor-Lévy, 1972. *Un Rêve québécois*. Montréal: Editions du Jour.

Bersianik, Louky, 1976. *L'Eugélionne*. Montréal: La Presse. *(The Eugélionne*, trans. Gerry Davis. Victoria: Press Porcépic, 1981).

——, 1979. *Le Pique-nique sur l'Acropole*. Montréal: VLB Editeur.

Blais, Marie-Claire, 1965. *Une Saison dans la vie d'Emmanuel*. Montréal: Editions du Jour. *(A Season in the Life of Emmanuel*, trans. New York: Gosset, 1966).

——, 1982. *Visions d'Anna*. Montréal: Alain Stanké. *(Anna's World*, trans. Sheila Fischman. Toronto: Lester & Orpen Dennys, 1985).

Boucher, Denise, 1979. *Les Fées ont soif*. Montréal: Editions Intermède. *(The Fairies are Thirsty*, trans. Alan Brown. Vancouver: Talonbooks, 1982).

——, 1978. *Cyprine: Collage pour être une Femme*. Montréal: L'Aurore.

Bourassa, Henri, 1925. *Femmes-hommes ou hommes et femmes? Etudes à bâtons rompus sur le féminisme*. Montréal: Imprimerie du Devoir.

Brossard, Nicole, 1977. *L'Amèr ou le chapitre effrité*. Montréal: Quinze. *(These Our Mothers*, trans. Barbara Godard. Toronto: Coach House Press, 1983).

——, 1985. *La Lettre aérienne*. Montréal: Editions du Remue-Ménage. *(The Aerial Letter*, trans. Marlene Wildeman, Toronto: The Women's Press, 1988).

Brossard, N., Marthe Blackburn, Marie-Claire Blais, Madeleine Gagnon, Luce Guilbeault, Pol Pelletier, and France Théoret, 1976. *La Nef des Sorcières*. Montréal: Quinze.

Gagnon, Madeleine, 1979. *Lueur: roman archéologique*. Montréal: VLB Editeur.

——, 1982. "My Body in Writing," pp. 269-82 in G. Finn and A. Miles (eds.), *Feminism in Canada: From Pressure to Politics*. Montréal: Black Rose Books.

Godbout, Jacques, 1976. *Un Couteau sur la table*. Paris: Seuil. *(Knife on the Table*, trans. Penny Williams, McClelland and Stewart, New Canadian Library, 1976).

Hébert, Anne, 1950. *Le Torrent*. Montréal: Beauchemin. *(The Torrent*, trans. Gwendolyn

Moore. Montréal: Harvest House, 1973).

——, 1982. *Les Fous de Bassan*. Paris: Seuil. *(In the Shadow of the Wind*, trans. Sheila Fischman. Toronto: Stoddart, 1984).

Hémon, Louis, 1975. *Maria Chapdelaine*. (1912) Reprint. Montréal: Fides. *(Maria Chapdelaine*, trans. W.H. Blake. Toronto: MacMillan, St. Martin's Classics, 1972).

Houde, Nicole, 1986. *La Maison du remous*. Montréal: Editions de la Plaine Lune.

Lalonde, Michèle, 1974. "Speak White." Montréal: L'Hexagone. ("Speak White," trans. D.G. Jones, p. 264 in Eli Mandel and David Taras (eds.), *A Passion for Identity: An Introduction to Canadian Studies*. Toronto: Methuen, 1987).

Massé, Carole, 1985. *Nobody*. Montréal: Les Herbes rouges.

Roy, Gabrielle, 1945. *Bonheur d' occasion*. Montréal: Beauchemin. *(The Tin Flute*, trans. Alan Brown. Toronto: McClelland and Stewart, New Canadian Library, 1982).

Théoret, France, 1982. *Nous parlerons comme on écrit*. Montréal: Les Herbes rouges.

Secondary Sources:

Godard, Barbara, 1985. "The Language of Difference," *The Canadian Forum* LXV(750) (June/July): 44-46.

——, 19084. "Ex-centriques, Eccentric, Avant-Garde: Women and Modernism in the Literatures of Canada," *Tessera, Room of One's Own* 8(4): 57-75. (Special issue on feminist criticism).

—— (ed.), 1987. *Gynocritics/La Gynocritique: Feminist Approaches to Writing by Canadian and Québécoise Women*. Toronto: ECW Press.

Gould, Karen, 1981. "Setting Words Free: Feminist Writing in Québec," *SIGNS* 6(4): 617-642.

Kamboureli, Smaro, and Shirley Neuman (eds.), 1987. *Amazing Space: Writing Canadian Women Writing*. Edmonton: Longspoon/NeWest Press.

Lewis, Paula Gilbert (ed.), 1985. *Traditionalism, Nationalism, and Feminism: Women Writers of Québec*. Westport: Greenwood Press.

Scott, Gail, 1985. "Finding Her Voice," *The Canadian Forum* LXV(750) (June/July): 39-44.

Simon, Sherry, 1980. "Feminist Writing in Québec," *The Canadian Forum* LX(701) (August): 5-8.

Smart, Patricia, 1978. "Women Writers in Québec," *Room of One's Own* 4(1 and 2): 7-18. (Special issue on Québec feminist writers).

——, 1987. "My Father's House," *The Canadian Forum* LXVII(774) (Dec.): 28-35.

——, 1988. *Ecrire dans la maison du Père: l'émergence du féminin dans la tradition littéraire du Québec*. Montréal: Québec/Amérique.

Chapter 13

Psychoanalysis and Feminism

Caryll Steffens

Psychoanalysis is both a theory and a method of therapy. As a theory it analyzes the nature of the unconscious. The unconscious has been defined in *Webster's New World Dictionary* (College edition) as:

> The sum of all thoughts, impulses, desires, feelings, etc. of which the individual is not conscious, but which influence his (sic) behavior; that part of one's psyche which comprises repressed desires and other matter excluded from, but often tending to affect the consciousness.

As a method of therapy it is based upon the assumption that unconscious conflicts can be resolved if we become aware of them. Dreams, fantasies, and free associations are the primary tools used to help us gain this awareness.

Psychoanalysis was developed by Sigmund Freud in Vienna during the early part of the twentieth century. In this paper I will describe his analysis of "masculinity" and "femininity" and then I will discuss feminist responses to this analysis.

Freud's Theory

Women sometimes dream that they have a penis; men, on the other hand, sometimes dream that they are giving birth. How do we make sense of dreams like these? Freud (1905, 1914, 1925, 1933) believed that they reveal a bisexual unconscious and point to the complexity of gender formation: in order to become masculine or feminine we must repress part of our psychic nature.

Both boys and girls begin life within a mother's body. Freud believed that after birth we have difficulty in perceiving our caretaker as an autonomous human being. We experience ourselves either as omnipotent or as in a state of blissful union with our mothers. Freud called this state "primary narcissism." Our mothers may co-operate in maintaining these narcissistic illusions by seeking to replicate the intra-uterine relationship during the first hours and days of our life. Around four to five months of age, this state is followed by a separation-individuation phase during which we begin to be aware that our mother is a separate person and to individuate from her. Freud believed that both boys and girls experience primary narcissism and early identification with the mother. Gender differences emerge in response to the Oedipus complex. The Oedipus complex is named after a Greek mythological figure who killed his father and married his mother. The complex emerges when we discover the father and perceive him as a rival to our intense relationship with our mother. It involves conflict between love for our mother and competition with our father for her love. In our society, the presence or absence of a penis is central in the resolution of this conflict. The boy, who has a penis, fears that this father might castrate him in retaliation for his angry competitive feelings. It is this fear (castration anxiety) that motivates him to resolve the conflict. He does this by abandoning his close relationship with the mother and identifying with the father. This allows him to vicariously "be" the father. The boy thus acquires "masculinity" by separating from the mother and assuming the father's values and beliefs, which become his superego. The superego consists of the conscience (what we feel guilty about) and the ego-ideal (our values and aspirations).

The little girl does not have a penis and is not encouraged to identify with the father. She, therefore, is less motivated to abandon her narcissistic identification with the mother. Freud sees her as being less individuated than the boy and as having a weaker superego. The girl responds to her lack of a penis by experiencing penis envy. She blames her mother for her "lack." However, her envy and anger may elicit feelings of guilt which make her feel she should be punished. Freud saw this as the basis for female masochism. Thus, for Freud, "femininity" involves narcissism, penis envy, a weak superego, and masochism.

Feminist Responses

Biological Essentialism

Much of the feminist reaction to psychoanalytic theory has been about the relative importance of biology and culture in the development of differences between men and women. Biological essentialists argue that biological differences between people necessitate specific psychological differences. Freud has been thought of as a biological essentialist. His famous statement, "Anatomy is destiny," has been interpreted as meaning there are essential psychological differences between men and women which are biologically determined. Juliet Mitchell (1975) has argued that this is an incorrect understanding of his position. Her argument is that Freud was describing gender differences created by specific social-historical childrearing practices and values. She criticizes those psychoanalytic theorists who interpret "castration anxiety" and "penis envy" as biologically determined experiences. She (1982) cites a letter by Freud to such theorists in which he states, "I object to all of you (Horney, Jones, Rado, etc.) to the extent that you do not distinguish more clearly and cleanly between what is psychic and what is biological... I would only like to emphasize that we must keep psychoanalysis separate from biology just as we have kept it separate from anatomy and physiology..." (1982, 7).

There are clear biological differences between the sexes; however, these differences are made "meaningful" by socially constructed normative-belief systems.[1] Normative systems are culturally-provided rules which prescribe appropriate ways of behaving. Our normative system tells us the appropriate ways for girls and boys to behave and the appropriate ways to interpret these behaviours. Belief systems legitimize these rules. Gender differences may be defined as sacred requirements: violations, then, are seen as sin. Or they may be defined as biologically essential: violations, then, are seen as illness. However, anthropologists have shown that normative-belief systems differ from one society to the next. They are constructed within particular historical-material situations by motivated individuals. Norms and beliefs are the products of social negotiations. When some agreement is achieved, the rules may become "externalized," i.e., they become accepted as unquestioned "external" guides for behaviour. Ultimately they may become "reified", i.e., people "forget" that they were socially constructed and come to believe that they are "natural," objectively correct ways of behaving. In families, people usually decide upon some division of labour: for example, Mary will work at home; John will work for wages outside the home. There may or may not be disagreement and discussion about this, but when a decision is made it becomes a "norm," a rule, within that family. The rule has been socially constructed; it is the product of social negotiation. It may then become "externalized:" Mary and John follow the rule automatically; it has "external" force. Rules like these may become "reified." They may be treated as "objective" laws of nature not as social constructions. People may come to feel that it is natural for women to rear children and for men to work for wages. The normative belief systems which define "femininity" and "masculinity" may thus come to be experienced as biologically determined. Religious systems may be constructed which legitimate this division of labour as "God's will." Anthropologists like Mead (1935), however, argue that our definitions of "femininity" and "masculinity" have been socially constructed by motivated people. Some of these motivations may have been unconscious. One of the tasks of a feminist psychoanalysis is to uncover these unconscious motivations.

Why did the presence or absence of a penis come to have its current meaning?

Shared Parenting

Some feminists have responded to Freudian theory by modifying it to explain why people might be motivated to create sexist normative-belief systems. Dorothy Dinnerstein (1976) and Nancy Chodorow (1978) are two of these theorists. Each sees the traditional family, in which the child's primary caretaker is a woman, as providing emotional support for sexism and each argues that men should be more actively involved in childcare.

Dinnerstein focuses on the negative experiences associated with maternal childcare. She argues that no one can understand or anticipate all of an infant's needs. No caretaker can avoid sometimes opposing an infant's will. The child, therefore, must experience frustration. In our culture the source of this frustration is usually a women. For the infant, the caretaker is the most powerful person he or she will ever know. For both sons and daughters, the first experience with dependency and power is with a woman who is absolutely essential to their survival. Dinnerstein sees the anger elicited by frustration and the extreme dependency of the infant as providing the emotional base for misogyny.

In the traditional family, sons and daughters respond in different ways to maternal power. The son is encouraged to identify with his father and to separate from his mother. Although he begins life as part of his mother's body and his most intense early experiences are with a woman, he must repress this knowledge. He is required to be unlike the "feminine" nurturing caretaker and to be like the "masculine" father whom he sees relatively infrequently. He sees the father as being the "boss" in the family (the mother has promised in her wedding vows to obey him). By identifying with the father, the son can cope with his dependency on the mother by aspiring to ultimately become a "boss" in his own family. Dinnerstein, however, argues that he takes with him into adulthood unconscious pre-Oedipal anger at, and fear of, women.

Daughters are, of course, not encouraged to identify with their fathers. They may maintain their close identification with the mother. However, because both sons and daughters experience maternal frustration and respond with fear and anger, both may be motivated to construct normative systems that control women's interpersonal power in male/female relationships and women's social power by limiting their access to powerful positions within the social system. This process may be unconscious and denied.

Dinnerstein suggests that this provides emotional support for a social system in which powerful positions are controlled by men. These men have been required to repress "feminine" nurturing aspects of their personalities and to separate from the emotionally intense mother-child relationship. Dinnerstein believes this has contributed to the creation of an individualistic value system in which the needs and feelings of others are relatively unimportant.

Chodorow focuses on another aspect of this process: the consequences of the close identification between mothers and daughters. Mothers see their daughters as being "like" them, as having the same needs, desires, and interests. Girls, therefore, may find it difficult to clearly separate their interests from those of others. I, for example, find it difficult to play competitive games. If I win and the loser is hurt, I experience her or his suffering. However, if I lose I may experience my own suffering. Chodorow suggests that it is this ability to closely identify with others that motivates women to nurture. It is what motivates women to mother. In order for a woman to be a "good enough" mother she must be able to emphatically respond to her child's needs. She must put these needs before her own wishes. She must be both willing and able to do this. Unconscious pre-Oedipal identification with the mother prepares her for this work.

Chodorow believes that if men shared in caring for young children they would develop nurturing skills and would provide nurturing male models with whom their sons could identify.

Both Dinnerstein and Chodorow agree that men who reject the "feminine" part of their personalities create social systems which are not nurturing. Men who are not required to nurture fail to develop and to value nurturing skills. Men who reject the "feminine" part of themselves create social systems in which "femininity" and women are undervalued and are not encouraged to individuate.

Dinnerstein and Chodorow have been criticized for describing only one family type (the traditional European patriarchal family with a nurturing mother and an authoritarian father). Clearly there are many different types of family. However, it is still true empirically that regardless of family type, in our society most children begin life nurtured by a woman. The medium in which children are socialized is one in which early experiences with frustration and dependency are with a woman who perceives her sons as being "unlike" her and her daughters as being "like" her. There are undoubtedly unconscious responses to this situation.

Both Dinnerstein and Chodorow believe that involving men in childcare will reduce misogyny. Men will not be required to repress the "feminine" parts of themselves; and neither men nor women will be able to associate early childhood frustrations only with a woman. Dinnerstein and Chodorow are interested in understanding the emotional motivation for sexism and for co-operation with sexist practices. They have focused on child-rearing practices which demand that men and women repress parts of themselves. Men are required to reject their "femininity" while women must deny their need to individuate. Judith Lorber (1981) rejects this focus. She believes that sexism serves economic interests. Some people benefit financially by having women available as a cheap and flexible source of labour. She sees the greed of these profiteers, not misogyny, as providing the motivation for sexist practices. She believes that men are less likely than women to become full-time parents because it would involve greater financial sacrifice for the family if they leave the paid labour force than if the woman, who is usually poorer paid, leaves. She says:

> If you want to change the kinds of men and women you produce, do not change the parenting arrangements: change the social structure that produces the parenting arrangements. Do not worry about men's psychological capacities for parenting but give women and men a chance to earn equal incomes so that it will be as costly for women to be full-time parents as it is now for men. Then, I predict, parenting will be shared—and not just by biological parents but by communities of interested adults (486).

It is clear that there are many different reasons for constructing particular normative belief systems. Dinnerstein, Chodorow, and Lorber can each be right. Women can be assigned to low status occupations both because of unconscious misogyny elicited by early childhood experience and because of a conscious desire to financially exploit women. Women can mother both because they desire to mother and because it is easier for them than for their husbands to leave the labour force. The more desires (conscious and unconscious) a particular action satisfies, the more "natural" it may seem.[2]

It is also clear that shared parenting requires changes in other social structures; e.g., both paternity and maternity leave have to be available. The reduction of sexism will require changes in all our socially constructed institutions.

I believe that male involvement in the care of infants is a prerequisite for a truly humane society. Complete human beings are both "feminine" (emotionally involved, interpersonally sensitive, and nurturant) and "masculine" (capable of individuated, assertive behavior). Because I believe this, I feel uncomfortable using the terms "feminine" and "masculine" because embedded in the terms is the assumption that girls are "feminine" and boys are "masculine." Both boys and girls begin life intensively identified with a nurturant caretaker (if the caretaker isn't nurturant enough, the child dies), and both must cope with the fact that this caretaker cannot automatically provide for all their needs. However our current sexual division of labour demands that boys repress their nurturant desires and that girls repress their desire to individuate. While it doesn't seem to me that shared parenting will automatically produce more complete human beings, it does seem possible, and perhaps even probable, that shared parenting is most likely to be practised in families where both a husband and a wife are committed to a "meritocracy" ideology: an ideology stressing the importance of individualistic achievement of status, income, and power in a competitive, stratified, technocratic society. In these families both parents may reject "femininity." If this is the case, both sons and daughters would be raised to be individualistic, competitive, unemotional, and unco-operative. Shared parenting will not have automatic effects. Its effects are mediated by the values, beliefs, specific behaviours, and assumptions of the caretakers.

Chodorow and Dinnerstein recommend shared parenting as a structural determinant of psychic realities. Lorber seems to believe that offering women economic opportunities equal to those of men will automatically produce other desirable changes, including the sharing of parental activity. Each of these positions is, in its own way, "essentialist." Each argues that social structure (the family type or the economy) has meaning independent of the interpretive activities of men and women who find themselves trying to cope with contradictory demands and desires. One objective of psychoanalytic sociology is that it can help us to understand these interpretive activities and the place of unconscious desires and practices in producing and reproducing them.

Reflexivity

People generally take their perceptions of "reality" for granted. However, sociologists have shown that people may interpret the same "reality" very differently. Our perceptions are reflexive; i.e., they are at least partially a reflection of our socially acquired assumptions and beliefs. Some of these assumptions may be unconscious. Dinnerstein and Chodorow suggest that early experiences with a female caretaker influence these assumptions. They believe that these experiences result in a consistent undervaluing of women. Feminist theorists have tried to show how these assumptions are reflected in the work of theorists (like Freud) who consistently interpret "femininity" as inferior to "masculinity."

Carol Gilligan (1982) has reviewed the literature on moral development. In this literature and in her own research she has found differences between male and female moralities. She has also found that "female" morality is consistently viewed as inferior to "male" morality. Mature male morality was found to be based upon an ethic of abstract justice which precedes from the premise of equality. Mature female morality was based upon an ethic of care which rests on a premise of non-violence: no one should be hurt. Women were more likely than men to define themselves as immoral if they failed to help someone who was suffering. Their sense of morality was based upon a principle of nurturance rooted in their ability to identify with others. Male morality was rooted in individuation and separation.

One of the examples she offers of "male morality" is the response of a twenty-five-year-old male participant in a study of morality:

> *What does the word morality mean to you?* Nobody in the world knows the answer, I think it is recognizing the right of the individual, the rights of other individuals, not interfering with those rights. Act as fairly as you would have them treat you. I think it is basically to preserve the human being's right of existence. I think that is the most important. Secondly, the human being's right to do as he pleases, again without interfering with somebody else's rights.

> *How have your views on morality changed since the last interview?* I think I am more aware of an individual's rights now. I used to be looking at it strictly from my point of view, just for me. Now I think I am more aware of what the individual has a right to (19).

The man's response was based on an abstract principle of justice. She contrasts this with the response of a twenty-five-year-old woman in a similar study:

> *Is there really some correct solution to moral problems, or is everybody's opinion right?* No, I don't think everybody's opinion is equally right. I think that in some situations there may be opinions that are equally valid, and one could conscientiously adopt one of several courses of action. But there are other situations in which I think there are right and wrong answers, that sort of inhere in the nature of existence, of all individuals here who need to live with each other to live. We need to depend on each other, and hopefully it is not only a physical need but a need of fulfilment in ourselves, that a person's life is enriched by co-operating with other people and striving to live in harmony with everybody else, and to that end, there are right and wrong, there are things which promote that end and that move away from it, and in that way it is possible to choose, in certain cases, among different courses of action that obviously promote or harm that goal.
>
> *Is there a time in the past when you would have thought about these things differently?* Oh, yeah, I think that I went through a time when I thought that things were pretty relative, that I can't tell you what to do and you can't tell me what to do, because you've got your conscience and I've got mine.
>
> *When was that?* When I was in high school. I guess that it just sort of dawned on me that my own ideas changed, and because my own judgment changed, I felt I couldn't judge another person's judgment. But now I think even when it is only the person himself who is going to be affected, I say it is wrong to the extent it doesn't cohere with what I know about human nature and what I know about you, and just from what I think is true about the operation of the universe, I could say I think you are making a mistake.
>
> *What led you to change, do you think?* Just seeing more of life, just recognizing that there are an awful lot of things that are common among people. There are certain things that you come to learn promote a better life and better relationships and more personal fulfilment than other things that in general tend to do the opposite, and the things that promote these things, you would call morally right (20-21).

The woman's response was based not on the principle of individual rights but upon a sense of being responsible to other people in the world.

Gilligan argues that the dialogue between men and women can be seen as a dialogue between fairness and care which is ultimately beneficial. Mature morality incorporates both concerns. A morality based upon interpersonal sensitivity which is untempered with an abstract sense of justice can result in painful self-sacrificing behavior, while a morality based only upon abstract justice can be cruel. Both care and justice are involved in moral behavior. Gilligan sees our sexual division of labour as being complementary. Her critique of theories of moral development, as in Freud's, is that they define "male" morality as superior. They fail to acknowledge the equal validity of "female" morality. She does not believe that the differences she and others have found between men and women are biologically determined. She believes that they emerge in response to the social situations boys and girls find themselves in. She offers no explanation for the consistent interpretation of "femininity" as inferior.[3]

Paula Caplan (1985)[4] looks at another aspect of Freud's interpretation of "femininity." She questions Freud's conclusion that "femininity" implies masochism. The concept of "masochism" describes behaviour which is motivated by the desire for pain. Caplan describes the types of female behaviour that have been called masochistic. These include the abilities to delay gratification (to sacrifice short-term pleasures for long-term gratification), to put other people's needs ahead of their own and to try to earn happiness through these efforts. These are skills associated with a close identification with the needs of others, not with a desire to suffer. (Behaviour may also seem masochistic when women remain in painful situations. Caplan argues that they do this because there seems to be no alternative. When they become aware of alternatives, they leave).

Caplan, like Gilligan, looks at female behaviour from a different set of assumptions. Gilligan shows how female concern with interpersonal relations can be defined as morally inferior; Caplan shows how it can be defined as illness. Freud called it narcissism. "Femininity" is interpreted as either inferiority or illness.

Dinnerstein and Chodorow suggest that this is at least partially a function of our child-rearing practices which elicit unconscious assumptions used to create and interpret gender differences. At this moment in history, "masculinity" is consistently defined as superior to "femininity." Dinnerstein argues that both men and women have unconscious hostile pre-Oedipal memories of women who failed to meet all their infantile needs. Both men and women have an investment in freeing themselves from maternal power. Our interpretations of "reality" are partially a function of these and other unconscious feelings.

Sexual Contradictions
Psychoanalysis suggests that there are unconscious processes which affect how we perceive reality. It also problematizes assumptions about the unitary rational nature of the individual. Psychoanalysts see cognitions and affects as being interrelated in complex ways. They see the subject as having an essentially contradic-

tory psyche. Acquiring culturally prescribed roles is always problematic. Civilization always produces its discontents. It is ironic, therefore, that Freud ignored these observations in his analysis of femininity and masculinity. His account of male and female child development ignores the contradictions expressed consciously or unconsciously during this process as well as during later life.[5] These are the contradictions, of course, which provide possible sites of change. Dinnerstein, Chodorow, and Gilligan reproduce Freud's mistake, thus implying that it is possible to create a perfectly gendered, non-contradictory subject.

Conclusion

Our current normative-belief systems have been created in historical situations in which women have had fewer social and political resources than men. This does not mean that women have had no input into the construction of this system, but it does mean that they have been at a competitive disadvantage in defining "reality." We are currently in the process of constructing a new gender system. The task of a feminist psychoanalysis is to make explicit the implicit unconscious desires which seeks expression in this process. Dorothy Dinnerstein, Nancy Chodorow, and Carol Gilligan (as well as many others) have begun to do this. However, the task is clearly not completed.

Notes

1. For a good discussion of this see Berger and Luckmann, 1963.
2. Joanna Dean and Rosemary Murphy discuss their personal experience of "mothering" in Part One of this collection. The economics and politics of women's mothering is a recurring theme in other contributions as well. See Vickers, Smart, Downing, and Martha MacDonald in this collection.
3. Susan Sorrell talks about the relevance of Gilligan's ideas to her own life in this collection.
4. Caplan's work is also referred to in this collection by Bourgon and Guberman on social work intervention.
5. See Sayers (1986) for a good discussion of these contradictions.

References

Berger, P., and T. Luckmann, 1963. *The Social Construction of Reality*. New York: Doubleday.

Caplan, P., 1985. *The Myth of Women's Masochism*. New York: E.P. Dutton.

Chodorow, N., 1978. *The Reproduction of Mothering: Psychoanalysis and the Sociology of Gender*. Berkeley: University of California Press.

Dinnerstein, D., 1976. *The Mermaid and the Minotaur: Sexual Arrangements and Human Malaise*. New York: Harper and Row.

Freud, S., 1905. "Three Essays on the Theory of Sexuality," *Standard Edition* 7. London: Hogarth Press.

——, 1914. "On Narcissism," *Standard Edition* 14. London: Hogarth Press.

——, 1925. "Some Psychical Consequences of the Anatomical Distinction between the Sexes," *Standard Edition* 19. London: Hogarth Press.

——, 1933. "Femininity," *Standard Edition* 22. London: Hogarth Press.

Gilligan, C., 1982. *In A Different Voice*. Cambridge: Harvard University Press.

Lips, H., and A. Colwell, 1978. *The Psychology of Sex Differences*. New York: Prentice-Hall.

Lorber, J., R. Laubcoser, A. Rossi and N. Chodorow, 1981. "On The Reproduction of Mothering in a Methodological Debate," *SIGNS* 6(3): 482-514.

Mead, M., 1935. *Sexual Temperament in Three Primitive Societies*. New York: Dell.

Mitchell, J., 1975. *Psychoanalysis and Feminism*. New York: Random House.

——, 1982. "Introduction 1," in J. Mitchell and J. Rose (eds.), *Feminine Sexuality*. New York: W.W. Norton and Co.

Sayers, J., 1986. *Sexual Contradictions*. London: Tavistock Publications.

Chapter 14

On Hockey Sticks and Hopscotch Patsies: Reflections on the Sexuality of Sport

Naomi R. Goldenberg

One winter evening, my friend Eta and I were ordered to "get the hell away" from the snooker table at Canada's National Press Club, in Ottawa. Bob, who had brought us there as his guests, was reprimanded as well. "Get them out of here," an old journalist had shouted. Our host defended our right to be there, and we, with our sticks in our hands, stayed where we were.

Later the man who had been so rude apologized—he had had too much to drink, he had had a fight with his wife, etc., etc. A few weeks after that, I read about the difficulties female snooker champions had with being allowed to play in important tournaments. Even though one of them had sunk "144 balls in a row," men were still finding ways to keep her out of competition. Most professional snooker players clearly considered it a man's game. I had been thinking the same thing myself.

Snooker is played with sticks which are used to shoot balls into holes. The best snooker players are those who have the greatest control of their sticks and balls. They are those who can "call their shots," who can predict which ball they will shoot into which hole on a given shot. In the bars and billiard halls of the world, men take pleasure in competing with one another over the issue of who can best control his stick and sink the largest number of balls into a particular hole.

Snooker is not the only game in which men compete with one another over their ability to use sticks to control balls. Because I live in Canada, hockey leaps to mind. A hockey puck is a somewhat flattened version of a ball. The use of sticks in hockey is far more elaborate than in snooker. The sticks are not only used to shoot the puck into the hole (which in hockey is a framed opening made into a sac-like structure by means of a net) but are also employed to interfere with other players' efforts to control the puck. Players use their sticks for varying sorts of offensive and defensive purposes. A defenceman's chief function is to jealously

This paper was previously published in: *Returning Words to Flesh: Feminism, Psychoanalysis, and the Resurrection of the Body*, Naomi Goldenberg, (Boston: Beacon Press, August 1990). Used by permission.

protect his goal from approach by any member of the alien team. The goalie in hockey is permitted to use his whole body, as well as his stick, to prevent a foreign player from implanting the puck within the home goal sac.

As in the case of snooker, female hockey players have been strongly discouraged from playing on the male teams. While it is true that not many women have shown any inclination to play hockey with men, whenever one does, she is booted out of serious competition at a young age. Some years ago, officials ruled that females simply could not play in tournament games of the Junior Hockey League competition. A nine-year-old girl who was an ace hockey player was disqualified from playing with her team when this decision was made. Like the snooker table, the hockey field remains largely an all-male preserve.[1]

In Canada, hockey dominates the "world of sports." Millions of men are devoted both to playing the game and to keeping track of the doings of myriad teams. They watch the game on television, listen to it on the radio, read about it in the print media, and discuss it endlessly among themselves. Little boys as young as five and six are outfitted with costly equipment and trained in the skills required by the game.

This male passion for hockey causes vast amounts of money and effort to be expended. Star hockey players are heroes who receive enormous salaries. Cities construct arenas for the sport. Newspapers and magazines employ specialized staff to photograph the games and write about them in great detail. Radio broadcasters build careers on their ability to convey the excitement of hockey action. Television stations routinely postpone the late news in order to show viewers every minute of the hockey events being covered each week during the season and most nights during the playoffs.

This expenditure of money, energy, and resources on the propagation of male stick sports is one reason why women ought to pay attention to the games. In addition, because such sports seem to play a central role in the way men talk (and possibly think) about what they do on their "teams" in other arenas such as business and government, women need to see the games more clearly in order to better comprehend male culture beyond the playing field. We need feminist theory about sports because the exclusion of women from male groups occupied with using sticks to chase balls into holes parallels the exclusion of women from male groups doing more serious stuff elsewhere in culture.

We can begin our efforts at a deeper comprehension of the games men play by noting that, for the most part, it is men who are fascinated by both playing and watching the stick variety of team sports. I hasten to qualify this statement. I am well aware that women can and do play very fine hockey, lacrosse, polo, golf, etc. I am also aware that, to a certain degree, these sports are of interest to both sexes. Men and women enjoy using their bodies in ways that demand strength, agility, and endurance. In addition, both sexes appreciate watching members of either sex use their bodies in ways that challenge muscle and mind. However, I maintain that it is chiefly men who are drawn both to watch stick sports and to participate in them. Female players and female fans are less attracted to the dramatic configurations of the games than they are to the opportunity to observe human physical prowess. It is the male imagination which produced stick games. We women watch the sports and sometimes even play them simply because, very often, "it's the only game in town."

I suggest that all stick sports involve players and audience in intense phallic drama. Male sexual desire is portrayed as a force which must be channelled by elaborate sets of rules. The symbolism and organization of the games seem to depict an adolescent male's struggle to focus his sexual activities into the channels and goals which his culture condones. Perhaps the holes and goals of the various stick games represent the vaginas of the women with whom mating is permissible. If so, then placing the permissible goal in the foreign team's territory might be an expression of an incest taboo urging the male players to try for intercourse (to "score") outside their own family or tribe. Such a deeply-rooted incest prohibition might be operating in the rules of several types of stick sports and would explain why players are never allowed to shoot at the goals of their own teams. Only exogamous unions of ball and goal are permitted. Only they will be cheered by the crowd.

Such an incest taboo might also explain why, in snooker, the white cueball is forbidden to enter any of the pockets on the table. In this game, because any player may (theoretically at least) try for any pocket on any shot, the location of the goal sacs indicates nothing about endogamy or exogamy. All holes are open to all balls of all colors. Without restrictions on the white ball, perversion and promiscuity would seem to run rampant on the table. In such a situation, the white ball can stand for propriety and social order only if it remains completely chaste—aloof for immersion in any hole.

In addition to dramatizing the cultural fact that only certain orifices are considered to be appropriate spaces for male incursion, the phallic theatre of stick sports also depicts male concerns about competition among penises regarding issues of strength and agility. A young player learns that he must control the movement of his stick in order to aim it accurately. He must shoot well to direct his seminal fluid—that is, balls or pucks—into designated locations. Missed shots are like premature ejaculations, and, because semen never enters the goal cavity, everyone feels a bit disappointed. (Good sportscasters capture the collective sense of let-down in their commentaries.)

I believe that the hypothesis I am framing here—that phallic fantasies are at the root of stick sports—is equally valid for foot sports such as soccer, rugby, and football[2] as well as for hand sports such as basketball. I rely on an important psychoanalytic principle to support the transposition of symbolism from sticks to hands or feet: Freud notes that it is common for phallic symbolism to be "displaced" upwards or downwards from the genitals onto other body parts. In

Freud's explanation of *Oedipus Rex,* for example, Oedipus puts out his own eyes as a gesture symbolizing self-castration.[3] Further, the name *Oedipus,* which in Greek means "swollen foot," can itself be understood as alluding to the improper sexual act in which the unfortunate man's penis becomes involved. Thus, this classic drama about one man's wayward genitals illustrates both upward and downward displacement of phallic imagery. I think similar displacement is at work in sports in which the penis is symbolized by feet, hands, or even heads.

Although the phallus is imaged somewhat differently in the symbolism of foot and hand sports, I believe that the ball continues to symbolize seminal fluid, just as it does in stick sports. Nevertheless, there are times in football, rugby, soccer, and basketball in which the ball also seems to represent a penis: to be touched only by particular players in particular ways at particular times. In contrast, in the stick sports, the perpetually stiff piece of equipment which symbolizes the penis can usually be held continuously throughout the game.

In all male team sports, contact with the ball is subject to elaborate controls. If, as in basketball, hands are permitted to touch the ball rather freely, then kicking is absolutely forbidden. Or, as in soccer, if feet are allowed frequent contact with the ball, then many restrictions are placed on manual manipulation. These rules probably reflect cultural restrictions on touching the penis and/or on having erections in inappropriate places at inappropriate times. I have heard several men discuss the embarrassments they suffered as adolescents when they were unsuccessful at controlling the erections of their rambunctious organs. Some also felt much remorse at succumbing to urges to masturbate. No wonder that the games which men and boys learn when they are young dramatize their desire for mastery over the phallus! The fact that some forms of ball games (most notably rugby) have been cultivated in all-male British public schools supports this view of the games as exercises for teaching genital discipline.

The phallic drama enacted in such stick games as baseball and cricket is somewhat different from the other games I have discussed so far. In baseball, for example, each team member takes a turn at attempting to hit the ball instead of competing for the opportunity to make contact with it. The issues involving the bat seem to be the clear male genital concerns of all stick sports: how hard can the bat hit the ball; how far can the ball be made to go; how accurately can the hard-hitting bat direct the ball into areas that meet with social approval. The main focus of baseball would thus seem to be on the strength of the phallus of each individual player. A similar contest is acted out in carnivals when men swing mallets to see how far up a stick they can drive a ball. If the ball goes to the top ("all the way"), a bell rings.

In baseball, however, another issue comes into play besides that of pure phallic power. This additional concern relates to the contamination carried by the ball once a player has hit it. The ball/semen of the player must not actually touch that player once he has made contact with it. If the player is tagged with the ball he has hit, he is considered polluted and declared "out." Indeed, the ball must not even *symbolically* touch the player by arriving at a base before he does. As long as the ball is directed away from the player after his hit, he is safe and can cavort around the bases. But the fun is over as soon as the ball comes back to his body. Perhaps the avoidance of the ball in baseball is an expression of social prohibitions against masturbation that forbid men to be preoccupied with touching their own semen. Or perhaps the message is closer to one that I have already noted in stick games, that is, that sexual liaisons must be sought outside the home area with partners outside the tribe. Probably the symbolism is multi-layered and refers in a general way both to taboos against masturbation and incest.

One conclusion that could be drawn from this type of reflection about men's games is that all sports which take place either on a field (hockey, soccer, etc.) or on a table (pool, snooker) spring from phallic fantasies. Melanie Klein seems to have drawn just such a conclusion. In 1923, she writes that,

> in the cases of pleasure in motion—games and athletic activities—we could recognize the influence of the sexual symbolic meaning of the playing-field, the road, etc. (symbolizing the mother), while walking, running and athletic movement of all kinds stood for penetrating into the mother. At the same time, the feet, the hands and the body, which carry out these activities and in consequence of early identification are equated with the penis, served to attract to themselves some of the fantasies which really had to do with the penis and the situations of gratification associated with that organ.[4]

Although I understand why, given the prominence of phallic symbolism in Western games, Klein would reduce all bodily motion in sports to an identity with the phallus, I do think we must not be so quick to see phallic action as all there is (or all there could be) in organized play. For example, there are other things going on in net games such as tennis, badminton, volleyball, and ping-pong. These types of play might be expressive of a less specific sexuality than that displayed in the forms of sport I have looked at so far.

Although net and court games often make use of paddles and rackets, I think these implements are not quite equivalent to the phallic sticks of hockey and snooker. Although paddles and rackets certainly express some phallic symbol-ism, for the most part, they function as simple extensions of the hand by broadening the range of palms and fingers. I am more willing to consider games such as tennis, badminton, and volleyball as less focused on the phallus because these games are often played in circumstances that are not segregated by gender. (Think, for example, how men and women can be mixed on both sides of the net in volleyball—a game which is often organized when people come together for informal sporting exchange.) The fact that women and men frequently play net games together indicates to me that these sports emphasize something other than phallic competition among men in which women can only be symbolized by goal-sacs, posts, or pockets.

In net games, a ball or "birdie" is moved at a varying tempo across a net between the territories of two people or two teams. The analogy with sexual intercourse comes to mind. Perhaps the net is the body boundary between two people and the ball is a generalized symbol for the fluids and feelings which pass between people during sexual activity. Net games seem to be more concerned with the give and take of sexual relations between equals.

In some games of exchange such as handball, racquetball, and squash, the net has become a line which divides two players who stand next to one another instead of face to face. Such games are possibly expressive of homoerotic desires. Since these court games are most often played by pairs of only men or only women, the side-by-side arrangement might well be placing emphasis on the fundamental sexual sameness of the players. Of course, by speculating on the homoerotic quality of court games as opposed to net games, I am not implying that enthusiasts for any given game are predominantly either heterosexual or homosexual in their more literal sexual practices. A homoerotic sporting preference would probably prove compatible with a generally heterosexual lifestyle and vice-versa. Since we are all bisexual beings to differing degrees, it is quite natural for our civilized sporting life to express a spectrum of sexual feelings. Sports should be an arena in which a range of physical and fantasy experience can be enjoyed.

So far, I have proposed three sporting categories:

1. Adolescent male games which emphasize phallic competition among men: hockey, soccer, rugby, football, polo, basketball, baseball, cricket, golf, snooker, and pool.
2. Adult games which emphasize sexual exchange between the sexes: tennis, volleyball, badminton, and ping-pong.
3. Adult games which emphasize sexual exchange between members of the same sex: squash, handball, and racquetball.

These categories leave out something very important—the clitoris. If this theory about sexuality in sports has any validity, there have to be games that are built around the specifically female imagery of the clitoris. Examples of such games can be found. Consider a famous fairy tale about a young princess and her golden ball. I quote the beginning of Tom Robbins' version of the story from his novel, *Still Life with Woodpecker:*

> Once upon a time, a long time ago, when it was still of some use to wish for the thing one wanted, there lived a king whose daughters all were

beautiful, but the youngest was so lovely that the sun itself, who had seen so much and forgotten so little, simply marvelled each time it shone on her face.

This daughter had a favorite plaything, a golden ball, that she loved dearly. When the days were hot, she would go out into the dark forest near the palace and spend many an hour tossing and catching her golden ball in the shade of a leafy tree. There was a spring in the forest, and usually the princess played near the brink of the spring so that when her play made her thirsty she might take a cool drink.

Now it happened one day that the golden ball, instead of falling back into the maiden's little hands, dropped to the ground and bounced into the spring. The princess followed the ball with her eyes as it sank, but the spring was very deep, and it soon sank out of sight. The bottom of the spring could not be seen. Thereupon she began to cry, and she wailed louder and louder as if her little heart were broken.[5]

The princess does retrieve her golden ball. Almost immediately after the accident, a frog appears and promises to return the toy if the princess will let him be her companion—if she will let him eat with her, drink with her, and sleep with her. She promises and the creature fishes out the ball and returns it to her. However, the princess soon finds the frog too disgusting to have around and tries to break her promise. When the king insists that she keep her royal word, the desperate princess hurls the frog against a wall in a violent attempt to free herself from his repulsive presence. As soon as he hits the wall, the frog becomes a prince who marries the now-ecstatic princess. The two live happily ever after and we never hear another word about the golden ball.

Robbins speculates about the toy's disappearance: "Maybe the princess put aside the golden ball until her own children were old enough to play with it, or maybe once she had a prince to play with she simply abandoned her beloved toy... and it got packed away in an attic, thrown out with the garbage, stolen by a chambermaid, or donated to Goodwill Industries."[6] In any case, after the princess meets the prince, the ball no longer claims her attention. "Whatever happened to the golden ball?" remains an often-posed but never answered question for the characters in Robbins' novel.

According to the classic Freudian interpretation which Robbins mentions, the frog in the story is really a penis which, although initially repulsive to the young girl, soon becomes alluring to the young woman. Although Robbins does not explain the ball in psychoanalytic terms, it seems obvious that it is the clitoris—the clitoris which, according to a Freudian tale, has to give way to the vagina as the seat of sexual pleasure in order for a girl to develop a "proper" sexual response. Seen in this way, the story reads as a piece of patriarchal propaganda expressing a male wish for women to give up all pleasure in their own bodies and learn to take sole delight in the penis. From the prince's point of view, the princess's ball is to be forgotten. Presumably if she were to maintain her interest in her toy, she would be less involved with what her prince had to offer. I take it as a sign of Robbins' identification with his women characters that he is very curious to know "whatever happened to the golden ball?"

I know where we should look for the ball. I think it lives on in the play of little girls, who, year after year, generation after generation, bounce it around against walls and on sidewalks. It lives on in the games of jacks and hopscotch in which girls are fascinated with patterns of tossing and retrieving small rubber balls or roundish toys called "patsies." Most of these little ball games involve either hopping and jumping around a patsy (as in hopscotch) or tossing a ball under a leg and bouncing it against a wall or sidewalk. Often rhymes are recited to emphasize the rhythmic quality of such play. Having the ball between the legs seems crucial to these games. Even jacks, which involves hands and fingers more than it does legs, is a game which often takes place between a girl's legs as she sits on the sidewalk, tosses the ball in the air, and picks up the jacks in patterns of onesies, twosies, threesies, etc.

In all little ball games, there are elaborate rules about how and when things can be touched. Bouncing ball games involve rules about what must be done between bouncing the ball and catching it. For example, sometimes a girl must clap three times or turn around twice before she catches the ball she has thrown against the wall. In more complex games such as jacks, there are complicated restrictions on touching both the ball and the jacks. A girl playing jacks can only touch the jacks she intends to pick up while the ball is in the air. If, for instance, she touches a third jack while gathering up a pattern of twosies, she loses her turn. She can continue her play only as long as she can manage to touch some jacks and avoid others in the prescribed patterns.

Rules against improper touching are fairly intricate in hopscotch as well. A hopscotch player must throw the patsy within the space of each chalk-drawn numbered box. If the patsy touches a chalk line, the player usually loses her turn. (In some neighborhoods, she is given a second chance to toss the patsy within the chalk box.) Rules about touching also extend to instructions about picking up the patsy once the toss is made. The player must hop through the design of chalk boxes in numerical sequence without ever touching a line with her foot. When she stops to retrieve the patsy, she must use just one hand while she stands on one foot in an adjacent box. If she falters and touches the ground with her other hand, she loses her turn. Thus, a good hopscotch player is one who has learned to discipline her body so that she can toss and retrieve the patsy within a small and fairly rigid grid. Could this elaborate use of small spaces be one way little girls train to make maximum use of the restricted social territory in which they will have to move when they grow up? Little ball games warrant study as symbolic expressions both of young girls' psychosexual interests and of the socialization of those interests.

It is striking to note how many little ball games involve throwing and retrieving things. Perhaps this feature of these games shows female interest in an in-and-out movement of things. Or, perhaps tossing the ball and bringing it back might express the going and coming of the nourishing breast in particular or parental attention in general. Indeed, the variety of groupings (onesies, twosies, threesies, etc.) in a game such as jacks could indicate a basic plurality in female erotic interests. The psychoanalytic musings of Luce Irigaray, who theorizes about the complicated dynamics of female sexuality, might illuminate our understanding of little girls' games.[7]

In our culture, the golden ball is neglected, just as it was in the fairy tale. There are no international hopscotch tournaments. Public culture is built around male-run institutions that glorify the hockey puck and scorn the hopscotch patsy. While games expressive of female sexuality are confined to childhood, the phallic sports of boys are aggrandized to become major cultural obsessions. Girls, for the most part, must watch or play boys' games. As adults, women do not get to flesh out more expansive versions of the games they played as children. We cannot know what little ball games might become if girls were given the physical space and social encouragement to develop sporting patterns that resonate with their female bodies.

Freud once suggested that limitations on human thought could be traced back to restrictions placed on masturbation. He thought that the way we learn to direct physical energy affects the way we channel mental energy and that our sense of what is physically permissible affects what we allow ourselves to consider as intellectually possible. Perhaps the relative paucity of patterns of sports in our culture reflects both the rigid gender arrangements and the restricted sexual activities we practice.

But all of this could change. If our gender arrangements and sexual behaviours were to become less restricted and less stylized in the future, our ways of thinking about ourselves and of organizing our social interactions would change also. And, along with the groupings that we have yet to form and the thoughts we have yet to think, there are games we have yet to play. Who knows? One day at the Super Bowl, the princess's golden ball might reappear.

Notes

1. Between 1981 and 1986, sports were exempted from the gender provisions of the Ontario Human Rights Code. The case of Justine Blaney changed this—she challenged the exemption and the ruling was changed in December 1986.
2. For some other psychoanalytic reflections on football, see Childe Herald's essay, "Freud and Football" in *Reader in Comparative Religion: An Anthropological Approach,* 2nd ed., William A. Lessa and Evon Z. Vogt, eds. (New York: Harper & Row, 1965), 250-252.
3. Sigmund Freud, *The Standard Edition of the Complete Psychological Works of*

Sigmund Freud, ed. James Strachey, 24 vols. (London: Hogarth Press, 1953-1974), Vol. XXIII, 190, note 1.

4. Melanie Klein, "Early Analysis" in *Love, Guilt and Reparation and Other Works, 1921-1945* (New York: Delacorte Press, 1975), 86.

5. Tom Robbins, *Still Life With Woodpecker* (New York: Bantam Books, 1980), 136.

6. Robbins, *Still Life With Woodpecker,* 141.

7. Luce Irigaray, *This Sex Which Is Not One,* trans. Catherine Porter (Ithaca: Cornell University Press, 1977).

Chapter 15
Jocks and Jills: Women's Experience in Sport and Physical Activity
Helen Lenskyj

Ethel was born in Toronto in 1908 and played competitive basketball and softball from about age thirteen until she married in 1932. She still participates in a number of sporting activities. She was seventy-five years old at the time of the interview.

Deb was born in 1938. Currently a sports administrator, she holds several Canadian records in Masters' running events (age-class competition for athletes over age thirty-five). She was forty-seven years old at the time of the interview.

Chris was born in 1960. Of Japanese origin, she was one of the top Canadian women in the sport of judo until her retirement in 1985. She was twenty-six years old at the time of the interview.[1]

Although these three women represent three generations of athletes, they experienced many of the same frustrations and triumphs in sport. All three challenged the traditional attitudes and practices that barred girls' and women's participation in all but the most gentle and feminine of physical activities. Figure skating, calisthenics, and dance were permitted, but softball, basketball, judo, and distance running were not. However, the barriers of women's sporting participation were different in each historical period.

Ethel's experiences in the twenties and thirties were perhaps less constrained by societal expectations of feminine behaviour than Deb's experiences in the fifties. The twenties and thirties, sometimes termed the "Golden Age" of women's sport in North America, marked a period of relaxed sex roles and more liberal views on relationships between the sexes. As a result, women had more freedom in their occupational choices and in their leisure pursuits. They could now work or play in the public realm with less fear of being labelled "unladylike" or "hoydenish." The remarkable growth of women's team sports in this period attests to women's success in challenging the more rigid societal expectations of the era before World War I.

By the time Deb was growing up in the fifties, however, there was a post-World War II swing back to conservatism; this period has been termed the era of the "feminine mystique" (Friedan, 1963). During the war years, women had held jobs as factory and munitions workers and as members of the Armed Forces, assuming roles that had long been viewed as incompatible with femininity. There was a deliberate effort on the part of governments, schools, and churches in the late 1940s and 1950s to restore the traditional female role of wife and mother, with the result that many of the "Golden Age" gains in women's sport disappeared.

Growing up in the 1960s, Chris benefitted from the most liberal attitudes and practices surrounding women and sport in the past three decades, although she still faced the problem of competing in the male domain of combat sports. The contemporary feminist movement had its beginnings around the time of the publication of Betty Friedan's *The Feminine Mystique* in 1963, and by 1970 when Kate Millett's *Sexual Politics* and Germaine Greer's *The Female Eunuch* were published, the time was ripe for women in sport to join those women already working for equal rights legislation and an end to sex discrimination in the home, the workplace, and the education system (Millett, 1970, Greer, 1970).

During the past decade, human rights legislation in both Canada and the U.S. has aimed at ending sex discrimination in sport. Schools, universities, and sports organizations can no longer exclude girls and women from full participation in sport solely on the basis of sex. In the U.S., Title IX of the Education Amendments of 1972 prohibits any form of discrimination on the basis of sex in any educational program receiving federal funds. Sports programs carried out by schools, colleges, and universities are all affected by this legislation which requires co-educational physical education classes, provides for non-discrimination in athletics, and identifies such factors as the number of sports available, levels of competition, facilities, supplies, and coaching as indicators of equal opportunity in athletics.

In Canada, discrimination on the basis of sex is prohibited by provincial anti-discrimination laws (termed human rights codes in most provinces), the Canadian Human Rights Code and the Canadian Charter of Rights and Freedoms. This legislation *permits* sex-integrated sport but does not necessarily *require* it unless it can be shown that females are being denied equal opportunity if they are barred from the male sport. The position of Sport Canada on the issue of integrated versus single-sex sport is that sports should be open to both sexes at least up to puberty, and that sports organizations providing single-sex sport must not discriminate against females in terms of programs, competitive opportunities, facilities, equipment, coaching, etc. For their part, many women's sports organizations oppose integrated sport on the grounds that the future of the female sport is jeopardized if top female players abandon the female team. The issue is by no means easy to resolve (Lenskyj, 1985).

Restrictive social attitudes and discriminatory practices have been the pattern in sport for over a century. Historically, girls and women were permitted only a narrow range of sex-appropriate sports: activities believed to enhance their health and feminine attractiveness. The idea that physical activity was enjoyable and valuable in itself was rarely applied to female sport. Many of the restrictions, legitimized by medical rationales, were taken for granted and rarely challenged: for example, girls and women should not swim during menstruation because swimming causes menstrual problems; they should not do the high jump for fear of dropped uteruses; they should not do the broad jump because they will lose their virginity; they should not play team sports because a blow to the chest will cause cancer, or a blow to the abdomen will make them infertile; they should not do distance running because they will stop menstruating and will not be able to have babies; they should not play competitive sport because boys and men do not like aggressive women. The list is endless!

With such a strong tradition supporting the myth of "female frailty," it is not enough simply to remove the barriers through enactment of human rights legislation. Special programs are needed to encourage girls and women who lack the skills and confidence to enjoy the sport of their choice. Despite progress made by the feminist movement in recent years, males still have greater power and privilege than females in North American society. In the nuclear family, the woman is still the primary caregiver and partner responsible for most of the domestic labour, often in addition to her paid employment outside the home. In the workplace, females as a group earn approximately 60 percent of males' wages. In the education system, females are under-represented in high-paying positions of responsibility in schools and in tenured positions in universities. And in the political system, women continue to be a minority, with the result that issues of specific concern to women—for example, day care, reproductive freedom (issues of contraception and abortion), and pay equity—tend to be neglected by governments.

Males as a group have a vested interest in maintaining rigid boundaries and distinctions between the sexes in terms of behaviour, appearance, and personality because such sex-differentiation serves as a very visible rationale for maintaining the existing imbalance of power between the sexes. After all, the argument goes, we can see by women's appearance and behaviour that they are weaker, more emotional, more frivolous, uncommitted to training or careers, and naturally inclined towards home and family. In other words, women need the protection of the superior sex, men, and the current arrangements between the sexes are eminently sensible and "natural."

Traditional sex-appropriate divisions within sport serve as an effective means of achieving this end. Activities are classified as masculine or feminine according to their socializing functions: the masculine or manly sports make a boy into a man, while the feminine sports promote heterosexual attractiveness ("sex appeal") in girls and women. The displays of masculinity and femininity on the football field provide a good example. The male football player is pushing himself to the limits of his endurance, strength, and speed. He is a team member, bonded with his fellow players in body and mind, following orders from the captain and coach but not denying his own identity, initiative, and judgement. He is participating in a "war without weapons," an initiation rite into masculinity and a cult that gains part of its destructive power and mystique from the deliberate exclusion of females. In fact, if he is a professional player, he is probably forbidden from having sexual relations the night before the game, presumably because this association with his wife or girlfriend would drain him of his virility and contaminate the atmosphere of male bonding.

Consider, on the other hand, the cheerleaders. Although their performance may constitute an athletic activity in its own right, it is used merely as a foil to the display of machismo on the playing field—a show of femininity, sexiness, and passivity in contrast with the serious masculine business of winning the game. Nothing in the cheerleaders' performance challenges the myth of male athletic superiority. It could be argued that many so-called feminine sports perform functions similar to cheerleading. Figure skaters, gymnasts, and synchronized swimmers are all expected to devote considerable energy to charming audiences (and male judges) with their clothing, makeup, and youthfully sweet demeanor, wearing a smiling mask to conceal the more appropriate facial expression of physical strain. These are among the fastest growing female sports, yet there is no room in them for the mature female athlete or the athlete who does not meet prevailing standards of heterosexual attractiveness (Lenskyj, 1986).*

Recent research on the sex-differentiated socialization of boys and girls into sport and physical activity, together with the experiences of three women, Ethel, Deb, and Chris, who were able to achieve their personal goals in sport, will provide us with a better understanding of some of the factors that determine girls' and women's participation or non-participation in sport. I have identified five such factors: the family, teachers and coaches, the school, the media, and socioeconomic factors.

The Family

Sex-differentiated child-rearing practices—ranging from different ways of handling male and female infants to the provision of physically challenging toys and equipment for young children—all have important implications for early motor skill development and subsequent involvement in sport and physical activity. Girls are treated as if they were more vulnerable to injury. They are more carefully supervised and have less freedom to explore their environment, to run

---

* Naömi Goldenberg draws attention to the sexual symbolism of male and female sports in this collection.

and climb, to get dirty. While bicycles, construction toys, hockey sticks, and baseball gloves promote large muscle development in boys, the dolls, baby carriages, and domestic toys that are girls' staple playthings contribute little towards this kind of motor development, or, more importantly, towards confidence in one's body. When children reach school age and are exposed to activities such as softball, floor hockey, skating, and running, girls are already disadvantaged on account of their early socialization away from vigorous physical movement. Recent research suggests that sex differences in motor performance can be better explained by social learning influences than by biological factors (Greendorfer, 1983). The biological arguments that explain sex differences in motor ability still persist, however, particularly among critics who invoke the old "female frailty" myth to justify keeping certain sports exclusively male.

> *Chris (born 1960):* Where the majority of players are male, you have to be that much stronger in your cause. You have to make that much more effort to encourage women. There are some men who are still quite condescending about women's judo and don't see it as quite as important as men's. There are always those stereotypic attitudes like "you don't look feminine competing." But people are seeing women doing good judo and society is starting to come around as far as women and sport as a whole is concerned. Yet I think judo is one of those sports where it takes a long time.

Both parents play an important part in girls' successful socialization into sport and their level of involvement during childhood, adolescence, and adulthood, but the nature of each parent's influence differs. The generation of women and men who are parents of today's adolescent girls grew up at a time when there were rigid sex-differentiated rules for sporting participation. As a result, the fathers are more likely to participate in organized sport, while the mothers may focus on personal fitness activities and provide less direct encouragement to their daughters. These patterns are changing, however, as the young daughters of women born in the 1960s see their mothers active in a wide variety of sporting activities.

There are several aspects of the mother's influence that researchers tend to overlook: the behind-the-scenes work of buying and maintaining clothing and equipment, providing meals to fit around family sporting schedules, driving children to practices and games, tending to injuries, doing fundraising and other volunteer work for sport organizations, etc. In some families, fathers may share these responsibilities, but for the most part they are considered "women's work."

Young female swimmers in one Canadian study considered their mothers' influence to outweigh their fathers'. These girls came from privileged socio-economic backgrounds, and this may have been a factor in their mothers' high levels of encouragement. For example, their mothers may have had more leisure time to dedicate both to their own and to their daughters' sporting interests. A subgroup in the study—competitive swimmers—attributed their entry into sport to their fathers' influence, and this was particularly true of younger girls (Butt, 1980). Again, the father's involvement in a daughter's training may be more visible and direct, but the mother who cheers from the sidelines plays an equally important, motivating role. For example, when Chris was a competitive athlete, both her mother and her father were closely involved in her training.

Chris (born 1960): When I was about 6 months old, my father started a judo club. My brothers started judo at about that time, and I wanted to get into it because my brothers were doing it. My mother says I started as soon as I could walk, but I think I was about four. I have three older brothers and we're all very close in age, and I just wanted to always do things they could do. My whole family was into judo. My mother is a 3rd degree black belt, and our whole family has black belts now. Although my mother never competed in fighting competition, she has competed in kata [form] competition.

I started competing when I was about six years old. I got my black belt when I was sixteen years old—you have to be a minimum age of sixteen—and I just got my 4th degree black belt last summer. My mother used to be my personal coach when I was competing internationally. She's been very instrumental in my success in judo, as has my father, of course. It's been a big family thing. My mum would always look after everything for me so that I could just concentrate on competing. She would be at the side cheering me on and telling me what to do.

Studies of the influence of brothers and sisters on girls' sporting participation indicate that male siblings, like fathers, have had considerable influence in the past, probably because male family members have traditionally had greater personal expertise and experience in sport than females.

Ethel (born 1908): I was on a basketball team that played all over Ontario. I can remember Mother counting over a hundred bruises on me! We played boys' rules and we were a good team. To be in the Ontario championships, you really had to play. We won our district and then we went to play other districts.

The coaches for our girls' basketball team, and two of the coaches for our baseball team, came from the YMCA. My brother Ross coached the baseball team the first year. There was a definite division between women's and men's teams. It was probably the breakthrough when those teams that I played on had men coaches and changed to men's rules.

I was a pretty good hitter. When I was about thirteen or fourteen, my brother would stand me in front of the double garage doors that were mostly glass, and he'd say, "You can't miss it now, you know!" and I didn't miss it, we never broke a glass on that door. It made me concentrate, you see, and this is the whole thing, thinking down to your fingertips. If you can't think to your fingertips you can't do any kind of sport.

Different patterns began emerging in the 1980s. The encouragement of "significant others" is an important factor in adolescent girls' sporting participation. "Significant others" refers in this case to other girls or women who have close relationships with adolescent girls as friends, teachers, or coaches. This influence is distinct from, and probably more important than, the influence of role models, sportswomen who provide girls with positive examples of women's sporting capacities but who are not necessarily involved in their daily lives; for example, Chris Evert or Mary Lou Retton (Knoppers, 1980; Berlage, 1983; Butcher and Hall, 1983; Varpolatai, 1987).

Socializing influences on adult women's sporting activity were investigated in the Canada Fitness Survey *(Changing Times,* 1984). For all age groups and roles of females included in the survey, the availability of a partner (sex unspecified) was ranked second in changes likely to encourage more physical activity; this factor was particularly important for housewives and for the ten to nineteen age group. The factor listed most often by both sexes was more leisure time, but males ranked better facilities higher than the availability of a partner. The growth of women's community sport is also indicative of the role played by female peers. Women-only outdoor clubs, softball, and soccer leagues have been flourishing in Canada and the U.S. in the last fifteen years. For married working women, the influence of a husband who is active in sport is a decisive factor. Single women would be more likely to be active in sport than women married to non-participating husbands (Laberge, 1983).

Ethel (born 1908): At Christmas, we'd all go out on the Humber River and play hockey and I would be there, too. I was the tomboy. I'd probably be the only girl. I didn't feel any different. If they knocked me down just the same as they knocked each other down, that didn't bother me.

I didn't mind what my sister called "all the roughness, people sliding into you and hurting your shins"—that didn't bother me. Anything I did made my sister say I was just a tomboy. But I am and I'm not! I always had a lot of men friends, and my brothers and my husband were my friends. I could play tennis or badminton with them, I could go fishing with them or skate with them. Anything they could do, I could do too, and do it as well as they could.

Attitudes of family members towards women's leisure, sport and physical activity have implications for their sporting participation. The stereotypical view of the wife-and-mother role requires that women subordinate their own leisure interests to those of their husbands and children. As a result, they are more likely to be passive spectators than active participants in sport. In addition, values assigned to regular physical activity for the purpose of physical and mental health are affected by both social class and sex. Men with professions are over-represented in distance running, while dance, exercise, and fitness classes are more popular among middle-class than working-class women. It is probably not surprising that working-class men and women whose work lives are physically demanding choose less strenuous leisure activities such as bowling, bingo, or TV viewing.

The concept of women's leisure time is complicated for women whose work is carried out exclusively in the home where demarcations between "work" and "leisure" are invisible. Housewives are seen as having lots of leisure time because, after all, they don't "go out to work." Of course, the double workday of the employed woman, whose domestic workday begins again when she returns home each evening, makes what is called "working mother" the least likely candidate for leisure activities.

Social class also affects the amount of time and money available for sport and physical activity. The working-class woman is less likely to be able to afford childcare and house cleaning services, and therefore has fewer leisure hours available to her than her middle-class counterpart. Not surprisingly, lack of time was the prime factor identified by Canadian women as an obstacle to increased physical activity *(Changing Times,* 1984). Again, there is the expectation that a woman will put others' needs ahead of her own; she may pay a babysitter so that she can go to a baseball game with her husband but may hesitate to do so when she wants to go bowling with women friends. Even when family members are supportive, the physically active woman faces the problem of time.

> *Deb (born 1938):* I have to fit my training into a life that includes a full-time job plus family life including four children. They're all competitive athletes so the whole household revolves around fitting meals in to suit everybody's training schedules and everybody's school schedules. Everybody is very supportive of everybody else's training and competitive activities. They are all in different sports: we've got a kayaker, a rower, a hurdler, a board sailor, and a basketball player in our family.

Race and ethnicity are important factors in the life chances of Canadian women, and racial discrimination no doubt contributes to the under-representation of minority women—Black women, native women, women of colour, immigrant women, disabled women, and others—as athletes, coaches, and administrators. The presence or absence of role models, too, has implications for minority girls' sporting participation: in track and field, aspiring athletes can see examples of successful Black women who are world-class runners, whereas there are few role models for non-white girls in sports such as skiing or tennis where the prominent women are mostly white and Anglo-Saxon. Effects of social class and race/ethnicity are often inter-related, exacerbating the problems of working-class girls' access to sports like skiing and tennis in which expenses of instruction and equipment are high.

The more rigid sex-role expectations that operate within certain ethnic or cultural communities limit girls' and women's sporting participation to those activities defined as appropriate for females in that particular culture. For example, Greek or Italian parents may be concerned about their daughters' involvement in co-educational swimming, camping trips, or school excursions, fearing social and sexual impropriety as a result of inadequate supervision and chaperonage. Problems of clothing which satisfies religious requirements as well as the practical demands of physical activity may arise among girls and women of Muslim or Rastafarian backgrounds who are not permitted to have bare legs.

Teachers and Coaches

A study of girls' and women's perceptions of their coaches reported that emotional support was seen as the most important characteristic (Butt, 1980). Sex differences have been found in college athletes' perceptions of coaches: males believed that their coaches emphasized winning ahead of any other objective, while females believed that "playing well" was their coaches' primary emphasis, with skill development second and winning a distant third (Berlage, 1983). These findings suggest that coaches lower their expectations of success for female athletes.

Observations of high school physical education (PE) teachers and coaches have shown some sex differences in teaching styles: females talked more during PE instruction, protected the privacy of their students (in the showers, for example), and emphasized skill development more than male teachers. For most dimensions, however, there were no sex differences (Bain, 1978). In another study, girls' soccer coaches (mostly women) were found to provide more positive feedback and less technical instruction than boys' coaches (all men), whose feedback was more often specific and technical in nature. It was suggested that either female coaches had, or believed they had, less technical expertise to offer, or that male coaches were operating on the traditional assumption that the young boys were destined to have long careers in amateur sport and needed an early start in serious skill development (Dubois, 1981). The traditional belief in the superiority of male coaches is still held by a considerable number of young women (Coakley and Pacey, 1982).

There are anecdotal accounts that refer to the special rapport between female coaches and female athletes. Many women believe that a female coach is better able to establish a good balance between skill development, competitiveness, camaraderie, and simple enjoyment of the game. In view of Carol Gilligan's findings that women are more likely than men to see themselves in *relation* to, rather than *separate* from others, these differences in coaching styles are not surprising (Gilligan, 1982).*

> *Chris (born 1960):* I started teaching [judo] in my teen years. Now I teach two peewee classes and there is only one little girl in each class. Often, if they come as a family, the girls drop out and the parents don't push it, whereas they'd be more inclined to try to keep the boys in. I try to be a good role model, but it's hard, especially when girls reach adolescence.

The pressure on young women during adolescence and later have a variety of implications for women in coaching and sport administration. On the one hand, pressure towards heterosexual conformity dictates for many young women that all their social and recreational activities should be mixed. On the other hand, mixed sport can be a humiliating and demoralizing experience for many young women. Girls and boys rarely reach puberty with the same levels of opportunity and encouragement to take part in school and community sport. Girls are disadvantaged in their eye-hand co-ordination (catching, throwing, hitting a ball or puck), in their cardiovascular endurance (heart and lung capacity), and in their muscular strength (power to hit, sprint, jump). However, in terms of physiology alone, there are insignificant sex differences in sporting potential before puberty. In other words, if boys and girls received the same opportunities to learn and practice these skills, their performance before puberty would be almost identical.

> *Chris (born 1960):* All the judo classes are mixed. I tried to start a women's class but it didn't work out because the people were already coming here three times a week, and the ones who came out were the elite athletes training for competitions. I didn't advertise outside the club, which is probably what I will do the next time. I'm thinking of doing it because self defence is a big issue now with women. If they go to the classes, they still learn self defence, but it's a mixed class and I guess some women don't feel comfortable with that.

* See Caryll Steffens in this collection for more details on Gilligan's work.

Many women experience the emotional support and the solidarity among female athletes as significant motivating factors, particularly if they have taken up physical activity later in their lives.

> *Deb (born 1938):* One of the things that I have found most rewarding and which adds to my motivation to keep going is women who come up to me after a road race and say, "We haven't met before but I read about you and I thought, well, if she can go out there and do that, I can try it too." Or she'll say, "I want you to know that I've just finished my fourth 10K and it was my fastest time yet."
>
> I haven't had the feeling from them that there's any resentment that I won the race and they were 32nd. It's more a feeling that we were in the race together and I achieved my objective of running so many seconds faster that I did before, and she achieved her objective—in some cases, it may have been just to finish the race.
>
> I think it's wonderful how older women support each other when they do become involved. That's why I appreciate that there are awards in the 50 plus, in the 55 plus, in the 60 plus, in the 65 plus and so on. I can remember one woman saying, "I'm sixty-two years old and for the first time in my life I'm an athlete, I've won an award!"

The School

Many studies have shown that school plays a relatively small role in encouraging girls' entry into sport (Greendorfer, 1980). Family members, peers, and community sports leaders have greater positive influence than schools do on girls' successful socialization into sport. The school's hidden curriculum is not conducive to girls' sporting participation since it conveys to female students that their appropriate role is to be domestic and subordinate to boys and men. Sex-differentiation still exists in areas such as home economics and industrial arts; PE curricula, intramural and inter-school sport are clearly divided by gender, even in elementary grades. The school's organization symbolizes male authority, in the person of the principal, and female subordination, in the predominantly female teaching staff, especially in elementary schools. Most service providers in the schools—secretaries, nurses, teacher-librarians—are also female, while maintenance and janitorial work, predictably, is done by men. In these ways, the school reinforces and reflects parents' and society's expectations of traditional sex-roles and fails to challenge the idea that girls do not need or want access to the full range of sporting activities.

Several studies have revealed traditional sex-role behaviour in the kinds of spontaneous play and games engaged in by elementary school children. Girls, for the most part, participate in imaginative, unstructured activities ("let's pretend...") that require little physical activity, rather than vigorous, rule-governed team games (Lever, 1976, 1978; Best, 1983). Again, Gilligan's thesis helps to explain these play patterns. Many girls and women see the structure and aggression of team games as threats to the web of connection: the bonds that depend on mutual caring and communication. Males, on the other hand, tend to view the rules as a safeguard that contains their aggression while maintaining their separateness (Bredemeier, 1983). However, these patterns do not mean that girls and women do not enjoy team sports, but rather that these kinds of sports might attract more female participants if the current tendencies towards aggression and the win-at-all-costs mentality were modified.

While Ethel's and Deb's school experiences were quite different, as competent athletes they both experienced the frustration of school PE and sports programs that failed to challenge or motivate them.

Ethel (born 1908): The very first time I was on a girls' baseball team was at Humber Bay school, I think it was 1922, when I was about thirteen. Then I went to Central High School of Commerce. They had a very good boys' sport program and a smaller girls' program. We had gym exercises, and phys. ed., a couple of periods a week, but I used to just walk through those things, so it didn't leave any impression on me, I did it so easily. There wasn't anything to learn except basketball. I played on the girls' basketball team against other high schools. I won an Ontario gold medal for the standing broad jump. Those were the kinds of sports I could do. I could always throw the ball the farthest, but I didn't think that was any great achievement.

Deb (born 1938): If you can find the sport or activity that you'll do well in—and you're more likely to enjoy something that you do well—and if you are encouraged to do it and given the opportunity to develop those skills, it can lead to an appreciation of your body and its strengths. How many women can recall being put down in physical education classes at school because they didn't have co-ordination or speed or whatever, instead of being encouraged to try the activity that they have the capacity for? They just dropped out of sports and physical activity altogether.

School boards are currently making attempts to equalize opportunities for male and female students but inequities persist. Inter-school competition is offered in far more male sports than female sports, with male team sports such as football and hockey getting the lion's share of funding and prestige. Boys are offered a wider range of sports, and better equipment and facilities.

Studies have shown that, while girls' participation in community recreation programs remains relatively stable during adolescence, their participation in PE and intramural/interschool sport drops dramatically in high school (Butcher and Hall, 1983, Ross et al., 1985). It has been suggested that co-educational PE classes are partly responsible for this trend: girls' lower skill levels make them feel uncomfortable in PE classes with boys. On the other hand, community recreation programs, such as dance, exercise, or gymnastics usually have only female participants and therefore may be more appealing to adolescent girls.

An Ottawa study documented the low numbers of female role models—PE teachers and teacher/coaches—instructing girls' and co-ed programs (grades four to twelve) and thus confirmed that sport and PE in the schools remains a predominantly male enterprise. Programs to equalize opportunity and funding for females need to be accompanied by affirmative action initiatives: for example, women's coaching clinics which will increase the numbers and the expertise of female teacher/coaches (Quirouette, 1983). A project in Carleton Board of Education schools (Ottawa) provided "role model relationships" for girls in intermediate PE. Fitness classes, basketball, volleyball, and gymnastics competitions were organized, with teachers, mothers, and senior female athletes joining the girls (Spence, 1984).

The shortage of female teacher/coaches is partly related to their own early experiences in sport. Like Deb, many women growing up in the 1950s were actively discouraged from testing their physical limits.

Deb (born 1938): I participated in sport in my early teens and was on a national track team in 1954. I ran for Canada in the Commonwealth Games in the longest distance that women were allowed to run, the 200 yard dash, as they called it in those days. I did all right but I wasn't exceptional. I would rather have been running the mile but they wouldn't let me. So partly I got frustrated, partly I was discouraged. I was going to university and there was no track and field for women at the university. That was not the thing that a seventeen or eighteen year-old girl did. So I quit being an athlete at the age of sixteen and did nothing else competitive for twenty years. I got married and had four children between the years 1963 and 1970. During those years I gradually became more and more inactive.

The Media

There is considerable literature on the effects of general TV viewing on children's values, attitudes, and behaviour. A study of the effects of TV sport programs on young adolescents in Canada and the U.S. identified sex differences in favourite types of shows. For males, sport, comedy, and adventure were the top three choices, while females' first choices were comedy, mystery, and drama (McMillan and Moriarty, 1980).

An American opinion survey showed that 35 percent of women considered there was too much sport programming on TV compared to 24 percent of men. Over half of the respondents (both sexes) believed that men's and women's sports each received adequate TV and newspaper coverage *(Miller Lite Report, 1983).* Of the college athletes in another study, about 60 percent of males read the sport pages daily and watched TV sport often, compared to 32 percent and 49 percent of women respectively (Berlage, 1983). Clearly, the professional male sports that dominate the media—Hockey Night in Canada, for example—have limited appeal to women, even sportswomen. For many women, and for some men, professional hockey and football signify machismo, brute force, violence, and national rivalry; they have lost their appeal as displays of highly-skilled athletes testing the limits of their ability in a competitive setting.*

A survey of adolescents' views of what they "liked best" about sport revealed no sex differences in the first three choices (excitement, competition, exercise) but the fourth choice for females was friendship, and, for males, aggression (McMillan and Moriarty, 1980). Again, these findings support Gilligan's theory about women's concern with being *in relation* to others, a goal that sport can help them to reach.

In view of the predominance of American research in sport psychology and social psychology, it is also important to note that this study identified significant differences between Canadian and American youth related to violence and cheating in sport and to TV programs depicting aggression. American adolescents were more tolerant of these programs than Canadians, perhaps because of a longer history of exposure to TV violence and to the college sport scene, where rule-breaking is commonplace: as in, for example, abuses of the scholarship system where players continue on college teams despite their repeated academic failures.

Sex stereotyping is the dominant characteristic of media treatment of women, with serious implications for the portrayal of physically active females. The emphasis on domestic activities results in an absence of alternative role models: women who work outside the home, women who engage in sporting or recreational activities, and women with careers in sport. Instead, women are depicted as housewives and mothers preoccupied with dirty shirts or shiny floors, or as mindless sex objects whose only interests are fashion, makeup, and men.

The passivity that media portrayals attribute to girls and women is not conducive to enjoyment of, or success in, sport and physical activity (Courtney and Whipple, 1978). Women are not shown taking control of situations, exercising leadership, or performing work in a confident and assertive manner. There are exceptions, but most female TV characters remain dependent on men for approval, protection, and decision-making.

---

* Naömi Goldberg offers an alternative psychoanalytic reading of male and female sports preferences in this collection.

The 1980s trend towards using women clad in the dance exercise uniform of leotards and tights to sell products ranging from diet products to stereos was not a particularly progressive step because the image of heterosexual allure, not the image of strong, active women, predominates. And among the most offensive co-optations of the active woman image are the TV exercise shows where exercise serves simply as a guise for a display of sexually suggestive movements and commentary designed to titillate male audiences.

When more explicit sexuality is portrayed in the media, women are shown in decorative roles: while men *act* in sexually assertive ways, women simply *are* sexy. Current media images reflect a traditional male definition of female sexuality as a commodity to be subordinated to male desire and control. Passive heterosexual attractiveness is depicted as the only acceptable expression of female sexuality, and there is little media validation for alternative images based on strength, confidence, and independence, or for alternative expressions of sexuality such as lesbianism or bisexuality.* The sexual attractiveness of the athletic woman does not come from passivity, coyness, and charm. Rather, she is attractive because her body is strong and fit, and because there is harmony between her body and her mind.

Nationalism and sexism characterize much of the coverage of international sports events. North American commentators continue to make disparaging comments about the appearance and performance of female athletes from former Eastern bloc countries. The "masculinity" of Soviet women in track and field events is a popular topic, and these women are targets of speculation concerning steroid use. Many commentators focus more on female athletes' personal lives than on their sporting performance, as seen in the attention that has been paid to Martina Navratilova's friends and supporters. Male commentators give female gymnasts and skaters unqualified approval for their grace and femininity despite the fact that this may have been achieved through puberty-delaying drugs and starvation diets. But when a gymnast fails to conform to the smiling, charming image—Nadia Comaneci, for example—they are quick to criticize. And while the female athlete is expected to be feminine in appearance, her performance is invariably evaluated by male standards: i.e., is she as good as a man?

All of these trends in the coverage of women's sport both reflect and reinforce the assumption that sporting success and heterosexual appeal are incompatible, and that this combination in a woman is worthy of comment. The overt media preoccupation with women who are both athletic and attractive demonstrates the assumption that "unattractive" female athletes are commonplace, the rule rather than the exception. Athleticism is so clearly defined as a male attribute that its presence in women is automatically assumed to "masculinize" her, if she was not "masculine" at the outset.

---

* Susan Cole, in this collection, describes the effect of this kind of media image on women seeking to make a place for themselves in the pop music field.

And in this context, "masculinity" implies an absence of heterosexual appeal.

It has been well documented that the coverage of women's sport in American newspapers and sport magazines, averaging 10-15 percent of total sports coverage, is by no means representative of current female participation levels, which have steadily increased in the past twenty years in almost every sporting activity. Although the women's movement can take some credit for challenging sex discrimination in the male-dominated sports system, it is both ironic and unfortunate that a leading sponsor of women's professional tennis, Virginia Slims, is one of the worst offenders in its trivializing of women and feminism through its slogan, "You've come a long way, baby," which is both inaccurate and degrading (Hilliard, 1983). The use of the term "baby" in this context is particularly offensive because it destroys the image of the strong, independent woman that the ad sets up. Furthermore, women's progress towards self-determination is trivialized when it is measured by their so-called freedom to smoke their own brand of cigarette.

While some specialized publications like *Tennis* and *Runner's World* are more positive, *Sports Illustrated* not only neglects women's sport but also takes deliberate steps to present women as sex objects. Its annual swimsuit issue uses as models women whose sporting interests rarely go beyond the recreational. These models are obviously selected first and foremost for their traditionally sexy bodies. As well, *Sports Illustrated*'s regular advertising depicts women in the traditional subordinate, decorative role, serving men drinks and admiring men's cars (Bryant, 1980; Rintala and Birrell, 1984). At least one Canadian publication takes the same approach, presenting women as embellishments to men's sport rather than as athletes in their own right. The *Toronto Sun* sport section, while paying minimal attention to women in sport, has at various times housed that paper's advertisements for strippers, exotic dancers, and x-rated movies.

Commercial pressure resulting from sponsorship by cosmetic and cigarette companies is responsible in part for current conservative trends in advertising and journalism. Commercial sponsors like Avon or Virginia Slims require that an unmistakably feminine and heterosexually attractive image be projected by female athletes in the events they sponsor (Boutilier and San Giovanni, 1983). Such portrayals are both distorted and unrealistic, since female athletes are heterogeneous in physique and in appearance and a more progressive advertising approach would take this into account. Certainly, some sportswomen are small, slim, and conventionally attractive, but the tall, muscular women who predominate in many sports are unlikely to conform to society's image of heterosexual attractiveness. And, after all, heterosexual attractiveness is unrelated to any person's sporting ability, male or female: strength, endurance, and training are the key factors. However, as long as women's professional sports depend on corporate backing, we cannot expect to see major changes in media preoccupation with the sex appeal of female athletes.

Like female athletes, coaches, and administrators, women in sports journalism face significant barriers. While men have long felt qualified to report and comment on women's sport, there are few women who have been given the opportunity to do the same for men's sports. A 1984 study of 115 articles from American magazines dealing with international tennis players reported that all the articles on major championships, and all but two on male players, were authored by men, while women wrote less than half of the stories on female players and none of the reports on major events (Hilliard, 1984). There have been some changes in the past few years, and some Canadian newspapers now have female journalists covering both women's and men's sport: for example, Nora McCabe on tennis.

Socio-Economic Factors

In addition to the relationship between social class and the kinds of sports considered appropriate for females, the economic conditions of women's lives play an important part in determining the sports and physical activities, if any, in which they participate. Sports clothing, equipment, instruction, facilities rental, travel, and childcare are beyond the financial resources of many women, who, as a group, earn approximately 60 percent of men's average incomes. As well, large numbers work as wives and mothers in unpaid domestic labour. And with women's career paths typically interrupted by childbearing and childcare responsibilities, there are barriers to pursuing a career as an athlete, coach or sport administrator.

> *Chris (born 1960):* This opportunity to coach came up and I thought I should go for it because I wanted to start a career for myself. Athletes have a hard time. There's no money being an athlete: you're living on the poverty line. I was the only one on the women's national team that was carded [financially assisted] because I was the only one that placed in the top six in the World Championships. Other women did well in other international competition, but Sport Canada only uses World Championships to decide on carded athletes.

Deb's statement illustrates the benefits derived from sporting participation as well as the barriers confronting women in sport in a male-dominated society. Sport is still considered a male preserve, and girls and women are denied the benefits of activities that are physically challenging, that develop the mind as well as the body, and that promote friendship and fun. Some women are working on developing community sport controlled by women and meeting women's needs and interests. Other women are pressuring schools, universities, and governments to provide equal opportunity for females to participate in the sports of their choice and to sanction those organizations which consistently refuse to give girls and women a fair deal in sport.

> *Deb (born 1938):* Sometimes I think I've had to work twice as hard, partly because I'm a woman and partly because I'm older, to get a job. Sport administrators are basically young men with a formal education and experience in that sport, and I'm an older woman without that kind of specific formal education. I was trying to find some kind of career for myself, I wanted to make a change. If I hadn't had a clear picture of myself as a successful athlete, I wonder if I would have had the courage to quit my job and go back to school at the age of forty-four, which is what I did.
>
> I know that I have gained self-confidence and strength from my relative success as a runner, and I know that the time I have spent training very often has given me the time I need to think things out and try to figure where I am going and what I should do next.

Sport has traditionally been the context in which rigid definitions of masculinity and femininity have been reinforced and male domination has been rationalized. The feminist enterprise is to retain the valuable and healthy aspects of sport and to eliminate the practices that are destructive so that sport may become a way for all of us to celebrate the vitality and potential of our humanness.

Notes

1. These names are pseudonyms. The interviews were conducted in 1983 (Ethel) and 1985 (Deb and Chris).

References

Bain, Linda, 1978. "Differences in Values Implicit in Teaching and Coaching Behaviors," *Research Quarterly* 49(1): 5-11.

Berlage, Gai, 1983. "Differences in Male and Female College Athletes' Commitment to Sports and Its Implications," paper presented to the 4th Conference of the North American Society for the Sociology of Sport, St. Louis.

Best, Raphaele, 1983. *We've All Got Scars: What Boys and Girls Learn in Elementary School.* Bloomington: Indiana University Press.

Biddle, Stuart, and Cynthia Bailey, 1985. "Motives for Participation and Attitudes Toward Physical Activity of Adult Participants in Fitness Programs," *Perceptual and Motor Skills* 61: 831-34.

Boutilier, Mary, and Lucinda San Giovani, 1983. *The Sporting Woman.* Champagne, Illinois: Human Kinetics.

Bredemeier, Brenda, 1983. "Athletic Agression: A Moral Concern," in Jeffrey Goldstein (ed.), *Sports Violence*. New York: Springer Verlage.

Bryant, James, 1980. "A Two-Year Investigation of the Female in Sport as Reported in the Paper Media," *Arena* 4(May): 32-40.

Butcher, Janice, and M. Ann Hall, 1983. "Adolescent Girls' Participation in Physical Activity," Planning Services, Alberta Department of Education.

Butt, Dorcas, 1980. "Perspectives from Women on Sport and Leisure," pp. 70-88 in Cannie Stark-Adamec (ed.), *Sex Roles: Origins, Influences and Implications for Women*. Montréal: Eden Press.

Canada Fitness Survey, 1984. *Changing Times*. Ottawa: Canada Fitness Survey.

Changing Times: Women and Physical Activity, 1984. Ottawa: Canada Fitness Survey/ Enquete condition physique Canada.

Chelladurai, P., and M. Arnott, 1985. "Decision Styles in Coaching: Preferences of Basketball Players," *Research Quarterly* 56(1): 15-24.

Coakley, Jay, and Patricia Pacey, 1982. "How Female Athletes Perceive Coaches," *Journal of Physical Education, Recreation and Dance* 53(2)(February): 54-56.

Courtney, Alice, and Thomas Whipple, 1978. *Canadian Perspectives on Sex Stereotyping in Advertising*. Ottawa: Advisory Council on the Status of Women.

Dubois, Paul, 1981. "The Youth Sport Coach as an Agent of Socialization: An Exploratory Study," *Journal of Sport Behavior* 4(2): 95-107.

Friedman, Betty, 1963. *The Feminine Mystique*. New York: Dell.

Gilligan, Carol, 1982. *In A Different Voice*. Cambridge, Mass.: Harvard University Press.

Greendorfer, Susan, 1983. "General Socialization Processes," *Proceedings of the New Agenda Conference*. Washington: Women's Sport Foundation.

——, 1980. "Gender Differences in Physical Activity," *Motor Skills* 4(2): 83-90.

Greer, Germaine, 1970. *The Female Eunuch*. London: Palladin.

Hasbrook, C., 1988. "Female Coaches–Why the Declining Numbers and Percentages?" *Journal of Physical Education, Recreation and Dance* 59(6): 59-63.

Hilliard, Dan, 1983. "If You've Come a Long Way, Why Do They Still Call You Baby," magazine profiles of women professional tennis players. Unpublished paper presented to the 4th Annual NASS Meeting, St. Louis.

——, 1984. "Media Images of Male and Female Professional Athletes: An Interpretive Analysis of Magazine Articles," *Sociology of Sport Journal* 1(3): 251-262.

Knoppers, Annelies, 1980. "Androgyny, Another Look," *Quest* 32(2): 184-191.

——, 1985. "Professionalization of Attitudes: A Review and Critique," *Quest* 37(1): 92-102.

Laberge, Suzanne, 1983. "L'activité physique chez les femmes: des conditions d'existence qui font la différence," *Canadian Women's Studies* 4(3): 31-34.

Lenskyj, Helen, 1985. *Female Participation in Sport: The Issue of Integration versus Separate-but-Equal*. Ottawa: Canadian Association for the Advancement of Women and Sport.

——, 1986. *Out of Bounds: Women, Sport and Sexuality*. Toronto: Women's Press.

——, 1988. *Women, Sport and Physical Activity: Research and Bibliography*. Ottawa: Fitness and Amateur Sport.

Lever, Janet, 1976. "Sex Differences in the Games Children Play," *Social Problems* 23: 478-487.

——, 1978. "Sex Differences in the Complexity of Children's Play and Games," *American Sociological Review* 43(August): 471-483.

Mathes, S., and R. Battista, 1985. "College Men's and Women's Motives for Participation in Physical Activity," *Perceptual and Motor Skills* 61: 719-726.

McMillan, Paul, and Dick Moriarty, 1980. "A Comparative Canadian-American Study of the Effect of Television Athletics and Organized Sport on Children and Youth," unpublished paper presented to the 6th Annual Association for the Anthropological Study of Play, Ann Arbor.

Miller Lite Report on American Attitudes Toward Sport, 1983. Milwaukee Brewing Co.

Millet, Kate, 1970. *Sexual Politics.* Garden City: Doubleday.

Potera, C., and M. Kort, 1986. "Are Women Coaches an Endangered Species?" *Women's Sports and Fitness* 8(9): 34-35.

Quirouette, P. et al., 1983. Ottawa Board of Education Athletic Survey. Research Report 83-01.

Ross, J. et al., 1985. "After Physical Education . . . Physical Activity Outside of School Physical Education Programs," *Journal of Physical Education, Recreation and Dance* 56(1): 88-91.

Spence, J., 1984. "Role Model Relationship," *OPHEA Journal* 10(1): 29-39.

Uhlir, G.A., 1987. "Athletics and the University: The Post-Woman's Era," *Academe* 73(4): 25-29.

Varpolatai, A., 1987. "The Hidden Curriculum in Leisure," *Women's Studies International Forum* 10(4): 411-422.

Whitaker, Gail, and Susan Molstad, 1985. "Male Coach/Female Coach: A Theoretical Analysis of the Female Sport Experience," *Journal of Sport and Social Issues* 9(2): 14-25.

Chapter 16

Cuckoo in the Nest?
A Feminist in Sociology
Marilyn Porter

I am a sociologist. I teach sociology in a university sociology department. I publish in sociology journals and present papers at sociology conferences. I do sociological research and I have a Ph.D. in sociology. And yet I am profoundly ambivalent about this identity. Sometimes I even feel that it is a bluff, disguising my "real" identity. For I see myself also, and in many ways more importantly, as a feminist and a marxist. What I want to discuss in this paper is what these three identities mean to me, and how they relate to each other.

One critical difference between them is that marxism and feminism are both *political* commitments; they both involve not only analyzing society in certain ways but also developing a program of action to achieve political objectives. Marxism is most concerned with the inequalities of class and economic relations and with the development of an alternative socialist society free of economic exploitation. Feminism is woman-centred and woman-identified. Its concern is to understand how sexism and patriarchy operate to subordinate women and how women's concerns, priorities, and visions can take their rightful place in the world.

While there are many differences, and even conflicts, between marxists and feminists, they share the same passionate *need* to understand the world in order that they may change it. Sociology, on the other hand, is an academic discipline. It has defined a certain area of knowledge as being "sociology": very broadly, the way society works and the relationships between groups of people within it. In order to do this, sociology has developed distinctive "methods," styles, and ways of seeing things as "sociologically interesting." But sociology, as an academic discipline, has no end beyond understanding that part of the world that it defines as sociology.

Already you can see that there is considerable overlap between what sociology would define as part of its area of concern and the kinds of issues that

---

The cuckoo does not raise its own young but lays its eggs in the nests of other, smaller birds. The baby cuckoo, upon hatching, pushes the smaller birds' eggs and/or babies out of the nest, so that it will receive all the food brought by the dutiful parents. Even so, the adoptive parents can hardly keep up with the voracious appetite of the intruder.

would interest marxists or feminists, and indeed, many other people. For example, sociologists are interested in the way economic relations are patterned in society, how these patterns perpetuate themselves, and what consequences they have for groups of people. In other words, class analysis is one area of sociological interest. For marxists, an understanding of class structure is a crucial element in analyzing how capitalism works and thus challenging capitalist society. Similarly, sociology considers the family a sociological "institution": a grouping patterned more or less predictably and relating to other parts of society, so the "sociology of the family" has been an important area of sociological interest. Feminists are also interested in the family because women's place in the family is crucial in determining many other aspects of their lives.

In each of these cases you can see how marxists and feminists could share with sociologists a desire to understand a particular aspect of society but that marxists and feminists would do so from a particular perspective and with the intention of going *beyond* merely understanding.

These kinds of examples may help to explain why some marxists and feminists should choose to operate within the academic discipline of "sociology" rather than, say, math or folklore. But why should they want to do so at all? Why not simply be marxists or feminists and not bother with sociology? This is not an easy question to answer, except to say that obviously and rather superficially, there are not as many academic jobs in marxism or feminism although there are increasing numbers of jobs in Women's Studies.

When I attempt to answer the question for myself, I find that both the structure of academic knowledge and the history of education in universities is relevant. At the time I was developing my interests, sociology was more available and established than feminism or marxism. There was a department of sociology in my local university offering relevant courses and qualifications and prospects for jobs. My entry into sociology (1971) occurred at a time when sociology as a discipline was in a period of rapid expansion, both in terms of the numbers of people and institutions involved and also in terms of its range of interests. Because many of these interests, especially the ones having to do with class and gender inequality, coincided with ones I was developing personally, sociology seemed a comfortable and obvious place in which to establish myself. I still feel that way, and yet that is not the full answer. I find myself unsure whether I am a sociologist because sociology as a discipline has intrinsic value, or because it provides a particularly progressive and receptive environment, or simply because sociology is so nebulous that it has become the academic equivalent of the Liberian flag—a flag of convenience flown by all kinds of ships including those engaged in *notorious* activities. Am I really a sociologist or am I just using sociology as a useful cloak for my "real" activities as a marxist-feminist?

When I first went into sociology, circumstances—and sociology— were very different from the current situation, and it may be helpful at this stage to look back and see if my biography helps to explain my identity as a sociologist.

The year 1968 meant many different things to different people. All over the Western world it signified the crest of a new wave of radical activities and concerns. It was a time when the Beatles, four ordinary young men from Liverpool, transformed the popular music scene. The U.S. was torn apart by the calamity of the Vietnam War, and thousands of young Americans became radicalized in their protest against it. The "new style" was flamboyantly different: bell bottom trousers, long hair, flowers, marijuana, guitars, and bright colours became a kind of uniform for progressive young people in many countries. Apart from mere style, there was an increasing concern with peace, harmony, and freedom, seen in stark contrast with the competitive, aggressive, militaristic administrations that dominated the world. Included in the freedoms young people were claiming was sexual freedom. The increasing availability of the pill had for the first time opened up the possibility of (heterosexual) sex without the risk of pregnancy. However, it was mainly men who saw it as the basis for demanding freer, more satisfying and creative ways of relating sexually. While women relished the release from fear of pregnancy, for many of them what it actually meant was that they had to be more sexually available than ever before, something that could be experienced as pressure to conform rather than as freedom. In keeping with the upsurge of new ideas about lifestyles and relationships, utopian communes were established in great numbers. Some were transitory, some survive today; some were urban, some were rural; some had a religious basis; some stressed particular forms of relationship; some were devoted to economic self-sufficiency. But very few had women's needs or ideas at their centre, and many women who had joined communes, full of enthusiasm and high ideals, found themselves continuing to have babies and do the washing up but in much more uncomfortable and insecure circumstances than the traditional nuclear family had offered.

An important part of the "1968 experience" was what was happening in education, especially in the universities. The generally critical mood among young people, coupled with the ideals of freedom and innovation, meant that students took a new look at every aspect of their education: at the hierarchical and authoritarian structure of the institutions, at the formal and rigid methods of teaching, at the elitist composition of the universities, at the heavily traditional content of the courses, and at the narrowness of the exam system. The result was an upsurge of student revolts and sit-ins in all Western countries. They demanded very similar reforms, which included more relevant and interesting courses to be taught in less authoritarian ways and greater student participation in the running of the universities. Sociology and sociology students played a key role in this process, especially in France, where students of sociology had led the way in the revolts. Greater numbers of students and teachers in sociology were involved in the revolts, and this was mainly because the kinds of topics that sociology *said* it addressed attracted people who were interested in social reforms. In the heady atmosphere of 1968, the wave of disillusionment when these radicals found that the sociological establishment was not especially progressive and had little sympathy with the student demands led to particularly acute crises in many sociology departments. The upshot was that radical young teachers and students began producing new course materials and curricula; setting up alternative conferences, journals and workshops; and challenging at every opportunity traditional priorities and methods, both in what was taught and what was researched. Of course, sociology was not the only discipline profoundly affected by the 1968 revolution, but it was affected more than many others.

Meanwhile, I missed the "1968 experience." I had my first child in January 1968 and then went to teach in Botswana. It was only two years and another child later that I caught up sufficiently to look around for a way of restructuring my private life and re-entering the public world. By this time the Women's Liberation Movement in England was in full swing. It was dominated by heterosexual, middle-class, young, married women with children and by people who could, in the heady, post-1968 days, be said to be "on the left." The first meeting I attended was daunting, in that all the women there seemed to inhabit a different world— a much freer and more positive one than mine—and to be fluent in what sounded then like a complex and difficult language of ideas. But it struck an immediate chord. I wanted the knowledge and confidence these women had. I had become increasingly frustrated with my personal life, although there was nothing I could really complain about. In fact I was altogether too comfortable in a nice, middle-class environment, with two perfect children and a helpful husband. It left me profoundly unsatisfied in ways I found hard to express because I could not justify them. I also felt excluded from all the vigorous new activity I knew was going on around me. In the Women's Liberation Movement I found a place where I could express my anger, frustration, and need for companionship. Within the space of a few months I had learned to both name my problems and to begin to solve them. In the course of consciousness-raising, campaigns around particular issues, and women's cultural and social events, I learned a particular way of interpreting what was happening, especially from friends who were struggling to re-interpret the marxism they had learned in leftist groups and political parties.

Excited and committed, I was learning to call myself a marxist-feminist and I was also becoming acutely aware of how little we actually *knew* about the position of women in society and the ways in which they were systematically disadvantaged and how vital this was to formulating powerful strategies to life our oppression. The next step seemed to be to qualify myself to address these problems. I had a B.A. in history and a professional year in education but neither of these avenues seemed appropriate. I had already decided that the school structure and curriculum were too rigid and repressive to operate in, and history as a discipline seemed dominated by the history of dead men studied by very nearly dead men. Progressive historians I knew were getting short shrift in their departments; later, however, the feminist and radical historians became one of the strongest and most cohesive groups in the new feminist movement in England.

On the other hand, sociology did have a reputation for radical and progressive courses and research. In England it was a new discipline, not yet weighed down by conservative precedents and practices. My interests and concerns clearly fell within its general constituency. However, despite the effects of radical teachers and students in the previous two years, in 1971, when I took my "conversion course," the discipline remained firmly wedded to respectability and tradition. In the department where I took my course, there were no women on faculty, no courses on women, and no particular sympathy for the Women's Liberation Movement. In fact, the post-graduate "conversion course" I took was remarkably formal and traditional.

Nevertheless, a year later I knew a modicum of traditional sociology, rather more about marxism and political economy, and a very great deal about how the left in the U.K. worked and its fundamental blind spots with regard to feminism. Issues such as daycare or equal pay had still to be taken seriously. It has to be said that I didn't learn all this in my sociology department. What I learned there was firstly, that everyone in sociology picked and chose what they wanted to be interested in and involved themselves in political issues outside the university, and I could do the same, and secondly, that it was enormous fun to conquer a new body of literature and a new set of ideas and concepts. It was especially fun to take them back to my friends in the Women's Liberation Movement and to try to beat them into a shape useful to our overriding purpose of understanding what was happening to women. The rest I learned outside, in the white heat of political life in the England of 1970, in the conferences, demonstrations, debates, pickets, alternative publications, street theatre, sit-ins: in all of which feminists were increasingly demanding, and taking, a larger and stronger place. We were also building our own political life (complete with splits, fights, and tensions of our own) in which we were debating our struggles and situation more and more intensely. In all of these gatherings, people identified themselves first as feminists and only *then* as social workers, historians, journalists, trade unionists, party activists, or sociologists.

By the time I was ready to start my Ph.D. I knew it was going to be neither politically nor academically "sociology," but nonetheless my only possible academic home was going to be in sociology. And so it turned out to be. Looking back now, my research topic seems embarrassingly naïve and partial, but it was one of a whole range of attempts inside and outside sociology both to redress the imbalance caused by the omission of women and to apply feminist theory and politics to the disciplines in which we found ourselves. Thus, not only was I committed to doing a more complete form of sociology, but I also wanted to reshape it to answer the new questions we were beginning to pose. I was concerned with what we would now call the interaction of gender and class ideology in the working class. I wanted to see how people's identities as men and women, and their identities as workers, influenced their ideas. To do this I focused on a factory (employing mainly men) that had recently had a strike. What I wanted to do was to examine how the "class consciousness" and knowledge that the men had acquired in their experience of the dispute had been mediated to their wives. Conversely, I wanted to discover the roots of their wives' political ideas and how their experience as women helped to structure those ideas. I started, therefore, with men and their experience, something I would never do now. I focused on the "cereal-packet family"—the heterosexual married couple with dependent children and the husband as principal wage earner—a paradigm situation we have long since learned to see in a broader perspective, encompassing a much wider range of sexual preferences and living arrangements. Even with these limitations it broke new ground in the field of industrial sociology which had previously focused almost exclusively on male workers in male-dominated industries such as coal mining and automobile manufacturing. Even more daring, it challenged two contradictory assumptions: firstly, that only men had political consciousness and secondly, that if women did have it, it would be inherently conservative. The very idea of talking to *wives* was, therefore, innovative and, indeed, risky.

The results demonstrated a much more complex situation than had been assumed by male sociologists. As a result of the strike, the men had battered their way through to a new level of "trade union consciousness": an understanding of how they were exploited at work; but on the whole they were unable to develop this into a full-fledged political analysis of their entire situation. The women had been given very little information about the strike, and because of this and their own rather unhappy experiences with unions, they were inclined to be leery about trade unions and what they could contribute to their lives. On the other hand, they had developed a much more comprehensive and radical analysis of society that derived from their whole range of experience as women: as mothers dealing with health care, social services, and the school system; as active members of the community resisting environmental pollution and campaigning for better public services; and as workers in women's job ghettos in laundry, catering, or in Will's Tobacco Factory. In the course of their experiences, they had learned to understand and resist the inequalities, especially as they relate to class inequalities in society, and had developed clear analyses about who holds power over, for example, housing, and how that power is exercised. Many of them were able to explain how, in the course of their disputes with authorities, they had come to understand that their individual fight about repairs, say, was connected with the national politics they saw on television. In other words, the material allowed me to argue, albeit tentatively, that there was a specifically *women's* consciousness based on women's experience that was at least as potentially radical as the kind of political consciousness men developed in their workplaces. Sociology would have to pay attention to women, to women's experiences, and to women's ideas if it wanted to gain more than a partial, one-sided analysis of the working class. This kind of research was paralleled by attempts by other feminists working in social administration, history, and psychology especially. In all these disciplines, increasing numbers of feminists were producing substantial research demonstrating both the inadequacy of previous work, which was flawed by sexist bias, and the potential of taking women's perspective and women's experience seriously. But it was in sociology that the greater numbers of feminists enabled us to make the greatest impact.

In the early 1970s, feminists in sociology were principally concerned with developing a critique of both the omissions and the methods of sociology. They pointed out that women's work had been neglected; that the sociology of women's occupations was unwritten; that we knew nothing of women's "deviant" activities, let alone their contribution to crime; that we didn't know what happened to girls in school; or what happened to them in formal organizations; or what contributions they made in politics.

However, it soon became clear that this kind of "completing the record" was not enough. More and more studies, like mine, showed that the omission of women prejudiced the analysis. We soon came to see not only that previous studies had left women out and were thus incomplete, but that they were at best deficient and more often simply wrong. Class consciousness did not emerge so simply from male working-class experience on the factory floor. A notion of politics that stopped short of analyzing informal organizations at the grassroots levels, such as community protest groups and the complex influences of women on formal organizations, misinterpreted much of the political potential of a society. Above all, studies of the family that assumed the perspective of the father and based the analysis on his priorities, while ignoring the perspectives of women and children, produced a simplistic reading that was quite at variance with reality.

This kind of work went on in a host of different areas. What they had in common was that they started with women's *own* lives and experience, often based on feminist academics' own lives and experience. For the first time, not only were women visible, but the world was seen from their perspective. We were also beginning to challenge the distinction between the "knower" and the "knowee," the researcher and her research "subject."

The criticism embedded in these practical studies of concrete areas of experience soon led to other, even more fundamental, criticisms. These centred around methodology. It became clear that the way sociologists had traditionally set about discovering facts was riddled with sexism. One of the first targets was statistics, the staple diet of sociologists. Anne and Robin Oakley in England, looking at "sexism in official statistics," demonstrated all the points at which sexism could enter into the apparently objective process of collecting census statistics: for example, in the concepts employed, such as "head of household" or "family;" and in the processing of the statistics (the tabulations and break-downs chosen). They also showed how women had been rendered invisible in most official statistics and over-visible in certain areas, e.g., fertility and household composition. In Canada, similar work by Pat and Hugh Armstrong on Statistics Canada looked at "explicit and more often implicit, assumptions—built into the collection and tabulation of these data, assumptions which may serve to conceal, or distort, important aspects of women's work." They showed how the assumption that the person in a household who pays "rent, mortgage, taxes or electricity" is the primary economic provider means it is usually the man who is so identified rather than the woman, whose wages are associated with food, clothing, and services.

However, while the Armstrongs argued that because of the deficiencies of quantitative or survey data based on these kinds of facts, we should rely more heavily on "qualitative" or subjective methods, other feminist sociologists were arguing that we should develop totally *new* methods appropriately tailored to our feminist needs. Liz Stanley and Sue Wise argued that "feminist theory" and "feminist research" ought to be concerned with the implications of *feminism* itself. They argue that feminists, by virtue of their passionate involvement in their own lives, are in a better position to break through to that state of personal consciousness in which valid research can take place. For Stanley and Wise, then, the method of becoming intensely aware of one's own situation as a woman is the *only* way we can arrive at "feminist knowledge."

However, it was "macro" sociological theory—the grand abstractions—that posed a more immediate problem for feminists in sociology. Virtually all socio-logical theory had been written by men. The works of the "founding fathers"—Marx, Weber and Durkheim—formed the core of all undergraduate courses, and all subsequent sociological explanation derived from their nineteenth century, patriarchal views of the world. Thus was sexism compounded by sexism.

Clearly we could not have feminist studies done with feminist methodology set within a patriarchal theoretical framework. An interesting argument revolved around whether gender could be relevant at such a level of abstraction. Surely ideas, models, abstract constructs could not be sexist? Surely it didn't matter that Marx used the generic "man" throughout his writing if his analysis of capitalism was valid? But feminists argued that in the end sociological theory has to be accountable to the real world, and the real world consists of women and men and their experience. While we accepted Marx's essential analysis, we were aware of at least two different kinds of deficiencies. His ignoring of gender meant that he failed to analyze either the different place of women in the labour market or the value of their work outside the labour market, in the household. On a rather different level, feminists have joined with other marxists in questioning the stress on economic analysis to the exclusion of cultural or ideological factors. In other words, we felt that macro-theory was weaker because it had ignored gender and that there were ways in which the insights of feminism were directly relevant to the development of such theory.

In any case, we badly needed to theorize the new intellectual areas that were opening up, to understand and relate the new knowledge we were generating as the result of research feminists had been doing for the previous few years. And it is difficult to start cold. Some feminists did try: women like Shulamith Firestone (who tried to develop a new "dialectic") and Mary Daly (who is rewriting our language). All too often, especially in the analysis of class and gender, they turned out to be analogies of marxism. Theories tend to grow best if they are rooted in other theories, but those other theories were all contaminated by patriarchy. We had to first rework and cleanse such theories that seemed most useful and then work forward to develop our own feminist conceptual tools. The primary focus for this activity was Marx. This was partly because so many feminists had either begun their political careers in marxist groups or had been profoundly influenced by marxism when they were developing their feminism. And this was directly connected to the radicalism of the late 1960s when these feminists had been developing their ideas. It was also because so much of what Marx had written *had* proved useful. At any rate, compared to the volumes of debate on Marx's ideas, Weber, Durkheim and subsequent sociological "fathers" have attracted a mere few lines.

An important debate that reinforced this process was the so-called "domestic labour debate" and its successors. This debate should also illustrate just what feminists in sociology were concerned about when they talked about "theory." The "domestic labour debate" revolved around analysis of the unpaid and unrecognized work that women did in the home. It also involved reordering the economic analysis of women's contribution, a re-analysis of the household economy, and an attempt to rework Marx's "labour theory of value," so as to recognize women's contribution in terms of the "reproduction of labour power." These phrases are, of course, a kind of shorthand. Marx had argued that all economic value arose from the labour of human beings when they worked to transform materials into valuable goods. Feminists argued that an important part of this process was the work women did in the home to "reproduce" workers: both by feeding and clothing men, making them ready for work each day, and by bringing up children who would be the next generation of workers. While some feminists in sociology had been trying to analyze the family and, in particular, women's contribution and the nature of housework, the main impetus for the debate came from the women's movement.* The "domestic labour debate" and

---

* The necessity of including 'domestic labour' in economic and political analyses is discussed further by Joanna Dean and Martha MacDonald in this collection.

its successors are still productive of both political dispute and theoretical advance. Thus a debate that began in the women's movement about whether we should demand "wages for housework" became a theoretical debate about the relevance of certain marxist ideas. It found a home in sociology partly because so many feminists and marxists were sociologists and used the sociological journals and conferences to carry on the arguments. The consequences for sociology as a discipline were unambiguously good. The family—previously a rather stale area of sociology—re-emerged as a dynamic study and one which could no longer ignore feminist insights and concerns. It could not be assumed that the family existed for the benefit of males and that other members had either no say or a lowly contribution to make. The family was a complex, problematic institution that was central to women's experience, and its analysis was vital to understanding women's position. All sorts of hidden "pathologies" became visible and the object of scrutiny—wife battering, incest, and sexual abuse among them. The analysis of both the national economies of capitalist societies and the interactions of those economies with Third World countries was redirected by a consideration of the economic role of households and women's contribution to them. Thus, feminist concerns to understand the nature of the work women did in the home in order to improve women's economic position led to major breakthroughs in sociological analyses of a variety of problems and the development of more sophisticated theories.

Another area of marxist analysis that feminists contended with was that of class. Marxists, including marxist-feminists, understood that classes—especially the major classes of capitalists and the proletariat—were a central mechanism of capitalist society, enabling the owners of wealth to employ workers so as to accumulate even more profit. Class has thus always been an important issue for marxists. Curiously, Marx himself had remarkably little to say about actual classes in bourgeois society. In particular, he had left few clues as to the analysis of the so-called "middle strata"—that ambiguous group between the capitalists and the proletariat. However, subsequent marxist sociologists filled out a reasonably satisfactory account of the class structure of advanced Western societies. The problem was that they assumed a woman's class position was based on that of her father and/or her husband; women did not have class positions in their own right. This sweeping form of sexism was repeated in the census categories and other measures of "social class," especially in England.

The critique initially arose from the observation that such an assumption took no account of marriages in which the wife "came from" a class different than that of her husband or where the wife's occupation gave her a different social class position than that of her husband. Considering how much analysis is based on the concept of "social class," feminists argued that it should not have such a shaky foundation. It was not merely a problem of statistical convenience. Sociologists were fundamentally unable to incorporate women into an analysis of class. They were relegated to secondhand status; they were accorded class by proxy: they ended up with a derived class. Some feminists, such as Jackie West, argued that no analysis of class, certainly no analysis of the family as a placement agency, was possible without taking into account *women's* occupations and their economic and ideological contribution to the family. Others moved on from this position to argue that gender was itself a source of stratification and that to adequately theorize women's position we needed to take account of *both* gender *and* class divisions. Both these approaches led feminist theory into rich territory. The focus on women's occupational positions developed and extended the analysis of the so-called "new middle classes" (argued for by writers like Poulantzas and Olin Wright). The other focus proved both more interesting and more divisive. Some feminists had taken gender as a fundamental category of social divisions and had developed quite sophisticated analyses that replaced class with sex as the basis (e.g. Shulamith Firestone). But many marxist-feminists were reluctant to do this and so tried to develop an extension of marxist class analysis that would allow gender to be equally important. The problem was that either one ended up giving one or other category priority, sex *or* class, or one developed an analogous treatment of gender, for example, by describing a "patriarchal mode of production" and a "capitalist mode of production" as two parallel social structures (See Delphy, 1984). Just as capitalists exploited workers, so men exploited women. Most marxist-feminists were unhappy with such analogies, feeling that they diffused the original clarity of the marxist categories without actually analyzing women's experience any more exactly. Was men's treatment of women always and inevitably exploitative? How did the two structures of patriarchy and capitalism relate to each other? And probably the most important political question: was capitalism the real enemy of women, or was it men?

    In this example as well, we are not talking about disputes that originated in sociology. Class, and more particularly how we conceptualized women's economic and social position, was a problem that exercised feminists generally. It was important not only because, as feminists, we felt an urgent need to develop our theory but also because there were vital political decisions to be made about how we acted, and why, to challenge women's oppression. These questions were not matters of abstract speculation to feminists, as they were to many male sociologists and male marxists. They were matters of vital and absorbing concern. Not having a degree in sociology was no reason to disqualify women from contributing to the debate. Nor were feminist sociologists prepared to restrict themselves to discussing the matter in the close confines of the discipline. Sociology became *one* forum of a feminist debate that ranged over a much wider territory and involved many other disciplines. Once more it was sociology's gain. To the extent that it was prepared to give house-room to enthusiastic masses of feminists and feminist writing, its own debate was enriched and its theoretical understanding enlarged. I have indicated that sociology gained from allowing feminists to use the discipline as a forum. What did feminists gain from sociology? It has to be said, not a lot.

The male hierarchy is still grudging in its acceptance. Feminists in sociology still report greater difficulties than their male colleagues in getting their papers accepted by male-run conferences or publications; getting hired, tenured, and promoted in academic institutions; and getting the necessary support to extend feminist courses. Feminist caucuses have been active in national sociological associations (e.g., the British Sociological Association and the Canadian Sociology and Anthropology Association) and have brought pressure on the profession to set its own house in order. As a result, the associations have tried to work towards gender parity on committees and publications and conference presentations. Source books and bibliographies of non-sexist research have been produced (e.g., Eichler & Lapointe) and they have worked out guidelines for eliminating sexism in both practice and publications.

But there are inherent limitations to this kind of reform. One is the sheer scale of the enterprise. It is hard to arrive at gender parity when you start with such overwhelming male dominance. Few university sociology departments had more than a token one or two women on faculty in the early 1970s, and those women were not necessarily feminists. In order to achieve gender parity, departments would have had to appoint only women and appoint them at a great rate. Even in the much more affluent conditions that prevailed then, this was impossible. Now that universities are in a period of restraint and possible cutbacks, it is more important to *keep* the appointments we have. We have learned, in the meantime, that to be an effective influence in any department we need more than a token feminist. We have to achieve a "critical mass" of feminists: about three in a department of fifteen or twenty. This eases the pressure on each feminist, enables us to teach more courses, and ensures that there is at least debate about feminist issues at department meetings. More importantly, it allows us to act as a caucus. We can outlaw raucous male laughter and sexist jokes by acting as a boisterous counter influence. We can have passionate debates *in public* about things that matter to us. Quite rapidly, this changes the discourse in the halls. We cease to be visitors on trial and begin to take possession of the academic space. Parity would be nice: three is an essential minimum, but in too many departments even that remains a distant dream.

Meanwhile, another process has been gaining ground, one that is well illustrated by this book: that of interdisciplinary feminism or Women's Studies. Feminist sociologists writing and speaking in feminist conferences and publications relayed the kinds of advances they had been making and found them matched by advances made by feminist historians, economists, etc.

While this process and intermingling had been a feature of feminist scholarship at least since the early 1970s, the boundaries between feminist scholarship and our disciplinary bases have become increasingly fuzzy and less important, especially as a result of the kind of debates I have described here. Interdisciplinary research seminars began to spring up. Deliberately interdisciplinary Women's Studies programs have gained increasing credibility. Feminists in different disciplines began to meet each other more frequently and to develop common concerns and concepts. We started to work together on research projects and development of Women's Studies courses and materials. All this caused those of us who were "in sociology" to feel more "feminist" and consequently, perhaps, less "sociological."

In considering my position as a feminist in a sociology department, let me give you a recent example. This semester I am teaching a graduate reading course in feminist theory. Because of the interest of the students and my own feeling that it is an important area, I began with Simone de Beauvoir and pursued the subsequent writings of French feminists, which focus on existentialism, language, psychoanalysis, and structuralism. Thus we are studying the work of writers such as Kristeva, Iragaray, Cixous, and Wittig. This involves some background work on the discourses in which these writers have developed their ideas. We are also looking at other aspects of the debates on sexuality, including the work of writers such as Juliet Mitchell, Michel Foucault, Carol Gilligan, and American commentary on the "Pleasure and Danger" debate about sexuality and the place of sado-masochism in feminist practice (Vance, 1984). None of this is easy material. All of it is crucial to developing a feminist understanding of the relationship of power and sexuality in our patriarchal culture. The students find it relevant, exciting, and challenging. I was talking about the course to a male colleague, who said, in tones of mild despair rather than criticism, "I don't suppose you're going to teach them any sociology, are you?" It was not until that point that I realized, firstly, that at no point in setting up and teaching the course had I thought about how much "sociology" there would be; secondly, that when I looked through the considerable reading list for the course, I was quite unable to say which writers were formally "sociologists" and which were not; and thirdly, that I was both willing and able to continue to teach and *defend* such a course as being appropriate to sociology graduate students. I would argue that the study of gender is a crucial area of sociological knowledge, and that the course I taught would extend the students' understanding of the social aspects of gender as well as deepen their grasp of complex concepts and theories.

I think this incident exemplifies both the strengths and weaknesses of being a feminist in sociology. One of the strengths is, obviously, that to teach such a course in sociology is possible, if not exactly encouraged. The main weakness, I think, is that because it *is* possible, I am seldom forced to work out the boundaries, contradictions, and conflicts between feminism and sociology. It's as if feminism is the cuckoo in the sociological nest. It's getting bigger and bigger and more and more demanding, and its parents—our sociology fathers—don't quite know what it is, much less what to do with it. Perhaps at this point we should take wing. Certainly we should examine those parts of sociology to see how valid and relevant they are *as* sociology, not merely as a cover for feminism. Feminism is ready to stand independently, intellectually as well as in every other way. We no longer really need the flags of convenience of sociology and other "liberal disciplines." But would this mean that feminists in sociology fly the nest and set up independent of sociology or any other disciplinary base? For myself, I don't know. Some feminists are doing just that, and the growth of Women's Studies departments will encourage this. Others, like myself, are more hesitant. For one thing, our incessant demands and growing strength are compelling disciplines such as sociology to mend their ways. If we leave, will they not lapse back into un-reconstituted sexism? For another, I do still seek to understand the world—the whole world, men as well as women. My feminism will ensure that my understanding is gendered, but my marxism and my sociology have questions to raise and concepts to consider. And so I remain, at least for the moment, a feminist in sociology.

Notes
Further Reading:

There are very few *general* introductions to the study of gender that are specifically *sociological*. Anne Oakley's *Subject Women* (Pantheon 1981) is good, although it does use English material. Two interesting Canadian feminists in sociology, writing from very different perspectives, are Angela Miles and Dorothy Smith. For example, D. Smith, *The Everyday World as Problematic* (Northeastern University Press, 1987) and A. Miles *Feminist Radicalism in the 1980s* (New World Perspectives, 1985). M. Eichler and J. Lapointe *On the Treatment of the Sexes in Research* (Social Sciences and Humanities Research Council, 1985) has been adopted as the non-sexist guidelines by SSHRC.

If you would like to follow up the domestic labour debates, there are good collections of papers in B. Fox (ed.), *Hidden in the Household* (Women's Press, 1980) and E. Malos (ed.), *The Politics of Housework* (Allison & Busby, 1980).

One of the most interesting discussions of feminist methodology in sociology is L. Stanley and S. Wise, *Breaking Out* (Routledge, 1983). J. West's article "Women, Sex and Class," in A. Kuhn and A. Wolpe (eds.), *Feminism and Materialism* (Routledge, 1978) gives a good view, and you can follow up this topic in V. Burstyn and D. Smith *Women, Class, Family and the State* (Garamond, 1985).

For a good taste of the debate about marxist-feminism look at Armstrong et al., *Feminist Marxism or Marxist Feminism* (Garamond, 1985).

References

Armstrong, Pat, and Hugh, 1982 (December). "Beyond Numbers: Problems with Quantitative Data," paper presented in Winnipeg.

Daly, Mary, 1984. *Pure Lust*. Boston: Beacon Press.

Delphy, Christine, 1984. *Close to Home. A Materialist Analysis of Women's Oppression*. London: Hutchinson.

Firestone, Shulemith, 1971. *The Dialectic of Sex*. New York: Bantam.

Foucault, Michel, 1980. *The History of Sexuality* 1. New York: Vintage Books.

Gilligan, Carol, 1982. *In A Different Voice*. Harvard University Press.

Mitchell, Juliet, 1984. *The Longest Revolution*. New York: Pantheon.

Poulantzas, Nicoa, 1975. *Classes in Contemporary Capitalism*. London: New Left Press.

Rintala, J., and S. Birrell, 1984. "Fair Treatment for the Active Female: A Content Analysis of Young Athlete Magazine," *Sociology of Sport Journal*, 1(3) 231-50.

Vance, Carol (ed.), 1984. *Pleasure and Danger: Exploring Female Sexuality*. London: Routledge.

Wise, Sue, and Liz Stanley, 1983. *Breaking Out*. London: Routledge.

Wright, E. Olin, 1985. *Classes*. London: Verso.

Chapter 17

How Feminism Can Take the Crazy Out of Your Head and Put it Back Into Society: The Example of Social Work Practice

Michèle Bourgon
Nancy Guberman

Getting the Pointed Finger...

Lisa is told that her son's delinquency is the direct result of her inadequate mothering, Mary-Lou that her husband's infidelities are due to her sexual responses, and Beth that her romantic failures all stem from her unrealistic expectations of men...

These women, and thousands like them, are daily hearing such explanations from most of the therapists they turn to for help. Although the situations they describe may be different, there is a common denominator: they will all be told, more or less explicitly, that they are the cause of the problems they and their families are encountering.[1] The blaming will often be subtle. For instance, Beth may be asked why she always chooses men who are unavailable rather than receiving validation for her suspicion that developing an honest and trustworthy relationship with a man in today's society is a very stiff order. Regardless of the form the blaming takes (i.e., you're too fat/you're too skinny, you're undersexed/ you're oversexed, you're too attentive of others/you're not attentive enough of others, etc.), the result is always the same: women and girls are made to feel guilty for whatever happens to them and to those about them. The ideology of guilt in which female children are raised from very early on plays a most important function in maintaining our sexist society. Women tend to blame themselves for everything that goes badly—and attribute to chance or luck anything that goes well. This explains in part why they seldom have the time, the energy, and the know-how to examine and understand the unfair social and economic conditions under which they often must live. At her therapist's instigation, Lisa spends weeks examining her own psychological make-up to determine what might have stopped her from breastfeeding her now delinquent son when he was a baby, yet never once does this same therapist acknowledge that Lisa's psychological make-up may be directly related to her circumstances in this society. Ours is a society which supposedly values motherhood yet does not provide Lisa and other single mothers with the emotional support, social recognition, proper daycare, and decent income they need to be able to *contribute to (not* be totally responsible for) the well being of their children.

In this article we wish to present an alternate way of working with women and girls, one which avoids scapegoating and holding them responsible for situations which stem from present-day social relations[2] but rather, as we will show in the next few pages, understands their feelings, thoughts, and behaviours, as well as the behaviours, thoughts, and feelings of those about them in light of what it means to be a woman or a man in this day and age.

To do this, we will proceed in the following manner: first we will identify some basic premises which underlie the alternate approach we are trying to develop. Although this approach can apply to any of the "helping" professions, we will use it here on the practice of social work. To illustrate some of the important changes we wish to see promoted, we will examine some sequences from a first interview with Kristy, a fourteen-year-old girl who quite unwillingly finds herself in a social worker's office. Given the constraints of this chapter, we have chosen to focus on this initial stage of the social work process. We believe that the "contracting" that takes place at this moment is probably the single most important means of instituting change within the professional relationship. Finally, we will briefly identify a few stumbling blocks facing those who wish to intervene from a feminist perspective.

Premises...Premises...Premises...

Three basic premises which guide this alternative social work practice can be delineated.

1. First, we believe that *long term and in-depth transformation of the political, economic, and ideological structures which reproduce dominant social relations are needed in order for all people, regardless of sex, age, colour, creed, status ,or sexual orientation to have access to the resources they require to be in good physical and mental health.* By resources we mean not only the more obvious material resources such as money, food, and shelter, but also things like adequate non-sexist medical services, free and accessible contraception and abortion, equal pay for work of equal value, etc., which we call "hard resources." We mean, as well, those emotional and affective resources such as attention, respect, social recognition, self-worth, caring etc., which we call "soft resources." Because the socio-economic and ideological structures of patriarchy and capitalism are *sexist,* i.e., discriminatory against women, *classist,* i.e., discriminatory against working-class people, *racist,* i.e., discriminatory against non-whites, *heterosexist,* i.e., discriminatory against gays and lesbians, *ageist,* i.e., discriminatory against the old and the very young, these hard and soft resources are not made available to everyone on the same equal basis. Concretely

speaking, this means that in our society a white male between the ages of thirty and forty-five, who is middle class, heterosexual, and without any mental or physical disability, is considered more valuable than a non-white, working-class, disabled female. Being considered more valuable gives the man access to more soft and hard resources than the woman. This is so whether he wishes it or not. A study done in New Brunswick proves this point quite well. It clearly showed that in order *not to* have to consult a mental health professional in that province in 1986, one had best be a highly educated, employed, English-speaking, married man. On the other hand, being an unemployed, single or divorced, French-speaking Acadian woman with little official schooling greatly increased one's chances of having to visit, sooner or later, a mental health clinic for help.[3]

2. A second premise underlies the approach we are developing and it is that *the first and foremost purpose of social work intervention is to obtain as many resources as possible for the women with whom we work.* This means that social workers must develop a consciousness and a belief that women are, objectively, in a specific difficult situation, and that this situation is at the core of an understanding of "their" problems, be they psychological or otherwise. On a very concrete level, this implies that workers must *believe* women when they tell them how hard it is to be a mother or a daughter or a single woman or a lesbian in our society, rather than discounting their complaints as examples of women exaggerating or wallowing in self-pity. If Freud had believed the many women who told him they had been abused as little girls, rather than interpreting their stories as hogwash or fantasies resulting from unresolved conflicts with their fathers, we would be one psychoanalytical theory poorer but perhaps a lot closer to understanding and acting upon how patriarchal relations breed incest and sexual abuse of female children (see Rush, 1980, and Caplan, 1985). It also means they must make clear right from the start what they, as professionals, can and cannot do within the confines of their offices. While they might be able to offer some of the soft resources which women need so badly—caring and a listening ear, for example—most often they will be unable to obtain many of the most needed hard resources. In many cases these resources simply don't exist, as in the "break-away-from-it-all" week-end for single mothers paid for by the state in recognition of the important work they do in raising children. When the resources do exist they are in insufficient quantity, as is the case with non-sexist medical services.

3. Closely linked to this last premise, we advance a third and final one, which is that *many complementary levels of intervention—individual, group, and community—from a common analytical perspective, are needed to obtain those resources which women lack.* Work with individual women or with small groups of women can offer the sharing, support and validating which they have determined they need. Work with communities can lead to large-scale changes, such as setting up a women's health and referral centre. It must, however, be pointed out that social work intervention alone can never change that which

underlies the lack of resources now facing most women in this society. This requires an active political movement, like the women's movement, which works to change those mentalities, laws, policies, and practices which interact to create and maintain situations in which women suffer.

In terms of social work practice, these three premises imply major changes on at least two conceptual issues. First of all, it means questioning the dominant view which exists in social work. This view regards the people involved in the social work relationship as individuals who are and do *what they want to be and do*, instead of as social actors[4] whose acts, feelings, and ideologies reflect who they are in our society. Many women are submissive, emotional, and guilt-ridden not because they are born that way but because they lack the soft and hard resources to be otherwise. Nicole, a battered woman with whom we worked recently, offers a good example of this. Confronted with her husband's violence for many years, she acted differently on the situation, which in her case meant leaving him, when she gained access to those resources which she specifically needed in order to do so. For her, it meant support and caring from five other battered women who understood and shared her psychological anguish over leaving a man with whom she had experienced so much—good and bad—for over fifteen years. It also meant obtaining an income of her own (welfare) and a roof over her head in a subsidized housing project. The fact of women remaining in battering situations for many years is given as an example of women's submissiveness, guilt, and lack of motivation to change. We interpret it differently. As we have already stated, all women in this society are raised in the ideology of guilt, and many of them might never gain access to those resources, i.e., support, self-worth, recognition, etc., which they need to *not* feel responsible for beatings when they occur.

The premises we have previously outlined also imply that social workers question the popular belief that holds that the social work relation is a "helping relationship" between a neutral and benevolent "helper" and a needy and problematic "helpee," who basically agree from the start on why they are working together. Rather, we believe it to be a *political* and *ideological* relationship between social actors whose experiences of the world are very different from each other. This means that workers must consciously acknowledge and act upon the fact that as young, middle-class, white, professional women they have access to more resources and therefore more power than the women and girls they work with, and that because of this they probably also have a very different definition of what the vague term "helping" means. Although we might consider it immensely helpful for the woman in front of us to get in touch with her anger, the woman herself, for whatever reason, might not agree. If we use the power invested in us by this society because we are white and she is Black or because we are professionals and she is not to impose our view of what "help" should be and interpret her disagreements with our view as "resistance to change" rather than expression of a reality most likely very different from, but as valid as, our own, then we are in fact reproducing, on a small scale, the racist and classist relations that bring women to social workers' offices in the first place. If, on the other hand, we understand the political and ideological nature of the relationship between ourselves and the woman we are working with, we can begin to transform it. This can be done, for instance, by questioning the popular belief that experts always know what is best for you regardless of what your own feelings and thoughts on the subject might be.

With the three premises we have stated in mind: *(1) the necessity of long term and in-depth transformation of the political, economic, and ideological structures which reproduce dominant relations; (2) the role of social work in procuring the resources women need to be in good mental and physical health; and (3) the necessity of multi-level social work intervention from a common analytical perspective,* let us now look at the opening sequence of an interview with fourteen-year-old Kristy who, after a fight with her father, ran away to a friend's house where she hid out for three days. She has since returned home, but her parents, worried about her behaviour, have forced her to see a social worker.

M: Hello Kristy. My name is Michèle. I'm a social worker here and I'm the one who received your file. The secretary gave it to me this morning so I've only just had a chance to look at it now. And that's why I'm here, because I'm the one that got your file...

K: But, why am I here?

M: That's a good question. You're wondering why you're here...

K: Yeah. My mother told me I had to come here, but nobody told me why.

M: Okay. What I can show you is the information I have here. All I know about you and why you're here is what's written on this paper. We can look at it together and we'll

Michèle begins her interview by acknowledging the political nature of the social work relation and the fact that both she and Kristy are political actors. What does this mean?

Michèle knows there is an objective power relation between her and Kristy, regardless of whether she wants it to be there or not. Michèle is a professional, backed by a social agency (the Children's Aid Society in this example) and has the status and power that accompany being a social worker. She is older than Kristy, has more education, probably comes from a different social milieu, has more money and access to material goods, and in our society, has more recognition and more value. If Michèle were a man, to boot, she would hold all the cards in have the same level of information. You see here that it's written that you ran away from home and that your mother is worried about you and that she wanted you to see a social worker because she thinks that you have some problems. That's all the information I have right now.

K: Did you speak to her?

M: No, I didn't talk directly to your mother. This information was taken down by a woman who works as an intake worker. That means that she takes all the incoming calls here at the Children's Aid. All I know about you, your mother, or your family right now is what's written on this sheet of paper we've been looking at.

the deck. These differences, and the power or lack of power they imply, are rarely acknowledged within the social work relation, but Michèle will deal with them throughout this interview.

Although this may be Kristy's first encounter with a social worker, she likely already knows the rules of the game since these rules are very similar to those she has experienced in her life in general up to now. She knows that, as a young person, she has very little real power in the final naming of her reality. She will be told who/what she is (a problem) and who and what she is supposed to become (a good girl). Her understanding and interpretation of why she is in a social worker's office will rarely be listened to, much less taken as a valid diagnosis of what's going on. Instead, what she says is most often filtered through an ageist and sexist prism which contains such premises as: young girls tend to over-react and manipulate and rarely know what they are talking about. In this way, the social work relation tends to reproduce the rules and social relations of the larger society. But this relation also contains the power to question these rules and relations.

● ● ● ● ● ● ● ● ● ● ● ● ● ● ●

M: Did your mother tell you she'd called here? Did she tell you why you were going to see a social worker?

How does Michèle attempt to question and act upon the social relations which exist between her and Kristy?

K: Well, she told me about it today when I got home from school.

M: Did she explain why you were coming here?

K: Not really... she said: you have to go there or else. You have to go. I said: why should I go? She said: you have to go, your father will tell you why. Then my father talked to me. But he didn't say much, just that if I didn't come he'd send me to reform school or something like that. I don't know. He said that I'm acting crazy.

M: That's pretty heavy, eh?

K: Yeah. I think he's a bit old-fashioned. He thinks his daughter should be Holy Mary, Mother of Grace. I'm the only girl in the family and I can't do anything. I can't even go out...

M: Um hum. And it's as if your having to come here this afternoon is more proof that you can't do anything. That I'm supposed to... What did they say that I was supposed to do exactly?

K: Oh they just said that I was fucked up and that I had to come to see you. That's all they said.

M: Do you get the feeling that I'm supposed to straighten you out?

K: Yeah. That's what I think. They said I'm fucked up and they want

First of all, she believes Kristy when she says she does not know why she is in this office and she also accepts that Kristy requires this information. She then proceeds to meet this need by giving Kristy complete access to all the information. She doesn't keep any hidden facts up her sleeve to better dominate Kristy and to get her to do what she believes is best for her. Rather, she shares all the information she has so that Kristy will know exactly where she stands and what she is up against.

All through this passage, Michèle checks Kristy's feelings and thoughts about coming to see her. She openly acknowledges that coming to see a social worker under "psychological duress" (threats of being sent away) is difficult and frustrating for her. She thus avoids labelling Kristy's justifiable reservations about being in this office as her unwillingness or resistance to change.

Here, Michèle ties in Kristy's visit to the more general situation of powerlessness in which Kristy often finds herself. In other words, she situates the social work relation in the global context in which it is taking place.

In this short passage, Michèle explicitly states the role social workers in social agencies usually play, that of straightening up "deviants" and in this way gives credibility to Kristy's understanding of what this me to be the way they think I should be. I thought you'd be like them. That's what social workers are there for.

M: You couldn't have been very anxious to see me then? (laugh)

K: Not at all. Not at all.

• • • • • • • • • • • • • •

M: If that's what you've been thinking, then you must be wondering what I'm going to do about all this and what I think of your situation?

K: Yeah...I thought you were going to give me a lecture.

M: You thought that's what I'm supposed to do?

K: For sure. In any case, all adults your age, try and talk to them. You can't really talk to them, they're always lecturing...

M: Am I about the same age as your parents?

K: Yeah....*(Silence)* But you don't seem so bad.

M: Why don't I seem so bad?

K: Well, you haven't yelled at me yet?

M: (Laugh) Were you afraid of that too?

adult will do to her. She also gives voice to Kristy's well-founded apprehension about being in this office.

Here Michèle deals explicitly with the different perceptions that currently exist around her role as a social worker. Kristy has every reason to believe that Michèle is going to lecture her, for in most cases that is exactly what social workers are expected to, and in fact, do. But, Michèle can choose to do this or not once the door to her office is shut. However, she must take into account that Kristy's perception is rooted in objective reality and recognize the fact that, in our society, having to see a social worker is tantamount to being labelled "a problem."

Michèle also openly acknowledges that the age difference between Kristy and herself is a significant social factor in an ageist society such as ours where the very young and the very old have unequal access to resources. Both Kristy and Michèle know this. By pointing this out, (I am an adult, much the same age as your parents), Michèle is saying that her relation to Kristy is structured by the "outside world"

K: Well, I'm always being yelled at.

and that the whole of society is present right here and now in this small office. In this way, she is countering the popular myth, reflected in dominant ideology, which says that there is a professional relationship between a social worker and a client which is devoid of such down-to-earth considerations as age differences, and that the professional "helper" is a disembodied, a political being whose only role is to bring her/his "helpee" to a higher level of insight and well-being.

Once again, Michèle believes Kristy when she tells of her experience of being yelled at and not listened to. She is describing what reality is like for a fourteen-year-old girl in our society, and in this sense she is speaking the reality of many other fourteen-year-old girls who have pretty much the same experience.

• • • • • • • • • • • • • • • • •

M: Would you like to know what I do? Because I get the feeling that that's bothering you a bit. You've been thinking: is she going to yell at me? is she going to lecture me? is she going to send me to reform school?

K: Yeah, I get the feeling I have no control over my life. It's them that decide. They can send me somewhere and I have no control over it.

M: That's what happened today, eh?

Another way in which Michèle directly addresses the political relation between herself and Kristy is by clarifying their respective roles within the relation.

It is important that this clarification be done by taking into account the more global parameters which define their relationship outside the four walls of the social worker's office (as an adult professional and a teenage girl who come with unequal status and power), because these parameters will continue to

K: That's right.

M: Okay. I'll explain what I do and after, if you have any questions, you ask them. Because, as you've noticed, I'm quite a bit older than you and you're right that sometimes our minds don't work in the same way. Okay?

K: Yeah.

M: The agency I work for is called the Children's Aid. We take calls from parents or children in difficulty. When we, when I, judge that a child is a danger for herself or for other people around her, that is, that she can hurt people around her or that she can be hurt by them, then my service intervenes. And we can indeed take a child out of her family. Or we can demand that the family come in and see a social worker, or we can simply suggest things.

K: So how come they're not here, my mother and father? Why is it just me who's here?

M: Okay. That's a good question. The only reason why you're here right now is because it's your mother who phoned and said: I want you to see my daughter. She ran away. And that you came to your appointment today.

define the relation in the future. Michèle does this by acknowledging Kristy's experience of powerlessness in having to come here today. She validates her well-founded fears and doubts about being here, for she knows that the social workers' institutional role rarely makes them popular with people in general and with young people in particular (at best they lecture and preach, at worst they take you away from your family and friends). Kristy has every reason in the world to be distrustful of Michèle who does, in fact, have the power to make decisions that can change Kristy's life, and in describing the agency she works for, Michèle makes this very clear.

..After recognizing Kristy's distrust as healthy and normal rather than as a symptom of resistance to change (a more typical social work interpretation of people's negative reactions to being obliged to see a social worker), Michèle can now give Kristy the information she needs to properly evaluate her own level of control over the situation. Kristy can then better decide where she wants to go within the relation.

Along with information-sharing, Michèle gives direct answers to Kristy's questions. She doesn't turn them around or throw them back at her, as is often done in such situations. (Why do you think your parents aren't here? You're the one in this office now, let's talk about you.)

These techniques of avoiding answering the "client's" questions are often used to trap them into admitting there's a good reason they are in a social worker's office (they have problems or, indeed, they are the problem). Michèle, on the other hand, recognizes that Kristy's questions are important and relevant, and she must have the right to ask them and receive answers if she is to make decisions about what she wants from Michèle, or if she wants anything within the context of the specific social work relationship.

● ● ● ● ● ● ● ● ● ● ● ● ● ● ● ●

K: Will you see her?

M: That will depend on what we do here this morning. As I said, the aim of this meeting is only to see what the situation is. I can't yet promise that I'll see you. I can't promise that I won't see you. I can't promise that I'll see your father, your mother, or brothers or sisters, just like I can't promise I won't. Okay? What we're doing here this morning is called an exploratory interview. We're exploring. We're like explorers. That means that you too explore. Because you're saying: what's this all about? And rightly so. And on my side I look and try to figure things out too. What can I do with this girl? What can't I do? Because I work in an agency that offers certain services and which doesn't offer others. This afternoon, we're trying to decide if we're going to work together.

In this important passage, Michèle explicitly clarifies the purpose of today's encounter. She is aware that social workers, like most other professionals, tend to develop language codes that only they can understand, (often without realizing it, but which in fact enable them to better dominate the people they work with, whether they intend to or not). She will thus use terms she is pretty sure Kristy is familiar with. She also clarifies what she, as a social worker, can and cannot do in this relationship.

She does not make any false promises in order to win Kristy's trust. Kristy has a right to know the rules of the game; rules which, by the way, have not been defined by Michèle but by others (thus Michèle has little or no power to change them) and which Michèle, in ac-

And if we don't, is there someone else you'd like to see? And if we do, what are we going to do together? What do you think of all that?

K: Well, uh...I mean, what am I supposed to do in all that? Is it going to be like at home... I tell you something and you say: yeah, yeah... and then you do whatever you want? Like my mother? She says: you know you can always talk to me... and then I talk to her and she doesn't do anything about it.

M: So you're saying that I could listen to you and after that do what I please, is that it?

K: Yeah.

• • • • • • • • • • • • • • • •

M: Okay. What I can promise you is that when you leave here you'll know what's up. I won't make any decision without telling you and I'll ask your opinion on everything. I have a role to play, I have recommendations to make... that's my job. But, I'll always let you know what's happening. If you don't agree, you can say so. You can even write it. It's your right to write comments on my report.

K: What will it give me to write things?

M: Well, it will show that you don't agree with me.

cepting to do this job, has agreed to respect. Michèle does, however, make very clear how these rules will be applied within the context of their relationship.

Here, Michèle specifically clarifies the power of each actor within the relation. She admits that she has more objective[5] power than Kristy in this relation because of her status as a social worker. She can, for instance, remove Kristy from her home against her will in specific circumstances because she has to administer a law. Kristy, on the other hand, has the power of the oppressed and dominated; that is, the power to disrupt and "bother" through her "delinquent" and "deviant" behaviour.

Michèle attempts to address the objective[5] nature of this political and ideological relation by openly

K: And if you make a decision I don't agree with, you'll do it anyway?

M: The only decision (hesitation)... I'm trying to imagine what decision I could make today that you wouldn't agree with. The only decision we have to make is where we're going

.

K: But what if I continue with you and you make decisions later that I don't agree with?

M: The only thing that could justify my going against your will would be if I thought you were in danger. There's a law that exists and as a social worker I have to administer it. Other than that I won't intervene if you don't want me to. That's a promise. And if I have to break it, I'll let you know and we'll discuss it.

negotiating and explicitly putting on the table those decisions which are, in fact, open to negotiation. Michèle does not give Kristy the illusion that she has more power than she actually has in this particular situation. Michèle will not agree to everything Kristy wants. For example, if Kristy is being sexually abused by an adult, she cannot agree to remain silent even though Kristy might want her to. If such a situation should arise, however, Michèle has the obligation to help Kristy assume the consequences that revealing such a situation would have on her life.

It is important that Michèle give Kristy the power to make decisions wherever possible and, on a more general level, help her name the political, ideological, and economic stakes at play when such negotiation cannot take place.

• • • • • • • • • • • • • • • •

M: Is there part of you that wanted to be here today?

K: Well... I don't know what to do any more. It's awful at my house. I'm tired of always being yelled at. I'm only fourteen. I have no money... I need something to live on...

M: Are you going to school?

K: Sometimes.

M: Do you have a job?

Because Michèle has previously encouraged Kristy to express her anger and resentment about being in her office, she can now check to see if Kristy might at the same time have something to ask her and therefore identify what she would like to get out of the social work relation. In this way she can develop a vested interest in the process and turn an unfavourable situation (being forced to see a social worker) into one over which she has some power, if she so desires.

K: No.

M: So you really have nothing to fall back on. It's as if you're caught in a cage. Is that it?

K: That's it. Sometimes I think about finding a boyfriend and taking off...

M: You'd like to leave home.

K: Maybe that's why my father doesn't want me to go out with boys.

M: What do you mean?

K: Well, he's afraid I'll leave home. He'll miss his slave.

M: In what way are you his slave?

K: Well, I won't be there to do the housework or the other things any more. He won't be able to yell at me and treat me like a piece of shit.

In this passage, Michèle also checks Kristy's access to resources—both hard (money, school, job) and soft ones (recognition, support, care). If subsequent interviews take place, Michèle will check the presence or absence of these resources in a much more detailed manner since she believes that access to these resources greatly determines the way Kristy thinks, feels, and acts towards herself and others and towards the societal institutions around her that she must deal with (i.e., school, Children's Aid, church, her family, etc., etc.).

● ● ● ● ● ● ● ● ● ● ● ● ● ● ●

M: It's not been easy for you, Kristy? I can better understand why you didn't want to come here today. You must be wondering what I'm going to do with all that, eh?

K: There's nothing to do anyway. I'm stuck. I don't know what you can do. Can you do something?

M: That depends. What do you mean by something?

In the following two excerpts, Michèle is openly negotiating the parameters of the work she and Kristy can do together within the given context that they have previously defined. Michèle has stated her institutional role, has recognized and validated Kristy's apprehension about being in her office, and has made perfectly clear the nature of the political relation, i.e., who has the power to do what, to whom, and for what reason. Kristy knows where

K: Well, can you... can you help me get out of there?

M: You want me to help you leave home? Is that it?

K: I'd like that... but I'm afraid...

M: You'd like us to look at that together?

K: Yes.

M: Leaving home, what it takes, what you need to leave home... is that it?

K: Uh huh.

she stands and can now better judge what she can and cannot get out of this relation. Because these clarifications have been made, Kristy is now ready to contract with Michèle on their work together.

Contacting is, in our opinion, one of the most important means of instituting change in the social relations which exist between the social worker and the woman in front of her. Contracting, for us, means coming to a *shared* understanding of why, when, and how a social worker and the other person are going to work together and what they are going to work on. Contracting explicitly defines the boundaries within which the people involved will function. This amounts to the "client" giving permission to the social worker to ask certain questions and to deal with certain issues which, in any other situation where two strangers meet, would be uncalled-for and downright indiscreet. With how many other strangers would you discuss the intimate details of your sex life? It also means that when the social worker asks these questions, the "client" either sees their relevance or else can refer to the contract to ask for clarifications. Before the contract has been established, the social worker does not have permission to pick up on the different issues that the "client" (we do not like this term but are having difficulty finding an alternative) might discuss. Any questions that the social workers asks, at this stage, are posed with the sole purpose of arriving at a contract. For example, Michèle does not attempt to understand Kristy's motivation for wanting to leave home, nor how she feels about her parents, because such information would not be relevant to defining the terms of their contract. The contract, that is their agreed-upon working objective (in this case looking together at the possibility of Kristy's leaving home), will determine which questions and issues Michèle can, and will, raise in future interviews.

● ● ● ● ● ● ● ● ● ● ● ● ● ● ●

M: Do you want to come back, Kristy?

K: Well... yeah...

M: You're still hesitant?

K: Well, I don't really know what I'm getting into here... It's a bit scary...

M: You're right Kristy. It is a bit scary. But I kind of think you've been in scary situations before and pulled out alright.

K: Yeah, I guess so...

M: Listen, how about if we just agree to meet a couple of times and see if I can help you get the things that you need to make your decision about leaving home or not. Then we can see together if your coming here

In winding up the interview, Michèle once again acknowledges Kristy's reluctance to enter the relation as well-founded and reflects this reluctance in her contract. She does not expect Kristy to blindly embark on a long-term adventure over which she would have little control. Rather, she offers her a short-term deadline, after which both she and Kristy will evaluate their work together. Kristy thus becomes an active partner in the relation and gains that power which the limits of this type of situation can give her.

is helping you any. If you have any
complaints, you tell me. If you don't
agree with what I'm saying or doing, you tell me. If you appreciate
our work together, tell me. How
about that? Is that a deal?

K: Yeah. Okay.

Issues for Feminist Intervention

In our opinion, the premises underlying the social work approach illustrated in
the above interview sequences address two very important issues facing
feminist practitioners today.

1. *Putting your practice where your theory is...*
A major challenge facing practitioners with a feminist perspective is that of
translating their analyses into concrete practice with women. Most other non-
feminist approaches tend to define the person seeking help as *the problem* or
at least fall into the trap of implicitly blaming them for the situation they are
in. The ensuing intervention thus seeks to change the person (be it their
behaviour, their attitudes, their feelings, or their ideas: called consciousness by
some) as its *end goal*. Since feminist practice often borrows techniques from
these other approaches, there is the danger of also borrowing the analysis that
underlies these techniques and in so doing implicitly holding women responsible, once again, for the difficult situations in which they find themselves.

For example, many interventions developed to help battered women lean
heavily on behaviour modification approaches[6] and have as their end objective
the changing of women's learned victimized behaviour.[7] Implicitly at least,
this gives women the message that they are battered because of their non-
assertiveness or their victimized behaviours. As such, these approaches most
often neglect to take into account that these behaviours, which include
passiveness, lack of assurance, and lack of assertiveness in and of themselves
are not the cause of the problem. When behaviour change is the goal, the
underlying analysis seems to be that if women were, for example, more
assertive, or if they no longer adopted victimized behaviour, they would not be
battered. Such explanations tend to neglect the fact that violence towards
women by men is *not* a behavioural phenomenon but a socio-political one
which has its roots in patriarchy itself. As we have already stated, in a society
based on patriarchal and capitalist relations, women are most often deprived
of the hard and soft resources they need to leave or change a battering situation.
Obtaining those resources should be the only goal of a feminist intervention.

This does not mean we are opposed to working with women to change their behaviours, attitudes, etc. How our approach differs from others is that, first of all, it gives the women in front of us the power to define which behaviours, thoughts, feelings they wish to change and how they want us to help them bring about these changes. Secondly, it always situates these changes as *means* rather than as *final goals*. We will work with women towards changing themselves if these changes will help procure some of the resources they need, such as self-love and self-worth, but we will do this only after it is clear to them why such changes are necessary to partially (never totally) change their situations. Changes in individual behaviour, feelings, or consciousness can only do so much to secure a better deal for women. For the most part, these changes help obtain certain soft resources on a short-term basis, but rarely do they obtain the hard resources on which these soft resources depend in the long run. For example, developing one's feelings of self-worth can be important if this will help attain another needed soft resource, like nurturing friendships. But it is rarely enough to get you a valued job or decent income, without which your feelings of self-worth may not endure in a society such as our own.

For us, then, a feminist analysis translated into practice means avoiding blaming women for their problems. We aim instead at acknowledging the difficult socio-political situation of women with an understanding that women's behaviour, attitudes, feelings, and ideas/consciousness are direct products of that situation; this means working with them to obtain as many of those resources of which they have been deprived as possible while at the same time aiming to empower them within the social work relation so that they can name and act on their reality outside our offices.

2. *Building the needed bridge...*

A second and closely-related issue which confronts us is how to intervene in the power relations between individual men and women while talking about and acting upon the social institutions, such as the family, the schools, the churches, etc., within which these individual power relations take form and signification.

As we have already stated, our analysis of problem situations is based on our understanding of what it means to be a woman or a man in today's patriarchal and capitalist society. This means taking into account the dominant ideological messages about our respective places in the world which serve to reproduce our present social order. It also means recognizing the important role that soft and hard resources play in the existence of the problem situations which individual women and men must face. Our work with women will lead us, if they wish, to try to identify the resources they need to act on the world they live in and on their future. It will also lead us to identify which of the needed resources exist (i.e., support groups for women) and which must be created.

But neither we, nor the women we work with, *by ourselves,* can change the socio-political and economic reasons for the lack of resources which we face. If we continue to work on a one-to-one or small group basis only, these women will face the same limits over and over again. As well, we will have no impact on the other women in our society in similar problem situations but who do not come or are not forced to come to our offices for "help."

It is for this reason that another objective of our intervention is to create collective activities which offer some of the soft and hard resources many women lack *while at the same time questioning why, under present-day dominant social relations, such resources do not exist for all women in the first place;* for example, setting up a self-help group which offers single women the support they need to "survive" in this couple-oriented society while teaching them to question dominant messages that say you are not a real woman if you do not have a man, that you need to be married to have a child, or that only "the love of a good man" can make you feel beautiful. It also means linking the need for these resources to the struggles of the women's movement and encouraging support of its demands whenever possible in our private and public lives.

We feel the approach we are developing and have presented here can provide some of the attention and care which women so lack and are entitled to, without dominating them by exacting allegiance to our feminist analysis of their problems and ways to solve them. At the same time that this approach supports women and addresses their needs, it simultaneously addresses and attempts to change, on a small but very important scale, the social relations and difficult objective situation of women within those social relations which push them to seek help in the first place.

Notes

This article was written five years ago, and the authors no longer agree with all they have said here. It is included because it marks an important point in their continuing development of a feminist perspective for social work theory and practice.

1. Caplan gives a good example of this phenomenon when she quotes a former mental health patient who says: "(After my suicide attempt) I started seeing Dr. L., a white man, who I also liked a lot. He's really helped me. But you know, no matter what I say, he brings it back to me. If I got the bubonic plague it would still be my fault." Caplan, Paula, *The Myth of Women's Masochism*, Signet, 1985, p. 199.

2. Social relations are the dominant and dominated political, economic, and ideological relations between social groups which define a society at a given moment in history. At the present time, the dominant social relations in our society are patriarchal and capitalist.

3. Wery, Anne, 1986. *Santé mentale en Nouveau-Brunswick qualques données descriptives.* Moncton: Texte inédit.

4. We are indebted in this part of our analysis to Frédéric Mispelblom, a French sociologist who developed the socio-historical approach in social work.
5. By objective power or the objective nature of the relation, we mean that this power or this relation exists outside the thoughts and feelings of the people involved. Whether Michèle likes it or not, she concretely has more power than Kristy and she is in a social work relation with her. (They are not just friends). Subjectively, or in her mind, she might want to have equal power with Kristy, or another type of relation, but their unequal power and the nature of their relation exist because of who they are in society and cannot be wished away.
6. According to behaviour modification approaches, behaviour represents the totality of one's personality, and there is no other reality than that which our senses can capture. In other words, since you cannot hear, see or feel your subconscious, it does not exist. Only observable behaviours are real. Thus, these approaches aim at helping people with problems by working through a system of rewards and punishments to change those behaviours which are considered to be inappropriate and thus the causes of their problems.
7. According to a theory developed by Leonore Walker (1979), learned victimized behaviour refers to the idea that battered women have learned to be victims. Walker claims that learning to be feminine develops learned powerlessness in women and sets them up as victims. Walker, Leonore. *The Battered Woman*. Harper and Row.

References

Bograd, M., 1987. "A Feminist Examination of Family Therapy: What is Women's Place?" in D. Howard (ed.), *A Guide to Dynamics of Feminist Therapy*. New York: Harrington Park Press.

Brook, Y., and A. Davis, 1985. *Women, The Family and Social Work*. London: Tavistock.

Burden, D., and N. Gottlieb (eds.), 1987. *The Woman Client*. New York and London: Tavistock Publications.

Caplan, P., 1985. *The Myth of Women's Masochism*. Signet.

Goldner, V., 1985. "Feminism and Family Therapy," *Family Processes* 24: 31-47.

Greenspan, M., 1983. *A New Approach to Women and Therapy*. New York: McGraw-Hill.

Hale, J., 1983. "Feminism and Social Work Practice," in B. Jordan and N. Parton (eds.), *The Political Dimensions of Social Work*. London: Basil Blackwood.

Hare-Mustin, R., 1987. "The Problem of Gender in Family Therapy Theory," *Family Process* 26: 15-27.

——, 1978. "A Feminist Approach to Family Therapy," *Family Process* 17: 181-192.

James, K., and D. McIntyre, 1983. "The Reproduction of Families: The Social Role of Family Therapy,"*Journal of Marital and Family Therapy* (April): 119-129.

Kravetz, D., 1976. "Sexism in a Women's Profession," *Social Work* 21: 448-454.

Levine, H., 1978. "Feminist Counselling: A Look at New Possibilities," *The Social Worker*, Special Issue.

Miller, J.B., 1976. *Toward a New Psychology of Women*. Boston: Beacon.

Mispelblom, F. "'socio-historiques' en travail social," *Revue internationale d'action communautaire* 8/48: 177-189.

Norman, E., and A. Mancuso (eds.), 1980. *Women's Issues and Social Work Practice*. Itasca, Ill.: F.E. Peacock.

Robbins, J.H., and R.J. Siegel (eds.), 1983. *Women Changing Therapy–New Assessments,*

Values and Strategies in Feminist Theory. New York: Hawthorn Press.

Rush, F., 1980. *The Best Kept Secret: Sexual Abuse of Children.* New York: Prentice-Hall.

Russell, M., 1979. "Feminist Therapy: A Critical Examination," *The Social Worker* 7(2-3).

——, 1984. *Skills in Counseling Women: The Feminist Approach.* Springfield: Charles C. Thomas.

Stephens, M.K., 1980. "One Women Among Many: A Structural Approach to Social Work," *Canadian Journal of Social Work Education* 6(2-3): 45-58.

PART FOUR

The Politics of Feminism:
Am I That Woman?

Introduction

The last words in this collection have been reserved for the voices of women who are most systematically silenced in our society, in this case the voices of lesbian women and women who are citizens of North America's First Nations. As indicated in the Introduction to this book, our experiences as women, as subordinates in the hierarchy organized by sex, are always mediated by our experiences of, and statuses within, other political hierarchies founded on other differences, like race, class, colour, creed, age, ability, language, locale, and sexual orientation. This is not to suggest that systems of discrimination and oppression based on race, class, colour, creed, age, ability, language, locale, and sexual orientation are secondary to, or derivative of, sexual oppression but that all of these systems of power and privilege work together and intersect with the particularities of our birth and nurture to determine the quality of our individual lives as women and our experience and understanding of the politics of sexism: its structures and mechanisms, its limits and scope, its causes and effects. So, although *as women* we share a position in the social and political hierarchy organized by and for male dominance, we do not share a position in, or experience of, other hierarchies of privilege and power founded on and for other orders of difference, like race, religion, class, age and sexual orientation, all of which converge to shape our individual experiences and understandings of sexism and our unequal stakes in the political systems which support it.

These differences among women, of experience, understanding and de-sire—of stakes and shares in contemporary patriarchy—are often obscured or minimized by mainstream feminisms which have tended to take the experiences of the most visible and therefore already most privileged and voiced women (privileged enough to have a voice that can be heard) as their point of departure and object of concern: that is, the experiences, knowledge and concerns of white, educated, European, heterosexual, middle-class women. Demands for "equal-ity" with men, for example (of access to work, pay, childcare services, and political representation) make sense for these relatively privileged women whose male "counterparts" occupy ruling positions in our society. But they make less sense for women of colour, or immigrant women, or working-class women, or differently-abled women, or women who are citizens of North America's First Nations, or lesbian women; for women, that is, whose male "counterparts" are not in ruling positions but, like themselves, are in positions of relative powerlessness: of exclusion and silence, subordination, exploitation and oppression.

All the contributors to this collection acknowledge these facts of political difference among women and the specificity of their own experiences and knowledges as women to particular places, persons and times. They take care not to generalize their experiences "as women" to all women and to position themselves as participants in a conversation among women which is just beginning, rather than as authorities of knowledge *about* women which is already in place. Nevertheless, the "voice" of this collection is predominantly white, educated, middle-class European, able-bodied and heterosexual. The discussion of "mothering" in Part One, for example, clearly speaks from this experience, and mothers who are not white, middle-class, heterosexual, able-bodied, or graduates of Canadian universities may not recognize themselves or their concerns in it. This does not *discredit* the knowledge and experiences of the women presented here but contextualizes and qualifies them as local and particular, reminding us that other women in other contexts will experience their "womaning" and in this case their "mothering" differently and will, therefore, have a different understanding of what structures their oppression "as women" and what will count as liberation from it.

This is certainly the case for Judy Brundige whose experience is presented in chapter 22. Judy describes herself as a *traditional Native woman* and regards her knowledge, experience and status as "mother" in particular as a strength rather than a liability in the Native community and in its struggle for sovereignty and survival. She believes being a "mother" empowers her for speech and action in that struggle rather than silencing her on its sidelines. Judy did not always know this. She came to this conclusion only after spending considerable time and energy fighting for a Native women's voice in the more conventional arenas of mainstream politics. To some extent we could say that Judy tried "our" ways—our white, educated, middle-class, "feminist" ways—and having discovered their limitations, found greater hope and strength in the traditional ways of her own people. She describes some of these ways, as well as her own journey towards them and her present practices of them. She speaks of the status, strengths and powers of First Nations women, past and present—as "mothers" of the tribe, as healers and as spiritual leaders—and of their specific political responsibilities for the family and, in particular, for the raising of the children who will be the adults of the next generation.

Joy Fedorick, whose poetry and prose conclude chapter 22, this section and this book, also tried "our" ways: "our" white, middle-class, "feminist" ways of making change and improving the status of women; and she, too, found them not just lacking, but actively and relentlessly racist. In a conversation we had in Toronto in June 1988, at the annual conference of the Ontario Native Women's Association, Joy described her experiences of both institutionalized racism in the feminist community (discussed in more detail by Patricia Monture in chapter 18) and personalized acts of racism directed specifically at her and their debilitating and demoralizing effects on her physical and mental health. Like Judy, she gave up on white feminism and white politics and returned to both her own abilities as a writer and to the Native community itself for the resources and strengths needed for their mutual, individual and collective, survival, creativity and control. Joy now works on *Earthtones North*, a community-based Aboriginal writing and publishing project which she founded in 1989 in North Bay, Ontario. The project has two principal objectives:

> To prevent the loss of the Cree and Ojibway languages through the development of a minimum of two hundred and fifty books in each language by the year 2000.

and the development of a community voice:

> Combining community development, desk-top publishing and modern transmissions, *Earthtones North* goes where the words are: remote and Northern Aboriginal communities in Ontario. From these visits, which actually are writing workshops that give voice to community people, community-based books are developed and produced.[1]

We can all learn from the experiences of Judy and Joy: about the complex intersection of race, sex, and class in the determination of both our personal and political lives (personal *as* political and political *as* personal); and about the necessary partiality and provisionality of any individual person's (or group's) vision and voice. Judy's and Joy's stories underline, that is, the absolute indispensability of dialogue and difference to social movements, like feminism, which claim commitment to *collective* rather than mere self-serving individual change.

Being visible is a necessary, though not in itself sufficient, condition of being "voiced" and thereby of asserting oneself and one's difference against the totalizing distortions, exclusions, and silences of dominant and dominating political discourses. The invisibility of lesbian women in patriarchal society (like the invisibility of Native women in post-colonial society) is both a sign and an instrument as well as an effect of patriarchy's subordination and control of women in general and of its "compulsory heterosexuality"[2] in particular.* Heterosexuality keeps women's attention, energy, and love focused on men

---

* See Helen Lenskyj in this collection.

instead of women and directs our psyches, sexuality, and desires towards servicing men's projects and men's needs (physical, emotional, social, sexual, and reproductive) instead of our own and those of other women.

Mary Eaton and Anna Lattanzi (in chapters 19 and 20 respectively) speak of their own experiences of being invisible as *lesbians* both inside and outside feminism and of the difference this makes to their understanding of patriarchal power in general and its heterosexism in particular, and to their understanding of what is at stake for them, therefore, in the feminist struggle against it. Their stories reveal how mainstream feminist politics tend to presuppose the heterosexual woman as the implicit or explicit norm and value of feminism and to disappear and silence lesbian women *as lesbians* though not as women (as Mary Eaton explains) from the presentation of feminism's public face. Feminism thus reproduces patriarchy's heterosexist prescriptions for women even as it purports to struggle against their effects, and thereby colludes in and reinforces the disappearance and denial of lesbian women which patriarchy requires.

Becoming visible is not, however, a sufficient condition of being "voiced" but only a first step in the struggle to speak and be heard in a language which has accomplished your exclusion, invisibility and silence. Patricia Monture (chapter 18) and Anna Lattanzi (chapter 20) address this issue directly: Patricia with reference to the historical and political complexities and contradictions of speaking as an "Indian," and Anna with reference to the historical and political complexities and contradictions of speaking as a "lesbian," when both "Indian" and "lesbian" function as categories of exclusion and dismissal in post-colonial heterosexist patriarchal society.* They are terms which classify individuals according to definitions, criteria, and assignations determined from "above"— from the standpoint and on behalf of the oppressor—and they carry the authority and weight of the state behind them, as both Anna and Patricia explain. Making the oppressor's language work for you and your experience *as* an "Indian" and/ or as a "lesbian" so that it is neither assimilated into "just like 'us'" nor erased into "not like 'us' at all" but included and responded to as part of what constitutes "us," is both difficult and painful, as their stories show. Patricia Monture and Mary Eaton describe the risk and pain involved in making themselves visible as "Native" and "lesbian" women respectively within the feminist community and of subsequently being held responsible by white heterosexual feminists for the racism and heterosexism their visibility both solicited and testified to!

Again, there are lessons for all of us here, particularly for those who are "white" and/or heterosexual and often forgetful of that fact in the formulation of our feminism(s): forgetful of the political privilege these contingencies confer upon us and thus of the specificity and partiality of our experiences "as women." White women speak from the standpoint and privilege of their whiteness and reproduce racism whenever they fail to recognize, problematize and politicize

---

* 'Woman' works the same way, as I clarify below and as all these essays indicate.

that fact. In the same way, heterosexual women speak from the standpoint and privilege of heterosexuality and reproduce heterosexism whenever they fail to recognize, problematize and politicize their heterosexuality. As these essays show, racism and heterosexism are "our" problems, i.e., problems of and for white heterosexual women as much as they are problems of and for women who are lesbians or citizens of North America's First Nations. The struggle against heterosexism and racism must, therefore, be part of any and every feminist agenda.

The subtitle of this last section "Am I That Woman?" is intended to draw attention to the fact that the category "woman" is a complex, unstable, and shifting *political* category (rather than a category of "natural" history) which organizes women's subordination in complex and often contradictory ways in conjunction with other equally diverse and shifting orders of dominance and control. The category "woman" does not, that is, designate an essence, identity, or nature which all women have in common by virtue of their genes and a shared biological constitution which differentiates them from men.[3] On the contrary, (as all these essays have argued) the category "woman" designates a "place" in society, a "position" of subordination organized by and on behalf of sexual difference, to which *all* women are assigned and which *all* women, therefore, must and do negotiate. This is what women have in common: not our experiences or knowledge as such, but our status as subordinates in a sexual hierarchy which touches every aspect of our lives and a corresponding interest in understanding how it works, either to negotiate it efficiently and successfully on its own terms (to survive as best we can), or to dismantle and transform it on ours. Feminism aims to do both: to strengthen the position of women *within and against patriarchy at the same time.* This means that feminism cannot but be as complex and contradictory and as decisive and diverse, and as difficult to understand and sustain, as the various systems of power it struggles against. Political, personal, practical and theoretical struggles *among* women are both inevitable and indispensable to feminism, as are similar struggles *within* individual women themselves. This is because, as I have already suggested, no woman is only or all "woman" but always embedded within and constituted by a complex set of social and political relations which determine the quality and direction of her life.

In chapter 21 Susan Sorrell describes some of the personal and political conflicts she has struggled with over the last several years "as a Woman and as a Feminist." Like Peggy Kelly's reflections on "Technology and Pornography," Susan's essay was originally written as a term paper for a course I was teaching in the Women's Studies Program at the University of Ottawa. Susan used the materials and the context of the course as an occasion for reflecting on experiences in her recent "feminist" life which had been accompanied by intense feelings of anxiety, terror, self-loathing, powerlessness, guilt, and/or resentment. She identifies four distinct but related sources of these anxieties: a fear of intimacy tied to a more basic fear of "losing" her "self" in others in intimate relationships; an internalized misogyny revealed in her contempt for and impatience with signs of "feminine" weakness in herself and others; a fear of responsibility and a corresponding difficulty in making decisions and value judgments for herself; and a sense of anomie, of not being "true" to her "self" whenever she was outside the circle of "like-minded" friends.

Although the experiences and events which activated these anxieties were particular to Susan and to the specificity of her own life history, Susan's analysis shows how the anxieties themselves were rooted in and inseparable from her social constitution and status as "a woman" in patriarchal society. Her analysis shows, that is, how "the personal is political" in this particular case. She started with a problem which was absolutely personal, that of her own intense feelings of anxiety in certain "feminist" situations, which she at first neither understood nor wanted to acknowledge, and through systematic analysis and reflection informed by her readings in philosophy and feminism, arrived at an understanding which linked her personal pain to political realities we can all recognize and in which we are all in some way implicated. As such, Susan's essay exemplifies how new knowledges can be and are being produced for women and from the *standpoint of women* which I characterized in the Introduction to this collection as the distinguishing mark of feminism and Women's Studies. As I said there, the feminism espoused by this collection designates not so much a set of shared beliefs about the world as a common standpoint towards it. The standpoint is that of women. I hope we have inspired you to join us in assuming that standpoint and continuing the project of its collective exploration.

Notes

1. From *Earthtones North* publicity brochure.
2. From Adrienne Rich, 1980. "Compulsory Heterosexuality and Lesbian Existence," *SIGNS* 5(4).
3. Women are, of course, biologically different from men. We have a distinctive relationship to–and experience and knowledge of–human procreativity, which is not shared by men. But this biological specificity does not *by itself* "woman" us, i.e., differentiate us from and subordinate us to men. Culture, not biology, does this. Culture, not biology, determines our social and political destinies and the meanings of the biological differences (of race and sex, for example). See, for example, Mary O'Brien, *The Politics of Reproduction*, Routledge and Kegan Paul, 1981, and Ruth Hubbards et al. (eds.), *Women Looking at Biology Looking at Women*, Cambridge: Schenkman, 1979.

Chapter 18

I Know My Name:
A First Nations Woman Speaks
Patricia A. Monture

What's in a Name?

"Sekon."[1] That is a greeting in my language. It is larger than a "hello." Here it is a recognition that for the next few pages we will be sharing our experiences. I have been taught by the Elders and traditional teachers that it is always important to begin things in a good way. Also they have taught me that it is essential that we always remember who we are: citizens of specific First Nations.

I am a member of the Ho-Dee-No-Sau-Nee Confederacy. The Confederacy is a "political"[2] union which is a democracy in the truest sense of the word. For many years, our nations were known as the Iroquois. But this is not how we call ourselves. There are six nations which make up the Ho-Dee-No-Sau-Nee Confederacy. We are the Seneca, Oneida, Onondaga, Cuyaga, Mohawk, and Tuscarora. I do not like to say that I am a "Mohawk" woman. A friend recently told me that Mohawk means "man-eater" in one of the European languages. This is not a nice way to be known. This is not what being "Indian" means to me. I am a proud member of my nation and this is a good way to be. It is a difficult experience to have your true name taken away from you. This is just one good example of the colonialism and oppression forced upon First Nations in Canadian society.

When I was growing up, the word I learned to describe who I was was "Indian." Since then, I have learned that it is not, in fact, an accurate way to refer to myself. The word "Indian" is technically a legal definition. An Indian is a person who is entitled to be registered under the definitions in the *Indian Act*.[3] This is not a good way to refer to ourselves because this definition has been forced on us by the federal government. Since coming to this realization, I have struggled to learn how constructs and processes such as naming support racism, colonialism, and/or oppression.

Language is a power tool which can operate to perpetuate racism, colonialism, and oppression.[4] Understanding the power of language and naming will help us overcome these injustices. The names which have been put upon us include

"Indian," "Native," and "Aboriginal." An examination of these labels helps us identify important parts of the processes by which we are oppressed.

Not only is the term "Indian" one that is technical and legal, it has forced Indian women into a situation of extreme discrimination. In 1974 the Supreme Court of Canada[5] heard the appeal of two Indian women, Jeanette Lavell and Yvonne Bedard, who had lost their status under the *Indian Act* as a result of their marriages to white men.[6] Former section 12(1)(b) of the *Act* provided that Indian women who "married out" (married non-Indians) were no longer considered Indians under the *Indian Act*. This legal provision treated Indian men who married non-Indian women in a different way. These non-Indian wives *gained* Indian status when they married Indian men. Both Mrs. Lavell and Mrs. Bedard, who had married out, challenged this racially and sexually discriminatory provision of the *Act* and lost.

The legal challenge by Mrs. Bedard and Mrs. Lavell was based on provisions of the *Canadian Bill of Rights,* which guaranteed equality under the law to both women and racial groups.[7] In essence (and this is not intended to be an analytic legal comment), the highest court in the land found that as neither *all* Indians nor *all* women were being discriminated against, just the combined group, Indian women, then no lawful discrimination existed. So-called "double discrimination" amounted to no discrimination in the eyes of the court. Indian women across this country were dismayed by the Supreme Court's decision which effectively denied them equality under the law and foreclosed all domestic legal recourse on the issue.

A number of years after the *Lavell and Bedard* case, the case of Sandra Lovelace[8] was heard by the international human rights tribunal of the United Nations. In 1981, Canada was cited in contravention of international declarations prohibiting discrimination against cultural groups. It is important to note that the basis of this international decision was *not* gender discrimination even though Mrs. Lovelace's claim included gender as one source of the discrimination complained about. Despite the efforts of many Indian women, both in domestic and international legal forums, it was only with the provisions entrenched in section 15 of the *Charter of Rights and Freedoms* that section 12(1)(b) of the *Indian Act* was repealed by legislation in June of 1985.

The federal government is fond of representing the 1985 amendments as having removed the discrimination from the *Indian Act*. This is not true! Indian women who lost their status *are* reinstated. Their children, however, receive a limited status which cannot be passed on to the disenfranchised woman's grandchildren. Therefore, the grandchildren of Indian women who married out are *not* entitled to be reinstated. The children and grandchildren of any marriage in the male line have *never* lost their status. The consequences of the 1985 amendments amount to treating unequally both sets of grandchildren, determined by whether they are descendants in the male line or the female line. This is not removing the sexual discrimination from the *Indian Act*. It merely shifts the burden and consequences by two generations.[9]

This is only one way in which the current *Indian Act* continues to discriminate against Indian women and their descendants. The 1985 amendments also distinguished, for the first time, between band membership[10] and Indian status.[11] An Indian woman who married out may be entitled to regain her Indian status but not her band membership. She can, therefore, be excluded from returning to the reserve to live, owning property on the reserve, inheriting from her parents, or raising her children in the cultural milieu of her choice. Remember, men are not subject to these consequences as they were never disenfranchised for their choice of spouses. The consequences of a government believing they have the authority to name another nation's citizens are far-reaching for my people. It is a heavy burden that has been carried by our women.

The 1985 amendments to the *Indian Act* also contain provisions whereby Indian bands can now draft their own membership codes.[12] Many First Nations assert and firmly believe that we are sovereign peoples and always have been. I do not believe the federal government has the authority, legal or otherwise, to define who we are as citizens of the First Nations. The Ontario Native Women's Association, the political voice of First Nations women in Ontario, believes that "the major obligation of the federal government is to relate to Indian people as a collectivity, on a nation to nation, government to government basis."[13] Membership, as provided for by the *Indian Act,* is defined as something less than citizenship. "Membership" fails to meet even the first obligation of the federal government to First Nations.

The amendments to the *Indian Act* are viewed by many as yet another effort to undermine First Nations beliefs in the sovereignty of our nations. Ours is a struggle against colonial rule to ensure that our birthright (in my case that is the right to live as a citizen and as a female citizen of the Mohawk nation) is retained and is respected. It must also be remembered that the *Indian Act* was forced upon First Nations people without our consent or consultation. To know who I am means that I must understand and survive colonial rule and only then live fully as a member of a sovereign nation. It means rejecting the false authority of the *Indian Act* and the name "Indian."

When the Canadian constitution was entrenched on April 17, 1982, a new legal word entered popular usage. We became "Aboriginal" peoples: that is, Indian, Inuit, and Métis.[14] In the summer of 1988 a traditional teacher explained to me that this term is a misleading one. When traced to its linguistic roots, "abo" means, among other things, "away from."[15] We are not people away from the original peoples of this land we call Turtle Island (North America). For me, understanding this is symbolic of the struggle First Nations have faced for so long. It is the struggle *not* to be assimilated, *not* to be erased, *not* to be made invisible. It is the struggle to survive. Even the words used to describe us (Indian or Aboriginal) erase or disappear us. The struggle that First Nations now face is, symbolically and politically, the recovery of our names. We must know in both our hearts and our minds who we are.

The word Native is sometimes used to describe my people. This is a confusing term as those who are not First Nations individuals but were born on Turtle Island also consider themselves native Canadians. I, therefore, prefer to use the terms *First Nations* or *original peoples*. This is a political choice intended to remind ourselves and others that we are indeed nations and were the first to live in harmony on this land. This is a political choice as well as a personal one. When referring to the situation of the original peoples around the world, the term Indigenous is often used.

This entire discussion about naming is only necessary when it is confusing to use my own language (in which I am not fluent). Imagine how it feels when you cannot even determine what to call yourself! The boundaries of the discussion have been set by others, and they exclude us from that discussion. Their boundaries exclude us from the very beginning: we are lost, not knowing who we are. This shows you how racism operates. Fortunately, discovering traditional teachings is a way to stop being lost. I am no longer disconnected from this land or from myself. I know my name.

How Racism Works

If, as people with different cultural histories, we are going to speak to each other in an honest and true way, there is another word we must understand. That word is racism.[16] Racism is a word which inspires fear and denial in those who hold privilege because of their race. In this society that is white people. Racism, as a word, has taken a hard knock. The definition of racism is misunderstood to mean an individual who lacks good intent (picture the "Archie Bunker" type). But racism is not about "bad" people willfully inflicting harm. It is simply about people who do not understand. And not understanding is not "bad." Not understanding *does* require an admission that one who is privileged does *not* know. One cannot speak to experience one has not had. White people, because of their skin colour, cannot be the *objects* of racism. I will not be silenced for my use of the word racism. Understand, then, that racism between individuals does not involve intent. And absence of intent does not excuse racism. That is one of the powers of racism: you cannot name it because people cannot get past their personal emotions and defences. Their ears are shut and they cannot learn. If racism continues unnamed, then there can be no hope for change. Only if we can rise above our defensive posturing on this issue will all of our lives be enriched, as only then will we be able to share and celebrate our differences.

It is difficult to discuss or write about racism because it is a subject potentially hurtful to other individuals.

Racism as a phenomenon has been personalized. People look at their skin colour and think "she is talking about me." As long as racism remains personalized, it is nearly impossible to do anti-racism work. The threat of your pain and hurt hangs over my head and makes it difficult for me *not* to be silenced. The traditional ways of my people are kindness, gentleness, and patience: I have no right to hurt or offend anyone; I have no right to interfere in anyone's life or their ways. But so many First Nations people are suffering because of racism, I *must* talk about it, even though I am still struggling to understand exactly what it is and how it operates. Hurting or offending someone defeats my purpose and allows the cycle of racism to continue. What I struggle to expose is how racism has become institutionalized and how our social institutions perpetuate racism.

Racism is not about individuals alone. When someone makes a racial slur (the "Archie Bunker" type again), this is only a small part of the experience of racism.[17] It is the visible part. The racism inherent in the values and beliefs of this society's social structures remains largely invisible. This is called systemic discrimination. If our anti-racism work focuses solely on individual acts such as racial slurs and acts, then we have failed to address the manner in which racism is learned and entrenched. Essentially, placing the focus on the visible edge conceals the very real costs and social harms of racism. Institutional, or systemic, racism is legitimized in this society. To end the perpetuation of racism we must learn how it is taught and socially sanctioned. It is only through careful examination that we realize that height and weight restrictions can exclude women and some racial groups from certain jobs; that educational requirements exclude those groups who have limited access to financial resources and positive role models; that certain aptitude tests (such as IQ tests or the Law School Admission Test) are culturally bound and therefore exclusionary.

Oka

The effect of long-standing exclusionary policies and practices was felt in Mohawk Territory in the summer of 1990. One of the things that troubles me greatly about the "Oka Crisis" is that I do not perceive the source of the conflict as a land dispute. The source of the conflict, as far as I am concerned, is hundreds of years of oppression. The sources of the oppression are racist beliefs, entrenched in Canadian social and legal structures, and the way in which Canadians have chosen to govern themselves. Land disputes are only one manifestation of the long-standing oppression of Mohawk people. During the Oka Crisis, evidence of racism and hatred surfaced in visible acts such as the burning of effigies of Mohawk warriors and the stoning of the old people, women, and children. Those incidents are only the visible edge of racism; they conceal the really damaging aspects of the oppression of Mohawk people. For some Canadians, those overt acts of racism, which were brought into their living rooms by television, provided their first opportunity to witness the racism First Nations have lived with for decades.

Consider that my people have been actively excluded from the decision-making institutions in this country. We never consented to the imposition of the Canadian legal system on our lives. Canadian laws such as the *Indian Act* forcefully replaced First Nations forms of government with the band council system. Canadian criminal laws result in the disproportionately high rate of imprisonment of my people. Just these examples of the many injustices result in two phenomena: Our youth are confused and do not know who they are; they have lost the strength of our traditional ways. Our people also feel a great sense of powerlessness. Some turn to the power of a gun. I do not condone that, but I certainly understand. And as the mother of two young sons, I have a deep sense of pain for the young men who felt they had no choice but to pick up guns. As long as racist beliefs are allowed to continue, as long as my people are viewed as inferior or less civilized or as having lesser status or fewer rights, the threat of Oka still hangs over all our heads. And I do not see where there has been any fundamental shift toward "nation to nation" discussions which could lead me to the hope that the practice of oppression and subordination of First Nations people has ended. It is not Mohawk people I hold accountable. They acted in the only way an oppressed people can act when every other option for peaceful resolution is removed. I look to the Canadian government and their years of oppressing my people. And I want to know why the Oka crisis was allowed to happen.

It is not just First Nations who carry the burden of oppression and racism in this country. The other nations that have come to this land and made it their home suffer with us because they are denied the opportunity to share in the natural ways of my people. We are collectively denied the opportunity to celebrate our difference. And this, too, is accomplished through the power of racism. Those natural ways were given to us by the Creator when she[18] put us on this land as caretakers. These natural laws were not given solely for the benefit of First Nations people, but for all those who make their home on the land to whom the law belongs.

Consider what we have already discussed about the *Lavell and Bedard* case. The decision in that case amounted to "double discrimination" (sex and race), but the Supreme Court found that to mean no discrimination at all. That court decision effectively denies my reality, it completely erases it. In order to understand the full effect of racism in the lives of First Nations women, I will examine the relationship between sexism and racism and its impact on my own life and experiences. I cannot separate what happens to me "just because I am a woman," or "just because I am an "Indian." My experience is not about *no* discrimination, as the Supreme Court held, nor is it about "double discrimination." It is about "discrimination within discrimination."[19] My experience of discrimination is layered like the layers of an onion.

First Nations' Women and the "Women's" Movement

It is no secret that relations between First Nations women, as well as other women of colour, and the women's movement have been tumultuous. The First Nations women I know largely do not consider themselves feminists.* We do not need to be feminists because we were born equal. It was after the European form of government was forced on my people through the *Indian Act* regime that our women and children lost the franchise (the right to vote).[20] We lost our voice in the political realm as a direct result of the settler people's desire to civilize us, not because our own culture or ways oppressed us! Discrimination against women has its roots across the ocean and not on Turtle Island. A second difficulty is that trust has not been developed between First Nations women and the feminist collectivity. Our experience of that movement is that, at a minimum, it is white and middle class. It does not speak to our issues, experience, or concerns.

The women's movement was not shaped through the efforts of First Nations women any more than it was shaped in consultation with Black women and their experience.[21] Therefore, logically, it does not reflect our perspectives. The most acute example of this is the belief that women share a single, common, and unifying experience. The notion of the commonality of all women is not agreeable to the First Nations perspective. My identity flows from the fact that I am first and foremost a Mohawk. My women's identity flows from my race. It is even said in this order. I am a Mohawk woman not a woman Mohawk. This is also true when you speak in the languages of the First Nations. It is in the traditional teachings which speak to and of creation that my understanding of woman rests. What the feminist movement has expected me to do is to invert my experience so they can talk to me. I am not willing to stand on my head for them. In fairness, the feminist movement has recently begun to question this assumption.

In making this distinction about the sense of my woman's identity, I am also aware that I do not speak for all women of colour. I do not even speak for all First Nations women, or even all Mohawk women. I speak only for myself and mine is a voice that is privileged. I am a law professor and have the privilege of both income and education.

What white women know is their own experience. Their experience is not just as women but also as white people. And I wish they would tell me about what that is and what it means. I do not believe that their "whiteness" has nothing to do with their experience of being women. I do not know if "whiteness" is only about privilege or if it is also about "culture." The women's movement, until it focuses on its own "whiteness," is a movement of privileged women who refuse to consider their privilege. If we are to share common ground, not only must my

---

* See Joy Fedorick and Judy Brundige in this collection.

experience be understood but I must understand yours. Perhaps together we can further deconstruct racism and sexism.

My involvement in the feminist movement as a First Nations woman has centred around explaining, "I am not you" (read that as "I am not white"). This allows that I may only define my existence in a negative way, as measured against the norm (yours and white). There is no place within the women's movement for a First Nations woman to focus on "I AM ME." There is no place for me to discuss difference with Black women, immigrant women, or any other women of colour. I am always reacting to the agenda white women have set.

Defining the realm and experience of First Nations women is, and must remain, a First Nations woman's responsibility. As a First Nations woman with an academic and political profile, I come to the attention of the feminist movement. I am not necessarily representative of the "average" First Nations woman in this so-called country. I do not wish to be the "token Indian woman." First Nations women who do not tread in the mainstream still remain largely invisible to the women's movement. Granted, this is beginning to change.

First Nations women do not tread in the mainstream for a number of reasons: lack of education; lack of employment; lack of economic power; lack of social status. And there are those of us who do not tread in the mainstream by choice. As well, First Nations women who reside in the remote and semi-remote north, as well as non-urban and non-white communities, are also invisible to the feminist movement. Our invisibility to this movement and to society in general ensures our insulation while denying us a voice. It is not possible to label this reality as either simply "good" or "bad." It has clear advantages as well as disadvantages. The socially constructed boundaries of the feminist movement and the lives of many First Nations women have never crossed. My voice, that of a well-educated Mohawk woman, must also be heard as the voice of privilege.

Let me try to explain this in another way, because I feel this is a very important understanding for us to develop. Recently, I had some unpleasant experiences with "affirmative action" programs. We must consider the philosophy behind the initiatives we choose to support. Critics of affirmative action describe these programs as reverse discrimination. I do not believe in such a phenomenon because to discriminate we must first wield power. Logically, those without power cannot meaningfully discriminate. More important, what action or movement are we aspiring towards in an affirmative action initiative? The norm we sanction is that of the "white male." This does not affirm my experience or reality! It is not likely I will wake up tomorrow and discover I have become a white male! What we need to consider are programs of "equity." Equity is what is just or what *should* have been all along. This description brings us around full circle, back to paying careful attention to language and the related power of naming.

Why Sovereignty?

When a person is lost, as so many of our First Nations citizens are, they are left without pride or dignity. Institutional processes and structures have contributed to so many of our people being lost and not knowing who they are. The residential schools*, child welfare laws, and the children's aid movement are all good examples. Lost people are susceptible to other social difficulties (I hesitate to use the word problem) such as over-representation in the criminal justice system, participation in events such as the Oka Crisis, high rates of alcohol and drug abuse, high suicide rates, high unemployment rates, lack of education, and so on. Rather than seeing these situations as symptomatic of a people who have been oppressed, we blame these people. We view them as less than ourselves. Canadian people and their history created what is known as the "Indian problem." This construction of the situation confronting First Nations people cries for a solution which looks unfortunately like assimilation: "If only Indians would be more like white people!" But we are not white people. "White" is only one way of being and I do not accept it to be the best way. This is yet another example of how racism is perpetuated in this society.

The First Nations have a different solution to the "Indian problem." We do not want to be blamed and victimized further. We want to be responsible for our lives and our futures. It is better to view this so-called "Indian problem" as a challenge which confronts us all. That challenge is First Nations sovereignty. First Nations must continue to live in sovereign ways, learning and living the law the Creator gave to us. That is our responsibility. The complementary responsibility rests with Canada—Canada must find a respectful way of accommodating our aspirations within its social, governmental, and legal structures.

This word, sovereignty, has caused First Nations many problems. Prime Minister Brian Mulroney said during and after the Oka crisis that sovereignty is not a realistic goal for First Nations to pursue. Such statements are not just problematic because they are paternalistic: he is not willing to carve up this country for our benefit. To Canadian politicians, sovereignty means, first and foremost, territory. And I cannot, nor would I, deny that there is a significant relationship between land claims and our version of sovereignty. However,

---

* Until the 1960s, and later in some northern communities, First Nations children were transported from their homes and schooled in "Indian Residential Schools." These schools isolated First Nations children from both their home communities and the public schools in urban centres. This removal from parents and home communities effectively trapped these children between their own culture and that of the dominant (white) society. After a few years they "belonged" nowhere. The effects were similar to the child welfare laws which caused hundreds and hundreds of First Nations children to be removed from their parents' care.

from a traditional perspective, I have been taught that sovereignty means the right to self-determination — the right to live in a good way, as the Creator made me, a Mohawk woman.

Sovereignty in a Mohawk sense begins with the individual living in a self-disciplined way which includes respecting the Great Law of Peace. It is upon those self-disciplined individuals that our families, clans, and nations are built. The Mohawk view of sovereignty is, therefore, a request for respect as responsible and self-disciplined individuals. I struggle to understand why the federal and provincial governments have had so much difficulty in respecting the desire of a people to be responsible. I think it is because they are so worried about *their* ownership of land that they cannot see what our claim of sovereignty is really about. To me, that makes the conversation about greed and *not* about nationhood.

No matter where we begin—First Nation's citizens in prison, alcoholism and substance abuse, the potential for another Oka, family violence, lack of employment, low income,[22] poor quality of education—the circle always completes itself with sovereignty.[23] Until we have control of our lives the cycles of abuse will not end. You must recognize the scope of the abuse that exists to truly begin to understand the oppression my people have faced in this country. Only then can you consider respectfully our notion of sovereignty for First Nations.

In 1980, only 20 percent of First Nations individuals had a post-secondary education compared to 40 percent of the non-First Nations population. First Nations individuals, if they do have any post-secondary education, are more likely to have training in a vocation or trade.[24] Ten percent of the Canadian population has a university degree. Less than 5 percent of First Nations people has a university degree.[25] Great gains have been made in this area since the 1960s, however: in 1961, only 0.3 percent of the registered Indian population held a university degree.[26] Although the education attainment has continued to improve since 1980, recent cutbacks by the Department of Indian Affairs and the cap placed on available funding have caused First Nations grave concern. To limit financial access to education before a situation of equity has been reached is neither sensible nor wise.[27]

Family violence in First Nations communities, as one study indicates, is eight times the national average.[28] This means that out of every ten First Nations Women, eight live or have lived in a violent family situation. This direct threat of violence in our daily lives has an overwhelming effect. It is deplorable that such a threat exists.

The rate of violent death for First Nations individuals is three times the national average. The suicide rate is six times the national average and is especially high among young people. Child welfare apprehensions are five times the national average.[29] The amount of physical and psychological violence we tolerate in our everyday lives is overpowering. There are more statistics available. The picture painted is already chilling.

The situation for First Nations people in general is appalling. The Canadian Human Rights Commission has likewise concluded that:

> The sorry list of statistics on the socio-economic plight of Aboriginal people in Canada has of late received considerable attention. Aboriginal people have not shared in Canada's enviable progress in wealth and well being. Instead, they have remained what many observers have called our "Third World." The condition of Indians, Inuit and Métis in this country, despite recent studies in health, housing, and education standards, is still deplorable. Without specific policy action to combat poverty, ill health, and illiteracy, both on and off reserve, Canada will remain seriously wanting in its legal and moral obligations toward Aboriginal people.[30]

The picture for First Nations women is even worse. First Nations and non-First Nations women work in the same job areas; however, First Nations women earn less and have higher rates of unemployment.[31] First Nations women earn less than any other group in Canada, including First Nations men. In 1980, the majority of First Nations women earned less than $5,000. Nearly 20 percent of First Nations men earned over $20,000 in that year. For First Nations women, less than 5 percent earned over $20,000 in that same year.[32] An examination of the 1986 Census data reveals that Aboriginal People's[33] access to income has *not* greatly improved. For men, 13.3 percent had a total income in excess of $20,000. Only 5.1 percent of women had incomes this great.[34] The average income for Aboriginal People in 1986 was $12,899, compared to $18,188 for the average Canadian. Aboriginal women earned only $9,828 on average, easily less than half the total income ($23,265)[35] of the average Canadian male. Although a small increase in access to income had been demonstrated by Aboriginal women, it is likely not great enough to offset the effects of inflation over the six years between 1980 and 1986. The net gain was therefore negligible and not a cause for celebration. Federal government statistics for their employment equity initiative indicate the same general trends regarding access to employment.[36] We, the women of the original peoples, are the poorest group in this country.

The composition of First Nations families further compromises the reality reflected in the income statistics. Twenty percent of First Nations families are single-parent families.[37] Of these, 80 percent are headed by women.[38] These figures are significantly higher than national rates. A further general trend in composition of First Nations families is that we generally have more children.[39] The birth rate for the original peoples continues to be significantly higher than the national average and our population is increasing.[40] And the solution for us is not simply to have fewer children. First Nations women have already endured a period in history of forced sterilization. The reality is that First Nations women support larger families on fewer dollars.

The conclusion is clear: First Nations women occupy the lowest rung in Canadian society. We earn less, have less education, bear sole responsibility for larger families, and confront the reality of racism and sexism daily. But we continue to struggle for our rightful place in this society. We struggle for a good future and for our children and for those to come.

I want to return for a moment to some more general statistics because these are the ones I find most disturbing. Ten percent of the federal prison population are First Nations citizens; yet we are only two percent of the population nationally.[41] In 1983, the First Nations inmate population at the only federal prison for women in Canada accounted for 31 percent of the total inmate population.[42] The situation in provincial institutions is no better. In fact, it is worse. In Saskatchewan, a Native man is 25 times more likely to be admitted to a provincial correctional centre than a non-Native man.[43] The fact of our over-representation in incarceration rates should not be trivialized. Imprisonment is a violation of individual freedoms. It cannot be rationalized by assuming that "Indians" are innately more criminal ("bad"). That is a ridiculous justification which plays on the "Indians are savages" stereotype. Such a rationalization amounts to blaming the victim, again. The question we are left to face is what, in real terms, can be done? Let me give you one example of what can happen when the government and First Nations work together along with other Canadians.

In 1989, the Solicitor General's Ministry struck a task force to examine the situation of federally sentenced women.[44] On any given day in Canada, there are approximately 10,500 federally sentenced men and less than 500 federally sentenced women. Thus, until the 1989 task force,[45] federally sentenced women were a correctional afterthought in the federal system. All correctional policies were drafted with the male prisoners' needs in mind. Comprising 25 percent[46] of the less than 500 federally sentenced women (again, please note their dramatic over-representation), First Nations women do not wish to be a second correctional afterthought, with their culturally-specific needs lost behind the needs of women generally.

In examining potential policy goals during the government's first attempt to identify what women prisoners' needs are, some startling statistics were collected on the First Nations federally-sentenced women. Ninety percent of these women reported an incidence of physical abuse during her life, compared to the 82 percent found within the total population, including First Nations women.[47] First Nations women had usually experienced physical abuse over long periods of time. Only 61 percent of non-First Nations women reported histories of abuse.

The research study of First Nations women's experience is described in the report as follows:

> The women spoke of violence, of racism, and of the meaning of being female, Aboriginal, and imprisoned. They spoke of systemic violence throughout their lives by those they lived with, those they depended on, and those they loved and trusted. Twenty seven of the thirty-nine women interviewed described experiences of childhood violence, rape, regular sexual abuse, the witnessing of a murder, watching their mothers repeatedly beaten, and beatings in juvenile detention centres at the hand of staff and other children...
>
> For Aboriginal women, prison is an extension of life on the outside, and because of this they find it impossible to heal in prison. They asserted that, for them, prison rules have the same legitimacy as the oppressive rules under which they grew up. In ways that are different from the world outside, but are nevertheless continuous with it, prisons offer more white authority that is sexist, racist, and violent. Those few "helping" services in prison that are intended to heal are delivered in ways that are culturally inappropriate to them as women and as Aboriginal people. Physicians, psychiatrists, and psychologists are typically white and male. They, therefore, symbolize the worst experiences of the Aboriginal women. As a result, Aboriginal women express anger at these caregivers, refuse to become involved, and then are further punished because they fail to seek treatment.[48]

The picture that becomes clear through examination of this report (merely one example of the picture I have been trying to paint throughout this article) is one of deplorable life experiences and intolerable institutional experiences in a supposedly free and democratic society. The solution mandated by the task force was a new policy direction based on providing women with meaningful choices. For First Nations women this means culturally relevant programming, servicing, and housing. It means allowing them to control their own lives. One way these goals are to be realized is through creation of a "Healing Lodge," a culturally distinct institution. Such an initiative is merely one example of the ways in which First Nations aspirations can be accommodated in the existing system to allow us to be both self-determining and self-disciplined. The idea of providing meaningful choices for First Nations citizens may indeed be a generic precondition for solutions to many of the issues challenging us today. The ideology of choices is one that bears further thought.

First Nations individuals, who are traditional people, have the knowledge necessary to heal our nations. But we have never been fully allowed the opportunity to pursue, with support, our rights and our ways. As a woman of the

First Nations, I walk in front of seven generations to come. I have a responsibility to the little ones who are not yet here to see that there is a good place for them when they come. I hope you will take my hand and we can all walk to that good place together, in respect and as equals. Nia:wen.[49]

Notes

1. Pronounced "say-go."
2. I am not using the word "political" in a Western sense. It is impossible to separate law (meaning living peacefully), government, spirituality (which is not the same thing as religion), and education in the traditional ways of my people. Life and experience are holistic (they have a beginning and ending like a circle and *not* like a straight line). All experience is connected. Traditional ways focus on teaching "relationships" and "connection" and *not* "individualism" and "separation." This is not to say that individualism is a "bad" or "wrong" way. Simply, it is not the First Nation's way. You cannot learn the traditional teachings of my people by reading one article. I have provided a selective bibliography of works not contained in the footnotes for the interested reader. Please respect that the ways of my people cannot be learned from books or writing alone. It is a lived experience. It is vastly complex. What you can likely learn is that the ways of the First Nations are different from those you grew up with and those differences do not make you or I better.

   I believe that Black feminism has labelled the struggle to make English work for their experience as "recreating the pencil" every time you wish to write. [See Audre Lorde, *Sister Outsider*. (New York: The Crossing Press, 1984) at 78]. This is an accurate description of my experience of the process of writing.
3. R.S.C. 1970, c 1-6, as amended in June of 1985.
4. In another article I have further developed this idea with specific reference to the law of discrimination. See "Reflecting on Flint Woman," in Richard Devlin, *Canadian Perspectives on Legal Theory*, forthcoming.
5. *Attorney General of Canada v. Lavell; Isaac v. Bedard*, [1974] S.C.R. 1349.
6. For a detailed discussion of the 12(1)(b) provision and its effect on Indian women, see: Kathleen Jamieson, *Indian Women and the Law in Canada: Citizens Minus* (Ottawa: Supply and Services Canada, 1978).
7. 1960, R.S.C. 1985, App. B.
8. *Lovelace v. Can.*, [1981] 2 H.R.L.J. 158, [1983] *Can. Human Rights Yearbook* 305 (U.N.H.R.C.).
9. The 1985 amendments to the *Indian Act* are discussed at length in the publication of the Native Women's Association of Canada, *Guide to Bill C-31* (Ottawa: Native Women's Association of Canada, 1986).
10. A band, as defined by the *Indian Act*, is a group of Indians who have reserve lands and are recognized by the federal government to have band status. Membership in a band means you are entitled to be registered on the band list. The band list controls who may live on reserve lands.
11. The Department of Indian Affairs also maintains a list of status Indians, or people who meet the definitional requirements of the *Indian Act*. With the exception of reserve residency and attached privileges, Indian status entitles the individual to participate in the benefits of the *Indian Act* regime.
12. See section 10 of the amended *Indian Act*.

13. Ontario Native Women's Association. *Presentation to the Standing Committee on Aboriginal Affairs on Bill C-31.* (Thunder Bay: Ontario Native Women's Association, 1988): 3.

14. The *Constitution Act 1982,* Part III, Section 35(1) recognizes and affirms existing Aboriginal and treaty rights. Section 35(2) defines Aboriginal Peoples and the Indian, Inuit, and Métis. Note in the original text the word "Aboriginal" is not capitalized. As this refers to my nation (such as English and French), I find it offensive. It is a similar feeling to that expressed earlier (see note 2) of having to re-create the pencil.

15. Professor Nicholas Deleary, Native Studies Department, University of Sudbury, shared this interpretation with us at the Annual Assembly of the Native Women's Association of Canada, August 1988, held in Winnipeg, Manitoba.

16. I have also discussed the meaning of this word and its silencing power in "Reflecting on Flint Woman," *supra.*

17. My understanding of the specifics of what racism is (individual acts versus institutionally-based action) has been significantly influenced by lively discussion with, and the patience of, Blaine Hanson.

18. I refer to the Creator as she. This is not accurate. In many of the languages of the First Nations this word mans neither he nor she. It means both. This is the way of creation: both male and female energies are required. I use "she" rather than "he" simply as a way to bring attention to this shortcoming of the English language and its corresponding implications.

19. Verna Kirkness, "Emerging Native Women," *Canadian Journal of Women and the Law* 2(2), 1987-88, 408: 413.

20. *bid.*: 414.

21. See bell hooks, *Ain't I A Woman: Black Women and Feminism* (Boston: South End Press, 1981); Audre Lorde, *Sister Outsider* (New York: The Crossing Press, 1984); Esmeralda Thornhill, "Focus on Black Women!" *Canadian Journal of Women and the Law* 1(1): 153, 1985.

22. For a discussion of "disadvantage versus dispossession," see Patricia A. Monture, "Ka-Nin-Geh-Heh-Gah-E-Sa-Nonh-Yah-Gah," *Canadian Journal of Women and the Law* 2(1): 159, 1986.

23. My ideas on the importance of sovereignty and self-determination have been significantly influenced by Shirley O'Connor, Past President, Ontario Native Women's Association and Mary Ellen Turpel of the Dalhousie Faculty.

24. These statistics should *not* be read with a predetermined value judgement, such as "professions (university education) are better than trades or vocations." What is essential is the relationship between education and access to disposable income.

25. Pamela M. White, *Native Women: A Statistical Overview* (Ottawa: Native Citizen's Directorate, 1986): 16.

26. James Frideres, *Native People in Canada: Contemporary Conflicts,* 2nd Edition (Scarborough: Prentice-Hall, 1983): 132.

27. There was considerable First Nations resistance to the new post-secondary education policies put forward by the Department of Indian Affairs in 1989. In Canada's national newspapers, you can follow the story of our resistance, commencing in March 1989.

28. Ontario Native Women's Association, *Breaking the Cycle of Aboriginal Family Violence: A Proposal for Change,* Final Draft (Thunder Bay: Ontario Native Women's Association, 1989): 17. As this study was only completed in communities where the sponsoring organization had "locals" (active comunity-based groups), it is

impossible to generalize the results to anything more than the Ontario Native Women's Association member groups. This is not a statistically significant national or provincial finding. I rely on a flawed research report *only* because national and/or provincial studies have not yet been undertaken. The lack of research resources committed to this issue is a further example of the oppression First Nations women face.

29. Michael Jackson, *Locking Up Natives In Canada* (Ottawa: Canadian Bar Association, 1988):6. Professor Jackson is citing from the report, *Indian Self-Government in Canada*, Report of the Special Committee on Indian Self-Government (The Penner Report), 1983: 14-15.

30. *Canadian Human Rights Commission*, "A New Commitment: Federal Aboriginal Policy," released November 21, 1990: 7.

31. White, *Native Women: A Statistical Overview*: 17.

32. *Ibid.*:19.

33. I am not using the language of First Nations here because I have chosen to reflect the structure imposed by the data collectors, Census Canada.

34. Aboriginal Peoples Output Program: 23.

35. *Ibid.*

36. Employment and Immigration Canada, *Employment Equity Act Annual Report* (Ottawa: Supply and Services, 1989): 39.

37. It is my own suspicion there is a relationship between the oppressive policies of the *Indian Act* and this figure. Issues about First Nations are under-researched and there is no study available to confirm my suspicions.

38. *Ibid.*: 22.

39. *Ibid.*: 24.

40. Frideres, *supra*: 132.

41. Correctional Law Review, *Correctional Issues Affecting Native Peoples*, Working Paper No. 7 (Ottawa: Ministry of the Solicitor General, 1988): 3.

42. Carol LaPrairie, "Native Women and Crime In Canada: A Theoretical Model," in Ellen Adelburg and Claudia Currie (eds.), *Too Few To Count: Canadian Women in Conflict With the Law* (Vancouver: Press Gang Publishers, 1987): 103.

    Current figures (the Correctional Law Review reports a figure of 13 percent) indicate that the figure of 31 percent I have cited is high. Through personal contact at the Prison for Women, I am not convinced that there has been an actual decrease, let alone a *dramatic* decrease in the incarceration rates of First Nations women. What I believe to be reflected in the decrease in the statistical rate of incarceration is how Native, Aboriginal, or Indian is defined. By way of example, the incarceration rate for Indians (remember the *Indian Act* narrowly defines who is and is not an Indian) would be lower than the rate of incarceration for all First Nations (including Indians, both status and non-status, Inuit, and Métis). Further, the systems which operate within the prison require that First Nations people self-report their racial status. Many prisoners choose not to do this as it is often not to their advantage but clearly to their disadvantage.

43. Jackson, *supra*: 3.

44. The provisions in Canada's constitution which divide the powers between the federal and provincial governments create the situation where prisoners whose sentence is two years or longer are federal responsibilities. If a sentence is two years less a day, that prisoner is the responsibility of the provincial government in which the sentence

was passed.

45. Solicitor General of Canada, *Creating Choices: The Report of the Task Force on Federally Sentenced Women* (Ottawa: Solicitor General, 1990).
46. *Ibid.*: 53.
47. *Ibid.*: 52.
48. *Ibid.*: 65-66.
49. This is a traditional closing. The literal translation is merely "thank you," but it is also a wish that the words we have shared have been good.

References

Akwesasne Notes (eds.), 1986. *A Basic Call to Consciousness*. New York: Akwesasne Notes.

Allen, Paul Gunn, 1986. *The Sacred Hoop: Recovering the Feminine in American Indian Traditions*. Boston: Beacon Press.

Armstrong, Jeannette C., 1985. *Slash* (Penticton, B.C.: Theytus Books.

Benton-Banai, Edward, 1981. *The Mishomis Book.* Saint Paul, Minn.: Indian Country Press.

Brant, Beth (Degonwadonti), 1984. *A Gathering of Spirit: Writing and Art by North American Indian Women*. Vermont: Sinister Wisdom Books.

Canadian Women Studies, 1989. Special Issue on Native Women 10(2-3)(Spring/Fall).

Hale, Janet Campbell, 1981. *The Jailing of Cecilia Capture*. Vancouver: Press Gang Publishers.

Harris, Michael, 1986. *Justice Denied: The Law Versus Donald Marshall*. Toronto: McMillan of Canada.

Maracle, Lee, 1988. *I Am Woman*. Vancouver: Write-On Press Ltd.

Monture, Patricia A., 1989. "A Vicious Circle: Child Welfare and First Nations," *Canadian Journal of Women and the Law* 3.

North American Indian Travelling College (eds.), 1984. *Traditional Teachings*. New York: North American Indian Travelling College.

Chapter 19

Equality and Lesbian Existence

Mary Eaton

I have a few things I'd like to mention before starting.

First of all, I just wanted to say that I am particularly pleased that the lesbian voice has been given some space at this conference. Most lesbians are painfully aware that this doesn't happen all that often. So I am very glad to be here and am very glad to be here as a lesbian feminist.

Secondly, I want to own up to something,which I suppose is always good feminist process, and that is: I have the "willies" like you wouldn't believe! Speaking in a forum like this is new to me and so I have this sense of just plain fear. But I am also quite nervous about the content of my talk. It's not enough to have a lesbian, or a woman of colour, or a working-class woman, etc., speaking; it also matters what they say. I hope you all know that strong words don't equal trashing and trust that you won't trash me in return.

Now that I have come out to you all, I could move on to something we could all relate to: something, let's say, lesbian-neutral, if there is such a thing. But I don't want to do that. I am here to talk to you about my experience *as a lesbian*. The prospect of doing this talk in this way has been keeping me awake at night.

These are hard words to speak.

I am on this panel, as you are probably aware, as a student. I am here, presumably, to articulate the student vision of what feminism in the legal profession is, and could be, like. Feminism, in its real sense, is supposed to be about equality in its real sense. Without attempting the definitive statement on what "real equality" means, let me just say this: for some women, equality as a concept loses its meaning, and its appeal, when it is treated as a synonym for equal treatment. All women are not treated equally because all women are not the same; we are as diverse a group as one could imagine. When we talk about equal treatment, what we are really talking about is treating one group of women like we treat one group of men. Many women are lost from this equation. Some women will never be a part of it, and others simply don't want to be. Real equality for lesbians begins with mere existence. To understand what this means, to appreciate how deeply this reality runs in living one's life

---

This chapter was a conference address given at Ideals and Reality: Feminism in the Study and Practice of Law, Kingston, Ontario, January, 1988.

as a lesbian is central to any understanding of how equality for lesbians will look.

Lesbians do not exist unless they make themselves known. That is what is distinct about lesbian oppression. That is what distinguishes our experience from that of other groups of women. The impact of this absence, which is our lives, has many dimensions and processes. I am only going to talk about a few of these. I am an out lesbian law student. I am here to tell you about my experience.

I am here, then, firstly to speak to other lesbians, to reaffirm our existence by my presence on this panel, and to say in "public" those words we don't dare say in private; not in the law schools, not in our feminist collectives, not to our lovers, not to ourselves. I am here to say these words so that we can find each other—so that we know we exist—so that we are no longer isolated within our collectives, from our lovers and friends, and from ourselves.

I am also here to raise hell. I have been told, by reliable sources, that lesbians talking as and about lesbians in legal-type circles is a rare thing, almost revolutionary, I'm told. One of the reasons for this unhappy state of affairs is, I suppose, that lesbian talk makes some people, including some women, feel ever so uncomfortable. For those of you who feel that way, I am here in the hope that you will leave those reactions behind and listen to my story of what your discomfort does to me and my lesbian sisters.

I want to start off with the idea that physical force (or the threat thereof) as the primary manifestation of oppression is misguided at best, and at worst is violence itself. It is also a particularly male way of viewing oppression: that is, that oppression consists only of rape, pillage, and plunder, and nothing less. I want to offer a very simple proposition: the dynamics of oppression are, in large part, played out in the politics of everyday life; in everyday language and conversation, in everyday work and play, in everyday love and friendship.

Getting a grip on this idea is central to any understanding of what I was speaking of moments ago. Lesbian oppression is about silence and invisibility, about being forced to conform to heterosexual norms, and about wiping out our tradition, our knowledge, our existence. The politics of lesbian existence have always been about denial, and silencing, and annihilation, and isolation—and never about liberal conceptions of choice or legal conceptions of personal "sexual orientation."

None of this is to say that lesbians don't experience, as a condition of their oppression, actual physical violence. I certainly don't want to be misunderstood as saying that violence is not part of our daily lives. No one ever forgets being queer-bashed. No one ever forgets being civilly committed for loving women. No one ever forgets rape—rape of our bodies and rape of our minds—as the ultimate attempt to make us straight. While I am talking about a different aspect of lesbian existence today, I want you to remember this other part as well. In fact, I would like us all to take a moment of silence for a specific group of our sisters: those lesbians who have been and are now incarcerated in psychiatric institutions and who have or will receive the many and various benefits of psychiatric treatment such as electro-convulsive "therapy."

To get a sense of how absent the lesbian voice is, we should consider the following problem. The silence of women in the classroom has been documented on a number of occasions. Dale Spender's work, in particular, has been invaluable in helping us uncover the ways in which our male classmates mute our voices. There are degrees of silence, however. Approximately one in ten women are lesbian. At Queen's Law School, for instance, there are about two hundred women. If you can do math as well as I can, you will figure out that there ought to be some twenty lesbian students at Queen's Law School. I have never met one (though it has been suggested to me by one of my colleagues that one particular woman, described as "unattractive" and "awkward" with poor taste in clothes, is probably a lesbian).

Those other nineteen women are as silent as silent can be. They are invisible. We ought, I think, to keep this in mind when we talk about silence as oppression.

What happens to lesbians who make themselves visible? Over the last few years, I have been trying to make sense of my experience, and now I am here trying to make sense of my life for you. I will be speaking on a few of the elements of heterosexual discourse as they relate to lesbians, including: (1) construction of the lesbian as deviant; (2) sexualization of the lesbian; (3) proprietization* of lesbian oppression by the egalitarian women's movement; and (4) silencing of articulation of lesbian experience through lesbopressive reactionism. Each of the above discourses actively enforces and reinforces the heterosexual woman as the norm.

Construction of the Lesbian as Deviant

Real lesbians do not exist in this world. You and I, as lesbians, exist only among ourselves; that is, we exist where we make room for one another. Otherwise, we are completely absent, or alternatively, we are constructed in such a way that one may well wonder how that social product and ourselves could ever be taken to be the same thing. That is, where the lesbian does occasionally appear, she is variously portrayed as a lonely, ugly, pathetic creature who can't get a man, or who wants to be one. In this latter regard, it has been said in the "scientific" literature that lesbians have extra-large clitorises (resembling the penis, you might note) hence giving rise to the theory that lesbians are really the result of some biological mix-up.

So lesbians are deviant, we are told. It is "natural" to be affectionally and sexually attracted to men, but it is not "natural" to feel so inclined towards women. The "sickness" of the lesbian has led to her frequent incarceration in

---

* Turning into property. This will be clarified below.

psychiatric institutions. When we look at the alarming rate of heterosexual violence against women and children, like the one in ten women who is battered by her male partner; the one in four children who has been sexually abused; and that another woman is raped in this country every seventeen minutes, we ought to wonder what is so "healthy," so "normal," about the pursuit of heterosexual relations.

Personality problems of various sorts are also attributed to lesbians. If she is despairing, call her suicidal, manic-depressive, or any other psychiatric catch-all phrase. It ain't easy not existing, and there is very little reason to smile about your own absence. Of course, if you do smile, there cannot be anything wrong; all must be well. The scope of emotion lesbians are permitted to experience without political repercussions is severely circumscribed. Because the "condition" of lesbianism has historically been linked to psychosis, the expression of lesbian feeling is often associated in the same way. In short, lesbians are not permitted to *feel* as individuals in the world without being labelled unstable.

Sexualization of the Lesbian

Similarly, the lesbian suffers from chronic masculinity, as we all know: if they would just be more feminine, they wouldn't have so many problems. Particularly in political discussions, lesbian-feminism is often attacked for being aggressive, adversarial, and just plain uppity: all attributes associated with male styles of discourse.

But anger is legitimate.

As marginalized women, lesbians suffer from the peculiar condition of not existing. We must struggle to be seen and heard. We must fight against the constant threat of annihilation. We must understand that struggle is necessary to our very presence.

Yet the lesbian struggle is consistently construed as masculine or male. There is nothing inherently male about struggle, just as there is nothing inherently female about submission. Empowerment is not penile.

Masculinization of lesbians in general, and of lesbian discourse in particular, is an undoing tactic, a way to keep us in line. It is a methodology by which het (heterosexual) women can coerce us into solidarity with them. It is a label much feared in a *gendered* world, a reality which no commitment to change can alter overnight. In essence, solidarity with heterosexual women on this level is a demand to pass—pass for feminine, pass for straight. And in the process, we have left buried lesbian herstory and culture.

Women, under conditions of patriarchal dominance, are almost entirely denied any capability other than sperm receptacle and sexual plaything: an object which is acted upon (in ways mostly sexual) and not one which acts for herself or is capable of acting for herself. The domination of the lesbian under these same conditions is sexualization with a vengeance. The lesbian is nothing but sex: sex drive, sex object, sex. The only thing that actually sets the lesbian apart from other women is that she sleeps with women but this fact becomes all encompassing of her identity. It is her primary determinant.

Women, who should know more than a little about the sexualization of women generally, actively impose this construction of lesbianism on lesbians all the time. Any lesbian who has ever tried to discuss Adrienne Rich's theory of "Compulsory Heterosexuality" has probably lived through this experience. The invariable reaction of non-lesbian women to the idea of the lesbian continuum is that they have no place on it; the reason being that they do not sleep with women and therefore can't possibly be lesbian in any way. Sex is all that we are, and we are nothing. Non-lesbian women do to lesbians precisely what men do to women all the time. They have learned their lessons well.

But lesbians know that the scope of lesbianism is infinite. They knew what women-positive and women-centred relationships were and created them, long before the feminist movement and long before heterosexual women appropriated from lesbians affectional relations between women and gave them heterosexual content. Lesbianism pre-dates feminism as patriarchy pre-dates capitalism. The appropriation of women-centred culture by heterosexual feminism had the effect of perverting lesbian culture, turning it into pornography, making eroticism between women dirty, bad, and sick. It left lesbians with nothing but sex. Lesbians have paid to make woman-connectedness possible; non-lesbian women have not. Listen to the battle cry of the feminist movement when it is labelled "lesbian." "We are not lesbians!" they say.

No, never.

Proprietization of Lesbian Oppression

Lesbian oppression has also become, in a sense, the property of the mainstream equality movement. By way of example, I was turned into pornography on the men's bathroom wall at the law school, twice to my knowledge. The second time was a remark in response to the pamphlet printed for this conference in which I was self-described as a lesbian feminist. Of course a number of people, both men and women, were outraged by this scandalous remark, though many admitted they were clueless as to what it was actually about. It was a remark levelled at my lesbianism. But in any case, the presence of this pornography spurred some people on to quasi-action. I say quasi-action because there was a big to-do about the whole thing, but in the end nothing was done. Despite the good intentions of those who took on the cause, a couple of truly astonishing transactions took place. Lesbian libel became, in effect, the property of the equalitists, because they "were offended too."

This transaction raised a frequent problem in coalitions between differently and differentially oppressed peoples. While we may be more familiar with it in other contexts, the dynamics of the problem are essentially the same. The problem is one of respect, participation, and control. Solving it requires great sensitivity and trust. And it requires discussion and naming.

In the pornography example, others had dibs on my public degradation and I was given, at best, an equal say in how the political action was to proceed. My pain became public property. My life became grist for the political mill.

Property notions also underlie that by-now-very-stale and boring debate between "I can't possibly know what your oppression is like because I'm not a lesbian," on the one hand, and "of course I know all about the conditions of your degradation," on the other.

As to the first of these, the "I can't possibly know" school, it is used more often than not as a cop-out. Because the adherents of this approach can't live with the limits of their own experience and understanding, they will do absolutely nothing. No work, no struggle, no pain.

On the other hand, the "yes we know" school of appropriation, those who hold heterosexual privilege assume that the content of our lives is available for their use, at their convenience. They know, because they've experienced oppression, too. After all, it's all just variations on a common theme.

I have come to believe that neither of these positions is legitimate, and that both are based on proprietary constructions of oppression. They both assume the heterosexual experience, not only as the norm, but also as the functional concept from which the experience of discrimination is to be measured. Neither allows lesbian existence status in its own right. Lesbians must make available for use the concrete conditions of our experience without any recognition that this process involves work. It is work, and pain, and sweat, and psychiatrized brains that makes this information available. The act of appropriating it for one's own use is called exploitation. Most of us ride on our privilege from time to time, sometimes consciously and sometimes not, but we would do better to learn to discover each other and the richness of experience we can offer, to learn to explore and respect our diversity rather than exploit one another.

Silencing the Articulation of Lesbian Experience

In closing, I would like to talk about a few of the more classic responses (which I call the Lesbophobic Hall of Fame) to the lesbian voice.

The first of these is the old reverse hierarchy ploy. Here, the lesbian, oddly enough, is glorified. She is the epitome of the revolutionary; she is counter-hegemonic beyond all belief. This construction will be imposed on the lesbian voice when it articulates the particularities of lesbian oppression. Whatever she says, she is more radical. Now, hierarchies being the nasty things they are, they must be dismantled whenever encountered, whether they are real or imagined. Hence the lesbian must get off her high radical horse and speak like the rest of us.

Conversely, the articulate lesbian feels far too sorry for herself. Her motives are to get people to feel sympathy towards her. She will likely be told that this kind of self-serving "oh poor me" type of behaviour is most unbecoming for a good radical. It makes a mountain out of a molehill, sees discrimination where it doesn't exist, and *creates* hierarchies of oppression, all to make the speaker out to be more oppressed "than thou."

When lesbians ask to be listened to, when we trust that equality matters to those we work with, we are likely to face the claim that we are asking far too much. To use popular jargon, we are asking for "special treatment." Now, the status of the special treatment philosophy these days is somewhat grim. It is regarded as a bad thing because it means that people may be treated differently, that the undeserving are pulling a fast one by claiming they are being discriminated against when they really aren't. Different treatment violates the great liberal concept of equality; namely, that once we treat everyone the same, we will have created a truly egalitarian community. The result of this ideological gibberish is that when the lesbian speaks as a lesbian, as opposed to as a member of the all-embracing category of "woman," she is demanding something she simply cannot legitimately be granted: different treatment. To do so would be, dare we say it, *unconstitutional.* Now, if the only way we know a woman is a lesbian is if she opens her mouth and tells us so, and if the inevitable consequence of a lesbian talking about her life as lesbian is that she is understood to be asking for special treatment, and if special treatment is unconstitutional, then we are driven to the conclusion that lesbians are unconstitutional.

Lesbians are, as well, just plain difficult to get along with. We are so disruptive, in fact, that our mere presence spells doom for equality for women. This is because lesbians are not really women. When lesbians are lesbians, this is called breaking solidarity with our heterosexual sisters, which is, of course, a horrible thing to do. When lesbians are not lesbians, they are women, and this is called building solidarity. Solidarity, it seems, is a synonym for assimilation.

The ordinary, run-of-the-mill lesbophobic reactions mustn't be left out, even if they do suffer from a severe lack of imagination. They include denials: "This is not about heterosexism or homophobia or any of that other stuff, it's about time pressures, or personalities, or differences of opinion." Also included is the attack which frequently occurs immediately consecutive to the denial. For example, the following responses may neatly fall under this category: *"You* are too demanding," *"You* are hurting people," *"You* are being unfair," and *"You* have no right to humiliate me like that."

Emotional coercion is also a useful technique for silencing even the most resilient radical dyke. Here, one must grapple with tears. They cry, but not over the damage they have done to you. They cry because, in demonstrating to them the effect their behaviour has on you, *you* have simply exhibited a lack of tact in the style department. You are just too mean/hostile/angry/aggressive, etc. In consequence, you want to console. And in dealing with their tears, what you have tried to explain is forever lost. You must change your focus. You must play the role of the good, ever-forgiving mother. You must heal the wound that you have supposedly created by—let's be straight about this—caring enough about someone to spend your time and energy explaining to them that perhaps they might pursue a less discriminatory course of conduct. I do not deny that being called on our biases in this way is painful. I suspect we all like to think of ourselves as good people who care about equality and who wouldn't dream of discriminating against anyone. But we do. What is important, I think, is how we deal with our own acts of domination and how we go about changing ourselves.

Lastly, the goodwill syndrome should probably be included. Here, the goodwill of the oppressor is conclusive of the question of whether an act of oppression has transpired. When a lesbian calls a person on their lesbophobic behaviour, she is likely to be quickly informed that she is mistaken. She is nothing less than wrong about the source of her pain since the oppressor didn't mean it that way. Because the oppressor was well-intentioned, the oppressed lesbian was not really oppressed, and to insist that she was is oppressive of the oppressor.

I want to finish with a few words on being in the closet and finding each other. The fear behind coming out is a rational one. Lesbians pay for being lesbians. This is especially true for those lesbians who also carry the weight of other oppressive forces endemic to our society.

Women who are the happy recipients of some unearned pleasures in life, like us white dykes for instance, would say that more is to be gained, and the benefit to all women is greater, when lesbians hide their lesbianism. Women of influence, in other words, often make the claim that they can exercise this influence in more productive ways if they stay in the closet. Such a position is dishonest to yourself and to your audience. As well, that position is virtually impossible to carry out without doing actual harm to our lesbians. The quest for credibility in this way reinforces and actively articulates heterosexual norms— it actively keeps lesbians down—and that position is never harm-free.

References

Allen, Jeffner, 1986. *Lesbian Philosophy: Explorations*. Palo Alto, CA: Institute for Lesbian Studies.

Cavin, Susan, 1985. *Lesbian Origins*. San Francisco: Ism Press.

Cornwell, Anita, 1983. *Black Lesbian in White America*. Tallahassee: Naiad Press.

Cruickshank, Margaret, 1982. *Lesbian Studies*. New York: The Feminist Press.

Freedman, Gelphi, Johnson, and Weston, 1985. *The Lesbian Issue: Essays from Signs*. Chicago: University of Chicago Press.

Frye, Marilyn, 1983. *The Politics of Reality: Essays in Feminist Theory*. Freedom, CA: The Crossing Press.

Kehoe, Monika, 1986. *Historical, Literary, and Erotic Aspects of Lesbianism*. New York:

Harrington Park Press.

Kitzinger, Celia, 1987. *The Social Construction of Lesbianism*. New York: Sage Publications.

Lorde, Audre, 1984. *Sister Outsider*. Trumansburg, N.Y.: The Crossing Press.

Rich, Adrienne, 1983. "Compulsory Heterosexuality and Lesbian Existence," in Snitow, Stansell and Thompson (eds.), *The Powers of Desire: The Politics of Sexuality*. New York: Monthly Review Press.

Spender, Dale, 1982. *Invisible Women: The Schooling Scandal*. London: Writers and Readers.

Chapter 20

Lesbians and Teddy Bears
Anna Lattanzi

Introduction

This is the first chapter of my honours paper, "Lesbianism and Teddy Bears: Notes Toward Understanding Lesbian Experience, or Can Teddy Bears Really Talk?" (Carleton University, 1988). It is a piece framed by the difficulties inherent in producing work by, for, and about lesbians within the confines of a patriarchal, heterosexist institution. Academia historically has been a purveyor of oppressive ideology concerning lesbianism, particularly in the fields of psychology, religion, sociology, and law. Today, through its codes, rules, techniques, and curriculae, it continues to close doors to the constructive research and understanding of lesbianism. To enjoin a creative process involving lesbianism means a struggle not only over meaning but over power and authority as well. In this sense, I feel this article contains a certain relevancy to the experience of lesbians within society generally.

The framework of "Lesbianism and Teddy Bears" is structured as an environment of struggle. The first difficulty I encountered was in defining terms. The word "lesbianism" conjures up any amount of savoury and unsavoury images in the minds of particular readers according to understandings gained through dominant discourse or lived reality. Moreover, it is an emotional word. No dry topic, this: people react emotionally to it. For the purposes of writing, my lack of control over the conveyance of meaning implicated a much larger and pre-existent struggle for power. It became obvious to me at this time that I needed to usurp the power of definition and this, primarily, is the purpose of this first chapter.

Perhaps, I thought, I could cancel out the emotions of prejudice with those of idealism and end up with something halfway honest. As I pondered the possibilities of this, a teddy bear jumped through my window and demanded her say, claiming that she was an expert in these matters. I agreed that her vision was an essential one and appropriate to my purpose. I chose her as an ally because it's hard to feel prejudice towards a teddy bear because teddy bears are associated with healing, and because I like them, or at least I used to.

I reminded myself that seeing definition as the obvious beginning was a choice made in reaction to a set of oppressive conditions; that, in fact, the necessity of definition was originally born out of the social desire to oppress and legislate us. Having been used more recently as a label of solidarity and rebellion, self-definition coincides in reality with the coming-out process.

Somehow, I felt, I had to create this definition as an approximation of that process or as a source of movement. I was thinking that, forced into using society's terms for a reality outside its experience, we have often narrowed meanings to get a point across and by this have distorted the shades of meaning which we understand because we live them. So it became clear to me that I needed to break down the concept of definition itself as it is understood within academia. I attempted to do this by interweaving creative and academic styles of writing.

I needed to retain the multi-focal, multi-layered nature of this word "lesbianism" and to create constellations of interconnected reality because this is what it feels like. And it is exactly the concept of a whole reality which is the first victim of oppression. Academic writing, with its self-proclaimed insistence on itself as authority, simply would not do. The teddy bear had already made this clear and it was she who became the "authority" in the paper because it was she who was coming to understand.

The knowledge in this paper[1] is presented through the relationship between the lesbian and the teddy bear. Knowledge is conveyed as process and as relational, rather than static and absolute. Difficulties I have found with this piece are its highly subjective nature and its short length. Many points only raised in the paper could and should be dealt with at greater length. There are many experiences which remain untold.

Lesbianism and Teddy Bears

This was how it was before I had her. Then, when she came it wasn't much different—at least not at first. So many people were there and even she wasn't clear till the very last moment. On the day she first came she was all boxed-in, tied-up, hidden under; secret. It was Christmas. She came in a box called love, wrapped like a mummy in layers of pretty, pretty paper. Very nice.

To tell you the truth, I could imagine better beginnings. But since I have promised to chronicle this honestly, I had best tell you the reality of what happened as I now understand it. It was hate at first sight.

As we sat the circle round; wishing, waiting, eyes cast down; under under, dead green tree; singing songs summarily.

And lo, there came a hand, risen from beneath the tree. And the hand was not empty. No, but held for each a box called love, proffered to each the box called love, and all partook. And each who received it mumbled, "Blessed be the evergreen," words of thanks and praise. For each time that the gift was taken, again the hand was risen; appearing from the hidden under, raised and filled with gift. And in my turn was given me. The hand stretched out and I was taken. And the hand said, "Of course we love you, you have been good; of course, of course and here is the proof bought with our love. We give this to you so that in times of need when we are not there, and sometimes we are not, because often we are here—in fact, often they were not, being neither here nor there—then, in times of need you may call on the box of love and the secret inside.

From us to you with love, for love, in love."

I opened slowly. And she appeared.

A brown, furry blob. Squishable, huggable, neutered bear. Her only distinguishing mark was a clump of hair, longer than the rest, on one side of her nose. A defect. One strongly in contradiction with that perfect hand which had given it. So, I thought, I will hide her away that no one may notice her ugliness. From one ear hung a cardboard bear on a string, "...a Stieff bear made in...", and underneath this the price. She embodied exactly the energy of love as it was given. The exact quantity of that energy was $29.95, plus tax.

The giver would have disagreed.

She would have said the gift was a symbol, a way of her speaking. That all of her gifts resounded, through the following day and the next, in the work she was doing, in the way she was cooking, and always in the moments of her caring. Like a recipe she would have said: a little of this, a little of that, and just enough spice to make it bearably interesting. And there you have sustenance. I do believe that she would have admitted, and on occasion she has, to sometimes getting the measurements wrong. But within the plenitude of endless sustenance, of selfless service, what can a little indigestion mean?

He would have said the gift was a symbol, a way of his hugging. That all of his gifts belonged, on the following day and the next, to the work he was doing, to the money he was making, and always to the moments of his solitude. Like a martini, he would have said: a little money, a little liquid, and just enough of each that it doesn't matter anymore. And there you have sustenance.

The sustenance of pure addition. The preparation of one-way life: a linear miracle, going off like a rocket. Proper remuneration to be received for each correct step. Each step to be measured at cost value. A multiplicity of steps, enumerated properly, will produce a line, like a chain stretched out tight. The weight of this chain of compilation, this one-by-one memory, forces the head back, fixing the gaze forward down a never-ending tunnel, and relegating the feet to obscurity. Ever-staring eyes fixed firmly forward, never blinking, till the walls fall away from vision and are seen no more. The perfect formula for happiness: the achievement of seamless living, stretching for miles in every direction and with no horizons. Only darkness. It could be anywhere, flat. It could be anytime, in an everlasting night.

There is giving and there is taking. There is nothing else. Seamless lives allow for the correct quantification of available resources and, with astute reasoning, the proper amount of giving and taking needed to ensure the continued stability of the market, and a reasonable profit.

...A phrase used in the literature that I like very much is MJP, maximum joint profit... What we want to stimulate in men and women is the desire and capability to negotiate for the maximum benefit of all parties concerned... And if they cannot establish the MJP, that is, the maximum joint profit negotiating patterns in advance (of marriage), they are far better off remaining unattached.[2]

Remember always to guard company secrets. Bid low in order to undercut your competitors. Improvement of the product is the key to greater market accessibility. Advertise! Advertise! Advertise! The market may fail or you may be replaced with a more advanced product. Know when to get out! Ensure your future. Good things come to those who wait! Someday, somewhere you may be heard.

This is your life. Start your engines.

The lying begins. Words given, not taken, lost in confusion. So much done in the name of omission. Things not looked for, not wanted, not found. For all, I concealed the spaces through pretty red paper imaginings and faced the silence with screams to the gods, properly repeated in careful monotone, tied up in bows of Christmas cheer. In this way, I presented myself: the necessary whole. In all I lost myself in layers and layers. The face exists to mask the eyes. The stories without endings and the silent march of hatred folded over again and again in the wrappings of endless sustenance, encapsulated all in the box of love for the very low cost of $29.95, plus tax.

In the beginning that was all I knew of her. Until she came there was no other. It was she, as she appeared. The shadow of my imaginings, the imaginings of my waiting.

I hated her, I ignored her. She sat in my room and I abhorred her. That was, of course, before I slept with her.

I had been watching the falling night, in the darkness of my room. The rising of dusk, the making of so many points of black, thrown together and strewn throughout the air. Shadows over my eyes. And she of whiteness, almost unbearable. It was she who gathered, taking all light into herself. The borders of her being were fuzzy, shattered, moving outward as the intensity grew. A slow reflection, brighter and brighter she became. And I thought, "It is she who brings this to me. She who gives me this night."

In the semi-darkness all space was given over to her. All who might have known were silence, hidden in expectation. The space between us eclipsed, and tendrils of light, of movement and sound, reached and spread before us, danced between us. Touching and retreating, each in movement toward the other, and underneath it all the solid drum of heartbeat. The playing of my body, over and over, till finally its form was lost and in haze I spread over the room.

In the darkness, the clump of hair on the left side of her nose gleamed red, glowed warmth and passion. A single, distinguishing beauty mark. A crack opens up the sky, breaks the horizon. The sun, and dawn. A time like a slipstream, open at both ends. Or like a secret passage. A light-year jump. An illumination. At least, I thought, I must look different.

The light enters my window in pulsating movement. A wave rising out of the sea like a last request, growing huge in the moments before it arrives, molding the beach into shadow like a reflection, obscuring everything but itself. It explodes in silence, creating nothing, and confounds time. There is no sound but the light, poised and tensed as a fist, till the sea, unclenching each finger one by one, raises a hand palm up to the surface in a gesture of acceptance. The water, now gurgling, returns like a sigh, ebbs like a slowly taken breath. And the next wave, reaching its full height, trembling before the plunge, waits to encounter its own shadow. An unbreakable calm fills my room in the moments before silence speaks.

She awoke beside me, in the cool morning light, smiling. Turning over, she looked at me intently. "Repeat after me," she said, "Say... lesbian."

"What!?!"

"Say it." She drew it out carefully, "Say llleessbbbiiiaaannn."

"Why?" said I, wrinkling my nose.

"Because, when you can say lesbian like I can say lesbian then you'll be thinking what I'm thinking about what we're being here together. You know, like this: lesbian, lesbian, lesbian..."

"You mean how it rolls off your tongue?"

"Better your tongue than your back."

"The imagery is fascinating."

She continued, "When you can say that, why you'll be over here where I am and we'll be thinking the same things about the same things, and you'll be one."

"A teddy bear?"

She paused. "Repeat after me..."

She lied to me sometimes. Well, not exactly lied. She left things out. That is, she'd know them but she wouldn't tell them. There she'd be, right in the middle of something, she'd be going on and then...boom! Just like after gym class when someone turned out the lights in the change room. Pitch black. Some nervous giggles, a scream or two, an ultra-normal voice saying, "Okay, turn them back on." And she'd continue, just like nothing had happened, her body coming slowly back into focus. Lying is easy when it's free. When you don't have to.

Or sometimes I'd just be sitting with her. Maybe she'd be talking or it'd be quiet, but she wouldn't be looking at me and I'd be watching her. Then, all of a sudden, I'd think, "Who am I sitting with? What am I doing here?" Just like I was in this strange place with this bear I'd never seen before. Light-years away. And then she'd turn to me and all of it was back, just like it had never been different. That was the thing about time between us. It was never there. It was always space.

There or not there, fading in and out. Apart or together, always going towards one or the other. A distance to traverse. A constant judgment to make about its measure; a weighing of pros and cons, benefits versus repercussions. Needing to find the ways. There are, after all, a thousand ways to remain a shadow, dim and unconquerable, or at least uncatchable. Fading in and out of someone else's reality. A perpetual flash, endless pictures. The keeper of underground bars and secrets, hidden so that only the initiated will know the ways there. Havens and prisons, safety and touch. "Bears have one secret," she told me, "If you were over here, I'd tell you what it is."

I was almost never there, where she was, because mostly I was here, and quite often neither here nor there. She would watch me sometimes doing something and then disappearing. She hated to see me go because something always went wrong. It started slowly. The anger red and rising, bubbling up; all light growing dim before me; my sight blurred by a rush of blood, a stream. Words—no words. My body shaking—terror, hatred rushing towards each other in floods, poured through either ear. When the flood waters met in the centre of my head, my brain exploded. Later, I found her lying in a jumble of toys. Something had tried to strangle her. She was pinned to the wall, her limbs splayed. A work of art.

I often found her like this in the daytime and always I healed her. In the night I could keep her safe, keep her near me. Being only her and me, I could be always there. And so it went on. Repetition. A pulsating beam. An endless circle. And within the circle, we were one—a unity. Arms around each other were only arms, our arms, inseparable, undecipherable. And in this we were alone. We of all, only we existed. In this place we were, the only place there was. A continuing. We always knew, like we had always known, like we always would. We gave this all, ceasing to exist in any other way. An endless, beginningless circle. A constant stream of light. How could we have been more faithful to each other?

Of course, we had our problems too. For one thing, the being over here and always having to go over there really got to be a strain on a person. Especially when a person is already having to go other places, which she always calling disappearing, I would have liked for her to come since she hated for me to go, but it just wasn't possible. Even that little clump of fur which I had clipped from the side of her nose, I had to hide away. And, of course, we never held hands in public.

One day I said to her, "Why is it there are so many places that I am going that you can't be coming?"

"Because," she said, "people cannot accept the fact that it's possible to have an emotionally satisfying relationship with a bear."

I looked at her disbelievingly, "How can that be so?"

She looked at me oddly, "I think it's time to tell you the secret." She paused momentarily, underlining the significance of her next words. "Some people think that bears have no outside seams. Others know that, in fact, there is one outside seam. It is hidden by the bow around my neck."

"Well, a seam is a seam is a seam...Isn't it?"

"To us, yes. But according to most people it means that we're not alive. And it's not possible to have an emotionally satisfying relationship with something that doesn't exist."

"But that's not it at all!"

"Sure, but there's no point in telling them any different. It just interrupts their seamless lives and causes their pupils to dilate. In our case, suspicion can be tantamount to strangulation."

"I don't believe it."

"You mean you don't want to believe it. Haven't you noticed that people look at you funny when you talk about me? And why is it that all your friends are beginning to look like bears? Face it, you're different. Not only are you weird, you're outright queer. Or hadn't you noticed?"

"Better outright than out wrong!"

"Have it your way."

From an island, you can look all around you. In every direction there is water and sky and the place where they meet. One line cutting the world in half, a border, a seam. Beyond this you cannot see, or be seen. If you were to stand in the centre, your arms outspread, you could catch the winds of two directions. And if you could hold them long enough, you would see their reflections, each in the other. The opposite of the same thing. Mirrors and magnets: finally they must dissipate or become infinite.

I bent to kiss her, lowering my head. Hers turned away. Joined in movement by a single thread. An ear, red hair, an outline. Why can't you say goodbye?

This final word not forthcoming. The bridge knocked out by a difference in price. Competition. Opposite in the sense that it depends on your point of view which one is worth more. That is, if you want quality or quantity. The role reversal of human and commodity. Teddy bears and life insurance have a lot in common. As a bear in a bullish market, you will want to keep your point of view a secret at times. This is sometimes called the double life. To live this particular life, you must first clone yourself, so that one of you can talk while the other one is watching from the shadows, anchored halfway between your mind and your mouth, halfway between you and this other.

On the border between you and you—and there is always a border—there is a place called safety. Here we can keep things which we don't want to lose, like honest laughter and tears. A space of safety based on deception requires at the very least imagination and at the most mobility. This is called cultural adaptation. It moves like a reflection. We are refracted. A space, both controlled and controlling. A refuge and a trap; safety and the illusion that we control its boundaries. Sometimes we call it home.

In fact, it lives in us. She and I and the box of love. Also known as the wild zone and just as quickly unknown. An underground full of secret passages. The ways we know each other. The ways we use what is used against us. A culture within a culture. Community and continuity. A legacy of codes, rules, and signs.

Apparently, we are quite distinct, the process of evolution having marked us as errant wanderers from the true path of progress: a sub-group, an oddity, a mutant gene, a congenital malfunction. So, for example, we are prohibited from joining the armed forces and the RCMP and from gaining higher levels of security clearance. When pressed for a reason, they say this is because we are too furry.[3]

She laughed when she told me that. "Hypocrisy," she said. Virginia Woolf reflected: "I thought how unpleasant it is to be locked out; and I thought how it is worse perhaps to be locked in..."[4] I thought of the beauty mark I kept safe in my pocket. We were, of course, still friends. Same bars and dances, same political ideology and organizations... we had a lot in common and would inevitably meet again. We marched together in a demonstration during International Teddy Bear Week. We walked together down the street, she doing most of the talking and I carrying a picket sign which read: "Beardom Not Boredom!"

"Hypocrisy," she continued, "It seems to me that there's far too many things judged according to this morality of right and wrong, this rule of retribution. After all, there's no such thing as objectivity. There's only data."

"Meaning what?" I asked.

"When they're being objective, we're the data." She pulled out a piece of paper, folded over several times. "Read this," she said, "It's from a government report on the applicability of human rights legislation to teddy bears."

I read:

> He's (sic) moved with panache from publishing to stationary and paper goods, from paper to plush, and finally from plush to a line of chinaware... Collectors especially are drawn to the Goebel line because the products are good-looking, realistically priced, and fully collectible. To a certain extent, collectibles go in cycles—but teddy bears renew themselves with every generation that comes along...[5]

"It's hard to believe that people can actually think those things," I remarked.
She smiled at me, "You're sure saying lesbian nicely these days."
"Quite nicely, thank you."
As I was walking home after the demonstration, a breeze sprang up. I stopped

and took out the beauty mark. Half of the fur I threw to the wind. "Be free," I whispered. Carefully replacing the remaining half, I continued on.

How can you tell just who's a lesbian? Lesbians are born with a microscopic radar in each ear which allows us to speak to each other secretly. The only time it becomes dysfunctional is during a lunar eclipse. So mostly we know—a kind of solidarity—who we are. I'll start off thinking, "I've seen her before." And, of course, it's quite possible that I've caught a glimpse of her somewhere or other. Or someone might say, "She looks like a dyke," which as far as I can tell means she's wearing comfortable clothes. And that's where the radar comes in.

People without radar tend to miss a lot. Consequently, we are quite often looked at without being seen. That is, they don't come very often to see us, since it's such a long way to go. They tell us we are not like normal bears. They say our bows are too big. Or too small. They seem confused on this point.[6] However, they're sure that something's not quite right. One time I asked one of these people how big hers was but she wouldn't tell me, or didn't know. All she said was, "Don't flaunt it." Apparently, a demonstration of frolicking ribbons could disrupt the social order.

They say we are different and I think we are. But they say we are more different than I think we really are, and in different ways. Sometimes it has to do with space: like where you happen to be. In a moment it can switch from safety to danger and back again. The flick of a camera lens can be fatal. Constant judgement. Then who is left to judge us anything but nasty, or dead? One day I called my bearfriend on the phone to ask her what she thought about all this.

"I'm spending a lot of time alone these days," she said.

"Where are all the people?" I asked.

"They're there."

"Where?"

"Over there where they always are."

"So, that makes you alone?" I asked.

"It makes me so alone that I have to leave the room."

"And where do you go?"

"I go someplace where I can be alone."

"Then you are still alone," I said decisively.

"Not as much," she replied, "I have a vivid imagination."

She told me that according to scientific theory we are different. Apparently, when we were invented around the turn of the century, a lot of people were shocked. A priest, voicing the general mood of the public "...denounced the Teddy Bear as destroying all instincts of motherhood and leading to race suicide."[7] All this because when we came out on the market we outstripped dolls and their sales declined radically.

We were invented to be prevented. A whole new discipline, called sexology, was drummed up to invent us (though it's true they did a lot of inventing, and not just for us). Basically, the sexologists invented us so the politicians could legislate us. To be invented by sexology was to be considered different and potentially dangerous. One of the sexologists, Havelock Ellis—a man of radical reputation and generally liberal character, so flexible as to be immovable—was most influential in our invention. And, being a typical creator, he tried to make us in his own image.[8]

He said that real teddy bears are like men, thereby propagating the most common stereotype used to distinguish us: the butch lesbian, also known as bulldagger, bulldyke, or just plain butch. A man in a woman's body, so to speak. A mismatch which could only be formulated through the static separation and enforced interdependence of women and men, and of masculinity and femininity. Incredible that the space between women, known only to women, must be so immediately usurped, used instead for a description of perverse masculinity. Sometimes designated as a third sex, we are parted from normalcy in heredity. Nature's way of saying "Oops."

But, beware! According to this theory, not all lesbians are real lesbians. Some have acquired lesbianism—collecting it like old bottles or being infected by it in a public washroom. They are straight women in disguise, or misguided. They can be saved—preferably with appropriate donations to the field of psychological research and therapy.

There was a catch to all this, however. The real lesbians were always getting together with the fake lesbians and confusing everybody. Therefore, rather than have everybody confused, it was decided that only lesbians should be confused. That's a problem with science: it's forever mistaking fuzziness for confusion. As my bearfriend concluded, "If we're different from other people, other women, and each other, then it's true we must be different, but not necessarily quite so often alone."

She continued, "Teddy bears, for example, live in icebergs and not always alone. They live in the centre of an iceberg just below the water line. In accordance with the temperature, the iceberg takes on or loses more ice. Concurrently, the teddies' fur grows longer or falls out. In this way, we can always approximate the temperature outside and dress accordingly. One possible explanation for the comfortable clothes."

"I am central to my iceberg," she said, "but what does this furriness, this invisible movement, this constant playing of boundaries mean in such a place? What basis of knowledge? What of communication and meaning? Whose reality?" She paused here, sighing as a tremor shook her body. "Teddy bears," she continued, "are the only ones who can live in this frigid environment because we are warm and furry."

We agreed to meet that Saturday night at the "Sand Bar," a place where lots of bears hung out a lot of the time. It was said that the "Sand Bar" was named for its remarkable ability to stay afloat. It was certainly beneath street level. Nevertheless, in this place I was destined to learn how to play pool and to dance.

When she and I got together there, I was spending a lot of energy trying to dance and she was spending very little energy playing pool. When we sat down together with drinks before us, she asked me how I liked it.

"It feels like coming home," I replied.

She laughed, "Cheap rent anyway."

"No, really," I insisted, "I can be myself here. I don't have to pretend."

"So many lies," she said, "it goes on and on. Look at us teddy bears. Here we are being so cute and cuddly, and they go and name us after a U.S. president whose favourite sport was bear hunting. It's the basic contradiction which plays through us all, through all our trying to understand this...," she threw out her arms, indicating the air around us, "...this place."

In the bar it seemed an obscene gesture. A kind of violation. "Let's go play some video games," I suggested.

She countered, "Let's go dance."

As we strode up to the dance floor, the conversation around us died. "Keep going," she said. When I reached the dance floor and turned around, I saw two cops walking in. Two male military types striding past tables of teddy bears; an incongruous sight. Moving my feet as best I could, I looked over questioningly at her.

She leaned towards me, still dancing, and yelled in my ear—a feat which, to this day, I consider astounding—"In for their weekly drink," she said wryly, "Freedom in disguise, always takes a bribe."

"But what about us?" I said, raising my voice above the music, pretending to dance. "What we have? It isn't like that. It's like a dream of what's possible. In a place of possibility there are so many borders and so many dreams. And even in this place. You can feel it here too."

We stopped dancing. "I live in a box," she said.

"I unwrapped you."

"This place is a wombroom," she continued, "but it's only partly real."

"But you are the teacher!" I was yelling at her now.

"That's right, I live in an iceberg. Who are you to be thinking that's all right, or even really different? What makes you so sure it will sometime blow away?"

"What makes you think it won't?"

"Look, all I'm telling you is that even when you know it, when you call it by its name, it still won't go away. It only moves over a fraction, so the light's hitting it just a tiny bit differently. Sometimes it means that you get to be just a little more honest and a little less safe. The basic contradiction remains untouched, indifferent, intransigent."

"But then, does nothing every change?"

"Change is rhythm. It happens when the silence speaks music."

The song had ended and we parted our ways. As the evening ended, we came together again. Walking towards the door, she turned and pointed back the way we had come.

"See that couple over there? Don't they look the way that guy Havelock Ellis described them?"

"You mean one's a fake?"

"Well, I wouldn't be saying anything about that. If she or she says that she is what she is, I wouldn't do anything but believe her and her."

"But then those over there aren't like her and her," I observed.

"Yes, but don't you know that in science, if a couple of datas don't fit, you can see fit to pretend they don't exist? For the sake of the seamlessness of science."

"So what's the truth of the matter?"

"The truth is that the butch is a writer, not doing very well at it, I'm afraid, and the femme works in construction and teaches self-defence. You figure it out."

"Hmmm," I said musingly, "There used to be a lot of butch-femme couples at one time, but people now just figure they were role-playing. Doing what the scientists told them to do. But they sure were loud in their playing. Almost everybody heard them at one time or another, heard them in their ways of being. They told it in their ways of knowing. Even we who hadn't been born then, we heard them."

"Yes," she commented, "they played their different games, trusted that this was what they were doing, and understood each other quite well. When night fell, they played the loudest. And sometimes this meant trouble for them."[9]

She continued, "Living through difference, under hatred... isn't that really what we're working for, the freedom to love? To be connected in ways that have meaning? It's easy to hate, or to disappear, but we have given too much already to think we can get away with nothing, to not let each other be, knowing we are being. And that's what we've always done, break boundaries by living in them, through them. We take the tools forged for other hands and use them to our own purpose. Weapons used against us are melted down and remade. The only way to fight hypocrisy and ignorance is with paradox and laughter."

"And they say we are mirrors: teddy bears and lesbians. But what else could we seem to each other in a seamless place? It's true we're always struggling like that. Mirrors are always looking both ways."

We walked out the door of the bar and into the cool, summer night air. Before us, a group stood in the street talking. Outlines in the dimly lit night. Vagire was slipping an arm into her jacket as we started on our way. "How long does it take to...?"

Before she could finish, the street exploded with shouts. I looked towards the noise where the group had stood in the streets. A whirling mass of fighting bodies met my eyes. I looked over at Vagire. A low moan had started from her and she hopped from foot to foot, the pitch of her voice rising. I reached out and grabbed her jacket. After a few seconds, I let her go. In a moment she had disappeared into the mayhem and I lost sight of her.

The fight was over in seconds. One group just ran off down the street leaving the other to themselves. I ran across the street to where two women were lying. Some others, Vagire among them, were with the first woman. I and one other reached the second almost simultaneously. She lay there sobbing convulsively. I felt her frustration, despair, futile anger. The noise she made was barely human. A rising and falling death cry tearing down my mind. Then it rose into one long steady cry, louder. She started hitting her head viciously on the curb. Thud, thud. It hit twice before I could get my hand between her head and the concrete. I remember it sounded like a baseball hitting a glove. The third time her head came down on my hand. I grabbed her with my other hand.

At the same moment, a woman ran up. "What the hell are you doing, Sherri? Stop that! Don't be stupid!" She stopped momentarily beside the woman and waited until she calmed down. Then she went to check on the second woman.

A few minutes later, with no sound, Sherri started hitting her head again. As we held her, her friend yelled over from where she was. Sherri stopped struggling and her crying finally started.

I glanced up at Vagire. She was there, by the other woman, just a short distance away. She was watching me. In her eyes, she looked lost. I felt it too, felt useless against the sounds around us. The absence of violence was no mercy.

Someone else had brought a car up and Sherri and her two friends left. Vagire was standing beside me as we watched them leave.

"I just went in and grabbed this guy," she said, pointing at where she had been fighting. "I just pushed him back and said: 'You don't ever hit a woman.' I think I surprised the hell out of him."

The rest of the women stood around us. I began to hear their voices, too. "Fucking gaybashers, fucking assholes." The anger was rising as the shock began to wear off. We walked down the street in a group. Behind us, two gay men ran up. Holding out a piece of paper, one of them said, "Karen wrote down all the information here. Will one of you call the cops and report this?"

At first no one appeared to hear him. He looked startled for a minute by this state of affairs but recovered quickly. "Hey now, girls, settle down. Just calm down now," he said.

"Why don't you call the cops?" one woman asked impatiently.

"I can't use my name. Come on, which one of you will take this?"

He held the paper out. It floated there in the middle of the circle, all eyes looking on it. No one spoke.

Notes

1. I would like to thank Jody Berland, Barb Freeman, Bonnie Ferguson, and Nicole Laviolette for their assistance with this paper.
2. From a lecture on "Negotiation Within the Family, now that Women are Becoming 'Equal'." It was given at the "Program in Human Sexuality," held at a "highly

influential and respected' centre for sex research in the United States. During this conference, input by gay and lesbian participants was shunted aside on the basis that it destroyed the level of trust needed to maintain an atmosphere of openness and safety. Quoted in: Carole S. Vance, "Gender Systems, Ideology, and Sex Research," in Ann Snitow, Christine Stansell and Sharon Thompson (eds.), *Powers of Desire: The Politics of Sexuality*. New York: Monthly Review Press, 1983: 377.

3. According to an Armed Forces report, the number discharged from the Armed Forces on the basis of homosexuality was 37 in 1981, 45 in 1982, 44 in 1983, and 38 in 1984. The Commissioner of the RCMP, R.H. Simmonds, in articulating the justifications for the exclusion of homosexuals from his organization, said: ". . . there are few members of any police organization that are comfortable at this point in history with people of that persuasion in their midst." Cited in the *Equality Rights Committee Minutes*, 18:32 and 6:8 respectively.

Darl Wood, a lesbian discharged from the Armed Forces questions: "If security is the main reason for not recruiting or retaining homosexuals in the services, as we are lead to believe, why is security not the focus of their investigations and interrogations? The abuse we endured instead was literally hours of voyeuristic harassment for us to reveal the intimate details of our sex lives. For example, some of the questions that were asked of me were: Who have I had sex with? What did we do to each other? Did we engage in oral sex? When was the first time I had sex with a woman? Where did we go? Who else knew? It went on and on . . . questions about my sex life and threats. They constantly tried to force me to reveal other people I suspected of being lesbian. I was warned it would be better for me to tell them then–they would hate to have it come out later — if I knew someone. One woman shared her story with me. . . After months of harassment and twelve gruelling hours of mental abuse in their interrogations, they finally did break her down with the promise that she would not be released if she signed a statement admitting she was gay. They cannot even bring themselves to use the term 'lesbian'. " Cited in the *Equality Rights Committee Minutes*, 14:38-39.

4. Virginia Woolf, *A Room of One's Own*. Middlesex: Penguin Books, 1975: 25-26.

5. George Hancocks, "The Successful Marketing of a Bear," in *Canadian Dimensions*, September/October, 1987: 17-18.

6. "Lichtenstein's and Dickenson's claims that lesbians have large clitorises are directly contradicted by Havelock Ellis's contention that they usually have small clitorises; and all three are contradicted by Henry who insists that lesbians have both over- and underdeveloped labias and clitorises." ". . . aetiologies (for homosexuality) popularly advanced in up-to-date psychiatric literature (include) 77 variables, and . . . they are all phrased in terms of the 'faults, flaws and follies that lead people to be homosexuals'." Quoted in: Malcolm Macourt (ed.), *Towards a Theology of Gay Liberation*. London: SCM Press Ltd., 1977: 28-29.

7. Peter Bull, *The Teddy Bear Book*. New York: Random House, 1969: 36.

8. See: Carrol Smith-Rosenberg, "The New Woman as Androgyne: Social Disorder and Gender Crisis, 1870-1935," in *Disorderly Conduct: Visions of Gender in Victorian America*. New York: Oxford University Press, 1985.

9. See: Joan Nestle, "Butch-Femme Relationships: Sexual Courage in the 1950s," in *A Restricted Country*. New York: Firebrand Books, 1987.

References
Thanks are due to Cathy Jones for the use of the bibliography from her unpublished manuscript, "Remaking Love: Sexology and the Social Construction of Lesbianism, 1870-1920." Carleton University, 1988.

Bernikow, Louise, 1980. *Among Women*. Toronto: Fitzhenry & Whiteside Ltd.

Bland, Lucy, 1983. "Purity, Motherhood, Pleasure or Threat? Definitions of Female Sexuality 1900-1970's," in S. Cartledge and J. Ryan (eds.), *Sex & Love: New Thoughts on Old Contradictions*. London: The Women's Press.

Boswell, John, 1982-83. "Revolutions, Universals and Sexual Categories," pp. 58-59 in *Salmagundi*.

Brown, Rita Mae, 1972. "Take a Lesbian to Lunch," in K. Jay and A. Young (eds.), *Out of the Closets: Voices from Gay Liberation*. USA: Douglas Books.

Browne, Stella, 1977. "The Sexual Variety and Variability among Women and their bearing upon Social Reconstruction," reprinted in Sheila Rowbotham, *A New World for Women: Stella Browne-Socialist Feminist*. London: Pluto Press.

Bull, Peter, 1969. *The Teddy Bear*. New York: Random House.

Cook, Blanche Weisen, 1979. "'Women Alone Stir My Imagination': Lesbianism and the Cultural Tradition," pp. 718-739 in *SIGNS* 4(4).

Cruikshank, Margaret (ed.), *Lesbian Studies: Present and Future*. New York: The Feminist Press.

D'Emilio, John, 1983. *Sexual Politics, Sexual Communities: The Making of a Homosexual Minority in the United States 1940-1970*. Chicago and London: The University of Chicago Press.

Ellis, Havelock, and J.A. Symonds, 1975. *Sexual Inversion*. Reprinted. New York: Arno Press.

Equality Rights Committee Minutes of Proceedings and Evidence, 1985. Patrick Boyer, Chairman.

Faber, Doris, 1980. *The Life of Lorena Hickock, E.R.'s Friend*. New York: Morrow.

Faderman, Lillian, 1981. *Surpassing the Love of Men: Romantic Friendship and Love Between Women from the Renaissance to the Present*. New York: Morrow.

Foucault, Michel, 1978. *The History of Sexuality, I-III*. New York: Pantheon Books.

Freedman, E., B. Gelpi, S. Johnson, and K. Weston (eds.), 1985. *The Lesbian Issue: Essays from SIGNS*. Chicago and London: University of Chicago Press.

Grahn, Judy, 1978. *The Work of a Common Woman*. New York: The Crossing Press.

——, 1984. *Another Mothertongue: Gay Words, Gay Worlds*. Boston: Beacon Press.

Hancocks, George, 1987. "The Successful Marketing of a Bear," *Canadian Dimensions* (September/October): 17-18.

Harris, Bertha, 1973. "The More Profound Nationality of their Lesbianism: Lesbian Society in Paris in the 1920's," *Amazon Expedition*. New York: Times Change Press.

Hartman, Mary S., and L. Banner (eds.), 1974. *Clio's Consciousness Raised: New Perspectives on the History of Women*. New York, Hagerstown, San Francisco, London.

Hewitt, Nancy A., 1983. "Beyond the Search for Sisterhood: American Women's History in the 1980s," *Social History* 10(3): 299-321.

Hull, Gloria T., Patricia Bell Scott, and Barbara Smith, (eds.), 1982. *But Some of Us Are Brave*. New York: The Feminist Press, 1982.

Jeffreys, Sheila, 1985. *The Spinster and Her Enemies: Feminism and Sexuality, 1870-*

1930. London: Pandora.

Katz, Jonathan (ed.), 1978. *Gay American History: Lesbians and Gay Men in the USA*. New York: Avon.

——, 1983. *Gay/Lesbian Almanac: A New Documentary*. New York: Harper & Row.

Kinsman, Gary, 1987. *The Regulation of Desire: Sexuality in Canada*. Montreal: Black Rose Books.

Lorde, Audre, 1982. *Zami: A New Spelling of My Name*. New York: The Crossing Press.

——, 1982. *Sister Outsider*. New York: The Crossing Press.

Macourt, Malcolm (ed.), 1977. *Towards a Theology of Gay Liberation*. London: SCM Press.

Marks, Elaine, and Isabelle de Courtivron (eds.), 1981. *New French Feminisms*. New York: Schocken Books.

Morago, Cherrie, and Gloria Angaldua (eds.), 1983. *This Bridge Called My Back*. New York: Kitchen Table.

Mosse, George, 1982. "Nationalism and Respectability: Normal and Abnormal Sexuality in the Nineteenth Century," *Journal of Contemporary History* 17(2).

Nestle, Joan, 1987. *A Restricted Country*. New York: Firebrand Books.

Radicalesbians, 1972. "The Woman-Identified-Woman," in K. Jay and A. Young (eds.), *Out of the Streets: Voices of Gay Liberation*. USA: Douglas Books.

Rich, Adrienne, 1979. *On Lies, Secrets and Silence*. New York: W.W. Norton & Co.

——, 1980. "Compulsory Heterosexuality and Lesbian Existence," *SIGNS* 5(4): 631-660.

Ruehl, Sonja, 1982. "Inverts and Experts: Radclyffe Hall and the Lesbian Identity," in R. Coward (ed.), *Feminism, Culture and Politics*. London: Lawrence and Wishart.

——, 1983. "Sexual Theory and Practice: Another Double Standard," in S. Cartledge and J. Ryan (eds.), *Sex & Love: New Thoughts on Old Contradictions*. London: The Women's Press.

Smith, Barbara, 1979. "Notes for Yet Another Paper on Black Feminism, Or Will The Real Enemy Please Stand Up," pp. 123-127 in *Conditions Five, the Black Women's Issue*.

—— (ed.), 1983. *Home Girls*. New York: Kitchen Table.

Smith-Rosenberg, Carroll, 1975. "The Female World of Love and Ritual: Relations Between Women in Nineteenth-Century America," *SIGNS* 1(1): 1-29.

——, 1985. *Disorderly Conduct: Visions of Gender in Victorian America*. New York: Oxford University Press.

Snitow, Ann, Christine Stansell, and Sharon Thompson (eds.), 1983. *Powers of Desire: The Politics of Sexuality*. New York: Monthly Review Press.

Steiner, na., "In Lieu of a Preface," pp. 58-59 in *Salmagundi*, 1982-1983.

Vance, Carol S., 1984. *Pleasure and Danger: Exploring Female Sexuality*. Boston: Routledge & Kegan Paul.

Vicinus, Martha, 1982. "Sexuality and Power: A Review of Current Work in the History of Sexuality," *Feminist Studies* 8: 147-151.

——, 1984. *Independent Women: Work and Community for Single Women, 1850-1920*. Chicago: University of Chicago Press.

Weeks, Jeffrey, 1977. *Coming Out: Homosexual Politics in Britain, from the Nineteenth Century to the Present*. London: Quartet Books.

——, 1981. *Sex, Politics and Society: The Regulation of Sexuality since 1800*. London: Longman.

——, 1981. "Discourse, Desire, and Sexual Deviance: Some Problems in a History of Homosexuality," in K. Plummer (ed.), *The Making of the Modern Homosexual*. London: Hutchinson & Co.

Chapter 21

Personal and Political Conflicts as a Woman and as a Feminist
Sue Sorrell

It was not an easy exercise to review the past five years of my life, that span of time since I first encountered feminism.[1] The more I explored those years, the more anxious I became. It seemed more important to locate the source(s) of this anxiety than (temporarily?) to shelve it in favour of some sort of broad review. After considerable reflection, I concluded that my anxiety was integrally related to four conflicts which have emerged since my initial exposure to feminism. All four represent personal conflicts: three I have struggled with throughout the past five years, and one which emerged only a couple of years ago but has become increasingly pressing. While I suggest that all of these conflicts are "feminist-specific," I do not suggest they are common to all feminists. Hence, this discussion may not, in any way, be generalizable beyond myself.

Fear of Intimacy and Loss of Self

It is difficult to decide which conflict to discuss first, as all are connected. However, I will begin with the one I find the most "shocking." First a little background... A year ago I decided to become a volunteer at the women's centre where I attend university. One of the first exercises we do at each volunteer training session is referred to as the "click of feminism." Each member of the group is asked to try to recall a specific event in her life which motivated her toward feminism or to taking the fateful label itself. The instant I was introduced to the exercise, I broke out in a cold sweat and began trembling. I was caught completely off guard. Nobody had ever put this question to me in quite that way. Whenever anyone asked, "Why are you a feminist?" I always responded with a lofty rationale about being fundamentally opposed to all forms of oppression and that, as a woman, feminism seemed to be one of the struggles against such oppression with which I could most closely identify. Clearly this was not a rationale over which I should be having an anxiety attack.

Once I allowed myself to confront my answer to the question, rather than trying desperately to make up a "good" response, I was astonished at what exploded in my mind. My "click" to feminism had occurred four years earlier, the first time I had attended a meeting with other feminists; this was also the very first time I had ever seriously considered the movement at all. A rather sudden conversion, I now realize. What I had found so attractive about feminism was symbolized by the women gathered at this introductory meeting. They all appeared so strong, independent, self-assured, and most importantly, they all talked of feeling fulfilled with or without men in their lives. Not once during my twenty-four years had I ever conceived of being fulfilled outside a relationship with a man. Yet this was more than a novel idea. It presented itself as the ultimate protection against a recent fear that was overwhelming me...a fear of re-losing my self.

About a year before my meeting with these feminists, my husband had drowned in a fishing accident. I think our marriage had been quite typical. Throughout our three-year relationship we put into practice what the minister had only put into words... we two became one and that one was my husband, Brad. I adopted all of his interests: all of his hobbies became my hobbies; all of his friends became my friends, to the exclusion of anyone and anything else. When he died, I felt that I, too, had died. I was completely empty. He seemed to have taken both of us with him. For most of a year I walked around in a body newly glossed up with heavy make-up, blonde curls, and stylish clothing, desperately searching for "things" I could fill it with, things which, combined, I could call "me." My search was backed by a newly created rule by which I was determined to guide my life: once I finally had a "me" again, I would *never again* give it up; i.e., I would never again get so deeply involved with a man that I lost my self. I would erect impermeable barriers.

Yet at the same time, I was terribly lonely, missing the intimacy I had shared with Brad. I was terrified that the loneliness would override my new rule. The "feminism click" exercise revealed to me that my conversion to feminism (and a conversion it was) had been motivated by what I perceived to be its promise of a life of independence from men. This truth landed hard; it was very far from the lofty rationale I had previously put forth. But what was almost more disconcerting was the simultaneous realization that the original terror had not abated at all. I had somehow managed to shelve or effectively disguise a continued, debilitating fear of losing my fragile self in an intimate relationship with a man.

This is, I now realize, one of the battles I have been fighting during this past five years. It explains, to a large degree, the many dead-end relationships I have pursued. It explains why I am unable to establish the degree of intimacy the "lonely me" continues to crave, despite being in a relationship with a man in whom I find no significant faults. Intellectually, I felt I had come to terms with the "lonely me's" insistence on being in a relationship. Carol Gilligan, a feminist educational psychologist, helped me to understand this as a woman; the "lonely me," in her terms, is the "relational me."

Gilligan has built on Nancy Chodorow's work in the area of feminist psychoanalysis and object relations theory. Gilligan argues that the outcome of a girl's early, intimate relationship with her same-sexed parent (i.e., her mother) is an orientation towards relationship, attachment, and interdependence. According to her, girls, and later, women, define themselves in a context of human relationship and judge themselves in terms of their ability to care for others. A consequence of this definition, Gilligan argues, is that female gender identity is threatened by separation: i.e., outside the context of intimate relationships, women tend to experience anxiety and a loss of identity. Yet within such relationships women's orientation to attachment and interdependence often results in the merging of their selves with those with whom they are in relationship.

I learned from reading Gilligan that my own tendency to merge is responsible for my constant fear of re-losing myself in relationships. The part of me terrified of losing the self which I struggled so long and hard to regain is now being heard at a "more conscious" level. I also realize that my experiences as a feminist have established a much less fragile self than existed five years ago, a self I am now likely to surrender to another. Through sharing experiences with many other women, I have gained a clearer understanding of the ways in which patriarchal culture socializes women to believe they cannot be fully human unless they are in relationships with men, relationships in which they have been taught to subsume their needs and identities to those of their male partners.

While the "feminism click" exercise and the months of emotional processing which I have since undergone have put my relationships with men in a new light, they have also provided a new understanding of a relationship I had with a woman lover. This is a bit of a diversion at this point in the story, but it is too important to me to let structure dictate its exclusion. Three years ago, my closest woman friend came out as a lesbian and told me she was in love with me. Flattery and homophobia* battled for primacy, with homophobia initially winning out. After a few months of constantly confronting this homophobia, I was able to overcome it enough for my attraction to Erin to become increasingly sexual. We decided to become lovers. At first it was wonderful. I did not conceive of it ending. Then, for reasons I could not at the time grasp, I became rapidly and increasingly repulsed by her. I remember feeling a desperate need to end the relationship but not being able to provide either of us with a convincing explanation.

Now, looking back, I realize that the thing which literally drove me away from Erin was this same fear of losing myself. I had not considered protecting myself against a woman, in part, no doubt, because I had never before taken intimate relationships between women very seriously. Erin and I had been closest friends; as lovers there was no part of me which she left untouched. Unlike a man, there was no experience with which she could not empathize. We spent every

---

* Homophobia refers to fear and/or hatred of gays and lesbians. In my case, it also involved fear of *being* a lesbian.

spare minute together. Rethinking the relationship causes me to re-experience my panicked determination to flee her, a determination based on a perceived threat to self, a self I felt was increasingly merging with hers. While I realize I have not yet fully conquered homophobia, it is a great relief to realize there was much more behind the demise of our relationship than the fear of being a lesbian. I have renewed hope that a future relationship with a woman need not be disastrous.

My Own Misogyny

The second conflict I have struggled with at a "less-than-conscious" level took on the shape of words during a workshop I attended on working with incest survivors. We were asked to think of aspects of our mothers, and of our relationships with our mothers, which we found unpleasant. Again, the thoughts which rushed forward were not expected.

I realized that what I both loved and hated about my mother were her strengths. These conflicting feelings were related to personality traits of my mother which are not typically associated with women in our culture. My mother has so-called "masculine" strengths. She is very strong, responsible, independent, decisive, opinionated, and principled. My father was, in many ways, the "feminine" partner in their relationship. He was generally very gentle, passive, irresponsible, clingy, indecisive, and wary of conflict. As I grew up, I strived to emulate my mother. What I realized I had learned from her was to despise weakness. For example, six weeks after my husband drowned, she walked into my bedroom, announced that she had left me to mourn for long enough, and it was now time to get off my ass, remember I was a Sorrell, and stop feeling sorry for myself. I did as I was told.

The weaknesses I came to despise were those deemed intrinsically female, i.e., those characteristics possessed by my father but culturally associated with women. I came to hate and desperately try to hide these weaknesses in myself. A few years ago I was amazed to discover that my mother has the same so-called "feminine weaknesses" as I do and has spent much of her own life trying to deny them. The legacy of my relationship with my mother has been not only to despise my own "womanliness," but to also have very little tolerance for the "feminine weaknesses" in other women. It came as a shock to me at the incest workshop to realize that I, too, am misogynist. Suddenly I understood, in horror, why I was so impatient with the battered women I worked with who seemed "unwilling" to assert themselves, to strike out on their own.

My struggle to emulate my mother has likely been an additional factor in my attraction to feminism, with the movement's association with strong, independent, decisive women; the sort of woman my mother respects and the sort of woman I want to be seen as. Yet, ironically, this attraction is located in a sort of misogyny, a hatred of "femininity," a hatred of my "feminine" self, or rather, those qualities culturally assigned to women which have in turn been used to "prove" women's inferiority and justify women's oppression. Since the workshop I have been trying to understand why my mother hid her "weaknesses" and get to know her and love her as both a strong and vulnerable woman. In the process, I am also working at loving and giving expression to my own vulnerabilities. An outcome of this has been a very gradual increase in tolerance for women however they are. I attempt, on more than an intellectual level, to regard all women largely as products of their cultural and familial experiences. I also find myself taking much more seriously radical feminists' insistence on reinterpreting so-called feminine qualities as strengths and working towards socializing both sexes to possess these qualities rather than assuming inherent "superiority" of traditional male qualities. This is not to suggest that everything associated with femininity is inherently superior, but rather that qualities such as co-operativeness, nurturance, interdependency, and a contextualized orientation towards decision-making may be preferable to competitiveness, aggressiveness, individualism, and abstraction.

Fear of Making Value Judgments

The third conflict is the one which emerged only a few years ago and which has taken on increasing importance in the past few months. I refer to it as a fear of taking responsibility for my own values, beliefs, ideas, and actions, which, not surprisingly, leads to reluctance to assert my position on issues, to make judgments, and to take actions. I still manage to do all of these things and appear decisive in the process. However, on the inside I am struggling to remain above a tide of uncertainty.

When I earlier stated that I had been converted to feminism, I was referring to conversion in the "irrational" sense associated with religion or faith. I suppose because feminism represented to me a sort of salvation, along with a desperately sought-after explanation for WHY, I did not bother to question particular ideas or actions I encountered. As long as it was legitimized by the label feminist, I accepted it as true. I was not aware of the nature of my relationship to feminism until I was confronted with an unwanted pregnancy. I sincerely do not recall any "conscious" deliberation following the announcement that the pregnancy test was positive. It was as if there were a feminist equation: if unwanted pregnancy, then abortion. When the father asked me what I wanted to do about the pregnancy, I announced that of course I would have it aborted. I did not allow any room for discussion, defining as ludicrous any alternatives he presented. Naïvely, I had not expected any opposition to my decision.

My appointment with a general practitioner, necessary for referral to a gynecologist, was my first encounter with an opposing view. He treated me with contempt, informing me with a look of repulsion that he disapproved of what I was doing. The guilt began to emerge. Yet it was not a guilt which stemmed from a personally-held belief that what I was doing was actually morally wrong. Rather, the guilt seemed to be more of a reaction to the emergent realization that what I was doing was *seen* to be morally wrong by others in my present social context. This doctor, a person with social prestige, saw me as a horrible, selfish person and I did not want to be seen, or to see myself, as that kind of person.

During the two weeks before the scheduled surgery, the troubled feelings and the new and unexpected doubts grew and grew. I informed my mother of my decision. She said she understood but asked me not to tell anybody else because they would not approve. In the hospital I was put on the maternity ward, two doors away from the nursery. I could hear the newborns crying and the parents gushing over them. The nurses were very cold; two of the three would not even speak to me. Finally, the father, who had accompanied me only under duress, was very removed and left early the next morning. I did not hear from him for four weeks.

By this time I was filled with self-loathing, all-consumed by this context-inspired guilt. However, instead of trying to understand why I had decided upon abortion and trying to accept my decision, I directed all my anger at feminism. I blamed feminism for not giving me any other option and for not telling me I would feel this way; that having an abortion was actually a very selfish thing to do. I felt cheated, lied to. I decided I would not be a feminist any longer. However, I quickly realized that this would be no simple feat.

During the previous two years of looking at the world through feminist glasses, I had come to see sexism in every aspect of our society. I could not simply close my eyes to it. It became clear that I could not easily detach myself from past experiences and will myself to make uninhibited choices. I soon realized that feminism was not the problem: the problem was that I had unquestionably adopted all of what I perceived to be this objectively "true," homogeneous, feminist value system, in the manner of Simone de Beauvoir's "serious (wo)man" (de Beauvoir, 1948, 46).

According to de Beauvoir, the serious woman is one who considers values as ready-made things. In the presence of anxiety and doubt, the serious woman is afraid to answer the questions which have evoked these feelings of uncertainty. Many questions emerged following the death of my husband, and fear, anxiety, and doubt certainly characterized the state I was in when introduced to feminism. In addition, de Beauvoir's serious woman is concerned less with the object she prefers to her "free" self (in my case, feminism) than with being able to lose herself in this object. As mentioned earlier, when I attended my first feminist meeting, I was searching for protection from re-losing myself in relationships with other men. I have come to realize that because I had never questioned anything, or critically picked and chosen from varying feminist values and ideas, I had not taken responsibility for any of these values. I had not defined them as my own.

I was not familiar with de Beauvoir's discussion of the serious woman when

I was re-evaluating my feminism. Yet, while hers are not the concepts I employed during this process, I have since found them useful for explaining both the relationship I had to feminism and the nature of the process through which I established a new and more critical relationship. I began the painful reassessment of all of my feminist beliefs and values and exploration of those of other feminists, gradually discarding those I did not accept and owning those I did. The most painful issue was abortion. I had to accept that I had the abortion because I believed it to be the best thing to do at the time and that I blamed feminism because I could not bear to see myself as the uncaring, selfish woman that others saw me as. As a woman, I feel I have thoroughly internalized the taboo against female selfishness to such a degree that it has generally been easier to sacrifice myself than see myself as selfish.

Despite this process of re-evaluating values, beliefs, and attitudes, which is ever on-going, I still have difficulty taking responsibility for my particular values, beliefs, and attitudes. This is likely related, in part, to my reluctance to act "selfishly." To purposefully change one's values and (especially) to act on them, is to be selfish if one is a woman: as women we are taught to be accepting and to place others' concerns above our own. I think my difficulty with taking this responsibility is also related to other aspects of being female. I have been socialized to believe that women's ideas are inherently less worthy than men's and are best left unexpressed. As I mentioned, I have not escaped misogyny. I feel it is thus doubly difficult for me to take feminist stands; first of all, these are stands I hold as a (inferior) woman and, second, these are stands which have been formulated by other (inferior) women. On an intellectual level I am certain that women's ideas are not inherently inferior to those of men, but at a deeper level of "self" I am much less certain.

Since reading Sartre, the process of re-evaluating and taking responsibility for my own values has been stepped up. Unfortunately, the consequence has been even greater hesitancy in both my thinking and my actions. According to Sartre, because there is no God and therefore no source of absolute truth, there is nothing either inside or outside a person on which she can depend with any degree of certainty. If God does not exist, we are not provided with any values or commands that could legitimize our behaviour. Hence we must recognize that we, as people, are the source of the values we hold and must take responsibility for our actions based on these values.

While I did not need to read Sartre to be convinced of the non-existence of God, I had not seriously considered the consequences of there being no source of absolute truth; I had not accepted that I, alone, have to justify my particular values and behaviours to both myself and others around me. The realization that I am the ultimate source of justification for every position or action I take can be immobilizing. As a woman, I have been taught that I am a poor judge of anything and should defer to the judgements of my superiors (men). Yet, having accepted that there are no externally justified truths, I also have to accept that there is no one to defer to. While to some degree I find this realization personally empowering, at this point in the process of owning my ideas the weight of the responsibility often holds greater sway. Just as I could not suddenly stop seeing the world as sexist, I cannot suddenly transcend all of my past socialization.

I have found it somewhat difficult to abandon the notion that there are no absolute principles by which I can guide my beliefs and actions. When "pushed into a corner," I frequently find myself justifying my position by reference to particular principles, yet I have also come to realize that those principles are my own and support my vision of the "good society." I know I have to work consistently at ridding my self of notions of female inferiority, at coming to accept that my ideas are not inherently more or less valuable than other peoples' (men's) and asserting them with more confidence. This exercise is not only difficult for reasons of sex, but also complicated by its situation within a feminist framework, a political framework which challenges every aspect of the status quo. It is not easy to maintain a particular perspective on the world when the vast majority of people see it in a very different way.

Being a "Positioned" Subject

My existence as a member of a political minority, or more particularly my constant effort to remain "true" to my unpopular political perspective, is the fourth conflict I have identified as ongoing through my years in the movement. It is related to my difficulty with taking responsibility for my own values, beliefs, etc., but is not identical to that conflict. Sometimes, away from the sanctuary of like-minded people, I begin to feel very anxious. In a classroom where a professor makes a sexist comment, or presents androcentric paradigms* as the only legitimate perspectives in his/her discipline and I challenge his/her assertion, I increasingly find myself looking straight ahead or downward, rather than facing the all-too-familiar looks of aggravation, contempt, even hatred. Sighs and groans are more difficult to avoid.

Despite attempts to gain confidence about my challenge, I find myself struggling against a desire to defer to the "cult of expertise," and a nagging insistence that all these people cannot be "wrong." I find it is much easier to take Women's Studies courses than to tolerate the anxiety and tension of battling to make feminist inroads in "men's studies," although I often feel this is a cop-out.

The experience which best exemplifies this conflict of trying to remain "who I am," especially around groups of people who deny my "reality," occurred at a recent xmas, when my partner and I flew home to spend eight days with our families and old high school friends. My partner's family had actually agreed among themselves, prior to our arrival, that they would not talk to us

---

* Paradigms based on men, which take 'man' as the norm of humanity.

about certain topics, and they immediately changed the subject when either of us introduced anything remotely controversial. It was like our entire existences were being denied.

My family pretends not to hear me when I say something they find "absurd." They have decided that my politics are a manifestation of the bitterness I feel over losing my husband. Hence it was not surprising that the only aspect of my life they were willing to discuss was my relationship with my (thankfully) male partner. Old high school friends insist on relating to me as though we have continued since high school to have essentially similar experiences. After four or five days of being denied, and of being cast in a role I no longer identified with, I began to feel an incredibly frightening sense of anomie. I felt I was losing my grip on who I was and was succumbing to the role everyone else thought was more appropriate, more familiar. By the end of the eight-day visit, I was consumed by anxiety. When we reached the city where I had attended university, and I was re-united with friends with whom I had grown politically, I experienced an incredible sense of being "recognized," accompanied by a powerful resurgence of "me."

This whole experience remained classified under "must get back to later when I have a lot more time" until I read Sartre. I am not certain I read him correctly, or if his words were conveniently applicable to an experience that resurged and demanded attention. How I came to understand this experience relates to what Sartre had to say about being a positioned subject, along with other positioned subjects, in a context of "inter-subjectivity" in which all give to each other an identity.

According to Sartre, a person becomes aware of herself, of who she is, only in a context inhabited by other social beings. At the time when this awareness of herself occurs, Sartre maintains, she is not only simultaneously aware of the presence of these others, but recognizes that her existence, and any knowledge she can have of herself, is dependent upon their presence. She recognizes that she cannot be anything unless others recognize her as such. Hence, according to Sartre, she at once finds herself in a world of "inter-subjectivity." I felt this at xmas, in particular, and I feel it when I am alone among people with radically different "realities" in general: they begin to "give" me an identity in conflict with the one "given to me" in interactions with politically left and/or feminist people. Perhaps because I was out of my "element" for an extended period of time at xmas, the experience of changing "form" was more acutely felt.

The difficulty in remaining "true" to the "me" I respect may also be described as a desire to get along with people, to minimize conflict, to nurture rather than impede relationship. Gilligan helped me to understand the source of this anxiety. She explains how women's orientation towards relationship is embedded in an "ethic of care." Gilligan argues that women's approach to conflict involves a desire to avoid violence, to arrive at a resolution that will produce the least amount of hurt for others, and which will not destroy the relationship. In doing so, Gilligan maintains, women often find it easier to sacrifice their own needs to those of others rather than risk the relationship itself.

While Gilligan helped me to understand why I tend to avoid conflicts, her prescribed method of transcending this self-sacrificing approach is somewhat more difficult to implement, i.e., recognizing the importance of my own needs and the value of my own ideas while attempting to minimize the undesirable consequences of conflicts. In other words, Gilligan sees the possibility for a woman to act on her desire to assert herself while recognizing the needs of others and sustaining the relationship. My difficulty with this approach has already been explored with regard to my hesitancy to accept responsibility for my ideas and actions. I am working towards a "deepening" of what is now only a surface acceptance of Gilligan's views on this matter.

This concludes my discussion of the four primary sources of anxiety which interfered when I attempted to survey my past five years as a feminist. In many ways these conflicts, and their histories, combine to create a picture of what these years have involved. I realize they will inform all of my future experiences in ways which vary with the point I am at in the process of their resolution. I don't ever expect to have conquered all of these "fears," but I do expect to work with them in altering forms, towards transforming them into conflicts which are both more manageable and more productive.

Notes

1. This essay was written in 1988, and since that time this writer's reflections upon and practices of feminism have developed and, to some extent, changed. While she supports the publication of this article, it would be somewhat different were it to be written now.

References

Chodorow, Nancy, 1979. *The Reproduction of Mothering: Psychoanalysis and the Sociology of Gender*. Berkeley: University of California Press.

Cisler, Lucinda, 1970. "Unfinished Business: Birth Control and Women's Liberation," in Robin Morgan (ed.), *Sisterhood is Powerful*. New York: Vintage Books.

de Beauvoir, Simone, 1948. *The Ethics of Ambiguity*. Secaucus, N.J.: Citadel Press.

Eichenbaum, Luise, and Susie Orbach, 1983. *Understanding Women: A Feminist Psychoanalytic Approach*. New York: Basic Books, Inc.

Fritz, Leah, 1982. "Abortion: A Woman's Right to Live," in Pam McAllister (ed.), *Reweaving the Web of Life: Feminism and Non-Violence*. Philadelphia: New Society Publishers.

Gilligan, Carol, 1982. *In A Different Voice: Psychological Theory and Women's Development*. Cambridge, Mass.: Harvard University Press.

Miller, Jean Baker, 1976. *Toward a New Psychology of Women*. Boston: Beacon Press.

Pelrine, Eleanor Wright, 1977. *Abortion in Canada*. Toronto: New Press.

Rifkin, Janet, 1981. "Mediation From a Feminist Perspective: Promise and Problems," *Journal of Law and Inequality* 2: 21-31.
Sartre, Jean Paul, 1948. *Existentialism and Humanism*. London: Methuen and Co. Ltd.

Chapter 22

Fighting Two Worlds
Judy Brundige and Joy Fedorick
in conversation with Geraldine Finn.

I spoke to Judy Brundige and Joy Fedorick at the annual conference of the Ontario Native Women's Association, held in Toronto in June 1988. At the time, Judy and Joy were, respectively, Co-ordinator of the Annual Assembly and Executive Director of the Ontario Native Women's Association.

I told them about this book, *Limited Edition,* and asked if they would like to contribute their voices to the collection, specifically their thoughts on and experience of the relationship between the Canadian women's movement ("white" feminism) and the movement of Native women and their particular concerns. They had a lot to say and I came away with more than four hours of taped conversation. What follows is a condensation and selection of their comments, sometimes in their own words, sometimes in mine, which I hope does justice to the richness and complexity of their thoughts and experience as well as to the areas of convergence and difference between them. Judy spoke to me first that day, then Joy, so I follow that sequence here.

Judy

Judy considers herself a traditional Native woman, though she has not always thought of herself in this way. She began by telling me her story. She spent her early life in Dryden, Manitoba, where she lived with her adopted parents. They were not Native and Judy did not really meet Native people until she went to high school where the kids from the reserve called her "apple face" and "white Indian." As she says, she was "fighting two worlds" at the time and though she was a "whiz kid" in school, she ended up dropping out and moving to Winnipeg where she met more Native people. With only a grade nine education, she was married (to a non-Native man) and had three children before she was twenty. She lived in the U.S. for a while, where she worked sewing in a factory. During that time people would come to speak to Judy and she would listen. This marked the beginning of a pattern for her: of people talking to her and of personal reflection, which eventually led her back to her Native roots in Canada, and to a more traditional style of life.

We went home with one dollar in our pockets.

After separating from her husband, Judy returned to Canada with her children. She went back to school and eventually on to university. At the same time, she began to work with Native youth, which she continues today. She also became active in treaty negotiations for the Northwestern Ontario region. In the passage that follows, Judy begins by talking about these experiences.

> As a representative for the Western Ontario region I did a lot of travelling to Ottawa at that time. I got into the big thing of, here I am, you know, and I'm going to do all this for the Native women. At that time there were very few Native women in politics. So when I went to conferences and to negotiate with these groups in Ottawa, there were very few of us.
>
> I got up in conferences and made speeches on that specific thing: that women were part of our nation and we, too, should have a voice. There were times when I got almost rude and people turned up their eyes and walked away. Mostly men. Because the only women in the room were the secretaries; that would be it. I would be the only woman sitting at the conference table, and so when I got up to make a speech or to say something, it was sort of: "Who is this lady trying to become?" "Who is she?" So I would do a lot of shouting.

When you were doing that, did you think you were speaking on behalf of Native women in general?

> Yes, I did. Because I was looking at what was happening on the reserves, where Native women were considered second-class citizens. The only time anything was asked of them was when there was something happening on the reserve and they were needed to help, to do the banquet. They never asked your advice if you were a woman; you were never asked to participate other than as workers or helpers and I didn't like that. I thought that the Native women had a lot to offer our society, that we had minds. It was as if they were saying, the Native men are the strong ones, the leaders. You sit back and when we need you we will call on you; but we don't need you right now, so sit back and keep your mouths shut. That upset me because I had been raised differently and knew how to be aggressive. I became aggressive.

Do you mean aggressive or just assertive?

> Well, aggressive to the point where I would bang tables and scream and

holler and want my voice to be heard. Many people did listen and I did get many things started, youth groups where the girls as well as the guys would speak up. I would set up councils where the girls took part. In most councils at that time on the reserve, there were no women involved, only men.

Could you explain a little of what the function of the council is on the reserve?

On the reserve the band council consists of the chief and the councillors, and they make all the decisions about money and programs and whatever is to happen on the reserve. Very few Native bands had women on their councils. I wanted the youths to learn about the council, how it operated, so I started up the council within the youth group. And I had women on that council as well. The boys were not too happy about it, but they agreed.

Did the girls need any persuasion?

Yes, because they had been raised at home to take a back seat. We met every three weeks and once the girls started speaking up, the boys started respecting that, and that the girls do have something to say and that it is valid. Once that had been established there was no problem. *Another* problem cropped up, though: Ojibwa versus Cree, something that still happens within our nations. The only thing I said to the youth was: what are you going to do about me, because I have been raised differently? I have not been raised as a Native, neither Cree nor Ojibwa. I am Ojibwa. I am a Native Indian. I want the same as you do. Instead of sitting here haggling over who's better, Ojibwa or Cree, we should be working together as one, that way we'll get three times as much done. Then they started looking at it that way: Indian first, then whatever tribe you come from, then Canadian.

How important is it for Native people of Canada to consider themselves, or be thought of as Canadians?

This is my personal opinion on that. There are times when it is important to me to be a Canadian. But most of the time, no. I am a Native first. I am Native to my brothers and sisters to the south. I am closer to them than I am to many Canadians. And this is something I have felt for years and years: first I am Native, then the tribe I am from, and then I am Canadian. The Canadian people and the Canadian government have interfered with our culture, our traditions and our values so much, and caused them such hurt that our people have a hard time reconciling themselves to what has happened. And there are so many areas where we continue to be overlooked. I think we have much to offer, not only to the non-Native women's movement but to non-Native people as a whole. For instance, our issues are different from those of non-Native women: equal pay, for example, and equality with non-Native men. I don't think I, as a Native woman, am looking for equal pay with Native men. I am looking for recognition from them: to say they will listen to me and come to me if there are things happening; come to me as a Native woman, respect what I have to say and take it into consideration.

You get the idea from books that Native women were downtrodden in the past, that we did not have any say in the structure of our society. In one way that was true, but in another way it wasn't. We were always the strength of our society. Within the band, each individual had a position that was important. Two of the most important parts of the band structure were the elders and the children. The elders because they had the knowledge of years and years of living. They had wisdom and they were the teachers. And the children because they were tomorrow's Natives, the ones who would grow up to be the warriors, the medicine men, the women. And the women had a very important role because they were the ones who guided the children. The woman gave birth to the child and raised the child. She also held the household together. The whole household was the responsibility of the woman. Men had no say whatsoever within that household. She tore down the tepee whenever they had to move; she did the cooking... and everything in the household. Women became medicine "men" and shamans. And they also became elders and were looked upon for guidance.

So, when you look at it, things haven't changed that much for the Native woman. We are still the backbone of our society. A Native man said to me a few years ago: "Judy, I went through those last years!" I was looking at him and wondering what he was talking about. "You know, we Native people have to start realizing the strength of our Native women." It was strange to hear him saying this because he was a man in his mid-fifties and had gone through that macho-type Indian man era and I figured he was still there. He went on: "When the non-Native people put us on the reserves and took everything away and then said to us, 'Now, go out and drink,' the Native men went haywire. But who stayed and held the family structure together and kept the household? The Native woman. When the government came in and put us on reserves, the one who was hurt the most, who lost the most, was the Native man. His purpose was obliterated. He was no longer the breadwinner, so to speak, of the household. The white man had taken that away and never taught him how to adjust to it. For him, there was no reason to live. Before, he went out hunting. Now the white man had taken that away and would do it for him. 'What purpose do I have any more?' But the life of the Native woman did not change. The women still give birth, still rear the children, are still the head of the household, and still have their medicines. Their strength is still there. It has taken a long time for the Native man to realize that the Native woman still has that strength."

I think this causes a lot of frustration and a rift between our own people. Today, both men and women work outside the household. But when the women work, who raises the children? This is creating a rift between the man and the woman in the Native world. We are competing against the man's world and we don't have to. We shouldn't have to. We don't have to compete to get what is needed; we should work with what we have, with what is there. Take, for instance, our organizations today. We have Native women's groups at both the community and provincial levels. Then we have the Native men's associations. They are not really men's associations, *per se,* but we feel them as such because of the non-involvement of the women. We are setting them up with the same political structure as the non-Native world and we are competing. When I spoke before about being aggressive, I, too, was in that competitive world only to find that I got totally frustrated, and I finally turned to my cultural and spiritual Native values and beliefs. Now I understand how our society existed, self-governed, for so many years. It worked, and it can still work today. The old base hasn't changed and we don't have to change it. Native women play a very important role in helping our people return to that way. In many ways I think it can only be done through understanding the spiritual values of our tradition.

I guess I was always a traditional woman, but I never realized it until later on in my life. Things that I did and felt from a young age I have only begun to understand in the last ten years of working with my elders. One of them said to me: "Judy, you didn't lose it. It was always there. You laid it down for a while. Now you have picked it up again and you carry it." I met a lady in British Columbia who was very inspirational to me. I watched what she did around the house, sacred things from yesteryear, and I started looking and seeing *many* people who are still doing these things, these sacred ceremonies and traditions, and I started to learn them myself and to understand my own spirit working within me. One of our traditional beliefs is that we are the caretakers of this land, that each and every one of us has a role within our society to look after our land. Now, I feel quite strongly that we Native women were not put on this earth to be the political people that we are trying to become.

That doesn't mean we don't have a lot of political ideas and opinions. It's just that these ideas can be best recognized through the system that is already there: by Native women working as a support group for our Native men; by them going back to being the warriors and we being the mainstay of the family. Let them do the arguing and fighting and let us return to guiding and rearing the young. I have raised three children, now it is time for me to help other people raise theirs. I don't want to become a politician or an administrator. I want to work with the people. It is the people who are hurting, who have problems. What I'm trying to say is, we Native women can still be political, but from the ground up, from the root, through the raising of those children.

Judy finished her story by talking about her return to traditional medicine which focuses as much on the healing of spirit as on the body. To stay healthy she drinks cedar tea, goes to sweat-lodges, and does purification ceremonies. When she is sick, she goes to the elders for medicine since non-traditional medicines, like aspirin, make her ill. She hopes eventually to learn from the elders how to heal others as well as herself. But that will take a while, for traditional medicine covers such a vast area.

Just the same as non-traditional medicine: there is the psychological and the mental, as well as the physical, to understand. We understand the body system probably as well as non-Native people do. Maybe even better in some cases, because we do not have the tendency to abuse our bodies. Those who understand the traditional beliefs about the spirit will not abuse the body in the same fashion as others. That is why drinking is such a sad thing for our people and kills so many of us. Our spirit rejects it instantly. We become alcoholics because our spirits either leave or say I can't take this any longer—and the alcohol takes over. It takes non-Natives a lot longer than us to become alcoholics, because of our spirits.

• • • • • • • •

Joy

Joy is a writer and an activist. In fact, her writing *is* her activism and vice-versa, as her poems and stories show. Joy sent this material to me after we spoke in Toronto. The best I can do is let her powerful words speak for themselves.

Joy Asham Fedorick
Profile/Bio
Originally written for Remote Control, this is a somewhat folksy look at me—JAF
The hardest thing for a writer to do is to write about Self—to put word after linear word and have it reflect what I am about. An exotic perfume might be easier to analyze, identify, and label "Essence of Joy." Therefore, I ask you to participate.

Place one foot on asphalt and the other in boreal forest and whip up the
following:
Take one Cree
Add one second-generation British immigrant
Mix with traditional teachings from both previous ingredients
Shake fiercely in today's society
Add one husband
Fold in two children
Remove the husband
Let children and blend of first three ingredients stand alone

Revolutionize

Burn ingredients out in community organizations
Tempt with Civil Service to provide for children
Burn ingredients out in Civil Service
Let stand to find Self

Introduce awareness
Socialize
Add one Computer
Mix in the need to write
And an obsession with Aboriginal literature development
Set loose in Northern Ontario

I was born a Cree-Métis in a small, interlake community in Manitoba. A world-traveller due to my father's occupation (career in military service), I settled and married in London, Ontario. A few short years later, with two children, the marriage came to a close and I entered into single-parenthood.

Returning to school, I learned how to type and bookkeep and began to find a niche for the creative writing that had been my source of self-expression for as long as I could remember. Then I returned to Manitoba and sunk my teeth into the concerns of my home city: Winnipeg. I wrote poetry of the times: revolutionary poetry that pointed fingers at injustice. Short stories and journal articles examined the state of affairs of society. In the estimation of someone who experienced firsthand what life in the core area of Winnipeg had to offer a Métis woman, society was not excelling. My work seemed to get a fair amount of recognition then, in the early seventies, and I was offered a job as information officer with the Manitoba Civil Service—the first offer that would let me feed my children and pay for good daycare. I left community work and began writing full-time. For a while. And the contradictions of life became thoroughly in-rooted: I call it the clash of value systems. Once understood, my theory requires one to make a decision to either be part of the problem or part of the solution. When little shining faces hang in the balance, the decision sometimes takes a while...

Somehow, with kids, cats, and suitcases, I ended up working in Kenora for the Ontario provincial government. Transferred to Thunder Bay and the Ontario Women's Directorate in 1980 or so, I found active and energetic involvement in the women's community. Writing surfaced now and then with articles, poems, and short stories entwining in my social work life—and life-style.

Burn-out can be fatal I was told, and I went on long-term sick leave from the Ontario Women's Directorate in early 1986. In August of that year, I got an offer I couldn't refuse and left the provincial government once and for all to edit Native literature and write a fairly massive and complex document called *Languages Without Refuge* (LWR), within which I developed and detailed a methodology for an Aboriginal literature-of-the-people creation, a must for the retention of the Ojibwa and Cree languages. (Without the literature development, there will not be enough speakers to maintain the languages past the turn of the century.)

It probably isn't news to you, but the sun often sets on government-funded projects. Thus was the literature development project wounded—it set rapidly in the South. But it lingered on within me: the decision had finally been made, and I absolutely *knew* what I must do.

I have continued to strive for my goal of language retention through technology-assisted development of Aboriginal literature-populaire. As an editor, enabler, writer, technical hacker/specialist, I believe I have found ways to ensure that cultural expression of Native peoples does not end in the year 2000. Several groups and individuals believe I could be right: their contributions of energy and support encourage me to continue. The Ontario Arts Council and the Canada Council have also played major roles in the rejuvenation of hope and energy. My thanks to all.

House of Meekwun*

My early writings rattle around about the many issues faced by Aboriginal peoples. You name it, at one point in time or another (and usually with us, happening all at the same time), we struggle for what Abraham Maslow calls (within his "Hierarchy of Needs") "lower level needs." **

Today, Aboriginal people talk freely and assertively about "self-determination;" but first our basic needs have to be met. In "House of Meekwun," relying heavily on rhyme, rhythm, structure, which is very characteristic of my earlier work, I throw anger at remote north living conditions. With me, I see freedom from structure within my present work as a realization of "self-determination:" I am no longer writing with a style others determine for me, but with a style I have selected.

Nevertheless, "House of Meekwun" remains one of my personal favourites, probably because it wrote itself: I imagine that it was captured for a very long time in my pen, just needing my hand to pick it up and allow it to flow. I've never edited it—it was all just "there." This is also true of "Progress" which follows immediately on from "House"—and is the poem which others have chosen as their favourite.

"Progress" has been set to music, recorded, been featured in television documentaries on issues such as the Churchill River Diversion. I think it's the beat, the repetition, the way "Progress" does a three-sixty that appeals to others. I prefer "House,"...

Meekwun lies alone in his room
One he shares with seven others
The walls are cracked and peeling
Stained with artwork of his brothers

On the bare board floor before him
A ray of sunshine plays
On drab, gray soot and ashes
Piled high from yesterday
When blizzard swept the village
And the cookstove was stoked to brim
But all the wood they stoked it with
Could not keep the chills from him

---

* Meekwun (pronounced meek one) is our word for "feather." In this case, it is a small boy's name...

** From Abraham Maslow, Motivation and Personality, Harper & Row, 1954.

Through cracks in the wall it whistled
The wind with all its force
Government required insulation
Had been overlooked, of course
The one door in the building
Opens to the northwind's roar
An architectural genius
Had placed it thus, I'm sure

You know this is a new house
Just five or six years old
But I really think the older ones
Could more ably stand the cold
Though by Red hands they were built
And by Red hands were maintained
But the White Man had to show us
Just how much we had gained

They showed us by constructing
A row of high-class shacks
Out of Buffalo board, a little glue
Some mortar and thumbtacks
Then told us, "Look, we have done for you
Much more than we do for us
Why can't we then engender
A little bit of trust?"

Do you trust him, Meekwun?

Joy Asham Fedorick, 1974

Progress

O swish of paddle O beat of drum
The forest calls me and I will come

The silence of the silver night
The moon on glistening brook
The outline of a hawk in flight
I must have one more look

O swish of paddle O beat of drum
Your silence calls me and I will come

My mind sees beaver building dams
I hear the splash of trout in stream
I must return before I die
This is my heartfelt dream

O swish of paddle O beat of drum
Sweet nature calls me and I must come

My blood boils with longing
My feet trudge on to find
My home in actuality
Instead of just in mind

O swish of paddle O beat of drum
Lead me homeward and I shall come

I'm here at last! I see it now—
The water and the trees
What's this I see there also
Great Spirit spare me please!

Where once the beaver built his dam
There's now a toxic swamp
Where crystal stream once wandered through
There's now a garbage dump
And mercury has killed the trout
And hunters slain the hawk
They gave to us a treaty card
What right have we to balk?

We should sit back and let them end
This progress they've begun
But will their greed allow them to
Return to us the sun?

O swish of paddle O beat of drum
Call no more I cannot come
                                             Joy Asham Fedorick, 1973

The following excerpt is taken from a work-in-progress, soon to be a book: non-fiction, real, and I describe the larger work thus:

"A Random Sampling of One: a psychological self-profile of inner machinations leading through depression to recovery. Introspective in the extreme, but may prove useful to those involved either professionally or personally with cultural psychology. Explores what psychologist Abraham Maslow defines as "peak experiences" and finds convention and commonplace, indeed normalcy, for them within traditional Aboriginal vision quests. Examines these phenomena within the structure of "health" using styles and terminologies which best express the various situations and psychological reactions. Laced with trauma, personal development, armchair philosophy and celebration, this one will surely screw up all who read it."

This passage (no pun intended) is an incident which occurred in February 1985, at the very first signs of "trouble" in what was to be my most disastrous personal relationship to date. It also tells of why I felt the need to write: I physically felt it surging through my right arm...

This incident also provided the "light at the end of the tunnel"—resulting in a consistent and steady movement forwards to spiritual and emotional healing... enough introduction, except to the people herein:

Beth — my daughter, then nineteen

Rick — my son, then seventeen

The man of the moment—the one man I ever thought I would love, and love and love, and did, until 1987. His name is Bill.

In 1989, with two years of healing after the me/Bill relationship had ended, I met Jerome, who I loved and loved and loved even more. Turbulent times Jerome and I had, breaking up once in the summer of 1989, at which time I wrote "Disguise," the poem which follows this excerpt from A Random Sampling of One. Jerome and I reconciled in early fall of 1989, swearing undying love across the thousand miles that separated us (he lived in Toronto). And then he died, November 13, 1989. His last visit to me happened on November 30—but that's another story, best left for the book...

A Random Sampling of One... Excerpt, Chapter 11

...Since our move to the high-rise, I had spent increasing periods in darkness, before the balcony doors, where I had placed my favourite wicker chair and a work table. In the dark there, I would look over the lights of Fort William, (night light being one of the few things I like of "progress") and would review in my mind, over and over again, the few good things that were happening in my life. It was kind of a positive reinforcement time, a time to convince myself that somehow life could be endured. About that time a phrase had slipped into my daily jive: "A fate worse than life." Hmmm...

The chair gave me comfort. (It was a survivor of a fire we had had years before and its survival was a statement to me.) The lights gave me focus. The table propped me.

That night the intensity of my positive mute recitals was tenfold. Anything to block from my mind the unanswered question: "Where is he?"

I look back now and can still see... the hoop of light that came and hung before me, just on the other side of the glass doors. And it did only that for a while, hung there silently until its friendliness suffused me and trust overwhelmed me.

And then, it silvered forth, pausing to draw up my right hand. And it pulled. Gently, but firmly. Pulled. Attracted. Smoothed my arm upwards and through the glass. No tinkle. Just inconceivably *through*.

And I *knew*. I knew I could leave with it. I knew I could be happy with it. I knew I could be cared for with it. I knew I could be forever blessed with its companionship and selfless love.

I wanted to go. I cannot compare a feeling to that experience, except I so much wanted to go. For me. For every bit of security and warmth and kindness and awareness I had ever sought or imagined. I just plain, downright, at the risk of sounding tacky, wanted to go to the innermost fibre of my being.

And I gently wafted. I let it carry me. My arm was almost all the way through (to where?). Silver once more. This time the tinkle was present. In my head, a voice. *My* voice, young and not yet grown cigarette-husky.

"But what about your Rick?"

"But what about Beth?"

"But what about Dad?"

"But what about him?"

Because, I was also overcome with the extreme permanentness of the trip? odyssey? fatedness?

And somehow, in my awed and crumbling state, I managed to decide to stay. Yes, stay.

Now, my new friend, the foxy silver hoop, had other ideas. And we entered into the most gentle yet commanding struggle. On again, off again. Arm in, arm out.

Heavens.

The clock on the hooplit bookcase registered ten minutes and still no three-count had occurred. And we danced some more.

And, I *felt* another decision. This one not mine. *It* would stay. Until it was no longer so urgently needed.

The clock said twenty minutes had passed.

It was then about ten-thirty at night and I was exhausted. This is an unusual state for me: usually the hour when adrenalin really gets surging and I glory for six more hours, such as now, while I write this.

And I slept. Although perhaps sleep is not the right word. Dreamless, motionless, soulmending, fathomless, rejuvenating unconsciousness. Twenty hours of it.

I awoke in soaking sheets. My sleep had oozed almost all liquid through the pores of my body and my bed was drenched in sweat.

I weightlessly veered to the living room, the glass doors, and there stood my chair as I had left it, although something was different.

I couldn't quite register what it was. It wasn't physical, but it wasn't intangible. It wasn't smaller than a star, nor bigger than a breadbox.

It was just, well, the air doubled. Two thicknesses of air. An instant reply?

Anyway, the thick air hung around for two weeks, as did a reassuring tingle in my right arm. Every now and then, it would seem that this thick air would nod. Smile, Comfort.

The man of the moment re-entered my life the night of the wet sheets.

His reaction to my recounting of this was:

"That was real, you know..."

and,

"Beam me up, Scotty."

Perhaps our intermittent kindred-spiritness is exhibited here.

Dominion Over

I wrote this poem in the Dryden Husky House Restaurant, specifically for a reading I was to do at the Dryden Library the next night.

In Dryden, thoughts of trees (or rather, lack of them) are always present: Reed's Paper Mills, though long gone from the community, left behind the rampant pollution and destruction that Northern nightmares are made from. Greasy burger drizzling on napkin scratchings, nostrils assailed by leftover mercury aroma, my thoughts turned back to times I had spent gliding, soaring and horrified, nestled in the mechanized security and weightless comfort of sky-sailing in light planes... a gentle and pleasurable feeling, contrasted with the downward view...

Drifting through clouds
I float gently
Hugged by sky
Content with eyes upward
Through the cotton wool
of
Infinity

Restless with perfection
The roar of Cessna
Seeps through clouds and
Turns my eyes downward
(Spirit to follow)—

Veins of poison creep
Relentlessly
Relentlessly
Relentlessly
North

All life ends
Where this poison creeps

I look upon the land
Thoughts of Infinity
Crash
Downwards
As Cessna
d
i
p
s
to ground

The veins become more distinct
Glare at me their purpose

Logging roads
Slash cut and
Torn trees
Crush on heart and sigh

Defeat
Defeat of
Boreal forest
Muskrat swamp
Wild rice

By contrast
Lushness
Curves the highway
Providing masks
To passers-by

Masks that shield
the Northern martyrdom
Tell the world that
Bay Street isn't so bad
That the North seems well
That the forest is perpetually

There

As eyes turn upwards
Infinity no longer perfection
Spirit convinced that
Dominion Over
has no place
Can find no settling within me
Of Daunted Spirit

Veins of poison
Creep through soul...

Joy Asham Fedorick,
Husky House, Dryden,
October 29, 1989

Disguise

The disguise of love
Shies close to me
Warms loins and limbs
Whispers in
Longing phrases

Makes of me
A
Physical Being

This
This
Mask

Convention has told me
Love has indicators
Ways to measure
Love and Myth

The Myth tells me
Love has parameters
Tells me
of

Commitment
Responsibility
Fidelity
Security
Always, always
To be there

Sometimes the Myth tells me
A white horse awaits
As does the sunset
And the oneness that
Comes when two people
Fuse

What is real?
It for me has been this:

Loins, limbs
Moist memories
Interminable longing
And knowing
Knowing in my soul
That no white horse awaits

The acceptance of this has been hard
The hardest because
The myth is impenetrable
Surrounds me daily
Never stops to ask, measure or define
Love
In my life.

Maturity speaks of throwing these things
Like old shoes into incinerator
The limbs tell me
Oh, to entwine
To meld
To fuse
To lose
Myself
In Love

The disguise still exists
Love wears its mask well
Protecting, protecting
Illusion
Illusion of life
Illusion of self

Disguises at times
Can be saving graces
Not allowing Real emptiness to
be perceived

Maturity says
"I know these things"
Limbs, loins, heart, though
Welcome the disguise

Until Reality
Like
Time
Freezes
Freezes

And Icycles
Settle
in
Limbs
Loins
Heart
Settle, in Cold Truth

Within

Joy Asham Fedorick, July, 1989